teach®
yourself

panjabi
surjit singh kalra
and
navtej kaur purewal
with
sue tyson-ward

For over 60 years, more than 50 million people have learnt over 750 subjects the **teach yourself** way, with impressive results.

be where you want to be
with **teach yourself**

For UK order enquiries: please contact Bookpoint Ltd, 130 Milton Park, Abingdon, Oxon, OX14 4SB. Telephone: +44 (0) 1235 827720. Fax: +44 (0) 1235 400454. Lines are open 09.00–17.00, Monday to Saturday, with a 24-hour message answering service. Details about our titles and how to order are available at www.teachyourself.co.uk

For USA order enquiries: please contact McGraw-Hill Customer Services, PO Box 545, Blacklick, OH 43004-0545, USA. Telephone: 1-800-722-4726. Fax: 1-614-755-5645.

For Canada order enquiries: please contact McGraw-Hill Ryerson Ltd, 300 Water St, Whitby, Ontario, L1N 9B6, Canada. Telephone: 905 430 5000. Fax: 905 430 5020.

Long renowned as the authoritative source for self-guided learning – with more than 50 million copies sold worldwide – the **teach yourself** series includes over 500 titles in the fields of languages, crafts, hobbies, business, computing and education.

British Library Cataloguing in Publication Data: a catalogue record for this title is available from the British Library.

Library of Congress Catalog Card Number: on file.

First published in UK 2007 by Hodder Education, 338 Euston Road, London, NW1 3BH.

First published in US 2007 by The McGraw-Hill Companies, Inc.
This edition published 2007.

The **teach yourself** name is a registered trade mark of Hodder Headline.

Typeset by Macmillan India Limited

Printed in Great Britain for Hodder Education, a division of Hodder Headline, an Hachette Livre UK Company, 338 Euston Road, London, NW1 3BH, by Cox & Wyman Ltd, Reading, Berkshire.

The publisher has used its best endeavours to ensure that the URLs for external websites referred to in this book are correct and active at the time of going to press. However, the publisher and the author have no responsibility for the websites and can make no guarantee that a site will remain live or that the content will remain relevant, decent or appropriate.

Hachette's policy is to use papers that are natural, renewable and recyclable products and made from wood grown in sustainable forests. The logging and manufacturing processes are expected to conform to the environmental regulations of the country of origin.

Impression number   10 9 8 7 6 5 4 3 2 1

Year   2012 2011 2010 2009 2008 2007

iii

contents

Acknowledgements

The authors would like to thank a number of people who were involved in different capacities throughout the inception and production of this book. Thanks first go to Dr Virinder S. Kalra, Lecturer in the Department of Sociology, Manchester University, England, who gave invaluable guidance, moral and technical support and advice each step of the way. To Balbir K. Kalra and Amarjit K. Purewal for their patience and understanding during the entire process. Also, to J. S. Bhogal, Neelu Kalsi, G. S. Bhogal, Jaswinder Kaur and T. S. Nahal from California for their help and encouragement.

About the authors

Surjit Singh Kalra is founder and director of the Panjabi Language Development Board in Birmingham, UK, a voluntary organization dedicated to the promotion and development of the Panjabi language. He is the author of over 20 Panjabi teaching aids. He is a prolific writer and is widely published in the Panjabi press as well as having five books of short stories published. He retired in 1992 as head of the Community Language Service for Birmingham Education Authority. He is, at present, the Sikh representative on the Inner Cities Religious Council.

Dr Navtej Kaur Purewal is a lecturer at the University of Manchester in the Department of Sociology. She teaches Development and South Asian Studies. Her doctoral thesis was on Panjab.

Sue Tyson-Ward was formerly Subject Officer for Community Language examinations at a National Exam Board.

Symbols and abbreviations

▶	recording	plu.	plural
m.	masculine	lit.	literally
f.	feminine	form.	formal
v.	variable adjective	inform.	informal
sing.	singular		

introduction

Geographically, the present day area of Panjab is divided between the nation states of India and Pakistan (see Map 1). This division took place in 1947 upon the departure of the British from colonial rule of the sub-continent. While the language and culture of East and West Panjab are similar, there are religious differences, with Muslims being the predominant group in Pakistan Panjab, Hindus and Sikhs in Indian Panjab, and a substantial Christian minority in both parts. Panjab has come to some prominence in the West because of the long history of migration from the region to the four corners of the world.

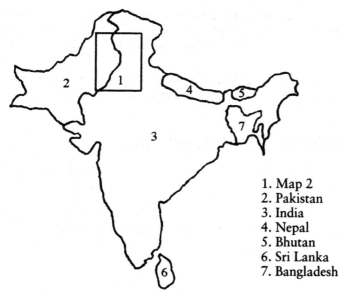

1. Map 2
2. Pakistan
3. India
4. Nepal
5. Bhutan
6. Sri Lanka
7. Bangladesh

Map 1   Indian sub-continent

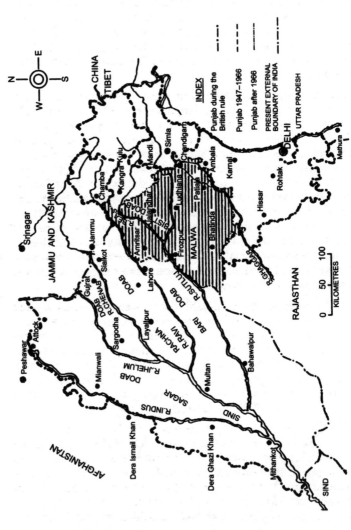

Map 2 Panjab and the 'Five Rivers'

There are, therefore, mainly three areas of the world where Panjabi is spoken; in East Panjab (India) where it is a state language, in West Panjab (Pakistan) where it is most widely spoken and in the diaspora, particularly Britain, North America, East Africa and Australasia. This wide geographic spread of the language is ironic given the fact that the word Panjabi – also spelt Punjabi – designates the language of the 'Panj – ab', the 'Five Rivers'. These are the Jhelum, Chenab, Ravi, Beas and the Satluj (see Map 2).

No accurate figures are available on the number of Panjabi speakers, either as a first or second language, but if the three Panjabs and various dialects are taken into account an approximation of 100 million would not be too far from the truth. One of the main problems with designating the exact number of Panjabi speakers is the presence of a large number of distinct dialects that are spoken across the large geographical area of East and West Panjab. There are some eleven recognized dialects of Panjabi: Majhi, Bhattiani, Rathni, Ludhianwi, Doabi, Patialwi, Powadhi, Malwi, Multani (Siraiki), Putohari and Hindko. The last three can arguably call Panjabi a dialect of themselves and are all spoken in the Pakistan part of Panjab. In the diaspora the most spoken form of Panjabi is the Doabi, and encompasses those speakers from the Jalandhar area of East Panjab.

Given the great variety of Panjabi there is some debate as to what is standard. This book is based upon the Majhi dialect which is the everyday form used in Lahore and Amritsar. The most important point is that once you have mastered the language using this book you will be understood across Panjab. The language used here is neither the colloquial rural nor the urban literary, as the focus of this course has been on developing an ability to communicate in as many different situations as possible.

One of the more interesting facts about the Panjabi language is that where it is numerically the most widely spoken, in Pakistani Panjab, it is hardly written at all. Panjabi is most often written in East Panjab in the Gurmukhi script. It is also possible to write the language in the Persian script often referred to as Shahmukhi in this context. However, in the last 100 years or so, Panjabi has become closely associated with Sikhs and Sikhism, thus Gurmukhi has also become associated with Panjabi. Gurmukhi literally means 'proceeding from the mouth of the Guru', and it is widely acknowledged that Guru Angad, the second Sikh Guru (AD 1504–1552), began the process of modifying existing scripts of the time laying the basis for the modern Panjabi alphabet that is used in this book.

Despite the modern day usage of Gurmukhi, the first Panjabi literature was written in Shahmukhi, and popular history associates this writing with Shaikh Farid and Goraknath. However, the literary period of the language begins with the sacred scriptures of the Sikhs, the *Guru Granth Sahib*. This collection of writings by the Sikh Gurus is probably the first manuscript of the Panjabi language. After the period of the Gurus, it was the Sufi poets who developed the Panjabi language. In fact it is the folk literature developed by the Sufis, and particularly the Quissa – love ballad form – which has had a long and lasting impact on the development of Panjabi literature. The stories of Heer-Ranjha and Mirza Sahiba are deeply embedded in the everyday life and culture of Panjab.

During the period of British colonial rule, the advent of the printing press saw the proliferation of the Panjabi language in the Gurmukhi script. Pamphlets, journals, novels and short stories all began to appear at the beginning of the twentieth century using the Panjabi typewriter. However, the official language of the time was either English or Urdu. The division of Panjab in 1947 between East (India) and West (Pakistan) and subsequently of East Panjab in 1966 led to the formation of the State of Panjab in the Indian Union. Panjabi is the official language of communication in East Panjab and the modern development of the language has been greatly accelerated by state patronage. Indeed, the development of Panjabi University in Patiala is one such example of state sponsorship.

Language may be the basis of culture, but there are many other aspects of Panjabi society and everyday life that impinge on the use of language. We have included a Commentary section in each unit which will introduce various aspects of the social and cultural life of the three Panjabs, although these are by no means exhaustive discussions of the rich culture of Panjab and the Panjabi diaspora.

how to use this course

Who is this course for?

This course in Panjabi has been designed for the absolute beginner who may or may not have studied a language before. The course will be useful for people who want to learn Panjabi in order to speak with their Panjabi friends and relatives, to communicate with Panjabi communities in relation to their work, to learn about aspects of Panjabi culture and society or to travel to Panjab itself. The course will also be useful for those who already know a little Panjabi but who may not have the confidence to speak and even for those fluent in spoken Panjabi but who wish to learn to read and write the Gurmukhi script. Throughout the course you will come across a number of different situations in which you will learn how to make requests, ask and give information and to express your feelings. The units include dialogues, language points and background information about Panjab and Panjabi people both in the region of Panjab as well as in other parts of the world where Panjabi communities have settled.

The course is divided into two parts. The first part (Units 1–10) is specifically designed for those who want to learn the basics of grammar and vocabulary in order to communicate in a simple manner and also enable you to read and write simple sentences. The second part (Units 11–16) will help you to expand your knowledge of spoken Panjabi further and is designed for those who are committed to becoming proficient in the Gurmukhi script.

Overall, the course introduces you to a wide range of vocabulary and covers the basic grammar of Panjabi. By the end of the course, you will be able to understand the spoken language, communicate in Panjabi in a number of everyday situations while also having a sufficient level of understanding of the written language to begin to read newspapers and to write letters. We hope that this course will be the beginning of your journey into the world of the Panjabi language.

How to use this course

The structure of the book is outlined in the contents pages. It is recommended that you read the introductory chapters before proceeding with the course. The Panjabi script and sound system follows this section and it is advisable to work through this section regardless of whether you intend to learn the script or not. Through this section you will gain practice of listening, speaking and reading which will help you for the rest of the course. After the script chapter, the book is divided into 16 units. The pattern of each unit is as follows:

- First there is an outline in English of what you will learn in the unit.
- ਗੱਲ ਬਾਤ gall baat (Dialogue): Each unit has two or three dialogue passages containing situations and commonly used speech which include the vocabulary and grammar to be covered in that unit. In the first part (Units 1–10) the dialogues use Gurmukhi, Roman script and English translations. In the remainder of the book (Units 11–16) the dialogues are only in Gurmukhi and English. However, Roman is maintained in the vocabulary sections throughout the book.
- ਸ਼ਬਦਾਵਲੀ shabdaavalee (Vocabulary): The vocabulary sections follow each Dialogue and include all new words, and sometimes key expressions, which appear in the dialogue text. All nouns are denoted according to their masculine or feminine (m. / f.) gender in parentheses and all adjectives which vary according to gender and number are identified with a (v.).
- ਅਭਿਆਸ abhiaas (Exercises): These follow the vocabulary and often make reference to the dialogues that they follow. There is a range of different exercises including true/false, matching, comprehension, 'fill in the blanks' and crosswords.
- ਬੋਲੀ ਬਾਰੇ bolee baare (Language points). These sections cover the main grammar points which appear in the dialogues. Each new grammar point is explained clearly using examples to illustrate. Often, English equivalents to the Panjabi are given alongside the explanations.
- ਵਿਆਖਿਆ viaakhiaa (Commentary): These sections introduce you to various aspects of Panjabi culture which have been

touched upon in the content of the dialogues. These will help you to become acquainted with colloquial speech, social etiquette and Panjabi history, traditions and customs.

• ਅਭਿਆਸ abhiaas (Exercises): Further exercises come at the end of each unit and review some of the main vocabulary, content and grammatical elements that were introduced in that unit. While the exercises that come after the dialogues in the units do not contain references to grammar, the exercises at the end of the units may test you on your ability to use the grammar you have learned.

At the end of the book there is a key to the exercises so that you can check your answers. There is also a Panjabi–English glossary which will be of use to you throughout the course in referring to the English definitions of Panjabi words which appear in the units.

How to study each unit

- Read the summary at the beginning of each unit to learn about what will be covered.
- Study the dialogues using the vocabulary lists for words that you do not understand and then read the dialogues out loud.
- Read the commentary section which will give you the relevant background to the dialogues.
- Complete the exercises which follow the dialogues and vocabulary. Check your answers with the key to the exercises at the end of the book.
- Go through the grammar sections to understand the new grammar points introduced.
- After learning the grammar, read the dialogue again to make sure that you fully understood the content.
- Go back to the dialogue and repeat it as often as you can, acting out the roles of the different characters.
- Complete the exercises at the end of the unit, checking your answers with the key to the exercises at the end of the book.

How to use the course with the recording

The book is accompanied by a recording which will help you to recognize and distinguish the Panjabi sound system and also to improve your listening and speaking abilities. While the book is in itself a complete course, the recording will be an added advantage for all Panjabi learners as it contains pronunciation exercises, dialogues from the units and oral comprehension activities based on the ਅਭਿਆਸ abhiaas (Exercises).

As you begin to go through the first part of the book (Units 1–10), you should listen to the recording of each ਗੱਲ ਬਾਤ gall baat (Dialogue) as you read it. Listen to it again without looking at the book once you have understood the general meaning. This will allow you to pay attention to the pronunciation and intonation of the speakers. Imitating the speakers in the dialogues is a useful way of picking up the language quickly. As you progress through the course to the second part (Units 11–16), you should try to listen to the dialogue on the recording without reading it in the book.

Introduction

Panjabi is most commonly written in the Gurmukhi script which is the most complete and accurate way to represent Panjabi sounds. Unlike English, the Gurmukhi script follows a 'one sound–one symbol' principle. There are a few exceptions to this rule and these will become apparent throughout the book. However, with some practice you will be able to recognize the characters and know their names and sounds. Ultimately, with even a basic knowledge of the sound system, you will be able to read and write Panjabi in the Gurmukhi script.

The Gurmukhi alphabet has 40 letters including 37 consonants and three basic vowel sign bearers. There are ten clear pure vowels and three auxiliary signs. The most striking characteristic of the Gurmukhi script, in comparison with English, is that, with the exception of five, all letters are joined by a line across the top. Like English and other European, Latin-based languages, it is written and read from left to right. However, there are neither capital letters in Panjabi nor articles such as 'a' and 'the'. Panjabi spellings are, for the most part, regular and relatively simple to learn, though you may come across variations in spellings of some words. However, as is the case in English, Panjabi spellings are not fully standardized.

Handwritten Panjabi, as with any script, differs from person to person in style. Some people prefer to write Panjabi without lifting a pen, making curves and having an irregular top line. It is up to the individual as to what sort of style he or she wants to adopt. Our advice to new learners is to follow the simple, clear style of lettering. There are a number of Panjabi fonts available on computer disk which have differing typefaces, some of which are very clear, attractive and decorative.

Equivalent sounds which have been given in Romanized (English) script are only approximate since the Gurmukhi alphabet has many unfamiliar sounds to the English speaker which often may not be exactly represented by the English alphabet. It is hoped that you will use the recording, attend classes, or seek help from a native speaker so as to perfect your pronunciation and to familiarize yourself with the sounds. In order to learn any language it is important to follow these basic rules: listen carefully, repeat out loud and distinctly, and do not worry about making mistakes. Apart from unfamiliar sounds, there are nasal and double sounds, intonation, stress and different dialects which might initially dishearten the student. However, with a little practice, you will begin to enjoy learning Panjabi.

Transliteration

The standard modern system of transliteration (the writing of Panjabi in the Roman alphabet) is used in this book with some modifications. As there are 40 letters, ten vowel sounds and three auxiliary signs in Panjabi, it is necessary to adapt the standard English alphabet. You will note two ways of distinguishing letters:

1 by a combination of two English letters such as rh, kh, bh, nh, etc. In those few cases where these letters appear together but *not* in combination, for instance, a 'r' and 'h' appear together, a '-' is shown between those letters.
2 by underlining, for example, the letter n (<u>n</u>) indicates nasalization or underlining ch (<u>ch</u>) indicates an aspirated sound.

Consonants
The Panjabi alphabet

South Asian languages are richly endowed with sounds and consonants. Sanskrit may have been one of the first languages to group the letters according to their sounds. At one time there were only 35 letters in the Panjabi script, but later five more letters were added in order to accommodate Urdu sounds correctly. This need arose because of the many loan words from Urdu used in Panjabi. More recently, an extra character (.ਲ l) was introduced, though it has not become popular and hence will not be included in this book. The complete Panjabi alphabet is given in Table A.

It is quite possible to learn the characters of the Gurmukhi script (ਗੁਰਮੁਖੀ ਲਿਪੀ gurmukhee lipee) and sounds of the language at the same time as, by and large, Panjabi is a phonetic language. It is more accurate to call the Panjabi writing system a syllabary because each character represents a syllable. It is important to note

Table A Panjabi alphabet

ੳ	ਅ	ੲ	ਸ	ਹ
—	a	—	s	h
ਕ	ਖ	ਗ	ਘ	ਙ
k	kh	g	gh	ng
ਚ	ਛ	ਜ	ਝ	ਞ
ch	<u>ch</u>	j	jh	nj
ਟ	ਠ	ਡ	ਢ	ਣ
t	th	d	dh	nh
ਤ	ਥ	ਦ	ਧ	ਨ
<u>t</u>	<u>th</u>	<u>d</u>	<u>dh</u>	n
ਪ	ਫ	ਬ	ਭ	ਮ
p	ph	b	bh	m
ਯ	ਰ	ਲ	ਵ	ੜ
y	r	l	w/v	rh
ਸ਼	ਖ਼	ਗ਼	ਜ਼	ਫ਼
sh	<u>kh</u>	<u>gh</u>	z	f

that two phonetic features of all North Indian languages are the system of contrasts between aspirated and unaspirated consonants and the contrast between retroflex and dental consonants. These do not occur in English. Aspirated consonants are accompanied by an audible expulsion of breath, whereas non-aspirated consonants are those produced with minimal breath. The letter 'k' in the word 'kit' and 't' in the word 'top' come close to Panjabi aspirated consonants. The problem for English speakers arises with non-aspirated consonants. To get an idea of the difference between the two, try saying the words 'kit' and 'top' while holding your breath. In dental consonants the tongue touches the upper front teeth, whereas with the retroflex consonants the tip of the tongue curls upwards against the palate (see diagrams in Appendix 2). The nearest approximations to English are the 't' sound in the word 'eighth' which is dental-like and the 'd' in the word 'breadth' which is retroflex-like.

There is a range of technical terms used to describe the pronunciation of Panjabi consonants. For those who are interested in technical, and linguistic matters these can be found in Appendix 1. The important thing is to be able to distinguish between the different consonants. The recording or the help of a native speaker are invaluable tools in this process.

Panjabi syllabary

The syllabary in Table B gives the Panjabi letters in groups, according to pronunciation.

Table B Panjabi syllabary

Gurmukhi	Transliteration	Pronunciation
ਸ	s	as 's' in 'sun'.
ਹ	h	this 'h' sound as in 'ahead' is the simplest form, although there is considerable variety, which will be discussed later.
ਕ	k	as 'k' in 'sky', but with less release of breath.
ਖ	kh	as 'k' in 'kit' but with stronger release of breath. No English equivalent.
ਗ	g	as 'g' in 'go' but with less release of breath.
ਘ	gh	as 'gh' in 'ghost' said quickly. No English equivalent.
ਙ	ng	as 'ng' in 'sing'. No English equivalent.
ਚ	ch	as 'ch' as in 'cheese' but with less release of breath.
ਛ	<u>ch</u>	strongly aspirated form of 'ch'. No English equivalent.
ਜ	j	as 'j' in 'jeer' but with less release of breath and with the tongue against the lower teeth.
ਝ	jh	the stronger aspirated counterpart of the above, somewhat like 'bridge'. No English equivalent.

ਞ	nj	representing the palatal nasal sound. No English equivalent.
ਟ	t	as 't' in 'train' but with the tongue further back and with less release of breath.
ਠ	th	the strongly aspirated counterpart of the above. No English equivalent.
ਡ	d	as 'd' in 'drum' but with tongue further back and with less release of breath.
ਢ	dh	strongly aspirated form of the above. No English equivalent.
ਣ	nh	representing the retroflex nasal sound. No English equivalent.
ਤ	<u>t</u>	unaspirated soft 't'. No English equivalent.
ਥ	<u>th</u>	as 'th' in 'thermos', strongly aspirated form of the above.
ਦ	<u>d</u>	as 'th' in 'then' with less release of breath.
ਧ	<u>dh</u>	strongly aspirated form of the above. No English equivalent.
ਨ	n	as 'n' in 'nice' but with the tongue flatter against the front teeth.
ਪ	p	as 'p' in 'spin' but with less release of breath.
ਫ	ph	as 'f' in 'fund', aspirated form of the above, though many Panjabi speakers pronounce 'ph' as 'f'.
ਬ	b	as 'b' in 'bin' but with less release of breath.
ਭ	bh	as 'bh' in 'club-house' spoken quickly. No English equivalent.
ਮ	m	as 'm' in 'mother'.
ਯ	y	as 'y' in 'yet'.
ਰ	r	as 'r' in 'motor.' This sound is always fully voiced and never lost like the English 'r'.
ਲ	l	as 'l' in 'life'.

ਵ	v / w	this sound lies between the English sounds 'v' and 'w'. However, unlike the English 'v' the lower lip hardly touches the upper teeth; unlike the English 'w' there is no lip-rounding. For transliteration purposes we only use 'v'.
ੜ	rh	no English equivalent.
ਸ਼	sh	as 'sh' in 'ship'.
ਖ਼	<u>kh</u>	similar to 'ch' in Scottish 'loch'. No English equivalent.
ਗ਼	<u>gh</u>	no English equivalent.
ਜ਼	z	as 'z' in 'zip'.
ਫ਼	f	as 'f' in 'find'.

Consonants with a dot

It is also important to note the distinction between plain consonants and those consonants which are marked by a dot, as shown in Table C.

Table C Consonants with dots

ਸ	ਸ਼	ਖ	ਖ਼	ਗ	ਗ਼	ਜ	ਜ਼	ਫ	ਫ਼
s	sh	kh	<u>kh</u>	g	<u>gh</u>	j	z	ph	f

These letters are named by adding the words ਪੈਰੀਂ ਬਿੰਦੀ **paireen bindee** to the name of the letter, so ਸ਼ is called ਸੱਸੇ ਪੈਰੀਂ ਬਿੰਦੀ **sasse paireen bindee,** which literally means sassa with a dot in its foot. Many Panjabi speakers do not make a distinction between ਖ ਖ਼, ਗ ਗ਼, and ਫ ਫ਼. There are two main reasons for this, first, their pronunciation is quite similar and second, they are used to differentiate borrowed words from Urdu, the knowledge of which is decreasing in East Panjab. You may come across written texts in which writers have not used the dot. In this book, however, we have maintained its use.

Subjoined consonants

Some Panjabi words require consonants to be written in a conjunct form, which takes the shape of a subscript to the main letter.

The second consonant is written under the first as a subscript. The reason for this is discussed after we have looked at Panjabi vowels. There are only three commonly used subjoined letters (see Table D) and to distinguish them from their normal forms the word ਪੈਰੀਂ **paireen**, which means *belonging to the foot,* is attached under the letter.

Table D Subjoined consonants

Full letter	Name of full letter	Subjoined letter	Name of subjoined letter	Transliteration
ਹ	ਹਾਹਾ haahaa	੍ਹ	ਪੈਰੀਂ ਹਾਹਾ paireen haahaa	h
ਰ	ਰਾਰਾ raaraa	੍ਰ	ਪੈਰੀਂ ਰਾਰਾ paireen raaraa	r
ਵ	ਵੱਵਾ vavvaa	੍ਵ	ਪੈਰੀਂ ਵੱਵਾ paireen vavvaa	v

For the purposes of transliteration there is no special sign for the subjoined character so you will have to pay careful attention to the Panjabi spelling.

Nasalization

There are five nasal consonants in Panjabi:

• ਙ ng • ਞ nj • ਣ nh • ਨ n • ਮ m

As shown in the syllabary, the nasal consonants belong to the five different classes of consonants. Nasalization is produced by directing a substantial part of the breath towards the nasal cavity as the letter is being uttered. In addition there are two nasalization signs in Panjabi which accompany consonants:

• ਬਿੰਦੀ bindee •   • ਟਿੱਪੀ tippee ੰ

These will be dealt with in detail later.

Pronunciation of consonants

Most letters in Panjabi have a fixed pronunciation, however some are variable and this depends on their position in a word. Consider the letters in Table E.

Table E Pronunciation of consonants

	ਘ gh	ਝ jh	ਢ dh	ਧ <u>dh</u>	ਭ bh
Sound at beginning of word	ਕ k	ਚ ch	ਟ t	ਤ <u>t</u>	ਪ p
Sound in middle or at end of word	ਗ g	ਜ j	ਡ d	ਦ <u>d</u>	ਬ b

Perhaps the most variable pronunciation of a single consonant in Panjabi is that of the letter ਹ *h*. Words beginning with ਹ *h* and those where no vowel precedes or affects it, carry the *h* sound as it would be used in English. For instance:

ਹਕੂਮਤ hakoom<u>t</u> *government* ਹਕੀਮ hakeem *doctor*

However, when ਹ *h* is used in the middle of a word following consonants and vowels its pronunciation is varied. We will return to this point after considering the vowel symbols and sounds.

Vowels

There are ten vowels in Panjabi in contrast to the English five (*a, e, i, o, u*). Panjabi vowels are generally pronounced as they are written, following the one sign – one sound rule. They are pure vowels making only one sound. However, there are two forms that vowels can take. The independent vowel form which does not require a consonant and the dependent form which is attached to a consonant. All consonants use the dependent form of the vowel. Tables F and G show the dependent vowels on their own and combined with the letter ਸ *s*.

Table F Dependent vowels on their own

	Vowel sign		Name of vowel	
1	invisible	a	ਮੁਕਤਾ	mu<u>kt</u>aa
2	ਾ	aa	ਕੰਨਾ	ka<u>n</u>naa
3	ਿ	i	ਸਿਹਾਰੀ	sihaaree
4	ੀ	ee	ਬਿਹਾਰੀ	bihaaree
5	ੁ	u	ਔਂਕੜ	au<u>n</u>karh
6	ੂ	oo	ਦੁਲੈਂਕੜੇ	<u>d</u>ulai<u>n</u>karhe
7	ੇ	e	ਲਾਂਵ	laa<u>n</u>v
8	ੈ	ai	ਦੁਲਾਂਵਾਂ	<u>d</u>ulaa<u>n</u>vaa<u>n</u>
9	ੋ	o	ਹੋੜਾ	horhaa
10	ੌ	au	ਕਨੌੜਾ	kanaurhaa

Table G Dependent vowels in combination with *s*

Consonant and vowel sign		Pronunciation
ਸ	sa	*a* in ahead
ਸਾ	saa	*a* in part
ਸਿ	si	*i* in it
ਸੀ	see	*ee* in see
ਸੁ	su	*u* in put
ਸੂ	soo	*oo* in food
ਸੇ	se	*a* in cake
ਸੈ	sai	*a* in man
ਸੋ	so	*o* in show
ਸੌ	sau	*o* in bought

You may note that the vowels are divided into five pairs. In the first three, the distinction is between a short and long sound, for example between *u* and *oo*. In the last two pairs the distinction is between closed and open sounds so *e* is closed and *ai* is open sounding.

Short *a* sound – 'muk̲taa'

We have seen that in Panjabi there are ten vowels and they are represented by nine symbols. The vowel **muk̲taa** has no equivalent sign to be used with consonants. The individual consonant expresses its own sound and also implies an *a* sound with it. This means that, unlike English, words can be formed with consonants only without using any visible vowel. Each consonant has an inherent sound, making it a syllable on its own. However, there is no symbol for this sound in Panjabi, though we have chosen to represent **muk̲taa** with the letter *a* for purposes of transliteration. Examples of the use of **muk̲taa** can be found in many borrowed words from English, for example: ਕਪ **kap**, *cup*, and ਮਗ **mag**, *mug*.

The inherent *a* is not pronounced in three main positions:

- at the end of a word, e.g. ਕਾਰ **kaar**
- with a subjoined consonant, e.g. ਸ੍ਰੀ **sree**
- at a syllable break, e.g. ਗਰਦਨ ਗਰ-ਦਨ **gar–d̲an**

Independent vowels

The independent form can occur in three ways. First, when the vowel comes at the beginning of a word or a syllable, second in those instances where two vowel sounds are required as a consonant cannot support two vowels, and third, in a diphthong – when two vowels are present in one syllable. In fact one of the features of Panjabi is the presence of many diphthongs, sometimes with three vowel sounds in one word with no consonants, for instance ਆਇਆ aaiaa (*he*) *came*.

Independent vowels are represented by dependent vowels carried by the first three letters of the Panjabi alphabet:

ੳ ਉੜਾ oorhaa   ਅ ਐੜਾ airhaa   ੲ ਈੜੀ eerhee

They are never used on their own and do not represent any consonant sounds. They *must* be accompanied by their allocated vowel signs. Their main function is to denote their own respective vowel sounds. They are founder, basic or parent vowel bearers representing the ten sounds.

However, the pronunciation of both independent and dependent vowels is the same (see Table H).

▶ **Table H   Independent vowel**

Formula		Example word	Transliteration	Meaning
─	u is added to ੳ to give ਉ	ਉਪਜ	upaj	*production*
═	oo is added to ੳ to give ਊ	ਊਠ	ooth	*camel*
◟	o is added to ੳ to give ਓ	ਓਟ	ot	*shelter*
	Invisible sign 'a' is added to ਅ	ਅਮਰ	amar	*immortal*
ਾ	aa is added to ਅ to give ਆ	ਆਟਾ	aataa	*flour*
◝	ai is added to ਅ to give ਐ	ਐਨਕ	ainak	*spectacles*
◟	au is added to ਅ to give ਔ	ਔਰਤ	aurat	*woman*
ਿ	i is added to ੲ to give ਇ	ਇਨਾਮ	inaam	*prize*
ੀ	ee is added to ੲ to give ਈ	ਈਸਾ	eesaa	*Jesus*
◟	e is added to ੲ to give ਏ	ਏਕਤਾ	ektaa	*unity*

Silent vowel signs

In English there are some silent or soft spoken consonants, for example *r* and *k*. There are no such consonants in Panjabi, however, there are silent vowels. These are not often found in modern Panjabi but occur often in the sacred language of Sikh religious texts. Silent vowels give special meaning to the word they are referring to. The most common use of the silent vowel you will come across is in the Sikh greeting ਸਤਿ ਸ੍ਰੀ ਅਕਾਲ sat(i) sree akaal.

Note that the **sihaaree** in the word ਸਤਿ has no effect on the pronunciation, however its presence does alter the meaning:

- ਸਤ sa<u>t</u> *extract* • ਸੱਤ sa<u>tt</u> *seven* • ਸਤਿ sa<u>t</u>(i) *true*

In this example we have included the silent vowel in brackets for purposes of illustration, however, throughout the rest of the book the silent vowel is not included in the transliterated text.

Tones

One of the unique features of Panjabi, in the variety of modern South Asian languages, is the presence of pitch contours. These change the meaning of the word depending on the way it sounds. In technical terms these are called 'tones' and there are three types: low, high and level. The Panjabi tone system is far less complex than Chinese, the best known tone language. The low tone is characterized by lowering the voice below the normal pitch and then rising back in the following syllable. In the high tone the pitch of the voice rises above its normal level falling back at the following symbol. The level tone is carried by the remaining words. Tones are not represented by any letters or symbols in the Gurmukhi script. In this course we are not marking words with tone signs, as we believe this will create confusion. The best manner to learn tonality is from repetition from the recording or listening and imitating native speakers.

Table I illustrates how tone can change the meaning of a word.

▶ **Table I   Tone illustrations**

Low tone	Level tone	High tone
ਝ jhaa *peep*	ਚਾਅ chaa-a *desire*	ਚਾਹ chaah *tea*
ਘੋੜਾ ghorhaa *horse*	ਕੋੜਾ korhaa *whip*	ਕੋਹੜਾ kohrhaa *leper*
ਘੜੀ gharhee *watch*	ਕੜੀ karhee *link of a chain*	ਕੜੀ karhhee *turmeric curry*

Return of ਹ 'haahaa'

We have already noted the variable pronunciation of the consonant ਹ *h*. Now that we have covered vowels and tones, we can return to look at some of the other varieties of **haahaa's** pronunciation.

1 When ਹ is preceded by a **sihaaree** the pronunciation of the vowel changes to resemble <u>dulaanvaan</u>. For instance the word

ਸ਼ਹਿਰ **shahir** is pronounced ਸ਼ੈਹਰ **shair**. The pronunciation of the word is therefore converted into a high tone.

2 When ਹ is accompanied by **aunkarh**, the pronunciation of the word changes to resemble **kanaurhaa**. For instance the word ਬਹੁਤ **bahut** is pronounced ਬੌਹਤ **bauht** once again changing the word to a high tone.

3 In a similar manner, when the letter preceding the ਹ has either the **aunkarh** or **sihaaree** vowel attached, then the pronunciation of the word changes so as to produce the **horhaa** and **laanv** vowels respectively. For example: ਸੁਹਣਾ **suhnhaa** is pronounced as ਸੋਹਣਾ **sohnhaa** and ਸਿਹਤ **sihat** is pronounced as ਸੇਹਤ **sehat**.

Subjoined consonants revisited

As we previously noted, a few Panjabi words require consonants to be written in a subjoined form, which takes the shape of a subscript to the main letter. The reason for this is to indicate that the inherent **muktaa** vowel is not present. Where vowels are present on the first letter, these are meant to be applied to the subjoined consonant. Therefore, in the word ਪ੍ਰੇਮ **prem**, there is no *a* symbol in the transliteration indicating the absence of the **muktaa**. The **laanv** vowel is applied to the *r* in the foot of the *p*. Note that the pronunciation of the subjoined consonant is the same as the normal consonant.

Auxiliary signs

The double sound ਅਧਕ 'adhak' ੱ

The function of the **ਅਧਕ adhak** ੱ is to allocate a double sound to the particular letter that it is assigned to. It should be placed above the preceding letter that is to be read twice, however, in practice it is placed between the two letters. Therefore, when the **adhak** occurs between two letters, it is the second of the two that is to be repeated. For example, in the Panjabi word for **thigh**, ਪੱਟ **patt**, the **adhak** affects the letter ਟ *t* changing the sound of the word from **pat** to **patt**. In some cases another vowel sound may come in between the two letters, but the **adhak** still affects the second letter, for example in the word ਬੱਚਿਓ **bachchio**, the **adhak** comes before the **sihaaree** vowel but still affects the letter ਚ *ch*, so it is pronounced **chch**. The **adhak** is a very important, though subtle device, as two letters without an **adhak** give rise to completely different meanings. For example ਪਗ **pag** means **foot**, whereas ਪੱਗ **pagg** means **turban**. A similar effect can be seen in English with the words **super** and **supper**.

Nasal sounds: ਬਿੰਦੀ 'bi<u>nd</u>ee' ∙ and ਟਿੱਪੀ 'tippee' ੑ

The **bi<u>nd</u>ee** and the **tippee** both serve to add a nasal sound to a particular vowel. The **bi<u>nd</u>ee** is used with **ka<u>nn</u>aa, laa<u>n</u>v, <u>d</u>ulaan-vaa<u>n</u>, bihaaree, horhaa** and **kanaurhaa** and the independent forms of vowels where ੳ is the bearer. For example: ਗਾਂ gaa<u>n</u> *cow.*

The **tippee** is used with the **mukṭaa, sihaaree, au<u>n</u>karh** and <u>d</u>u-lai<u>n</u>karhe. For example: ਖੰਡ kha<u>nd</u> *sugar.*

The sound of the **tippee** and **bi<u>nd</u>ee** is almost equivalent to the *n* in *pound* or *bangle.* However, their sound varies from the almost totally nasalized to a more fully pronounced *n* sound. For transliteration purposes the letter <u>n</u> is used for both the **tippee** and **bi<u>nd</u>ee.**

Panjabi loan words

The Panjabi language has a substantial number of words which have been borrowed from the English language, for example *school, college, telephone, bus, pen, pencil, chalk, ticket,* and *computer.* Moreover, some Panjabi words have been adopted by English, including *chutney, pandit, kebab, samosa, saree, dhobi,* and *guru.* Some English words borrowed by Panjabi have also been altered by Panjabi pronunciation and you will notice in the transliteration that English words and names have been written with this in mind.

Dictionary order

The letters in Panjabi dictionaries are arranged in the order of Table A, reading left to right, as are the order of words within each letter. The exceptions to this rule are those letters which are distinguished by a dot that is ਸ਼, ਖ਼, ਗ਼, ਜ਼ and ੜ, as these letters occur within the non-dotted form. Subjoined letters are not differentiated from the full form. Dictionary order in the Gurmukhi script is based upon phonology as vowels precede consonants. Therefore, the vowel signs follow **mukṭaa, ka<u>nn</u>aa, sihaaree, bihaaree, au<u>n</u>karh, <u>d</u>ulai<u>n</u>karhe, laa<u>n</u>v, <u>d</u>ulaa<u>n</u>vaa<u>n</u>, horhaa, kanaurhaa.**

Writing

Panjabi words are made up partly of consonants and partly of vowel signs. Letters are written first and then the sound symbols. Panjabi punctuation is similar to that used in English. However, one distinct difference is that in Panjabi a vertical stroke is used at the end of a sentence to mark a full stop. For example: *My name is Ritu.* ਮੇਰਾ ਨਾਮ ਰਿਤੁ ਹੈ।

There are ten vowels represented by nine signs. Their positions relating to consonants are as follows – = are written beneath the letter: ˆˋˊˋ are written above the letter; ਿ is written on the left of the letter while ਾ and ੀ are written on the right. The three auxiliary signs,ˇ · ˚ are written above the letter. Panjabi is best written on lined paper initially. In English the letters rest on the line, whereas in Panjabi the horizontal headstroke is written upon the line, the characters then hang from the line, in much the same way as clothes hang from a washing line.

Panjabi alphabet ਪੰਜਾਬੀ ਵਰਣਮਾਲਾ ਗੁਰਮੁਖੀ ਲਿਪੀ panjaabee varanhmaalaa gurmukhee lipee

Letter	Name of letter		Sign of letter
ੳ	ਉੜਾ	oorhaa	—
ਅ	ਐੜਾ	airhaa	a
ੲ	ਈੜੀ	eerhee	—
ਸ	ਸੱਸਾ	sassaa	s
ਹ	ਹਾਹਾ	haahaa	h
ਕ	ਕੱਕਾ	kakkaa	k
ਖ	ਖੱਖਾ	khakhkhaa	kh
ਗ	ਗੱਗਾ	gaggaa	g
ਘ	ਘੱਗਾ	ghaggaa	gh
ਙ	ਙੰਙਾ	nganngaa	ng
ਚ	ਚੱਚਾ	chachchaa	ch
ਛ	ਛੱਛਾ	<u>chachch</u>aa	<u>ch</u>
ਜ	ਜੱਜਾ	jajjaa	j
ਝ	ਝੱਜਾ	jhajjaa	jh
ਞ	ਞੰਞਾ	nja<u>n</u>njaa	nj
ਟ	ਟੈਂਕਾ	tai<u>n</u>kaa	t

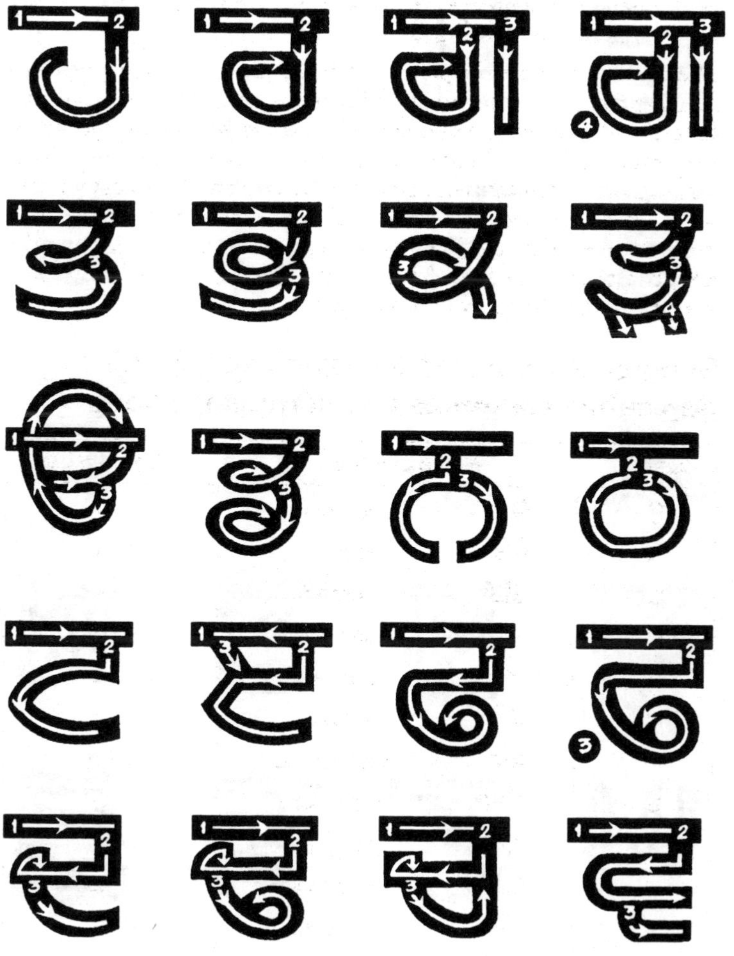

ਠ	ਠੱਠਾ	thaththaa		th
ਡ	ਡੱਡਾ	daddaa		d
ਢ	ਢੱਡਾ	dhaddaa		dh
ਣ	ਣਾਣਾ	nhaanhaa		nh
ਤ	ਤੱਤਾ	tattaa		t
ਥ	ਥੱਥਾ	thaththaa		th
ਦ	ਦੱਦਾ	daddaa		d
ਧ	ਧੱਦਾ	dhaddaa		dh
ਨ	ਨੱਨਾ	nannaa		n
ਪ	ਪੱਪਾ	pappaa		p
ਫ	ਫੱਫਾ	phaphphaa		ph
ਬ	ਬੱਬਾ	babbaa		b
ਭ	ਭੱਬਾ	bhabbaa		bh
ਮ	ਮੱਮਾ	mammaa		m
ਯ	ਯੱਯਾ	yayyaa		y
ਰ	ਰਾਰਾ	raaraa		r
ਲ	ਲੱਲਾ	lallaa		l
ਵ	ਵੱਵਾ	vavvaa		v
ੜ	ੜਾੜਾ	rhaarhaa		rh
ਸ	ਸੱਸਾ	shashshaa		sh
ਖ਼	ਖ਼ੱਖਾ	khakhkhaa		kh
ਗ਼	ਗ਼ੱਗਾ	ghaghghaa		gh
ਜ਼	ਜ਼ੱਜ਼ਾ	zazzaa		z
ਫ਼	ਫ਼ੱਫਾ	faffaa		f

Relationship between independent and dependent vowels:

Independent	ਅ	ਆ	ਇ	ਈ	ਉ	ਊ	ਏ	ਐ	ਓ	ਔ
Dependent	-	ਾ	ਿ	ੀ	ੁ	ੂ	ੇ	ੈ	ੋ	ੌ
Transliteration	a	aa	i	ee	u	oo	e	ai	o	au

Sample reading and writing lessons

1 ਮੁਕਤਾ ਅ 'muktaa a'

The vowel **muktaa** has no visible symbol in the Gurmukhi script. For transliteration purposes it is represented by the letter *a*.

Reading

1 ਕਰਮ, ਕਪ, ਕਮਰ
karam, kap, kamar
Karam, cup, Kamar

2 ਕਮਲ ਮਗ ਭਰ
kamal, mag bhar
Kamal, fill the mug.

3 ਅਮਰ, ਚਰਚ ਚਲ
amar, charach chal
Amar, go to the church.

4 ਮਲਕ, ਜਗ ਭਰ
malak, jag bhar
Malik, fill the jug.

Writing pattern

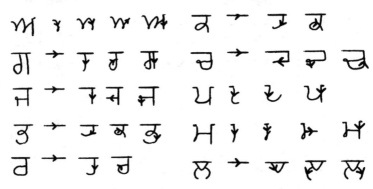

▶ Exercises

1 Read the following sentences out loud and check your pronunciation with the recording.

a ਕਪ ਭਰ ਕਰਮ

b ਮਗ ਭਰ ਕਮਲ

c ਭਰ ਜਗਾ ਮਲਕ

d ਚਰਚ ਚਲ ਕਮਰ

2 Write out the following words:

a ਕਮਲ

b ਚਰਚ

c ਜਗ

2 ਕੰਨਾ ਆ ਾ 'ka<u>nn</u>aa aa'

The dependent form of the **ka<u>nn</u>aa** vowel is placed to the right of the letter that is affected. For transliteration purposes it is represented by the symbol *aa*.

Reading

1 ਸ਼ਾਮ, ਨਾਨਾ, ਵਾਲ ਵਾਹ
shaam, naanaa, vaal vaah
Sham, grandfather, comb hair.

2 ਰਾਮ, ਬਸ ਫੜ
raam, bas pharh
Ram, catch the bus.

3 ਚਾਚਾ, ਘਰ ਆ
chaachaa, ghar aa
Uncle, come home.

4 ਕਾਕਾ, ਅਨਾਰ ਖਾ
kaakaa, anaar khaa
Baby, eat the pomegranate.

Writing pattern

ਸ → ੮ ੮ ਸ   ਹ → ੮ ੮ ਹ

ਘ → ੮ ੮ ਘ   ਨ → ੮ ੮ ਨ

ੳ → ੮ ੮ ੳ   ਬ → ੮ ੮ ਬ

ਦ → ੮ ੮ ਦ   ੜ → ੮ ੜ ੜ

ਸ → ੮ ੮ ਸ   ਖ → ੮ ੮ ਖ

▶ Exercises

1 Read the following sentences out loud and check your pronunciation with the recording.

a ਨਾਨਾ ਬਸ ਫੜ   c ਕਾਕਾ ਘਰ ਆ
b ਸ਼ਾਮ ਵਾਲ ਵਾਹ   d ਚਾਚਾ ਅਨਾਰ ਖਾ

2 Write out the following words:

a ਬਸ   b ਸ਼ਾਮ   c ਨਾਨਾ

3 ਅਧਕ 'adhak' ੑ

The ਅਧਕ 'adhak' ੑ should be placed above the preceding letter that is to be read twice, in practice, however, it is placed in between the two letters. Therefore, when the **adhak** occurs between two letters it is the second letter of the two that is to be repeated. For transliteration purposes the **adhak** has the effect of doubling the consonant effected.

Reading

1 ਅੱਖ, ਪੱਟ, ਲੱਤ
akhkh, patt, latt
eye, thigh, leg

2 ਸ਼ਾਮ, ਪੱਗ ਰੱਖ
shaam, pagg rakhkh
Sham, put on the turban.

3 ਅੱਠ ਹੱਥ
athth haththth
eight hands

4 ਸੱਤ ਨੱਕ
satt nakk
seven noses

Writing pattern

ਟ → ਟ ਟ੍ਰ   ਠ → ਠ ਠ੍ਰ

ਤ → ਤ ਤ੍ਰ   ਥ → ਥ ਥ੍ਰ ਥ

▶ Exercises

1 Read the following words out loud and check your pronunciation with the recording.

a ਸ਼ਾਮ ਪੱਗ ਰੱਖ   c ਸੱਤ ਹੱਥ
b ਅੱਠ ਨੱਕ   d ਅੱਖ, ਲੱਤ, ਪੱਟ

2 Write out the following words:

a ਪੱਟ   b ਅੱਠ   c ਹੱਥ

4 ਸਿਹਾਰੀ ਇ ਿ 'sihaaree i'

The dependent form of the sihaaree vowel is placed to the left of
the letter being affected. For transliteration purposes it is represented by the letter *i*.

Reading

1 ਕਿਰਨ, ਇੱਟ, ਇੱਕ, ਕਿੱਲ
kiran, itt, ikk, kill
Kiran, brick, one, nail

2 ਜਿੱਲ, ਸਿੱਧਾ ਲਿਖ
jill, si<u>dhdh</u>aa likh
Jill, write straight.

3 ਦਿਲਬਰ, ਰਿੱਛ ਗਿਣ
<u>d</u>ilbar, ri<u>chch</u> ginh
Dilbar, count the bears.

4 ਇਹ ਚਾਰ ਹਿਰਨ ਹਨ
ih chaar hiran han
These are four deer.

Writing pattern

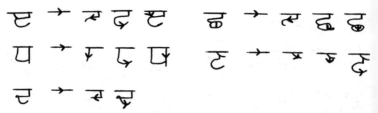

▶ Exercises

1 Read the following sentences out loud and check your pronunciation with the recording.

a ਇੱਕ ਇੱਟ   c ਦਿਲਬਰ ਕਿੱਲ ਗਿਣ

b ਕਿਰਨ ਸਿੱਧਾ ਲਿਖ   d ਇਹ ਚਾਰ ਰਿੱਛ ਹਨ

2 Write the names in Gurmukhi of the items in the pictures:

a ri<u>chch</u>   b kill   c hiran

5 ਬਿਹਾਰੀ ਈ ੀ 'bihaaree ee'

The dependent form of the **bihaaree** vowel is placed to the right of the letter that is being affected. For transliteration purposes it is represented by the letter *ee*.

Reading

1 ਸੀਟੀ, ਡੱਬੀ, ਵਾਲੀ, ਸੀਤਾ
seetee, dabbee, vaalee, seetaa
whistle, small box, earring, Sita

2 ਰੀਟਾ, ਗਲੀਚਾ ਸਾਫ਼ ਕਰ
reetaa, <u>gh</u>aleechaa saaf kar
Rita, clean the rug.

3 ਚਾਚੀ ਖ਼ਤਾਈ ਲਿਆਈ
chaachee <u>kh</u>a<u>t</u>aaee liaaee
Aunty has bought a biscuit.

4 ਈਸ਼ਰ ਦੀ ਬਿੱਲੀ ਕਾਲੀ ਸੀ
eeshar <u>d</u>ee billee kaalee see
Eesher's cat was black.

Writing pattern

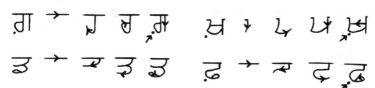

▶ Exercises

1 Read the following sentences out loud and check your pronunciation with the recording.

a ਰੀਟਾ ਬਿੱਲੀ ਲਿਆਈ   c ਚਾਚੀ ਗਲੀਚਾ ਲਿਆਈ
b ਸੀਤਾ ਖ਼ਤਾਈ ਲਿਆਈ   d ਈਸ਼ਰ ਸੀਟੀ ਲਿਆਈ

2 Write the names in Gurmukhi of the items in the pictures:

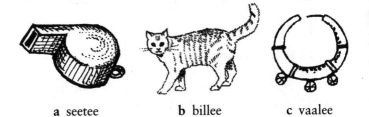

   a seetee   **b** billee   **c** vaalee

6 ਔਂਕੜ ਉ ◌ੁ 'auṉkarh u'

The dependent form of the vowel **auṉkarh** is placed under the
letter to be affected. For transliteration purposes it is represented
by the letter *u*.

Reading

1 ਦੁੱਧ, ਢੱਕਣ, ਸੁਖ, ਪੀ
<u>dudhdh</u>, dhakkanh, sukh, pee
milk, lid, Sukh, drink

2 ਉਪਕਾਰ, ਉੱਨ ਲਿਆ
upkaar, unn liaa
Upkar, bring the wool.

3 ਯੁਵਕ, ਜ਼ਬਾਨ ਨਾ ਕੱਢ
yuvak, zabaan naa kadhdh
*Young boy! Do not stick
out your tongue.*

4 ਗੁਲਾਬ, ਚੁੱਪ ਕਰ
gulaab, chupp kar
Gulab, keep quiet.

Writing pattern

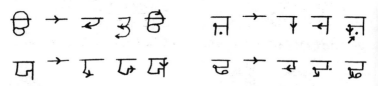

▶ Exercises

1 Read the following sentences out loud and check your pronunciation with the recording.

a ਸੁਖ ਢੱਕਣ ਲਿਆ   c ਯੁਵਕ ਦੁੱਧ ਪੀ
b ਗੁਲਾਬ ਉੱਨ ਲਿਆ   d ਉਪਕਾਰ ਚੁੱਪ ਕਰ

2 Write the name in Gurmukhi of the items in the pictures:

a dhakkanh   **b** zabaan   **c** unn

7 ਦੁਲੈਂਕੜੇ ਉੁ _ 'dulainkarhe oo'

The dependent form of the vowel **dulainkarhe** appears under the letter being affected. For purposes of transliteration the symbol *oo* is used to represent the **dulainkarhe**.

Reading

1 ਸੂਰ, ਫੜ, ਝਾੜੂ, ਭੂਪ
  soor, pharh, jhaarhoo, bhoop
  pig, hold, broom, Bhup

2 ਰੂਪ, ਆੜੂ ਖਾ
  Roop, aarhoo khaa
  Rup, eat the peach.

3 ਸਰੂਪ ਦਾ ਊਠ
  Saroop daa ooth
  Sarup's camel

4 ਅਨੂਪ, ਮੂਰਤ ਬਣਾ
  Anoop, moorat banhaa
  Anup, draw a picture.

Writing pattern

▶ Exercises

1 Read the following sentences out loud and check your pronunciation with the recording.

  a ਸਰੂਪ ਦਾ ਊਠ   c ਅਨੂਪ ਆੜੂ ਖਾ
  b ਰੂਪ ਮੂਰਤ ਬਣਾ   d ਭੂਪ ਝਾੜੂ ਫੜ

2. Write the names in Gurmukhi of the items in the pictures:

    a ooth   **b** soor   **c** jhaarhoo

8 ਲਾਂਵ ਏ ੇ 'laanv e'

The dependent form of the vowel **laanv** is placed on top of the affected letter. For transliteration purposes the letter e will be used to symbolize the **laanv**.

Reading

1 ਲੇਲੇ, ਪਿਆਰੇ, ਭੇਡ, ਮੇਰਾ
lele, piaare, bhed, meraa
lambs, beloved, sheep, my

2 ਇਹ ਛੇ ਮੇਜ਼ ਹਨ
ih che mez han
These are six tables.

3 ਉਹ ਜੇਨ ਦਾ ਸੇਬ ਏ
uh jen daa seb e
That is Jane's apple.

4 ਡੇਵਿਡ, ਸ਼ੇਰ ਦੇਖ
devid, sher dekh
David, look at the lion.

▶ Exercises

1 Read the following sentences out loud and check your pronunciation with the recording.

a ਇਹ ਛੇ ਲੇਲੇ ਹਨ
b ਲੇਲੇ ਪਿਆਰੇ ਹਨ

c ਇਹ ਮੇਰਾ ਸੇਬ ਏ
d ਉਹ ਭੇਡ ਏ

2 Fill in the blanks by writing the correct words in Gurmukhi:

a _____lele   b _____bhed   c _____seb

9 ਦੁਲਾਂਵਾਂ ਐ ੈ 'dulaanvaan ai'

The dependent form of the vowel **dulaanvaan** is written on top of the affected letter. For transliteration purposes the symbol *ai* is used to represent **dulaanvaan**.

Reading

1 ਸਵੈਟਰ, ਬੈਗ, ਜਰਨੈਲ, ਪੈਰ
svaitar, baig, jarnail, pair
sweater, bag, Jarnail, foot

2 ਇਹ ਐਨਕ ਲੈ
ih ainak lai
Have these spectacles.

3 ਅੱਜ ਐਤਵਾਰ ਹੈ
ajj aitvaar hai
Today is Sunday.

4 ਇਹ ਕੈਮਰਾ ਮੇਰੀ ਭੈਣ ਦਾ ਹੈ
ih kaimraa meree bhainh daa hai
This is my sister's camera.

▶ Exercises

1 Read the following sentences out loud and check your pronunciation with the recording.

a ਇਹ ਕੈਮਰਾ ਜਰਨੈਲ ਦਾ ਹੈ
b ਇਹ ਮੇਰਾ ਸਵੈਟਰ ਹੈ

c ਇਹ ਬੈਗ ਮੇਰੀ ਭੈਣ ਦਾ ਹੈ
d ਇਹ ਐਨਕ ਲੈ

2 Fill in the blanks by writing the correct words in Gurmukhi:

a _____bhainh   b _____aitvaar   c _____ainak

10 ਹੋੜਾ ਓ ੋ 'horhaa o'

The dependent form of the vowel **horhaa** appears above the affected letter. For transliteration purposes the letter *o* is used to represent **horhaa**.

Reading

1 ਖੋਤਾ, ਮੋਟਾ, ਘੋੜਾ, ਸੋਟੀ
khoṯaa, motaa, ghorhaa, sotee
donkey, fat, horse, stick

2 ਸੋਹਣ ਕੋਲ ਤੋਤਾ ਹੈ
sohanh kol ṯoṯaa hai
Sohan has a parrot.

3 ਰੋਟੀ ਖਾ ਮੋਹਨ
rotee khaa mohan
Eat your food Mohan.

4 ਆਓ ਬੱਚਿਓ ਮੋਰ ਦੇਖੋ
aao bachchio mor ḏekho
Come on children look at the peacock.

▶ Exercises

1 Read the following sentences out loud and check your pronunciation with the recording.

a ਸੋਹਣ ਰੋਟੀ ਖਾ
b ਖੋਤਾ ਮੋਟਾ ਹੈ

c ਮੋਹਨ ਕੋਲ ਘੋੜਾ ਹੈ
d ਆਓ ਬੱਚਿਓ ਤੋਤਾ ਦੇਖੋ

2 Fill in the missing letters in Gurmukhi:

a ___ ਤਾ khoṯaa   b ___ ਟਾ motaa   c ___ ੜਾ ghorhaa

11 ਕਨੌੜਾ ਔ ੌ 'kanaurhaa au'

The dependent form of the **kanaurhaa** vowel appears above the affected letter. For transliteration purposes the symbol *au* is used to represent **kanaurhaa**.

Reading

1 ਫ਼ੌਜੀ, ਪੌੜੀ, ਬਲੌਰ, ਦੌੜ
faujee, paurhee, balaur, ḏaurh
soldier, ladder, playing marbles, run

2 ਸ਼ਰਨ ਕੌਰ, ਚੌਲ ਉਬਾਲ
sharan kaur, chaul ubaal
Sharan Kaur, boil the rice.

3 ਉਹ ਔਰਤ ਕੌਣ ਹੈ
uh auraṯ kaunh hai?
Who is that woman?

4 ਇਹ ਮੇਰੇ ਖਿਡੌਣੇ ਹਨ
ih mere khidaunhe han
These are my toys.

▶ Exercises

1 Read the following sentences out loud and check your pronunciation with the recording.

a ਚੌਲ ਉਬਾਲ
b ਉਹ ਕੌਣ ਹੈ?

c ਉਹ ਫ਼ੌਜੀ ਹੈ
d ਇਹ ਮੇਰੇ ਬਲੌਰ ਹਨ

2 Fill in the missing letters and vowels in Gurmukhi:

a ___ ਲ chaul   b ਖਿ ___ ਨੇ khidaunhe   c ___ ਜੀ faujee

12 ਬਿੰਦੀ 'bindee' • and ਟਿੱਪੀ 'tippee' ੰ 'n'

The bindee and the tippee both serve to add a nasal sound to a particular vowel. For transliteration purposes, the letter **n** is used for both the *tippee* and bindee.

Reading

1 ਸਿੰਘ, ਚੁੰਜ, ਮੂੰਹ
  singh, chunj, moonh
  lion, beak, mouth

2 ਅੰਬ, ਜੰਞ, ਲੰਙਾ
  anb, jannj, lanngaa
  mango, marriage party,
  lame person

3 ਕਾਂ, ਗੇਂਦ, ਕੈਂਚੀ, ਮੀਂਹ
  kaan, gend, kainchee, meenh
  crow, ball, scissors, rain

4 ਹੋਂਠ, ਪੋਂਡ, ਉਂਗਲੀ, ਵਤਾਊਂ
  honth, paund, unglee, vataaoon
  lips, pound, finger, aubergine

Writing pattern

▶ Exercises

1 Read the following words out loud and check your pronunciation with the recording.

a ਸਿੰਘ, ਜੰਞ, ਕੈਂਚੀ   c ਮੂੰਹ, ਅੰਬ, ਮੀਂਹ
b ਚੁੰਜ, ਲੰਙਾ, ਉਂਗਲੀ   d ਕਾਂ, ਗੇਂਦ, ਵਤਾਊਂ

2 Fill in the missing letters and vowels in Gurmukhi:

a ਜ____jannj   b ਲ_____lanngaa   c ਵ_____vataaoon

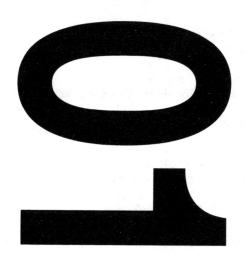

01

ਤੁਹਾਡਾ ਕੀ ਹਾਲ ਹੈ?

tuhaadaa kee haal hai?

how are you?

In this unit you will learn:
- how to use simple greetings
- how to introduce yourself
- how to ask how people are

▶ 1 *What is your name?*

ਗੱਲ ਬਾਤ ੧ ਤੁਹਾਡਾ ਕੀ ਨਾਮ ਹੈ?

gall baaṯ 1 ṯuhaadaa kee naam hai?

It is the first day of the new Panjabi class at Heywood College. Mr Charan Singh is the teacher and Jane, Henry and David are students.

ਚਰਨ ਸਿੰਘ **Charan Singh**	ਸਤਿ ਸ੍ਰੀ ਅਕਾਲ ਜੀ! saṯ sree akaal jee! *Hello! (see Commentary section)*
ਜੇਨ **Jane**	ਸਤਿ ਸ੍ਰੀ ਅਕਾਲ ਜੀ! saṯ sree akaal jee! *Hello!*
ਚਰਨ ਸਿੰਘ **Charan Singh**	ਮੇਰਾ ਨਾਮ ਚਰਨ ਸਿੰਘ ਹੈ। ਤੁਹਾਡਾ ਕੀ ਨਾਮ ਹੈ? meraa naam charan siṉgh hai. ṯuhaadaa kee naam hai? *My name is Charan Singh. What's your name?* *(to Jane)*
ਜੇਨ **Jane**	ਜੀ ਮੇਰਾ ਨਾਮ ਜੇਨ ਹੈ। jee meraa naam jen hai. *My name is Jane.*
ਚਰਨ ਸਿੰਘ **Charan Singh**	ਅੱਛਾ! ਤੁਹਾਡਾ ਕੀ ਨਾਮ ਹੈ? achchaa. ṯuhaadaa kee naam hai? *OK! What's your name? (to Henry)*
ਹੈਨਰੀ **Henry**	ਜੀ ਮੇਰਾ ਨਾਮ ਹੈਨਰੀ ਹੈ। jee meraa naam hainree hai. *My name is Henry.*
ਚਰਨ ਸਿੰਘ **Charan Singh**	ਸ਼ਾਬਾਸ਼! shaabaash! *Well done!*

David and Jane exchange greetings in an informal manner.

ਜੇਨ **Jane**	ਸਤਿ ਸ੍ਰੀ ਅਕਾਲ। ਮੇਰਾ ਨਾਂ ਜੇਨ ਏ। ਤੇਰਾ ਕੀ ਨਾਂ ਏ? saṯ sree akaal. meraa naaṉ jen e. ṯeraa kee naaṉ e? *Hello. My name is Jane. What's your name?*
ਡੇਵਿਡ **David**	ਸਤਿ ਸ੍ਰੀ ਅਕਾਲ। ਮੇਰਾ ਨਾਂ ਡੇਵਿਡ ਏ। saṯ sree akaal. meraa naaṉ devid e. *Hello. My name is David.*

ਸ਼ਬਦਾਵਲੀ shabdaavalee *Vocabulary*

ਤੁਹਾਡਾ	ṯuhaadaa	*your* (formal)
ਕੀ	kee	*what* / how
ਨਾਮ	naam	*name* (m.) (formal)
ਹੈ	hai	*is* (formal)*
ਸਤਿ ਸ੍ਰੀ ਅਕਾਲ	saṯ sree akaal	Sikh greeting (lit. God is truth)
ਜੀ	jee	honorific particle signifying respect (see Commentary)
ਮੇਰਾ	meraa	*my*
ਅੱਛਾ	achchaa	*OK, alright*
ਸ਼ਾਬਾਸ਼	shaabaash	*well done*
ਤੇਰਾ	ṯeraa	*your* (informal)
ਨਾਂ	naan	*name* (m.) (informal)
ਏ	e	*is* (informal)*

* The ways in which *is, am* and *are* are formed in Panjabi will be referred to in Unit 2.

ਅਭਿਆਸ abhiaas *Exercises*

After reading the dialogue and / or listening to the recording, try to do the following exercises.

▶ 1 True or false?

a ਤੁਹਾਡਾ ṯuhaadaa means *your* (True)/ False
b ਮੇਰਾ meraa means *my* (True)/ False
c ਅੱਛਾ achchaa means *well done* True / (False)

2 Arrange in correct word order.

a ਮੇਰਾ ਹੈ ਡੇਵਿਡ ਨਾਂ meraa-hai-devid-naan *My name is David.*
b ਤੁਹਾਡਾ ਹੈ ਨਾਮ ਕੀ ? ṯuhaadaa-hai-naam-kee? *What is your name?*
c ਨਾਂ ਏ ਕੀ ਤੇਰਾ ? naan-e-kee-ṯeraa? *What is your name?*

▶ 2 *How are you?*

ਗੱਲ ਬਾਤ ੨ ਤੁਹਾਡਾ ਕੀ ਹਾਲ ਹੈ ?

gall baaṯ 2 ṯuhaadaa kee haal hai?

Parveen and Talat meet each other in the city centre. Parveen is with her brother Rahim and sister Salma.

ਪਰਵੀਨ **Parveen**	ਅੱਸਲਾਮ ਅਲੈਕਮ । ਤੁਹਾਡਾ ਕੀ ਹਾਲ ਹੈ ? asslaam alaikam. ṭuhaadaa kee haal hai? *Hello. How are you?*
ਤਲਤ **Talat**	ਵਾਲੈਕਮ ਅੱਸਲਾਮ । ਮੇਰਾ ਹਾਲ ਠੀਕ ਹੈ । vaalaikam asslaam. meraa haal theek hai. *Hello. I'm fine.*
ਪਰਵੀਨ **Parveen**	ਇਹ ਮੇਰਾ ਭਰਾ ਹੈ ਅਤੇ ਇਹ ਮੇਰੀ ਭੈਣ ਹੈ । ih meraa bharaa hai aṭe ih meree bhainh hai. *This is my brother and this is my sister.*
ਤਲਤ **Talat**	ਕੀ ਤੁਹਾਡਾ ਪਰਵਾਰ ਠੀਕ ਹੈ ? kee ṭuhaadaa parvaar theek hai? *Is your family alright?*
ਸਲਮਾ ਤੇ ਰਹੀਮ **Salma and Rahim**	ਸ਼ੁਕਰੀਆ । ਸਾਡਾ ਪਰਵਾਰ ਠੀਕ ਹੈ । shukreeaa. saadaa parvaar theek hai. *Thank you. Our family is fine.*
ਤਲਤ **Talat**	ਖੁਦਾ ਹਾਫ਼ਿਜ਼ । <u>kh</u>udaa haafiz. *Goodbye.*
ਰਹੀਮ, ਸਲਮਾ ਤੇ ਪਰਵੀਨ **Rahim, Salma and Parveen**	ਖੁਦਾ ਹਾਫ਼ਿਜ਼ । <u>kh</u>udaa haafiz. *Goodbye.*

ਸ਼ਬਦਾਵਲੀ shab<u>d</u>aavalee *Vocabulary*

ਹਾਲ	haal	*condition* (lit.) (m.)
ਹੈ	hai	*is*
ਤੁਹਾਡਾ ਕੀ ਹਾਲ ਹੈ ?	ṭuhaadaa kee haal hai?	*How are you?* (see Commentary)
ਅੱਸਲਾਮ ਅਲੈਕਮ	asslaam alaikam	*Muslim greeting*
ਵਾਲੈਕਮ ਅੱਸਲਾਮ	vaalaikam asslaam	*response to Muslim greeting*
ਠੀਕ	theek	*fine / OK / alright*
ਇਹ	ih	*this*
ਭਰਾ	bharaa	*brother* (m.)
ਅਤੇ	aṭe	*and*
ਭੈਣ	bhainh	*sister* (f.)
ਪਰਵਾਰ	parvaar	*family* (m.)
ਸ਼ੁਕਰੀਆ	shukreeaa	*thank you* (m.)
ਸਾਡਾ	saadaa	*our*
ਖੁਦਾ ਹਾਫ਼ਿਜ਼	<u>kh</u>udaa haafiz	*Muslim departing phrase*

ਅਭਿਆਸ   abhiaas   *Exercises*

After reading the dialogue and / or listening to the recording, try to do the following exercises.

▶ 1 Begin the conversation.

a ਵਾਲੈਕਮ ਅੱਸਲਾਮ ।
vaalaikam asslaam.
Hello.

b ਮੇਰਾ ਹਾਲ ਠੀਕ ਏ ।
meraa haal theek e.
I am fine.

c ਜੀ, ਪਰਵਾਰ ਠੀਕ ਹੈ ।
Jee, parvaar theek hai.
The family is fine.

2 Match the expressions.

a ਮੇਰਾ ਭਰਾ	meraa bharaa	1	*our family*
b ਮੇਰੀ ਭੈਣ	meree bhainh	2	*my brother*
c ਸਾਡਾ ਪਰਵਾਰ	saadaa parvaar	3	*my sister*

ਬੋਲੀ ਬਾਰੇ bolee baare *Language points*

Possessive adjectives

1 Adjectives are words which describe people, places and objects. The words *my*, *your* and *his / her* are possessive adjectives. Unlike in English, the possessive adjective in Panjabi changes according to what is being possessed. In Dialogues 1 and 2 the word ਹਾਲ **haal** (*condition*) is grammatically masculine and therefore requires a masculine possessive adjective. Similarly, a woman talking about her children will use two forms of the

word *my*, distinguishing between her son and daughter. ਮੇਰਾ **meraa** would apply to the male and ਮੇਰੀ **meree** for the female. Note that it is the ending which changes. This distinction is the same even if the father were talking about his son and daughter.

Examples:

Mother talking about her children:

| ਮੇਰਾ ਲੜਕਾ ਠੀਕ ਹੈ। | meraa larhkaa theek hai. | *My son is fine.* |
| ਮੇਰੀ ਲੜਕੀ ਠੀਕ ਹੈ। | meree larhkee theek hai. | *My daughter is fine.* |

Father talking about his children:

| ਮੇਰਾ ਲੜਕਾ ਠੀਕ ਹੈ। | meraa larhkaa theek hai. | *My son is fine.* |
| ਮੇਰੀ ਲੜਕੀ ਠੀਕ ਹੈ। | meree larhkee theek hai. | *My daughter is fine.* |

You will have noticed that there is no difference between the sentences spoken by the mother and the father. The form of the possessive adjective does not depend on the gender of the possessor (i.e. whether male or female) but on the gender of what is being possessed. In addition to gender, possessive adjectives also change according to whether the possessed object is singular or plural. As both parents are talking about one person, the possessive adjective is in the *singular* form.

There are, therefore, three factors which need to be taken into account when selecting the appropriate possessive adjective:

- whether the object is masculine or feminine
- whether the object is singular or plural
- whether the situation is formal or informal

2 In addition to describing objects, possessive adjectives are also used to describe different states of being, i.e. how you are, how you are feeling or other personal descriptions such as your name. You will remember from Dialogue 2 that Parveen uses the possessive adjective *your* when asking her friend Talat *How are you?* The literal meaning of this question in Panjabi is *How is your condition?* Talat responds by saying *I'm fine*, literally *My condition is fine* with the possessive adjective *my*.

The following tables illustrate the way in which possessive adjectives are formed with singular, masculine and feminine objects. Note that the plural forms given here (*their*, *our*) refer only to the nature of the possessor, not of the object being possessed.

Possessive adjectives with singular masculine objects

1st person

| ਮੇਰਾ | meraa | *my* |
| ਸਾਡਾ | saadaa | *our* |

2nd person

| ਤੇਰਾ | <u>t</u>eraa | *your* (informal) |
| ਤੁਹਾਡਾ | <u>t</u>uhaadaa | *your* (formal) |

3rd person

ਇਹ ਦਾ / ਇਸ ਦਾ	ih <u>d</u>aa / is <u>d</u>aa	*his / her*
ਇਹਨਾਂ ਦਾ	ihnaa<u>n</u> <u>d</u>aa	*his / her* (formal) *their*
ਉਹ ਦਾ / ਉਸ ਦਾ	uh <u>d</u>aa / us <u>d</u>aa	*his / her*
ਉਹਨਾਂ ਦਾ	uhnaa<u>n</u> <u>d</u>aa	*his / her* (formal) *their*

Possessive adjectives with singular feminine objects

1st person

| ਮੇਰੀ | meree | *my* |
| ਸਾਡੀ | saadee | *our* |

2nd person

| ਤੇਰੀ | <u>t</u>eree | *your* (informal) |
| ਤੁਹਾਡੀ | <u>t</u>uhaadee | *your* (formal) |

3rd person

ਇਹ ਦੀ / ਇਸ ਦੀ	ih <u>d</u>ee / is <u>d</u>ee	*his / her*
ਇਹਨਾਂ ਦੀ	ihnaa<u>n</u> <u>d</u>ee	*his / her* (formal) *their*
ਉਹ ਦੀ / ਉਸ ਦੀ	uh <u>d</u>ee / us <u>d</u>ee	*his / her*
ਉਹਨਾਂ ਦੀ	uhnaa<u>n</u> <u>d</u>ee	*his / her* (formal) *their*

Further examples of possessive adjectives with plural objects will be illustrated in Unit 3.

▶ Formal and informal speech

There is a clear distinction between formal and informal speech in Panjabi. For instance, two sisters talking over the phone will use significantly different speech from two strangers meeting for the first time. Let us consider the example of a telephone conversation between Surinder and Mohinder who are sisters.

Surinder	ਕਿੱਦਾਂ ਮੋਹਿੰਦਰ ?	<u>kiddaan</u> <u>M</u>ohindar? *How are you, Mohinder?*
Mohinder	ਠੀਕ ਹਾਂ । ਤੇਰਾ ਕੀ ਹਾਲ ਏ ?	<u>theek haan</u>. <u>t</u>eraa kee haal e? *I'm fine. How are you?*

Now let's contrast this situation with two strangers meeting in an office.

Mr Sandhu	ਤੁਹਾਡਾ ਕੀ ਹਾਲ ਹੈ ਜੀ ?	<u>t</u>uhaadaa kee haal hai jee? *How are you?*
Mr Johal	ਧੰਨਵਾਦ । ਮੇਰਾ ਹਾਲ ਠੀਕ ਹੈ ।	<u>dh</u>annvaa<u>d</u> meraa haal theek hai. *Thank you. I am fine.*

If you compare these two example situations, you will notice that there are two Panjabi words for the same English word *your*. In the first meeting between Mr Singh and the Panjabi class at Heywood College, the words ਤੇਰਾ <u>t</u>eraa and ਤੁਹਾਡਾ <u>t</u>uhaadaa are used for *your*. Either word is used depending on who is being addressed. The word ਤੁਹਾਡਾ <u>t</u>uhaadaa is used normally when addressing more than one person (plural) or when addressing one person, male or female, formally as a sign of respect. Therefore, the word ਤੁਹਾਡਾ <u>t</u>uhaadaa serves two purposes:

- to address a singular male/female in a formal manner
- to address more than one person, male or female, in an informal or formal manner

Conversely, the word ਤੇਰਾ <u>t</u>eraa is used only in an informal manner to address a single person, male or female.

Here are two common examples of the formal and informal:

ਤੁਹਾਡਾ ਕੀ ਨਾਮ ਹੈ ?	<u>t</u>uhaadaa kee naam hai?	*What is your name?* (formal)
ਤੇਰਾ ਕੀ ਨਾਂ ਹੈ / ਏ ?	<u>t</u>eraa kee naa<u>n</u> hai / e?	*What is your name?* (informal)

Asking questions in Panjabi

In Dialogue 1 the word ਕੀ **kee** is used to turn a statement into a question. For example:

| *Statement* | ਤੁਹਾਡਾ ਪਰਵਾਰ ਠੀਕ ਹੈ। | ṯuhaadaa parvaar theek hai. | *Your family is fine.* |
| *Question* | ਕੀ ਤੁਹਾਡਾ ਪਰਵਾਰ ਠੀਕ ਹੈ? | kee ṯuhaadaa parvaar theek hai? | *Is your family fine?* |

However, you do not always need to use a question word, or interrogative, to turn a statement into a question. The use of intonation (rise and fall of the voice in speech) and emphasis can serve the same purpose. Raising your voice at the end of a sentence or using a questioning tone are equally effective. To ask the question *What is your name?* you can simply say:

ਜੀ ਤੁਹਾਡਾ ਨਾਮ?   jee ṯuhaadaa naam?   *Your name, please?*

The use of any question depends on the context of the conversation, the relationship between the speakers, and the number of people involved. You may have noted that the question *How are you?* is given as ਤੁਹਾਡਾ ਕੀ ਹਾਲ ਹੈ? <u>ṯuhaadaa kee haal hai</u>? <u>There are three</u> literal meanings of this sentence: *What is your condition?*, *How are you getting on?* and *How are you feeling?* The various forms of *How are you?* will be used throughout the rest of the book. So look out for them!

There are many ways of asking and responding to the question *How are you?* in Panjabi. Some of the possibilities are listed in the Commentary section. You do not have to learn all of these, but they are useful to know when trying to understand the speech of other Panjabi speakers.

ਵਿਆਖਿਆ   viaakhiaa   *Commentary*

1 How are you?

There are various ways of saying *How are you?* in Panjabi. Here are some examples:

- ਤੂੰ ਕਿਵੇਂ ਹੈਂ?   ṯoon kiven hain? (informal)
- ਤੇਰਾ ਕੀ ਹਾਲ ਹੈ?   ṯeraa kee haal hai? (informal)
- ਕਿੱਦਾਂ?   kiddaan? (colloquial)

Now let's have a look at the variety of responses to the question *How are you?*

- ਠੀਕ ਏ   theek e   *Fine.* (informal)

• ਤੁਹਾਡੀ ਕਿਰਪਾ ਹੈ	ṭuhaadee kirpaa hai	*By your blessings.* *(I am fine)* (formal)
• ਵਾਹਿਗੁਰੂ ਦਾ ਸ਼ੁਕਰ ਹੈ	vaahiguroo ḍaa shukar hai	*By the grace of God.* *(I am fine)* (formal)

It is common for Panjabi speakers to respond to *How are you?* reciprocally by asking the same of the enquirer:

• ਤੂੰ ਸੁਣਾ	ṭoon sunhaa	*You tell (how you are).* (informal)
• ਤੁਸੀਂ ਸੁਣਾਓ	ṭuseen sunhaao	*You tell (how you are).* (formal)

As in English when asked the question *How are you?* many people say *thank you* after replying with such responses as *I'm fine*. There are a few common ways of expressing *thank you* in Panjabi:

• ਧੰਨਵਾਦ	dhannvaaḍ
• ਸ਼ੁਕਰੀਆ	shukreeaa
• ਮਿਹਰਬਾਨੀ	miharbaanee
• ਤੁਹਾਡੀ ਕਿਰਪਾ ਹੈ।	ṭuhaadee kirpaa hai

▶ 2 Panjabi greetings

Panjabi greetings are chosen, not according to the time of day – as in cases such as *Good morning* or *Good evening* – but according to the religion of the speakers. All the world's main faiths are represented in Panjab. However, after the partition of the region, the main religious group in West Panjab (Pakistan) is Muslim, with a sizeable Christian minority, and in East Panjab there is a mixture of Sikhs and Hindus with a Christian and Buddhist minority. Throughout the remainder of the book, we have focused on the Hindu, Sikh and Muslim religious groupings.

Sikhs greet each other by saying: ਸਤਿ ਸ੍ਰੀ ਅਕਾਲ ਜੀ sa̱t sree akaal jee, or simply ਸਤਿ ਸ੍ਰੀ ਅਕਾਲ sa̱t sree akaal. There is an associated body language with each greeting. When saying ਸਤਿ ਸ੍ਰੀ ਅਕਾਲ sa̱t sree akaal the hands are, usually, joined together in front of the chest, with the head slightly bowed. In formal and respectful circumstances the suffix ਜੀ jee is added. The reply to the greeting is the same, ਸਤਿ ਸ੍ਰੀ ਅਕਾਲ sa̱t sree akaal. This is also used on departure, and may be combined with other sayings such as ਫਿਰ ਮਿਲਾਂ ਗੇ phir milaan ge (*See you again*) or ਰੱਬ ਰਾਖਾ rabb raakhaa (*May God protect you*).

The Muslim greeting is ਅੱਸਲਾਮ ਅਲੈਕਮ asslaam alaikam, which is taken from Arabic and means *Peace be upon you*. The reply to this is ਵਾਲੈਕਮ ਅੱਸਲਾਮ vaalaikam asslaam, which means *Peace be upon you also.* On departing a Muslim may say ਖ਼ੁਦਾ ਹਾਫ਼ਿਜ਼ **khudaa haafiz,** which means *May God protect you.* Men will greet each other by a shake of the hand and an embrace or by the raising of the right hand. Women would greet one another with an embrace or a clasping of the hand.

ਨਮਸਤੇ **namaste,** ਨਮਸਤੇ ਜੀ **namaste jee,** or ਨਮਸਕਾਰ, **namaskaar** are different forms of Hindu greetings. The greeting is from Sanskrit and literally means *I greet you respectfully.* The reply to ਨਮਸਤੇ **namaste** is ਨਮਸਤੇ **namaste.** Men may shake hands in greeting. However, to and among women the folding of hands and a slight bowing of the head is considered a mark of respect. There is no specific departing phrase.

It is considered good practice to use the greeting of the other person's religion on first meeting. Therefore if Mr Singh, who is a Sikh teacher, had a Muslim student in his class, he would greet him by saying ਅੱਸਲਾਮ ਅਲੈਕਮ **asslaam alaikam.** The student could equally reply ਵਾਲੈਕਮ ਅੱਸਲਾਮ **vaalaikam asslaam** or say ਸਤਿ ਸ੍ਰੀ ਅਕਾਲ **sat sree akaal** as a sign of respect. However, if you are not certain of the other person's religious background, it is advisable to use the westernized, secular greeting *hello* or *hello jee.*

ਜੀ **jee** is an extra added word known as an honorific particle, signifying respect. The use of the word ਜੀ **jee** is very common in the Panjabi language. It can be added to the end (and sometimes before) almost any sentence as a sign of respect in a formal context. To some extent **jee** is the equivalent of *please* and also of *sir/madam* in English.

ਅਭਿਆਸ   abhiaas   *Exercises*

1 Word search

Three words are hidden in the box. These words are ਅੱਛਾ **achchaa,** OK, ਸ਼ਾਬਾਸ਼ **shaabaash,** *well done,* and ਰੱਬ ਰਾਖਾ **rabb raakhaa,** *goodbye.* Find them by looking horizontally across each of the rows.

ਓ	ਰੱ	ਬ	ਰਾ	ਖਾ
ਮਾ	ਪਾ	ਰ	ਗ	ਚ
ਸ਼ਾ	ਬਾ	ਸ਼	ਕਾ	ਜ
ਜ	ਜ਼	ਖ	ਸ	ਬਾ
ਕੱ	ਲ	ਹਿ	ਅੱ	ਛਾ

2 Greeting response

How would you respond to someone who greets you with the following expressions?

a ਨਮਸਤੇ   namaste
b ਅੱਸਲਾਮ ਅਲੈਕਮ   asslaam alaikam
c ਸਤਿ ਸ੍ਰੀ ਅਕਾਲ   sat sree akaal

3 Use the appropriate formal and informal possessive adjectives in the following sentences.

a _Tuhadaa_ ਕੀ ਨਾਮ ਹੈ? _Tuhadaa_ kee naam hai?
     What is your name? (formal)

b _Teraa_ ਕੀ ਹਾਲ ਹੈ? _Teraa_ kee haal hai?
     How are you? (informal)

c _Teraa_ ਕੀ ਨਾਂ ਏ? _Teraa_ kee naan e?
     What is your name? (informal)

▶ 4 Complete the conversation.

You have just met Kiran, a new student in the Panjabi class. Following the English prompts complete the following conversation in Panjabi.

Kiran   ਸਤਿ ਸ੍ਰੀ ਅਕਾਲ ਜੀ। ਤੁਹਾਡਾ ਕੀ ਨਾਮ ਹੈ?   sat sree akaal jee. ṭuhaadaa kee naam hai?
       Hello. What is your name?

You   **Say hello, tell her your name and ask what her name is.**
     Sat srec akaal, merra naam Krista hai
     Tuhadaa kee naam hai?

Kiran   ਮੇਰਾ ਨਾਮ ਕਿਰਨ ਹੈ। ਤੁਹਾਡਾ ਕੀ ਹਾਲ ਹੈ?   meraa naam Kiran hai. ṭuhaadaa kee haal hai?
       My name is Kiran. How are you?

You   **Tell her you are fine and then ask her how she is.**
     Teek, Kee haal hai?

Kiran   ਮੇਰਾ ਹਾਲ ਵੀ ਠੀਕ ਹੈ।   meraa haal vee theek hai.
       I am fine too.

You   **Say goodbye.**
     raab raakhaa

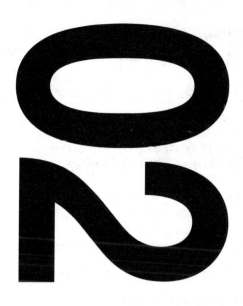

02

ਮੈਂ ਕਿਰਨ ਹਾਂ
main Kiran haan
I'm Kiran

In this unit you will learn:
- how to say who you are
- how to ask about and describe ethnicity or nationality
- about Panjabi sentence word order

▶ 1 *Are you English too?*

ਗੱਲ ਬਾਤ ੧ ਕੀ ਤੁਸੀਂ ਵੀ ਅੰਗਰੇਜ਼ ਹੋ ?

gall baat 1 kee tuseen vee angrez ho?

It is the second day of the Panjabi class at Heywood College. Mr Singh is the teacher and Henry, Jane, Ashok, Kiran and David are students attending the class.

ਚਰਨ ਸਿੰਘ **Charan Singh**	ਜੇਨ, ਕੀ ਤੂੰ ਜਰਮਨ ਹੈਂ ? jen, kee toon jarman hain? *Jane, are you German?*
ਜੇਨ **Jane**	ਨਹੀਂ ਜੀ, ਮੈਂ ਜਰਮਨ ਨਹੀਂ ਹਾਂ । ਮੈਂ ਅੰਗਰੇਜ਼ ਹਾਂ । naheen jee, main jarman naheen haan. main angrez haan. *No, I'm not German. I'm English.*
ਡੇਵਿਡ **David**	ਮੈਂ ਵੀ ਅੰਗਰੇਜ਼ ਹਾਂ ਅਤੇ ਮੈਂ ਵਿਦਿਆਰਥੀ ਹਾਂ । main vee angrez haan ate main vidiaarthee haan. *I'm also English and I am a student.*
ਚਰਨ ਸਿੰਘ **Charan Singh**	ਬਹੁਤ ਅੱਛਾ । ਅਸ਼ੋਕ, ਕੀ ਤੁਸੀਂ ਭਾਰਤੀ ਹੋ ? bahut achchaa. ashok, kee tuseen bhaartee ho? *Very good. Ashok, are you Indian?*
ਅਸ਼ੋਕ **Ashok**	ਮੇਰਾ ਦੇਸ਼ ਭਾਰਤ ਹੈ ਅਤੇ ਮੇਰੀ ਬੋਲੀ ਗੁਜਰਾਤੀ ਹੈ । meraa desh bhaarat hai ate meree bolee gujraatee hai. *My country is India and my language is Gujarati.*
ਚਰਨ ਸਿੰਘ **Charan Singh**	ਸ਼ਾਬਾਸ਼! ਹੈਨਰੀ, ਕੀ ਕਿਰਨ ਗੁਜਰਾਤੀ ਹੈ ? shaabaash! hainree, kee kiran gujraatee hai? *Well done! Henry, is Kiran Gujarati?*
ਹੈਨਰੀ **Henry**	ਨਹੀਂ, ਉਹ ਪੰਜਾਬੀ ਹੈ ਅਤੇ ਹਿੰਦੂ ਹੈ । naheen, uh panjaabee hai ate hindoo hai. *No, she is Panjabi and Hindu.*
ਚਰਨ ਸਿੰਘ **Charan Singh**	ਧੰਨਵਾਦ । dhannvaad. *Thank you.*

ਸ਼ਬਦਾਵਲੀ   shabdaavalee   *Vocabulary*

ਤੂੰ	toon	*you* (informal)
ਜਰਮਨ	jarman	*German* (m. / f.)
ਅੰਗਰੇਜ਼	angrez	*English* (m. / f.)
ਵਿਦਿਆਰਥੀ	vidiaarthee	*student* (m. / f.)
ਤੁਸੀਂ	tuseen	*you* (formal)
ਭਾਰਤੀ	bhaartee	*Indian* (m. / f.)
ਦੇਸ਼	desh	*country* (m.)
ਭਾਰਤ	bhaarat	*India* (m.)
ਬਹੁਤ ਅੱਛਾ	bahut achchaa	*very good*
ਬੋਲੀ	bolee	*language* (f.)
ਗੁਜਰਾਤੀ	gujraatee	*a person from Gujarat or of Gujarati origin* (m. / f.)
ਵੀ	vee	*also*
ਹੋਣਾ	honhaa	*to be*
ਮੈਂ	main	*I*
ਤੇ	te	*and*
ਨਹੀਂ	naheen	*no*
ਪੰਜਾਬੀ	panjaabee	*a person from Panjab or of Panjabi origin* (m. / f.)
ਅਤੇ	ate	*and*
ਹਿੰਦੂ	hindoo	*Hindu* (m. / f.)

ਅਭਿਆਸ   abhiaas   *Exercises*

After reading the dialogue and / or listening to the recording, try to do the following exercises.

1 True or false?

Say whether these statements about the students' ethnicities and nationalities are true or false.

a ਕਿਰਨ ਗੁਜਰਾਤੀ ਹੈ   kiran gujraatee hai   True / ~~False~~

b ਜੇਨ ਜਰਮਨ ਹੈ   jen jarman hai   True / False

c ਅਸ਼ੋਕ ਭਾਰਤੀ ਹੈ   ashok bhaartee hai   True / False

▶ 2 Listen to the recording and tick the correct box.

	Panjabi	English	Gujarati
Jeevan			
John			
Ram			

▶ 2 *I'm Kiran*

ਗੱਲ ਬਾਤ ੨ ਮੈਂ ਕਿਰਨ ਹਾਂ

gall baat 2 main kiran haan

Kiran and Ashok meet at the Hindu temple. They have only met once in the Panjabi class and are still unacquainted with one another.

ਕਿਰਨ **Kiran**	ਨਮਸਤੇ। ਮੈਂ ਕਿਰਨ ਹਾਂ। ਕੀ ਤੁਸੀਂ ਅਸ਼ੋਕ ਹੋ ? namaste. main kiran haan. kee tuseen ashok ho? *Hello. I'm Kiran. Are you Ashok?*
ਅਸ਼ੋਕ **Ashok**	ਨਮਸਤੇ। ਹਾਂ ਜੀ, ਮੈਂ ਅਸ਼ੋਕ ਹਾਂ। ਇਹ ਮੇਰੇ ਮਾਤਾ ਜੀ ਹਨ, ਮਿਸਜ਼ ਸ਼ਰਮਾ। namaste. haan jee, main ashok haan. ih mere maataa jee han, misaz sharmaa. *Hello. Yes, I'm Ashok. This is my mother, Mrs Sharma.*
ਕਿਰਨ **Kiran**	ਨਮਸਤੇ ਮਿਸਜ਼ ਸ਼ਰਮਾ। ਤੁਹਾਡਾ ਕੀ ਹਾਲ ਹੈ ? namaste misaz sharmaa. tuhaadaa kee haal hai? *Hello Mrs Sharma. How are you?*
ਮਿਸਜ਼ ਸ਼ਰਮਾ **Mrs Sharma**	ਮੈਂ ਠੀਕ ਹਾਂ। ਕੀ ਤੇਰੇ ਮਾਤਾ ਜੀ ਇੱਥੇ ਹਨ ? ਅਸੀਂ ਦੋਨੋਂ ਸਹੇਲੀਆਂ ਹਾਂ। main theek haan. kee tere maataa jee iththe han? aseen donon saheleeaan haan. *I'm fine. Is your mother here? We are both friends.*
ਕਿਰਨ **Kiran**	ਨਹੀਂ ਜੀ, ਉਹ ਇੱਥੇ ਨਹੀਂ ਹਨ, ਉਹ ਘਰ ਹਨ। naheen jee, uh iththe naheen han, uh ghar han. *No, she's not here. She's at home.*
ਅਸ਼ੋਕ **Ashok**	ਮਾਤਾ ਜੀ, ਕਿਰਨ ਤੇ ਮੈਂ ਦੋਨੋਂ ਇੱਕੋ ਕਲਾਸ ਵਿਚ ਹਾਂ। maataa jee, kiran te main donon ikko kalaas vich haan. *Mother, Kiran and I are both in the same class.*

ਸ਼ਬਦਾਵਲੀ   shabdaavalee   *Vocabulary*

ਇਹ	ih	*he, she, it, this, they, these*
ਮਾਤਾ ਜੀ	maataa jee	*mother* (f.)
ਮੈਂ	main	*I*

ਇੱਥੇ	iththe	here
ਅਸੀਂ	aseen	we
ਦੋਨੋਂ	donon	both
ਸਹੇਲੀ	sahelee	friend (f.)
ਉਹ	uh	he, she, that, they, those
ਨਹੀਂ	naheen	no
ਘਰ	ghar	house, home (m.)
ਅਸੀਂ ਦੋਨੋਂ	aseen donon	both of us
ਇੱਕੋ	ikko	same
ਕਲਾਸ	kalaas	class (f.)
ਵਿਚ	vich	in

ਅਭਿਆਸ   abhiaas   *Exercises*

After reading the dialogue and / or listening to the recording, try to do the following exercises.

▶ 1 Listen and give appropriate responses.

Kiran ਕੀ ਤੁਸੀਂ ਅਸ਼ੋਕ ਹੋ ? kee tuseen ashok ho?	Ashok
Kiran ਤੁਹਾਡਾ ਕੀ ਹਾਲ ਹੈ ? tuhaadaa kee haal hai?	Mrs Sharma
Mrs Sharma ਕੀ ਤੇਰੇ ਮਾਤਾ ਜੀ ਇੱਥੇ ਹਨ ? kee tere maataa jee iththe han?	Kiran

2 Arrange in correct word order.

a ਹਾਂ ਮੈਂ ਕਿਰਨ   haan-main-kiran   *I am Kiran.*
b ਹੋ ਅਸ਼ੋਕ ਕੀ ਤੁਸੀਂ ?   ho-ashok-kee-tuseen?   *Are you Ashok?*
c ਨਹੀਂ ਇੱਥੇ ਉਹ ਹਨ   naheen-iththe-uh-han   *She is not here.*

3 Crossword

Complete the crossword in English using clues taken from Dialogues 1 and 2.

1 ਕਿਰਨ _____ ਹੈ   kiran _____ hai

2 ਜੇਨ _____ ਹੈ   jen _____ hai

3 ਕਿਰਨ ਤੇ ਅਸ਼ੋਕ ਦੋਨੋਂ ਇੱਕੋ _____ ਵਿਚ ਹਨ   kiran te ashok donon ikko _____ vich han

4 ਅਸ਼ੋਕ ਦੇ ਮਾਤਾ ਜੀ ਦਾ ਨਾਮ _____ ਹੈ ashok <u>d</u>e maa<u>t</u>aa jee <u>d</u>aa naam _____ hai

5 ਕਿਰਨ ਦੇ ਮਾਤਾ ਜੀ _____ ਹਨ kiran <u>d</u>e maa<u>t</u>aa jee _____ han

ਬੋਲੀ ਬਾਰੇ bolee baare *Language points*

Subject pronouns

Pronouns are words used in the place of nouns, or naming words, which are used to refer to persons, places or objects. In English the words *I*, *you*, *he*, *she*, *it*, *they* and *we* are called subject pronouns. In Panjabi they are very important as the endings of verbs change according to which subject pronoun is being used, as will be seen in subsequent units.

Singular subject pronouns

First person	ਮੈਂ	mai<u>n</u>	*I*
Second person	ਤੂੰ	<u>t</u>oo<u>n</u>	*you* (informal)
	ਤੁਸੀਂ	<u>t</u>usee<u>n</u>	*you* (formal)
Third person	ਇਹ	ih	*he / she / it / this*
	ਉਹ	uh	*he / she / it / that*

Plural subject pronouns

First person	ਅਸੀਂ	aseen	*we*
Second person	ਤੁਸੀਂ	ṭuseen	*you*
Third person	ਇਹ	ih	*these, they* (near)
	ਉਹ	uh	*those, they* (far)

Unlike in English, but as in all the Latin-based languages, persons, places and objects (nouns) are grammatically either male or female in Panjabi. Even though some objects have ambiguous status in the sense that some people may refer to them as masculine and others as feminine, generally all nouns, even those with ambiguous status, belong to either the masculine or feminine gender. Some nouns can be used for both male and female, such as doctor. You will note in the vocabulary sections that we have given (m.), (f.) and (m. / f.) to represent the gender of a noun.

There is no gender distinction in the actual forms of subject pronouns, only in the verb endings that refer to the subject pronoun. For example, ਉਹ **uh** can refer to one man or woman or a group of either men or women. There is no way of distinguishing, by looking only at the subject pronoun, between *he, she* or *they* as the third person singular and plural forms are interchangeable. It is the verb ending which will enable you to recognize whether it is *he, she* or *they* being referred to. In Panjabi there is no equivalent to the word *it* which implies gender neutrality in English.

Use of subject pronouns

1 ਇਹ **ih** and ਉਹ **uh** literally mean *he/she/it* in the singular and *they* in the plural. There is however a recognizable distinction between the use of ਉਹ **uh** and ਇਹ **ih**. ਉਹ **uh** refers to a person or persons absent or at a distance, whereas ਇਹ **ih** is used when the person or persons are present or in close proximity.

2 In English the words these and those are called demonstrative pronouns. In Panjabi there are no specific equivalents. ਉਹ **uh** and ਇਹ **ih**, however, often translate into *those* and *these*, respectively, in many situations.

3 When talking about a singular person who is deserving of respect, such as Kiran's mother in Dialogue 2, it is grammatically correct always to use the plural form:

ਉਹ ਇੱਥੇ ਨਹੀਂ ਹਨ, ਉਹ ਘਰ ਹਨ। **uh iththe naheen han, uh ghar han.** *She's not here, she's at home.*

ਉਹ **uh** and ਇਹ **ih** are used in the plural, in this case, which is reflected in the use of the plural form of ਹੋਣਾ (ਹਨ) **honhaa (han)** instead of the singular ਹੈ **hai**, even though only one mother (she) is being talked about.

4 In a similar way, the word ਤੂੰ **toon** you is used informally and ਤੁਸੀਂ **tuseen** is used in both formal speech as well as in the plural form. These two forms of you require discretion in their application. ਤੂੰ **toon** is used between family members and close friends as well as when speaking to younger people. It is also used in public speech where a degree of informality is expected, such as when bargaining in the market or fixing the price of a taxi fare. ਤੁਸੀਂ **tuseen** is a more formal and polite form which is used between people of equal status and age as well as to people deserving respect due to age or social standing. However, when the distinction between the formal and informal use is not obvious, it is always safest to use the formal. Formal and informal speech is a crucial distinction in Panjabi and will crop up many times as you progress through the course. If you have some knowledge of French or Spanish, you will note the similarity here between the singular, informal use of *you*, *tu* and *tú* and the plural and singular formal forms of *you*, *vous* (French) and *usted* (Spanish).

The present tense of ਹੋਣਾ 'honhaa' *is*, *am* and *are*

Subject pronouns are assigned appropriate forms of the verb *to be*. This can similarly be compared with English: *I am*, *you are*, *we are*, *he is*, *they are*. In Panjabi *to be* is expressed in the verb ਹੋਣਾ **honhaa** which denotes states of being, conditions and existence. Note the following pairings of subject pronouns with their assigned forms of ਹੋਣਾ **honhaa**:

Singular

First person	ਮੈਂ ਹਾਂ	main haan	*I am*
Second person	ਤੂੰ ਹੈਂ ਤੁਸੀਂ ਹੋ	toon hain tuseen ho	*you are* (informal) *you are* (formal)
Third person	ਇਹ ਹੈ ਉਹ ਹੈ	ih hai uh hai	*he / she / it is* *he / she / it is*

Plural

First person	ਅਸੀਂ ਹਾਂ aseen haan	we are
Second person	ਤੁਸੀਂ ਹੋ tuseen ho	you are
Third person	ਇਹ ਹਨ ih han ਉਹ ਹਨ uh han	they / these are they / those are

Formal uses of possessive adjectives

The formal uses of subject pronouns in Panjabi also extend to possessive adjectives. In Unit 1 we saw how possessive adjectives are formed with singular masculine and feminine objects. Possessive adjectives used to describe people with respect or in a formal situation always take the formal form, even when the person being described is in the singular. Note the following examples where the possessive adjectives and forms of ਹੋਣਾ honhaa, *to be* change according to the formal and informal contexts in which they are used to describe singular people. In the following examples, note how ਮੇਰੀ meree (*my*) and ਤੇਰੀ teree (*your*) change into ਮੇਰੇ mere and ਤੁਹਾਡੇ tuhaade.

Formal   ਇਹ ਮੇਰੇ ਮਾਤਾ ਜੀ ਹਨ   ih mere maataa jee han
This is my mother.

Informal ਇਹ ਮੇਰੀ ਮਾਤਾ ਹੈ   ih meree maataa hai *This is my mother.*

Formal   ਕੀ ਤੁਹਾਡੇ ਮਾਤਾ ਜੀ ਇੱਥੇ ਹਨ ?   kee tuhaade maataa jee iththe han? *Is your mother here?*

Informal ਕੀ ਤੇਰੀ ਮਾਤਾ ਇੱਥੇ ਹੈ ?   kee teree maataa iththe hai? *Is your mother here?*

These examples illustrate how the plural in Panjabi can be used to make speech more formal. However, this is only one aspect of plural possessive adjectives. In these examples the object here is itself not in the plural (and the form of the adjective is being used in a formal situation). Unit 3 illustrates possessive adjectives with plural objects.

Word order

Note the word order of a simple Panjabi sentence – subject (person carrying out the action) first, verb (the action) last and the rest in between. The sentence *I am fine* is written in Panjabi as

I fine am, where *I* is the subject and *am* is the verb. For example:
ਮੈਂ ਠੀਕ ਹਾਂ   mai̱n theek haa̱n   *I am fine:*

ਮੈਂ	ਠੀਕ	ਹਾਂ
mai̱n	theek	haa̱n
I	*fine*	*am*
subject		**verb**

Word order in Panjabi is generally more flexible than it is in English. Note how the meaning does not change though the word order does in the following sentences:

ਤੁਹਾਡਾ ਨਾਮ ਕੀ ਹੈ ?   tuhaadaa naam kee hai?

ਤੁਹਡਾ ਕੀ ਨਾਮ ਹੈ ?   t̤uhaadaa kee naam hai?

Both examples mean *What is your name?* However, this does not mean that any word order is allowed. The form of the verb ਹੋਣਾ **honhaa (ਹੈ hai)** is still at the end of the sentence in both examples.

ਵਿਆਖਿਆ viaakhiaa *Commentary*

1 Where are you from?

The question of where someone comes from depends on who is doing the asking and where the conversation is taking place. For example, a person born in Panjab living in London will respond that they are from India if the questioner is an English person. However, if the questioner is a fellow Panjabi they may say the district or the village they are from. This apparently simple question becomes even more complicated when asked to diaspora South Asians. The response to the question *Where are you from?* can give rise to replies such as *Birmingham* or *New Jersey* which are quite legitimate responses. Increasingly, the use of a religious identity tagged onto a national identity is a form of self-identification used in the diaspora. Therefore, a young person responding to the question *Who are you?* may reply a *British Muslim* or *Canadian Sikh*. It is important to remember that Panjabi speakers come from a huge variety of national, religious and social contexts and this is reflected in the many possibilities that the questions *Where do you come from?* and *Who are you?* can evoke.

If you meet a Panjabi in England or North America, they are likely to live, or at least have relatives, in three areas which are known as centres of Panjabi settlement: Southall in England, Yuba City in California and Vancouver in Canada. Each of these areas is often called *Little Panjab*. Early Panjabi immigrants settled here and these places are still icons on the global map of Panjabi travels, serving as temporary embarkation ports to would-be emigrants. These areas are distinctive for the range of shops selling South Asian goods such as groceries, sweets, music, jewellery, clothing and food. Apart from being a central shopping area they are the focus of social, religious, political and cultural activities.

2 Names

South Asian names can provide many clues about a person's sex, background, country of origin and religious affiliation. These are often very important pieces of information, particularly when engaging in formal conversation.

Sikh names

Most Sikhs have three names: a personal name, a second name and a surname. The second name, 'Singh' for men and 'Kaur' for women is in fact a religious name and its addition is one of the main ways of distinguishing men from women. Otherwise first names can be the same for men and women. Surnames vary from representing someone's caste or the name of their village.

Hindu names

The Hindu naming system is similar to the English naming system, in that most individuals have one or two personal names followed by a common surname. First names are generally male and female specific. A middle name of Kumar or Chand is quite popular in North India and is a way of distinguishing a Hindu Panjabi from a Sikh.

Muslim names

Muslim names tend to be less fixed in the order of first and second name. There is also a tendency for women not to have the surnames of their husbands, but just to have the word **bibi** or **begum** attached, which means lady or woman. Muslim names tend to be a composite of Koranic names with some local flavour. Male and female names are distinguished.

Throughout the book you will come across a range of Sikh, Hindu and Muslim names. Try and see if you can distinguish them. It is worth remembering, however, that some names transcend religious boundaries, and also that you may come across a lot of nicknames.

ਅਭਿਆਸ   abhiaas   *Exercises*

1 Complete the box.

ਹਨ	han	
ਹੈ	*hain*	*is*
	ho	*are*

2 Say the sentences in Panjabi.

a Are you Ashok?
b Are you Kiran?
c I am Kiran.
d He is Ashok.

3 Refer to the dialogue and choose the correct forms of *to be* from the options given.

a ਕੀ ਤੂੰ ਜਰਮਨ _____ (ਹੋ, ਹੈਂ)?   kee toon jarman _____ (ho, hain)?   *Are you German?*

b ਮੈਂ ਵੀ ਅੰਗਰੇਜ਼ _____ (ਹਾਂ, ਹੈ)   main vee angrez _____ (haan, hai).   *I'm also English.*

c ਕੀ ਅਸ਼ੋਕ ਤੇ ਕਿਰਨ ਪੰਜਾਬੀ _____ (ਹੈਂ, ਹਨ)?   kee ashok te kiran panjaabee _____ (hain, han)?   *Are Ashok and Kiran Panjabi?*

4 Word search

Three words are hiddens in the box. These words are ਜਰਮਨ **jarman** *German*, ਪੰਜਾਬੀ **panjaabee** *Panjabi* and ਅੰਗਰੇਜ਼ **angrez** *English*. Find them by looking horizontally across each of the rows.

ਉ	ਜ	ਰ	ਮ	ਨ
ਕ	ਖ	ਪ	ਰ	ਲ
ਪੰ	ਜਾ	ਬੀ	ਸੀ	ਸਿ
ਟ	ਅੰ	ਗ	ਰੇ	ਜ਼
ਕੇ	ਕਾ	ਕਿ	ਕੀ	ਕੋ

03

ਇਸ ਦਾ ਸੁਆਦ ਕੀ ਹੈ?

is daa suaad kee hai?

what does it taste like?

In this unit you will learn:
- the names of vegetables and Panjabi food
- how to ask questions
- how to describe people and things

▶ 1 *What is this?*

ਗੱਲ ਬਾਤ ੧ ਇਹ ਕੀ ਹੈ?

gall baat 1 ih kee hai?

Mr Singh has taken the Panjabi class to Southall in order to give the students an opportunity to hear and speak Panjabi in a real situation. They are in a grocery shop.

ਹੈਨਰੀ **Henry**	ਇਹ ਕੀ ਹੈ? ih kee hai? *What is this?*	
ਦੁਕਾਨਦਾਰ dukaandaar **Shopkeeper**	ਇਹ ਕਰੇਲਾ ਹੈ। ih karelaa hai. *It (this) is a bitter gourd.*	
ਹੈਨਰੀ **Henry**	ਇਸ ਦਾ ਸੁਆਦ ਕੀ ਹੈ? is daa suaad kee hai? *What does it taste like?*	
ਦੁਕਾਨਦਾਰ **Shopkeeper**	ਇਸ ਦਾ ਸੁਆਦ ਕੌੜਾ ਹੈ। is daa suaad kaurhaa hai. *It has a bitter taste.*	
ਜੇਨ **Jane**	ਉਸ ਸਬਜ਼ੀ ਦਾ ਕੀ ਨਾਮ ਹੈ? us sabzee daa kee naam hai? *What is the name of that vegetable?*	
ਦੁਕਾਨਦਾਰ **Shopkeeper**	ਛੋਟੀ ਸਬਜ਼ੀ ਭਿੰਡੀ ਹੈ ਤੇ ਵੱਡੇ ਸ਼ਲਗਮ ਹਨ। chotee sabzee bhindee hai te vadde shalgam han. *The small vegetable is okra and the large ones are turnips.*	
ਜੇਨ **Jane**	ਕੀ ਸ਼ਲਗਮ ਮਿੱਠਾ ਹੈ ਜਾਂ ਕਸੈਲਾ? kee shalgam miththaa hai jaan kasailaa? *Are turnips sweet or bitter?*	
ਦੁਕਾਨਦਾਰ **Shopkeeper**	ਉਹ ਮਿੱਠੇ ਹਨ ਤੇ ਬਹੁਤ ਸਸਤੇ ਵੀ ਹਨ। uh miththe han te bahut saste vee han. *They are sweet and also very cheap.*	

ਸ਼ਬਦਾਵਲੀ   shabdaavalee   *Vocabulary*

ਕਰੇਲਾ	karelaa	*bitter gourd* (type of vegetable) (m.)
ਇਸ	is	*it, this*
ਦਾ	daa	*of*

ਸੁਆਦ	suaad	*taste* (m.)
ਕੌੜਾ / ਕਸੈਲਾ	kaurhaa / kasailaa	*bitter* (v.)
ਉਸ	us	*that*
ਸਬਜ਼ੀ	sabzee	*vegetable* (f.)
ਛੋਟਾ	chotaa	*small* (v.)
ਭਿੰਡੀ	bhindee	*okra* (type of vegetable) (f.)
ਵੱਡਾ	vaddaa	*big, large* (v.)
ਸ਼ਲਗਮ	shalgam	*turnip* (m.)
ਸਸਤਾ	sastaa	*cheap* (v.)
ਮਿੱਠਾ	miththaa	*sweet* (v.)
ਜਾਂ	jaan	*or*
ਬਹੁਤ	bahut	*very*

ਅਭਿਆਸ   abhiaas   *Exercises*

After reading the dialogue and / or listening to the recording, try to do the following exercises.

1 True or false?

a	ਭਿੰਡੀ	bhindee means *bitter*	True / False
b	ਕਰੇਲਾ	karelaa means *okra*	True / False
c	ਸ਼ਲਗਮ	shalgam means *turnip*	True / False
d	ਸਸਤਾ	sastaa means *expensive*	True / False
e	ਸੁਆਦ	suaad means *taste*	True / False

▶ 2 Mr Khan's shopping list

Mr Khan is at the local grocery shop buying vegetables. Listen to the recording to hear which items he has purchased from the shopping list that Mrs Khan has given him. As the items are spoken on the recording, tick them off the list. Don't worry if you can't recognize all the words.

ਕਰੇਲਾ	✓ karelaa	*bitter gourd*
ਸ਼ਲਗਮ	✓ shalgam	*turnip*
ਭਿੰਡੀ	✓ bhindee	*okra*
ਗਾਜਰ	gaajar	*carrot*
ਆਲੂ	aaloo	*potatoes*
ਗੋਭੀ	✓ gobhee	*cauliflower*
ਟਮਾਟਰ	✓ tamaatar	*tomatoes*
ਮਟਰ	✓ matar	*peas*

▶ 2 *Which sweets are good?*

ਗੱਲ ਬਾਤ ੨ ਕਿਹੜੀਆਂ ਮਿਠਿਆਈਆਂ ਚੰਗੀਆਂ ਹਨ ?

gall baat 2 kihrheeaan mithiaaeeaan changeeaan han?

After visiting the grocery shop, Mr Singh takes Jane and Henry to the Panjabi sweet shop (ਮਿਠਿਆਈ ਦੀ ਦੁਕਾਨ **mithiaaee dee dukaan**). Panjabi sweet shops are not like confectionery shops, because although they are most famous for the sweet dishes that they sell, they also provide a range of other dishes.

ਮਿਸਟਰ ਸਿੰਘ **Mr Singh**	ਇਹ ਬਹੁਤ ਚੰਗੀ ਮਿਠਿਆਈ ਦੀ ਦੁਕਾਨ ਹੈ। ih bahut changee mithiaaee dee dukaan hai. *This is a very good sweet shop.*
ਜੇਨ **Jane**	ਇੱਥੇ ਕਿਹੜੀਆਂ ਮਿਠਿਆਈਆਂ ਚੰਗੀਆਂ ਹਨ ? iththe kihrheeaan mithiaaeeaan changeeaan han? *Which sweets are good here?*
ਮਿਸਟਰ ਸਿੰਘ **Mr Singh**	ਸਾਰੀਆਂ ਮਿਠਿਆਈਆਂ ਚੰਗੀਆਂ ਹਨ ਪਰ ਲੱਡੂ ਖ਼ਾਸ ਸੁਆਦੀ ਹਨ। saareeaan mithiaaeeaan changeeaan han par laddoo khaas suaadee han. *All of them are good, but* ladoos *are especially tasty.*
ਹੈਨਰੀ **Henry**	ਪਰ ਲੱਡੂ ਮਹਿੰਗੇ ਹਨ। par laddoo mahinge han. *But* ladoos *are expensive.*
ਜੇਨ **Jane**	ਕੀ ਕੋਈ ਨਮਕੀਨ ਚੀਜ਼ ਹੈ ? kee koee namkeen cheez hai? *Is there anything salty?*
ਦੁਕਾਨਦਾਰ **Shopkeeper**	ਹਾਂ ਜੀ, ਪਕੌੜੇ ਤੇ ਸਮੋਸੇ ਹਨ। haan jee, pakaurhe te samose han. *Yes, there are* pakoras *and* samosas.
ਜੇਨ **Jane**	ਕੀ ਸਮੋਸੇ ਕਰਾਰੇ ਹਨ ? kee samose karaare han? *Are the* samosas *spicy?*
ਦੁਕਾਨਦਾਰ **Shopkeeper**	ਹਾਂ ਜੀ, ਸਮੋਸੇ ਬਹੁਤ ਕਰਾਰੇ ਹਨ। haan jee, samose bahut karaare han. *Yes, the* samosas *are very spicy.*

ਸ਼ਬਦਾਵਲੀ shabdaavalee *Vocabulary*

ਕਿਹੜੀ	kihrhee	*which, which one* (v.)
ਮਿਠਿਆਈ	mithiaaee	*Panjabi sweet* (f.)
ਚੰਗੀ	changee	*good* (v.)
ਦੁਕਾਨ	dukaan	*shop* (f.)
ਇੱਥੇ	iththe	*here*
ਲੱਡੂ	laddoo	a type of Panjabi sweet (m.)
ਖ਼ਾਸ	khaas	*especially*
ਸੁਆਦੀ	suaadee	*tasty*
ਪਰ	par	*but*
ਮਹਿੰਗਾ	mahingaa	*expensive, costly* (v.)
ਕੋਈ	koee	*any*
ਚੀਜ਼	cheez	*thing* (f.)
ਨਮਕੀਨ	namkeen	salty
ਹਾਂ ਜੀ	haan jee	*yes* (polite)
ਪਕੌੜਾ	pakaurhaa	a type of deep-fried pastry similar to fritters (m.)
ਸਮੋਸਾ	samosaa	*triangular stuffed pastry* (m.)
ਕਰਾਰਾ	karaaraa	*spicy* (v.)

ਅਭਿਆਸ abhiaas *Exercises*

After reading the dialogue and / or listening to the recording, try to do the following exercises.

1 Complete the table.

ਮਿੱਠਾ		*sweet*
ਕੌੜਾ	kaurhaa	
	suaad	*taste*

2 Arrange in correct word order.

a ਹੈ ਦੁਕਾਨ ਇਹ hai-dukaan-ih *This is a shop.*

b ਹੈ ਚੰਗੀ ਦੁਕਾਨ ਇਹ hai-changee-dukaan-ih *This is a good shop.*

c ਇਹ ਦੀ ਮਿਠਿਆਈ ਹੈ ਦੁਕਾਨ ih-dee-mithiaaee-hai-dukaan *This is a sweet shop.*

d ਹੈ ਦੁਕਾਨ ਦੀ ਮਿਠਿਆਈ ਚੰਗੀ ਇਹ hai-dukaan-dee-mithiaaee-changee-ih *This is a good sweet shop.*

▶ 3 *This is our sitting room*

ਗੱਲ ਬਾਤ ੩ ਇਹ ਸਾਡੀ ਬੈਠਕ ਹੈ

gall baat 3 ih saadee baithak hai

Mr Singh has taken his students to visit his house and is showing them around.

ਚਰਨ ਸਿੰਘ	ਇਹ ਸਾਡੀ ਬੈਠਕ ਹੈ। ਮਾਫ਼ ਕਰਨਾ, ਹਰ ਪਾਸੇ ਮੇਰੀਆਂ ਕਿਤਾਬਾਂ ਹਨ।
Charan Singh	ih saadee baithak hai. maaf karnaa, har paase mereeaan kitaabaan han.
	This is our sitting room. Sorry, my books are everywhere.
ਹੈਨਰੀ	ਤੁਹਾਡਾ ਘਰ ਵੱਡਾ ਹੈ। ਪੌੜੀਆਂ ਚੌੜੀਆਂ ਹਨ।
Henry	tuhaadaa ghar vaddaa hai. paurheeaan chaurheeaan han.
	Your house is big. The stairs are wide.
ਜੇਨ	ਕਿੰਨੇ ਕਮਰੇ ਹਨ?
Jane	kinne kamre han?
	How many rooms are there?
ਚਰਨ ਸਿੰਘ	ਚਾਰ ਕਮਰੇ ਹਨ ਅਤੇ ਦੋ ਗ਼ੁਸਲ ਖ਼ਾਨੇ ਹਨ।
Charan Singh	chaar kamre han ate do ghusal khaane han.
	There are four rooms and two bathrooms.
ਅਸ਼ੋਕ	ਬ਼ਗ਼ੀਚਾ ਲੰਬਾ ਹੈ ਪਰ ਰਸੋਈ ਛੋਟੀ ਹੈ।
Ashok	bagheechaa lanbaa hai par rasoee chotee hai.
	The garden is long but the kitchen is small.

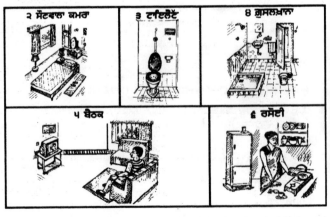

ਚਰਨ ਸਿੰਘ **Charan Singh**	ਇਹ ਸੱਚ ਹੈ, ਪਰ ਮੇਰੇ ਬੱਚੇ ਅਤੇ ਮੇਰੀ ਪਤਨੀ ਇੱਥੇ ਖ਼ੁਸ਼ ਹਨ। ih sachch hai, par mere bachche aṯe meree paṯnee iṯhthe <u>kh</u>ush han. *That's true, but my children and my wife are happy here.*	

ਸ਼ਬਦਾਵਲੀ **shabḏaavalee** *Vocabulary*

ਬੈਠਕ	baithak	*sitting room* (f.)
ਮਾਫ਼ ਕਰਨਾ	maaf karnaa	*sorry*
ਹਰ ਪਾਸੇ	har paase	*everywhere*
ਪੌੜੀਆਂ	paurheeaa<u>n</u>	*stairs* (f.)
ਚੌੜਾ	chaurhaa	*wide* (v.)
ਕਮਰਾ	kamraa	*room* (m.)
ਕਿੰਨੇ	ki<u>n</u>ne	*how many*
ਗ਼ੁਸਲ ਖ਼ਾਨਾ	<u>gh</u>usal <u>kh</u>aanaa	*bathroom* (m.)
ਬਗ਼ੀਚਾ	ba<u>gh</u>eechaa	*garden* (m.)
ਲੰਬਾ	la<u>n</u>baa	*long* (v.)
ਰਸੋਈ	rasoee	*kitchen* (f.)
ਸੱਚ	sachch	*true, truth* (v.)
ਬੱਚੇ	bachche	*children* (m.)
ਪਤਨੀ	paṯnee	*wife* (f.)
ਖ਼ੁਸ਼	<u>kh</u>ush	*happy*

ਬੋਲੀ ਬਾਰੇ **bolee baare** *Language points*

Interrogative words

Interrogative words change sentences into questions. In Panjabi
interrogative words generally begin with the letter ਕ **k** and may
appear at the beginning of the sentence or within the sentence.

ਕੋਣ	kaunh	*who*
ਕੀ	kee	*what*
ਕਿੱਥੇ	ki<u>th</u>the	*where*
ਕਿਉਂ	kiu<u>n</u>	*why*
ਕਿਵੇਂ	kive<u>n</u>	*how*
ਕਦੋਂ	ka<u>d</u>o<u>n</u>	*when*
ਕਿਹੜਾ	kihrhaa	*which**
ਕਿਹੜੀ	kihrhee	*which**

*Note that these two examples of which only apply to singular objects.

The endings of ਕਿਹੜਾ **kihrhaa** and ਕਿਹੜੀ **kihrhee** change according to the nature of the noun to which it is referring: whether it is singular or plural, or masculine or feminine.

Examples:

ਉਹ ਕੋਣ ਹੈ ?	uh kaunh hai?	*Who is he / she?*
ਉਹ ਕੀ ਹੈ ?	uh kee hai?	*What is that?*
ਉਹ ਕਿੱਥੇ ਹੈ ?	uh ki<u>thth</u>e hai?	*Where is she / he?*
ਉਹ ਇੱਥੇ ਕਿਉਂ ਹੈ ?	uh i<u>thth</u>e kiu<u>n</u> hai?	*Why is he / she here?*
ਉਹ ਕਿਵੇਂ ਹੈ ?	uh kive<u>n</u> hai?	*How is she / he?*
ਕਲਾਸ ਕਦੋਂ ਹੈ ?	kalaas ka<u>don</u> hai?	*When is the class?*
ਕਿਹੜਾ ਫਲ ? (m.)	kihrhaa phal? (m.)	*Which fruit?*
ਕਿਹੜੀ ਸਬਜ਼ੀ (f.)	kihrhee sabzee? (f.)	*Which vegetable?*

Nouns

In Panjabi, nouns are affected by gender, either masculine or feminine, and number, either singular or plural. Every noun in Panjabi, even an inanimate object, is assigned a masculine or feminine gender and has a singular or plural numerical character. The process of assignment of gender to nouns is quite arbitrary. There are no obvious reasons, for example, why ਕੁਰਸੀ **kursee** *chair* is feminine and ਮੇਜ਼ **mez** *table* is masculine. However, in logical terms, all nouns which represent males are masculine and those which represent females are feminine. For example, ਮੁੰਡਾ **mu<u>n</u>daa** *boy* is masculine and ਕੁੜੀ **kurhee** *girl* is feminine.

There are no steadfast rules about the distinction of the gender of inanimate objects. In Panjabi this is a matter of convention, whereby the gender of a noun is often simply understood. There is a general code that nouns ending in ਈ (ee) are feminine and nouns ending in ਆ (aa) are masculine, such as ਲੜਕਾ **larhkaa** *boy* and ਲੜਕੀ **larhkee** *girl*. Exceptions to this, however, are plentiful, with words such as ਹਾਥੀ **haa<u>th</u>ee** (*elephant*) masculine, ਮਾਂ **maa<u>n</u>** (*mother*) feminine and ਮਾਲਾ **maalaa** (*necklace*) feminine, all having endings which counter this general code. So be careful! You will learn more about nouns as you go along.

Type 1: Variable nouns

Variable nouns are those which change from the singular form when they are plural.

Masculine

Singular	ਮੁੰਡਾ	mundaa	*boy*
Plural	ਮੁੰਡੇ	munde	*boys*
Singular	ਚਾਚਾ	chaachaa	*uncle*
Plural	ਚਾਚੇ	chaache	*uncles*

Feminine

Singular	ਕੁੜੀ	kurhee	*girl*
Plural	ਕੁੜੀਆਂ	kurheeaan	*girls*
Singular	ਦੁਕਾਨ	dukaan	*shop*
Plural	ਦੁਕਾਨਾਂ	dukaanaan	*shops*

Type 2: Invariable nouns

Invariable nouns are those which do not change forms from the singular to the plural.

Masculine

Singular	ਆਦਮੀ	aadmee	*man*
Plural	ਆਦਮੀ	aadmee	*men*
Singular	ਹੱਥ	haththth	*hand*
Plural	ਹੱਥ	haththth	*hands*

Some other examples of invariable nouns:

ਮੋਤੀ	motee	*pearl*
ਹਾਰ	haar	*necklace*
ਨੱਕ	nakk	*nose*
ਦਰਿਆ	dariaa	*river*

Note that generally all feminine nouns are variable, that is feminine nouns change from the singular to the plural form.

Adjustable nouns

In Panjabi the same noun can often be used to represent both genders by simply changing the ending to express their femininity or masculinity. These types of nouns are irregular, though the pattern of endings that they take can be distinctly identified.

	Masculine			Feminine	
ਚਾਚਾ	chaachaa *uncle*		= ਚਾਚੀ	chaachee	*paternal aunt*
ਪੁੱਤਰ	puttar	*son*	= ਪੁੱਤਰੀ	puttaree	*daughter*

ਊਠ	ooth	*male camel*	=	ਊਠਣੀ	oothnhee	*female camel*
ਨੌਕਰ	naukar	*male servant*	=	ਨੌਕਰਾਣੀ	naukaraanhee	*maid*
ਬਾਲ	baal	*male child*	=	ਬਾਲੜੀ	baalrhee	*female child*
ਰਾਜਾ	raajaa	*king*	=	ਰਾਣੀ	raanhee	*queen*
ਮੋਚੀ	mochee	*male cobbler*	=	ਮੋਚਣ	mochanh	*female cobbler*

Some nouns are significantly different from their masculine / feminine counterparts:

ਭਰਾ	bharaa	*brother*	=	ਭੈਣ	bhainh	*sister*
ਮੁੰਡਾ	mundaa	*boy*	=	ਕੁੜੀ	kurhee	*girl*
ਬੰਦਾ	bandaa	*man*	=	ਜਨਾਨੀ	janaanee	*woman*

Nouns borrowed from English

Words borrowed from English are also classified in terms of gender and are pluralized according to the pattern of Panjabi nouns. For example:

Masculine

Singular			Plural		
ਕੈਮਰਾ	kaimraa	*camera*	ਕੈਮਰੇ	kaimre	*cameras*
ਟੈਲੀਫ਼ੋਨ	taileefon	*telephone*	ਟੈਲੀਫ਼ੋਨ	taileefon	*telephones*

Feminine

Singular			Plural		
ਪਲੇਟ	palet	*plate*	ਪਲੇਟਾਂ	paletaan	*plates*
ਪੈਂਸਲ	painsal	*pencil*	ਪੈਂਸਲਾਂ	painsalaan	*pencils*

Similarly, the plural of ਸਮੋਸਾ **samosaa** (*samosa*) is ਸਮੋਸੇ **samose** in Panjabi and *samosas* in English.

Adjectives

An adjective is a word that gives descriptive information about a noun, pronoun or another adjective. Generally, adjectives come before the noun and after the pronoun. Similar to nouns, adjectives are also either masculine or feminine and are used in singular and plural forms, reflecting the gender and numerical traits of the nouns that they are describing. There are two types of simple adjectives, variable and invariable.

Variable adjectives

Variable adjectives end in ਆ **aa** for the masculine and ਈ **ee** for the feminine such as ਵੱਡਾ **vaddaa** (masculine) and ਵੱਡੀ **vaddee** (feminine) *big*. They inflect (i.e. change their endings) with the number and the gender of the noun.

Masculine singular	ਵੱਡਾ ਲੜਕਾ	vaddaa larhkaa	*big boy*
Masculine plural	ਵੱਡੇ ਲੜਕੇ	vadde larhke	*big boys*
Feminine singular	ਵੱਡੀ ਲੜਕੀ	vaddee larhkee	*big girl*
Feminine plural	ਵੱਡੀਆਂ ਲੜਕੀਆਂ	vaddeeaan larhkeeaan	*big girls*

When the noun is the same for both genders and singular / plural forms, it is the variable adjective and / or the verb which will indicate the numerical and gender characteristics of the noun.

Examples:

Singular	ਇਹ ਵੱਡਾ ਮਕਾਨ ਹੈ	ih vaddaa makaan hai	*This is a big house.*
Plural	ਇਹ ਵੱਡੇ ਮਕਾਨ ਹਨ	ih vadde makaan han	*These are big houses.*

Variable adjectives also indicate the gender characteristic of the noun.

ਇਹ ਵੱਡਾ ਮੇਜ਼ ਹੈ	ih vaddaa mez (m.) hai	*This is a big table.* (m.)
ਇਹ ਵੱਡੀ ਕੁਰਸੀ ਹੈ	ih vaddee kursee (f.) hai	*This is a big chair.* (f.)

There are some exceptions regarding adjectives of this type. Some adjectives do not change their form according to the noun's gender and number associations, despite the fact that they end in ਈ **ee** or ਆ **aa** such as:

ਵਧੀਆ vadheeaa *superior*   ਗੁਲਾਬੀ gulaabee *pink*

You need to learn such exceptions as you go along.

Invariable adjectives

Invariable adjectives do not change according to the nouns that they specify and do not end with ਆ **aa** or ਈ **ee**, such as:

ਲਾਲ	laal	*red*
ਖੁਸ਼	khush	*happy*
ਸਾਫ਼	saaf	*clean*

ਖ਼ੁਸ਼ ਲੜਕਾ	<u>kh</u>ush larhkaa	*happy boy*
ਖ਼ੁਸ਼ ਲੜਕੇ	<u>kh</u>ush larhke	*happy boys*
ਖ਼ੁਸ਼ ਲੜਕੀ	<u>kh</u>ush larhkee	*happy girl*
ਖ਼ੁਸ਼ ਲੜਕੀਆਂ	<u>kh</u>ush larhkeeaa<u>n</u>	*happy girls*

The simple verb

Verbs indicate activity and are also called action words. Throughout the book the Panjabi verb is referred to in the infinitive form (i.e. the form *to*). The root of the verb plus the ending -ਣਾ **nhaa** or the ending -ਨਾ **naa** form the infinitive. Here are some common examples of verbs in the infinitive, or simple form:

Infinitive form (= 'to____')			Root		Ending	
ਲਿਖਣਾ	likhnhaa	*to write*	ਲਿਖ	likh	ਣਾ	nhaa
ਦੇਣਾ	<u>d</u>enhaa	*to give*	ਦੇ	<u>d</u>e	ਣਾ	nhaa
ਖਾਣਾ	khaanhaa	*to eat*	ਖਾ	khaa	ਣਾ	nhaa
ਆਉਣਾ	aaunhaa	*to come*	ਆਉ	aau	ਣਾ	nhaa
ਬੋਲਣਾ	bolnhaa	*to speak*	ਬੋਲ	bol	ਣਾ	nhaa
ਕਹਿਣਾ	kahinhaa	*to say*	ਕਹਿ	kahi	ਣਾ	nhaa
ਰਹਿਣਾ	rahinhaa	*to live, stay*	ਰਹਿ	rahi	ਣਾ	nhaa
ਕਰਨਾ	karnaa	*to do*	ਕਰ	kar	ਨਾ	naa

The simple verb is also used as a form of command particularly related to actions in the near future.

Examples:

ਜਲਦੀ ਆਉਣਾ	jal<u>d</u>ee aaunhaa	*come back quickly*
ਹੌਲੀ ਬੋਲਣਾ	haulee bolnhaa	*speak softly*
ਚਿੱਠੀ ਲਿਖਣਾ	chiththee likhnhaa	*write a letter*

The possessive particle ਦਾ '<u>d</u>aa' *of*

In Panjabi, possession is expressed through the particle ਦਾ. In English possession is not usually expressed using the word *of*, for example, *the pencil of the girl* would usually be written *the girl's pencil*. The particle ਦਾ <u>d</u>aa is therefore similar to the apostrophe *s* in English as it establishes the relationship between possessions. The particle ਦਾ <u>d</u>aa *of* should agree with the gender and number of the object being possessed. Generally, it takes the following forms:

| ਦਾ | <u>d</u>aa | masculine singular |
| ਦੇ | <u>d</u>e | masculine plural |

ਦੀ	dee	feminine singular
ਦੀਆਂ	deeaan	feminine plural

Words such as *of, in, to* or *from* are called prepositions in English and signify place or position. These words come before the noun and are therefore called prepositions.

In Panjabi these kinds of words come after the noun and are therefore called postpositions. This is also the second function of ਦਾ **daa** in that it dictates word order and acts as a grammatical point determining the endings of the nouns and adjectives associated with the possession.

Examples:

ਕੁੜੀ ਦੀਆਂ ਪੈਂਸਲਾਂ	kurhee deeaan painsalaan	*the girl's pencils*
ਆਦਮੀ ਦੀ ਦੁਕਾਨ	aadmee dee dukaan	*the man's shop*
ਮੇਰੀ ਭੈਣ ਦਾ ਕਮਰਾ	meree bhainh daa kamraa	*my sister's room*

Possessive adjectives with plural objects

In Unit 1 you learned about possessive adjectives with singular objects. When objects being possessed are plural, the endings of possessive adjectives change accordingly. The following tables illustrate the use of the possessive adjective with plural objects.

Possessive adjectives with plural masculine objects
1st person

ਮੇਰੇ	mere	*my*
ਸਾਡੇ	saade	*our*

2nd person

ਤੇਰੇ	tere	*your* (informal)
ਤੁਹਾਡੇ	tuhaade	*your* (formal)

3rd person

ਇਹ ਦੇ / ਇਸ ਦੇ	ih de / is de	*his / her*
ਇਹਨਾਂ ਦੇ	ihnaan de	*his / her* (formal) *their*
ਉਹ ਦੇ / ਉਸ ਦੇ	uh de / us de	*his / her*
ਉਹਨਾਂ ਦੇ	uhnaan de	*his / her* (formal) *their*

Possessive adjectives with plural feminine objects

1st person

| ਮੇਰੀਆਂ | mereeaa<u>n</u> | *my* |
| ਸਾਡੀਆਂ | saadeeaa<u>n</u> | *our* |

2nd person

| ਤੇਰੀਆਂ | <u>t</u>ereeaa<u>n</u> | *your* (informal) |
| ਤੁਹਾਡੀਆਂ | <u>t</u>uhaadeeaa<u>n</u> | *your* (formal) |

3rd person

ਇਹ ਦੀਆਂ / ਇਸ ਦੀਆਂ	ih <u>d</u>eeaa<u>n</u> / is <u>d</u>eeaa<u>n</u>	*his / her*
ਇਹਨਾਂ ਦੀਆਂ	ihnaa<u>n</u> <u>d</u>eeaa<u>n</u>	*his / her* (formal) *their*
ਉਹ ਦੀਆਂ / ਉਸ ਦੀਆਂ	uh <u>d</u>eeaa<u>n</u> / us <u>d</u>eeaa<u>n</u>	*his / her*
ਉਹਨਾਂ ਦੀਆਂ	uhnaa<u>n</u> <u>d</u>eeaa<u>n</u>	*his / her* (formal) *their*

Examples:

ਮੇਰੇ ਬੱਚੇ	mere bachche	*my children*
ਤੁਹਾਡੀਆਂ ਕਿਤਾਬਾਂ	<u>t</u>uhaadeeaa<u>n</u> ki<u>t</u>aabaan	*your books*
ਉਹਨਾਂ ਦੀਆਂ ਮਿਠਿਆਈਆਂ	uhnaa<u>n</u> <u>d</u>eeaa<u>n</u> mithiaaeeaa<u>n</u>	*their sweets*
ਸਾਡੇ ਲੜਕੇ	saade larhke	*our sons*

▶ Numbers

In Dialogue 3, you were introduced to the numbers **ਚਾਰ chaar** and **ਦੋ d̲o**. The following is the list of numbers from 1–20. The topic vocabulary list at the end of the book gives the remaining numbers up to 100.

੧	1	ਇੱਕ	ikk	੧੧	11	ਗਿਆਰਾਂ	giaaraa<u>n</u>
੨	2	ਦੋ	<u>d</u>o	੧੨	12	ਬਾਰ੍ਹਾਂ	baar-haa<u>n</u>
੩	3	ਤਿੰਨ	<u>t</u>i<u>nn</u>	੧੩	13	ਤੇਰ੍ਹਾਂ	<u>t</u>er-haa<u>n</u>
੪	4	ਚਾਰ	chaar	੧੪	14	ਚੌਦਾਂ	chau<u>d</u>-haan
੫	5	ਪੰਜ	pan<u>j</u>	੧੫	15	ਪੰਦਰਾਂ	pan<u>d</u>araa<u>n</u>

੬	6	ਛੇ	<u>ch</u>e	੧੬	16	ਸੋਲ੍ਹਾਂ	solhaa<u>n</u>
੭	7	ਸੱਤ	sa<u>tt</u>	੧੭	17	ਸਤਾਰ੍ਹਾਂ	sa<u>t</u>aar-haa<u>n</u>
੮	8	ਅੱਠ	a<u>thth</u>	੧੮	18	ਅਠਾਰ੍ਹਾਂ	a<u>th</u>aar-haa<u>n</u>
੯	9	ਨੌਂ	nau<u>n</u>	੧੯	19	ਉੱਨੀ	unnee
੧੦	10	ਦਸ	<u>d</u>as	੨੦	20	ਵੀਹ	veeh

ਵਿਆਖਿਆ viaakhiaa *Commentary*

1 *The vegetable seller* ਸਬਜ਼ੀ ਵਾਲਾ **sabzee vaalaa**

In Panjab, fresh seasonal vegetables are available in abundance. The land is rich and the climate is tropical. Vegetables can generally be bought from a variety of sources. A street hawker carrying vegetables in his hand-pulled cart will make his daily rounds in the streets, shouting the names of vegetables at the top of his lungs in a manner that signals his presence more than does the content of his wares. Vegetables can also be bought from the market (often called a ਮੰਡੀ ma<u>n</u>dee or even ਮਾਰਕੇਟ **maarket**) where dozens of greengrocery stalls and shops are situated next to each other. These stalls offer a wide variety of fresh vegetables (ਸਬਜ਼ੀਆਂ **sabzeeaa<u>n</u>**) according to the season. In Panjab, visiting the market, especially in the evenings, is more than just for shopping; it is also a social and entertaining experience. Prices are not displayed so that customers have to make enquiries to shopkeepers, comparing prices of different stalls and bargaining as they go along. An accepted and often time-consuming part of shopping in Panjab is bargaining. Once a bargain has been made, the shopkeeper uses his age-old technique of weighing the goods between two pans on his scale. Most shopkeepers are efficient in mentally calculating the price of the weighed goods and are keen to chat, pointing out the low prices of other vegetables on offer and generally to praise their goods. This is a contrast to shopping for vegetables in western countries which is usually impersonal and mechanical.

2 *The Panjabi sweet shop* ਮਿਠਿਆਈ ਦੀ ਦੁਕਾਨ mithiaaee <u>d</u>ee <u>d</u>ukaan

Sweet shops are an integral part of shopping areas catering for South Asian communities in England, America, Canada and other parts of the world. These sweet shops are not like confectionery shops or bakeries, as they are often attached to take-away restaurants and also offer a range of spicy snacks and nibbles. It is customary for most South Asians to exchange boxes of sweets among friends and family on happy occasions. These can range from weddings and birthdays to festivals. Sweet shops, therefore, remain busy throughout the year. There is an enormous variety of sweets from different regions of the Indian sub-continent. Most sweet shops in the diaspora offer about 50 of the more common types of sweets and savoury dishes. Here is a list of some of the more popular items.

Sweets

ਲੱਡੂ laddoo	a sweet round ball, generally orange in colour, consisting of tiny particles made of gram flour
ਗੁਲਾਬ ਜਾਮਨ gulaab jaamanh	a round soft brown ball made of milk powder soaked in a sweet syrup
ਬਰਫ਼ੀ barfee	a bar of milk powder, similar to fudge, which is cut into diamond and rectangular shapes and is also found in a variety of colours such as white, pink and green

ਜਲੇਬੀਆਂ	whirls of batter, yellow-orange in colour, which are
jalebeeaa<u>n</u>	soaked in a sweet syrup
ਰਸ ਗੁੱਲੇ	sweet round balls made of cheese soaked in a
ras gulle	clear sweet syrup
ਰਸ ਮਲਾਈ	sweet round balls made of cheese soaked in thick,
ras malaaee	sweet milk
ਗਜਰੇਲਾ	a sweet dish made from grated carrots
gajrelaa	
ਪਿੰਨੀਆਂ	sweet round balls made from ground lentils and
pi<u>n</u>neeaa<u>n</u>	gram flour

Savouries

There are about a dozen salty dishes which are available from sweet shops. These are the most common ones:

ਪਕੋੜੇ	seasoned and spiced vegetables covered in a
pakaurhe	gram flour batter which are deep fried in oil
ਸਮੋਸੇ	deep-fried triangular pastries filled with boiled
samose	peas, potatoes and sometimes minced meat

ਅਭਿਆਸ   abhiaas   *Exercises*

1 Choose the appropriate adjectives.

Bitter gourd and turnip are masculine and okra is feminine.

small

| ਛੋਟਾ | <u>ch</u>otaa | ਛੋਟੀ | <u>ch</u>otee |

big

| ਵੱਡਾ | vaddaa | ਵੱਡੀ | vaddee |

a **ਇਹ ਕਰੇਲਾ _____ ਹੈ।**   ih karelaa _____ hai.
  This bitter gourd is small.
b **ਇਹ ਕਰੇਲਾ _____ ਹੈ।**   ih karelaa _____ hai.
  This bitter gourd is large.
c **ਇਹ ਭਿੰਡੀ _____ ਹੈ।**   ih bhi<u>n</u>dee _____ hai.
  This okra is small.
d **ਇਹ ਭਿੰਡੀ _____ ਹੈ।**   ih bhi<u>n</u>dee _____ hai.
  This okra is large.

e ਇਹ ਸ਼ਲਗਮ _____ ਹੈ ।   ih shalgam _____ hai.
This turnip is small.

f ਇਹ ਸ਼ਲਗਮ _____ ਹੈ ।   ih shalgam _____ hai.
This turnip is large.

ਕਰੇਲਾ   ਭਿੰਡੀ   ਸ਼ਲਗਮ

▶ 2 Who has ordered what?

Mr Singh, Jane and Henry have each ordered several food items. Listen to the recording and tick the box to show who has ordered what.

	ਸਮੋਸਾ samosaa	ਲੱਡੂ laddoo	ਪਕੌੜੇ pakaurhe	ਰਸ ਮਲਾਈ ras malaaee	ਭਿੰਡੀ bhindee	ਗੋਭੀ gobhee
Mr Singh	✓		✓		✓	
Jane	✓	✓	✓			
Henry				✓	✓	✓

3 Who am I?

After reading the Commentary section, try to guess who I am from the descriptions given below.

a I am sweet, full of syrup, round and dark brown in colour.

b I am sweet like fudge, in diamond and rectangular shapes and come in a variety of different colours such as white, pink and green.

c I am a very popular savoury snack, triangular in shape, covered in pastry, filled with potatoes and peas, and deep fried.

d I am like a fritter, dipped in a batter of gram flour mixture, and deep fried. My core ingredients are usually cauliflower, potatoes and aubergine.

4 Insert the correct possessive adjectives.

(Remember that the forms of possessive adjectives change not only in terms of who is in possession of the object, but also by the gender and number of the object being possessed.)

a _____ ਸਮੋਸੇ ਸੁਆਦੀ
ਹਨ।

samose suaadee
han.

*Their samosas
are tasty.*

b _____ ਲੜਕੇ ਕਿੱਥੇ ਹਨ?

larhke kiththe han?

*Where are my
sons?*

c _____ ਕਿਤਾਬਾਂ ਹਰ
ਪਾਸੇ ਹਨ।

kitaabaan har
paase han.

*Our books are
everywhere.*

d _____ ਮਿਠਿਆਈਆਂ
ਸਭ ਤੋਂ ਚੰਗੀਆਂ
ਹਨ!

mithiaaeeaan
sabh ton
changeeaan han!

*Your (formal)
sweets are
the best!*

04

ਵੜੀ ਖੁਸ਼ੀ ਦੀ ਗੱਲ ਹੈ!

barhee
khushee
dee gall hai!

that's very good news!

In this unit you will learn:
- how to introduce yourself and others
- how to ask and answer questions about work
- how to ask and respond to questions about place of origin
- how to talk about your family
- how to describe actions and objects in the present

▶ 1 *What do you do?*

ਗੱਲ ਬਾਤ ੧ ਤੁਸੀਂ ਕੀ ਕਰਦੇ ਹੋ ?

gall baat 1 tuseen kee karde ho?

Dr Singh and Mrs Sharma are travelling on a train going from Birmingham to London. They are meeting for the first time.

ਮਿਸਜ਼ ਸ਼ਰਮਾ **Mrs Sharma**	ਸਤਿ ਸ੍ਰੀ ਅਕਾਲ । ਕੀ ਇਹ ਸੀਟ ਖ਼ਾਲੀ ਹੈ ? sat sree akaal. kee ih seet khaalee hai? *Hello. Is this seat vacant?*
ਡਾਕਟਰ ਸਿੰਘ **Dr Singh**	ਸਤਿ ਸ੍ਰੀ ਅਕਾਲ । ਹਾਂ ਜੀ, ਖ਼ਾਲੀ ਹੈ । ਬੈਠੋ ਜੀ । sat sree akaal. haan jee, khaalee hai. baitho jee. *Hello. Yes, it's vacant. Please sit down.*
ਮਿਸਜ਼ ਸ਼ਰਮਾ **Mrs Sharma**	ਧੰਨਵਾਦ ਮੇਰਾ ਨਾਮ ਮਿਸਜ਼ ਸ਼ਰਮਾ ਹੈ । ਸਰਦਾਰ ਸਾਹਿਬ, ਤੁਹਾਡਾ ਕੀ ਨਾਮ ਹੈ ? dhannvaad. meraa naam misaz sharmaa hai. sardaar saahib tuhaadaa kee naam hai? *Thank you. My name is Mrs Sharma. Sardar Sahib, what is your name?*
ਡਾਕਟਰ ਸਿੰਘ **Dr Singh**	ਮੇਰਾ ਨਾਮ ਅਜੀਤ ਸਿੰਘ ਹੈ । ਮੈਂ ਡਾਕਟਰ ਹਾਂ । ਤੁਸੀਂ ਕੀ ਕਰਦੇ ਹੋ, ਮਿਸਜ਼ ਸ਼ਰਮਾ ? meraa naam ajeet singh hai. main daaktar haan. tuseen kee karde ho, misaz sharmaa? *My name is Ajeet Singh. I'm a doctor. What do you do, Mrs Sharma?*
ਮਿਸਜ਼ ਸ਼ਰਮਾ **Mrs Sharma**	ਮੈਂ ਅਧਿਆਪਕ ਹਾਂ ਅਤੇ ਮੈਂ ਬਰਮਿੰਘਮ ਵਿਚ ਰਹਿੰਦੀ ਹਾਂ । ਤੁਸੀਂ ਕਿੱਥੇ ਰਹਿੰਦੇ ਹੋ ? main adhiaapkaa haan ate main barmingham vich rahindee haan. tuseen kiththe rahinde ho? *I am a teacher and I live in Birmingham. Where do you live?*
ਡਾਕਟਰ ਸਿੰਘ **Dr Singh**	ਮੈਂ ਵੀ ਬਰਮਿੰਘਮ ਵਿਚ ਰਹਿੰਦਾ ਹਾਂ । ਮੈਂ ਕੀਨੀਆ ਤੋਂ ਹਾਂ । ਕੀ ਤੁਸੀਂ ਪੰਜਾਬ ਤੋਂ ਹੋ ? main vee barmingham vich rahindaa haan. main keeneeaa ton haan. kee tuseen panjaab ton ho? *I live in Birmingham too. I am from Kenya. Are you from Panjab?*
ਮਿਸਜ਼ ਸ਼ਰਮਾ **Mrs Sharma**	ਨਹੀਂ ਜੀ । ਮੈਂ ਦਿੱਲੀ ਤੋਂ ਹਾਂ । naheen jee. main dillee ton haan. *No. I'm from Delhi.*

ਸ਼ਬਦਾਵਲੀ   shab<u>d</u>aavalee   *Vocabulary*

ਸੀਟ	seet	*seat* (f.)
ਖ਼ਾਲੀ	<u>kh</u>aalee	*empty, vacant*
ਬੈਠਣਾ	baithnhaa	*to sit*
ਬੈਠੋ ਜੀ	baitho jee	*please sit down* (formal)
ਸਰਦਾਰ ਸਾਹਿਬ	sar<u>d</u>aar saahib	*Mr* (see Commentary)
ਡਾਕਟਰ	daaktar	*doctor* (m. / f.)
ਅਧਿਆਪਕਾ	a<u>dh</u>iaapkaa	*teacher* (f.)
ਬਰਮਿੰਘਮ	barmi<u>ng</u>ham	*Birmingham* (m.)
ਰਹਿਣਾ	rahinhaa	*to stay, to live*
ਕੀਨੀਆ	keeneeaa	*Kenya* (m.)
ਤੋਂ	<u>t</u>on	*from*
ਪੰਜਾਬ	pa<u>n</u>jaab	*Panjab* (m.)
ਦਿੱਲੀ	<u>d</u>illee	*Delhi* (f.)

ਅਭਿਆਸ   abhiaas   *Exercises*

After reading the dialogue and / or listening to the recording, try to do the following exercises.

1 Fill in the blanks.

Following the first example, fill in the blanks with the Panjabi phrases according to the English ones given to you. You may borrow phrases from the dialogue.

a ਮੈਂ ਡਾਕਟਰ ਹਾਂ।   mai<u>n</u> daaktar haa<u>n</u>.   *I am a doctor.*

b _____   *Is this seat vacant?*   _____ *Yes, it is.*

c _____   *I'm a teacher.*

d _____   *What do you (formal) do?*

2 Arrange in correct word order.

a ਵੀ ਮੈਂ ਬਰਮਿੰਘਮ ਰਹਿੰਦਾ ਹਾਂ।   vee mai<u>n</u> barmingham rahi<u>nd</u>aa haa<u>n</u>.   *I live in Birmingham too.*

b ਦਿੱਲੀ ਤੋਂ ਮੈਂ ਹਾਂ।   <u>d</u>illee <u>t</u>on mai<u>n</u> haa<u>n</u>.   *I am from Delhi.*

c ਤੁਸੀਂ ਹੋ ਕਰਦੇ ਕੀ?   <u>t</u>usee<u>n</u> ho kar<u>d</u>e kee?   *What do you do?*

3 Remarks and responses

The following conversation is between two unacquainted passengers on a train. Put the responses of Passenger B into order according to Passenger A's remarks by using the correct corresponding number.

Passenger A		Passenger B
1	ਕੀ ਇਹ ਟਰੇਨ ਲੰਡਨ ਜਾਂਦੀ ਹੈ ? kee ih taren landan jaandee hai?	a	ਮੈਂ ਲੀਡਜ਼ ਰਹਿੰਦਾ ਹਾਂ main leedz rahindaa haan
2	ਤੁਸੀਂ ਕਿੱਥੇ ਰਹਿੰਦੇ ਹੋ ? tuseen kiththe rahinde ho?	b	ਮੈਂ ਅਧਿਆਪਕਾ ਹਾਂ main adhiaapkaa haan
3	ਤੁਸੀਂ ਕੀ ਕੰਮ ਕਰਦੇ ਹੋ ? tuseen kee kanm karde ho?	c	ਹਾਂ, ਇਹ ਟਰੇਨ ਲੰਡਨ ਜਾਂਦੀ ਹੈ haan, ih taren landan jaandee hai
4	ਕੀ ਤੁਸੀਂ ਹਿੰਦੀ ਬੋਲਦੇ ਹੋ ? kee tuseen hindee bolde ho?	d	ਮੈਂ ਪੰਜਾਬ ਤੋਂ ਹਾਂ main panjaab ton haan
5	ਕੀ ਤੁਸੀਂ ਪੰਜਾਬ ਤੋਂ ਹੋ ਜਾਂ ਦਿੱਲੀ ਤੋਂ ਹੋ ? kee tuseen panjaab ton ho jaan dillee ton ho?	e	ਮੈਂ ਹਿੰਦੀ ਅਤੇ ਪੰਜਾਬੀ ਬੋਲਦਾ ਹਾਂ main hindee ate panjaabee boldaa haan

▶ 2 *That's very good news!*

ਗੱਲ ਬਾਤ ੨ ਬੜੀ ਖ਼ੁਸ਼ੀ ਦੀ ਗੱਲ ਹੈ।

gall baat 2 barhee khushee dee gall hai!

While Dr Singh and Mrs Sharma chat on the train going from Birmingham to London, Fatima Khan boards the train at Coventry. Mrs Sharma and Fatima Khan know each other. Fatima Khan addresses Mrs Sharma by her first name, Sita.

ਫ਼ਾਤਿਮਾ ਖ਼ਾਨ **Fatima Khan**	ਨਮਸਤੇ ਸੀਤਾ। ਤੇਰੀ ਸਿਹਤ ਕਿਵੇਂ ਹੈ ? namaste seetaa. teree sihat kiven hai? *Hello Sita. How's your health?*
ਸੀਤਾ ਸ਼ਰਮਾ **Sita Sharma**	ਨਮਸਤੇ! ਮੇਰੀ ਸਿਹਤ ਹੁਣ ਬਿਲਕੁਲ ਠੀਕ ਹੈ। ਮਿਹਰਬਾਨੀ। namaste! meree sihat hunh bilkul theek hai. miharbaanee. *Hello! My health is perfectly fine now. Thank you.*
ਫ਼ਾਤਿਮਾ ਖ਼ਾਨ **Fatima Khan**	ਬੜੀ ਖ਼ੁਸ਼ੀ ਦੀ ਗੱਲ ਹੈ! barhee khushee dee gall hai! *That's very good news!*

ਸੀਤਾ ਸ਼ਰਮਾ **Sita Sharma**	ਤੇਰੇ ਪਰਵਾਰ ਦਾ ਕੀ ਹਾਲ ਹੈ ? tere parvaar daa kee haal hai? *How is your family?*
ਫ਼ਾਤਿਮਾ ਖ਼ਾਨ **Fatima Khan**	ਸਾਰੇ ਠੀਕ ਹਨ। ਮਿਸਟਰ ਖ਼ਾਨ ਮੌਜਾਂ ਕਰਦੇ ਹਨ। ਸਾਡਾ ਬੇਟਾ ਅਤੇ ਬੇਟੀ ਕਾਲਜ ਵਿਚ ਪੜ੍ਹਦੇ ਹਨ। saare theek han. mistar <u>kh</u>aan mauj<u>aan</u> kar<u>d</u>e han. saadaa betaa ate betee kaalaj vich parhh<u>d</u>e han. *Everyone is fine. Mr Khan is enjoying life. Our son and daughter are studying at college.*

(Sita Sharma introduces Dr Singh and Fatima Khan to one another.)

ਸੀਤਾ ਸ਼ਰਮਾ **Sita Sharma**	ਡਾਕਟਰ ਸਿੰਘ, ਇਹ ਮੇਰੀ ਸਹੇਲੀ ਫ਼ਾਤਿਮਾ ਖ਼ਾਨ ਹੈ। ਫ਼ਾਤਿਮਾ, ਇਹ ਡਾਕਟਰ ਸਿੰਘ ਹਨ। daaktar si<u>n</u>gh, ih meree sahelee faa<u>t</u>imaa <u>kh</u>aan hai. faa<u>t</u>imaa, ih daaktar si<u>n</u>gh han. *Dr Singh, this is my friend Fatima Khan. Fatima, this is Dr Singh.*
ਡਾਕਟਰ ਸਿੰਘ **Dr Singh**	ਅੱਸਲਾਮ ਅਲੈਕਮ asslaam alaikam. *Hello.*
ਫ਼ਾਤਿਮਾ ਖ਼ਾਨ **Fatima Khan**	ਵਾਲੈਕਮ ਅੱਸਲਾਮ। vaalaikam asslaam. *Hello.*

(Sita addresses Fatima.)

ਸੀਤਾ ਸ਼ਰਮਾ **Sita Sharma**	ਫ਼ਾਤਿਮਾ। ਅਗਲੇ ਹਫ਼ਤੇ ਨੂੰ ਸਕੂਲ ਦੀਆਂ ਛੁੱਟੀਆਂ ਸ਼ੁਰੂ ਹੁੰਦੀਆਂ ਹਨ। ਬੱਚਿਆਂ ਨਾਲ ਬਰਮਿੰਘਮ ਆਉਣਾ। faa<u>t</u>imaa, agle haf<u>t</u>e noo<u>n</u> sakool <u>d</u>eeaa<u>n</u> <u>ch</u>utteeaa<u>n</u> shuroo hun<u>d</u>eeaa<u>n</u> han. bachchiaa<u>n</u> naal barmi<u>n</u>gham aaunhaa. *School holidays start next week. Come with the children to Birmingham.*
ਫ਼ਾਤਿਮਾ ਖ਼ਾਨ **Fatima Khan**	ਇਨਸ਼ਾ ਅੱਲਾ। inshaa allaa. *We'll try.* (lit. If God wishes.)

ਸ਼ਬਦਾਵਲੀ   shab<u>d</u>aavalee   *Vocabulary*

ਬੜੀ	barhee	*very* (v.)
ਖ਼ੁਸ਼ੀ	<u>kh</u>ushee	*good* (f.) (lit. happiness)

ਗੱਲ	gall	*matter, news (f.)*
ਸਿਹਤ	siha<u>t</u>	*health (f.)*
ਹੁਣ	hunh	*now*
ਬਿਲਕੁਲ	bilkul	*absolutely, perfectly*
ਸਾਰੇ	saare	*everyone, all (v.)*
ਮੌਜਾਂ ਕਰਨਾ	maujaa<u>n</u> karnaa	*to enjoy*
ਬੇਟਾ	betaa	*son (m.)*
ਬੇਟੀ	betee	*daughter (f.)*
ਕਾਲਜ	kaalaj	*college (m.)*
ਪੜ੍ਹਨਾ	parhhnaa	*to read, to study*
ਸਹੇਲੀ	sahelee	*friend (f.)*
ਅਗਲਾ	aglaa	*next*
ਹਫ਼ਤਾ	haf<u>t</u>aa	*week (m.)*
ਸ਼ੁਰੂ ਹੋਣਾ	shuroo honhaa	*to start, to begin*
ਸਕੂਲ	sakool	*school (m.)*
ਛੁੱਟੀਆਂ	<u>ch</u>utteeaa<u>n</u>	*holidays (f.)*

ਅਭਿਆਸ   abhiaas   *Exercises*

After reading the dialogue and / or listening to the recording, try to do the following exercises.

1 True or false?

a ਮਿਸਜ਼ ਸ਼ਰਮਾ ਬਰਮਿੰਘਮ ਰਹਿੰਦੀ ਹੈ।   misaz sharmaa barmi<u>n</u>gham rahi<u>n</u>dee hai.   True / False

b ਮਿਸਜ਼ ਸ਼ਰਮਾ ਅਧਿਆਪਕਾ ਹੈ।   misaz sharmaa a<u>dh</u>iaapkaa hai.   True / False

c ਮਿਸਜ਼ ਸ਼ਰਮਾ ਡਾਕਟਰ ਹੈ।   misaz sharmaa daaktar hai. True / False

▶ 2 Talking about yourself

You have just met someone for the first time. Listen to their questions on the recording and / or read them from the following list and respond with information about yourself.

a ਤੁਹਾਡਾ ਨਾਮ ਕੀ ਹੈ?   <u>t</u>uhaadaa naam kee hai?   _____

b ਤੁਸੀਂ ਕੀ ਕਰਦੇ ਹੋ?   <u>t</u>usee<u>n</u> kee kar<u>d</u>e ho?   _____

c ਤੁਸੀਂ ਕੀ ਇੰਗਲੈਂਡ ਤੋਂ ਹੋ?   kee <u>t</u>usee<u>n</u> inglai<u>n</u>d <u>t</u>on ho?   _____

d ਤੁਸੀਂ ਕਿੱਥੇ ਰਹਿੰਦੇ ਹੋ?   <u>t</u>usee<u>n</u> ki<u>thth</u>e rahi<u>n</u>de ho?   _____

ਬੋਲੀ ਬਾਰੇ bolee baare *Language points*

The present tense

The simple present tense is used to describe either actions which are habitual (i.e. done on a regular basis) or objects which have permanent or fixed qualities. It is formed by adding the appropriate endings to the root of the main verb followed by a corresponding auxiliary verb. The 'ingredients' for constructing the present tense are, therefore, as follows:

subject + main verb (simple present) + auxiliary verb
= present tense

ਦਾ <u>daa</u>, ਦੀ <u>dee</u>, ਦੇ <u>de</u> and ਦੀਆਂ <u>deeaan</u> are the endings which are added to the root of the main verb to reflect the gender, person and number of the subject.

The auxiliary is formed by use of the simple present of the verb ਹੋਣਾ honhaa *to be* (see Unit 2 where it is used for *is, am* and *are*). The auxiliary verb operates at three levels:

1 helping the main verb

ਮੈਂ ਕਰਦੀ ਹਾਂ   mai<u>n</u> kar<u>d</u>ee haa<u>n</u>   *I do*

2 functioning independently

ਮੈਂ ਠੀਕ ਹਾਂ   mai<u>n</u> theek haa<u>n</u>   *I'm fine*

3 showing the existence of the object or situation being described

ਕੀ ਕੋਈ ਕਿਤਾਬਾਂ ਹਨ ?   kee koe ki<u>t</u>aabaa<u>n</u>   *Are there any*
                       han?   *books?*

Now we can look at examples of the simple present tense. The verb ਕਰਨਾ karnaa (*to do*) is used here as an illustration. Verb root ਕਰ kar:

ਮੈਂ **mai<u>n</u>** *I* (1st person singular masculine) + ਕਰਦਾ **kar<u>d</u>aa** *do* (present form of *to do*) + ਹਾਂ **haa<u>n</u>** *am* (auxiliary, 1st person singular) = ਮੈਂ ਕਰਦਾ ਹਾਂ **mai<u>n</u> kar<u>d</u>aa haa<u>n</u>** *I do*:

Singular

Masculine	Feminine	
ਮੈਂ ਕਰਦਾ ਹਾਂ mai<u>n</u> kar<u>d</u>aa haa<u>n</u>	ਮੈਂ ਕਰਦੀ ਹਾਂ mai<u>n</u> kar<u>d</u>ee haa<u>n</u>	*I do*
ਤੂੰ ਕਰਦਾ ਹੈਂ <u>t</u>oon kar<u>d</u>aa hai<u>n</u>	ਤੂੰ ਕਰਦੀ ਹੈਂ <u>t</u>oon kar<u>d</u>ee hai<u>n</u>	*you do*
ਇਹ / ਉਹ ਕਰਦਾ ਹੈ ih / uh kar<u>d</u>aa hai	ਇਹ / ਉਹ ਕਰਦੀ ਹੈ ih / uh kar<u>d</u>ee hai	*he, she, it does*

Plural

Masculine	Feminine	
ਅਸੀਂ ਕਰਦੇ ਹਾਂ aseen karde haan	ਅਸੀਂ ਕਰਦੀਆਂ ਹਾਂ aseen kardeeaan haan	*we do*
ਤੁਸੀਂ ਕਰਦੇ ਹੋ tuseen karde ho	ਤੁਸੀਂ ਕਰਦੀਆਂ ਹੋ tuseen kardeeaan ho	*you do*
ਇਹ / ਉਹ ਕਰਦੇ ਹਨ ih / uh karde han	ਇਹ / ਉਹ ਕਰਦੀਆਂ ਹਨ ih / uh kardeeaan han	*they / these / those do*

The example of **ਕਰਨਾ** shows the manner in which verb roots ending with consonants are formed in the simple present tense. However, those roots which end in vowels follow a slightly different pattern. The nasal consonant is placed between the root and the present tense endings. Here, the verb **ਪੀਣਾ peenhaa** (*to drink*) is used to illustrate. Note that the **bindee ·** follows the **bihaaree ੀ ee** of **ਪੀਣਾ peenhaa**.

Simple verb: **ਪੀਣਾ peenhaa** *to drink*. **Verb root: ਪੀ pee:**

subject + (object, where appropriate) + simple present + auxiliary = present tense

ਮੈਂ main *I* (subject) (1st person, singular feminine) + **ਪਾਣੀ paanhee** *water* (object) + **ਪੀਂਦੀ peendee** *drink* (present of *to drink*) + **ਹਾਂ haan** *am* (auxiliary) (1st person singular) = **ਮੈਂ ਪਾਣੀ ਪੀਂਦੀ ਹਾਂ main paanhee peendee haan** *I drink water*:

Singular

Masculine	Feminine	
ਮੈਂ ਪਾਣੀ ਪੀਂਦਾ ਹਾਂ main paanhee peendaa haan	ਮੈਂ ਪਾਣੀ ਪੀਂਦੀ ਹਾਂ main paanhee peendee haan	*I drink water*
ਤੂੰ ਪਾਣੀ ਪੀਂਦਾ ਹੈਂ toon paanhee peendaa hain	ਤੂੰ ਪਾਣੀ ਪੀਂਦੀ ਹੈਂ toon paanhee peendee hain	*you drink water*
ਇਹ / ਉਹ ਪਾਣੀ ਪੀਂਦਾ ਹੈ ih / uh paanhee peendaa hai	ਇਹ / ਉਹ ਪਾਣੀ ਪੀਂਦੀ ਹੈ ih / uh paanhee peendee hai	*he, she, it drinks water*

Plural

Masculine	Feminine	
ਅਸੀਂ ਪਾਣੀ ਪੀਂਦੇ ਹਾਂ aseen paanhee peende haan	ਅਸੀਂ ਪਾਣੀ ਪੀਂਦੀਆਂ ਹਾਂ aseen paanhee peendeeaan haan	*we drink water*
ਤੁਸੀਂ ਪਾਣੀ ਪੀਂਦੇ ਹੋ tuseen paanhee peende ho	ਤੁਸੀਂ ਪਾਣੀ ਪੀਂਦੀਆਂ ਹੋ tuseen paanhee peendeeaan ho	*you drink water*
ਇਹ / ਉਹ ਪਾਣੀ ਪੀਂਦੇ ਹਨ ih / uh paanhee peende han	ਇਹ / ਉਹ ਪਾਣੀ ਪੀਂਦੀਆਂ ਹਨ ih / uh paanhee peendeeaan han	*they drink water*

Here are a few more examples of other verbs in the simple present:

ਮੈਂ ਸੋਚਦੀ ਹਾਂ	main sochdee haan	*I think*
ਬੱਚੇ ਖੇਡਦੇ ਹਨ	bachche khedde han	*the children play*
ਅਸੀਂ ਉਰਦੂ ਬੋਲਦੀਆਂ ਹਾਂ	aseen urdoo boldeeaan haan	*we speak Urdu*

Subject–verb agreement

The verb in a sentence must agree with the gender and number of its subject (with a few exceptions in the past tense which will be discussed in Unit 10). If the subject is feminine and singular, then the verb must also be feminine and singular. As you should have noticed in the previous section on the simple present tense, there are two verbs: one is the main verb which indicates the action and the other is the auxiliary verb (a form of ਹੋਣਾ *to be*). The main verb changes according to the gender and number of the subject, and the auxiliary verb must also agree with the subject but only changes according to the person (1st – *I*, 2nd – *you*, 3rd – *they*) of the subject.

In the following examples note how the verbs (main and auxiliary) are in agreement with the subject:

ਮੈਂ	ਜਾਂਦੀ	ਹਾਂ	main	jaandee	haan
ਉਹ	ਜਾਂਦੇ	ਹਨ	uh	jaande	han
ਤੁਸੀਂ	ਜਾਂਦੇ	ਹੋ	tuseen	jaande	ho
ਮੁੰਡੇ	ਜਾਂਦੇ	ਹਨ	munde	jaande	han

Notice that the main verb and the auxiliary verb agree with one another in the singular and plural aspect of the subject. This is an essential element of forming sentences in Panjabi, and it should therefore be understood how verbs change accordingly.

Simple postpositions

You will recall from Unit 3 that the particle ਦਾ **daa**, in addition to showing possession, can be used as a postposition. Simple postpositions can be used to denote a number of different senses. In Panjabi the most common simple postpositions are as follows:

ਵਿਚ, ਦੇ ਵਿਚ	vich, de vich	*in, inside*
ਤੋਂ	ton	*from*
ਤੇ	te	*on*
ਤਕ	tak	*until, up to*
ਨਾਲ, ਦੇ ਨਾਲ	naal, de naal	*with*
ਨੂੰ	noon	*to*

Here are some simple examples of the uses of postpositions:

ਬਾਗ਼ ਵਿਚ	baagh vich	*in the garden*
ਪੰਜਾਬ ਤੋਂ	panjaab ton	*from Panjab*
ਮੇਜ਼ ਤੇ	mez te	*on the table*
ਅੱਜ ਤਕ	ajj tak	*until today*
ਇੱਥੇ ਤਕ	iththe tak	*up to here*
ਪਰਵਾਰ ਨਾਲ	parvaar naal	*with the family*
ਕਲਮ ਨਾਲ	kalam naal	*with a pen*
ਅਮਰੀਕਾ ਨੂੰ	amreekaa noon	*to America*
ਸ਼ਾਮ ਨੂੰ	shaam noon	*in the evening*

Nouns in the oblique

Panjabi nouns can be used in three different cases (modes of expression): the vocative, direct, and oblique. Each has its own corresponding way of formation. The vocative case reflects direct speech and will be dealt with in Unit 8. Direct nouns only change according to gender and number, as has been explained in Unit 3, and are not affected by any postposition. In contrast, the oblique case refers to the changes that some nouns undergo when affected by postpositions. In the examples of nouns with postpositions, all of the nouns are in the oblique case, though their forms do not reveal this because they are either invariable or are feminine in gender (see Unit 3). All nouns before a postposition, whether or not in a changed form, take on the oblique case. Generally, proper nouns such as names of people and places are not inflected by the postposition which follows them. In addition, masculine and feminine nouns have noticeably different formations in the oblique. You will note that feminine nouns in the singular and plural do not change in the oblique. Only masculine nouns change form when followed by postpositions.

Masculine singular

Direct			Oblique		
ਮੁੰਡਾ	mundaa	*boy*	ਮੁੰਡੇ ਨੂੰ	munde noon	*to the boy*
ਘੋੜਾ	ghorhaa	*horse*	ਘੋੜੇ ਤੇ	ghorhe te	*on the horse*
ਕਮਰਾ	kamraa	*room*	ਕਮਰੇ ਵਿਚ	kamre vich	*in the room*

Masculine plural

Direct			Oblique		
ਮੁੰਡੇ	munde	*boys*	ਮੁੰਡਿਆਂ ਨੂੰ	mundiaan noon	*to the boys*
ਘੋੜੇ	ghorhe	*horses*	ਘੋੜਿਆਂ ਤੇ	ghorhiaan te	*on the horses*
ਕਮਰੇ	kamre	*rooms*	ਕਮਰਿਆਂ ਵਿਚ	kamriaan vich	*in the rooms*

Feminine singular

Direct			Oblique		
ਤਸਵੀਰ	tasveer	*picture*	ਤਸਵੀਰ ਵਿਚ	tasveer vich	*in the picture*
ਕੁੜੀ	kurhee	*girl*	ਕੁੜੀ ਨੂੰ	kurhee noon	*to the girl*
ਜਨਾਨੀ	janaanee	*lady*	ਜਨਾਨੀ ਤੋਂ	janaanee ton	*from the lady*

Feminine plural

Direct			Oblique		
ਤਸਵੀਰਾਂ	tasveeraan	*pictures*	ਤਸਵੀਰਾਂ ਵਿਚ	tasveeraan vich	*in the pictures*
ਕੁੜੀਆਂ	kurheeaan	*girls*	ਕੁੜੀਆਂ ਨੂੰ	kurheeaan noon	*to the girls*
ਜਨਾਨੀਆਂ	janaanee aan	*ladies*	ਜਨਾਨੀਆਂ ਤੋਂ	janaaneeaan ton	*from the ladies*

Adjectives in the oblique

Adjectives must agree with the nouns they describe. Therefore, it is only logical that adjectives should also change form when attached to a noun followed by a postposition. In a similar manner to the oblique forms of nouns, adjectives are inflected in the oblique case, in addition to carrying the feminine or masculine, singular or plural nature of the nouns which they qualify. When adjectives are attached to oblique nouns, they also become oblique. Invariable adjectives, however, do not change. Notice the pattern of inflection of the adjectives in the following examples:

Direct		Oblique	
ਵੱਡਾ ਬੇਟਾ vaddaa betaa	elder son	ਵੱਡੇ ਬੇਟੇ ਨੂੰ vadde bete noon	to the elder son
ਵੱਡੇ ਬੇਟੇ vadde bete	elder sons	ਵੱਡਿਆਂ ਬੇਟਿਆਂ ਨੂੰ vaddiaan betiaan noon	to the elder sons
ਵੱਡੀ ਬੇਟੀ vaddee betee	elder daughter	ਵੱਡੀ ਬੇਟੀ ਨਾਲ vaddee betee naal	with the elder daughter
ਵੱਡੀਆਂ ਬੇਟੀਆਂ vaddeeaan beteeaan	elder daughters	ਵੱਡੀਆਂ ਬੇਟੀਆਂ ਨਾਲ vaddeeaan beteeaan naal	with the elder daughters
ਲਾਲ ਗੱਡੀ laal gaddee	red car	ਲਾਲ ਗੱਡੀ ਵਿਚ laal gaddee vich	in the red car
ਲਾਲ ਗੱਡੀਆਂ laal gaddeeaan	red cars	ਲਾਲ ਗੱਡੀਆਂ ਵਿਚ laal gaddeeaan vich	in the red cars

ਵਿਆਖਿਆ viaakhiaa *Commentary*

Employment and the Panjabi diaspora

There has been a long history of labour migration from Panjab to all parts of the world. The descendants of officers in the British Indian police force formed the core of the community in

Malaysia and the Philippines, while political migrants at the beginning of the twentieth century formed the core of the old community in Vancouver, Canada. In Britain, migration occurred after World War II and was primarily into the old industrial heartlands of the Midlands and the North, with a sizeable group also working in London. From a predominantly rural background to urban Britain, Panjabi men went from tilling the land to toiling on factory floors.

In the 1960s in Britain a Panjabi man would almost definitely be working in a factory or foundry in labouring or semi-skilled occupations. This is in contrast to migration to America in the 1960s where, due to the operation of quotas, only professionals such as doctors and engineers were allowed entry from the Indian sub-continent.

As communities have settled and the old industrial manufacturing sector has gone into decline, Panjabis are now found in all walks of life in Britain and North America. However, there is a concentration in certain parts of the economy, particularly in traditional professions such as law, medicine and engineering as well as self-employment. A large number of Panjabis are also involved in business ventures in textiles, food processing and retailing, the most popular niche markets. At the same time there is an increasing diversity of occupational and class profiles of Panjabis, from the long-term unemployed to multi-millionaires.

ਅਭਿਆਸ abhiaas *Exercises*

1 True or false?

a ਸਿਹਤ	sihat	means *health*	True / False
b ਬਿਲਕੁਲ	bilkul	means *alright*	True / False
c ਅਧਿਆਪਕਾ	adhiaapakaa	means *doctor*	True / False
d .ਖੁਸ਼ੀ	khushee	means *fine*	True / False

2 Who made the statements?

Reread the dialogues, then look at the following:

a ਇਹ ਡਾਕਟਰ ਸਿੰਘ ਹਨ। ih daaktar singh han. *This is Doctor Singh.*

b ਮਿਸਟਰ ਖ਼ਾਨ ਮੌਜਾਂ ਕਰਦੇ ਹਨ। mistar khaan maujaan karde han. *Mr Khan is enjoying life.*

c ਮੈਂ ਵੀ ਬਰਮਿੰਘਮ ਰਹਿੰਦਾ ਹਾਂ। main vee barmingham rahindaa haan. *I live in Birmingham too.*

3 Oblique or direct?

The following sentences contain adjectives and nouns which have been underlined. Identify which ones are direct and which ones are oblique.

a ਕੀ ਇਹ <u>ਤੁਹਾਡੀ ਬੇਟੀ</u> ਹੈ?   kee ih <u>tuhaadee betee</u> hai?   *Is this your daughter?*

b <u>ਤੁਹਾਡੇ ਬੇਟੇ</u> ਦਾ ਨਾਮ ਕੀ ਹੈ?   <u>tuhaade bete</u> daa naam kee hai?
What is your son's name?

c <u>ਕਮਰਾ</u> ਸਾਫ਼ ਹੈ।   <u>kamraa</u> saaf hai.   *The room is clean.*

d ਕੁੜੀਆਂ <u>ਕਮਰੇ ਵਿਚ</u> ਹਨ।   kurheeaan <u>kamre vich</u> han.   *There are girls in the room.*

e <u>ਅਗਲੇ ਹਫ਼ਤੇ</u> ਨੂੰ ਆਉਣਾ।   <u>agle hafte</u> noon aaunhaa.   *Come next week.*

▶ 4 Subjects and verbs into plural forms

Listen to the following sentences and / or read them in the following list. The sentences are in the present tense. Change the subjects and verbs from the singular to the plural. Remember that the verbs (both main and auxiliary) must agree with the subject. The first one has been done for you.

a ਮੈਂ ਲੰਡਨ ਵਿਚ ਕੰਮ ਕਰਦੀ ਹਾਂ।   main landan vich kanm kardee haan.
I work in London.
ਅਸੀਂ ਲੰਡਨ ਵਿਚ ਕੰਮ ਕਰਦੀਆਂ ਹਾਂ।   aseen landan vich kanm kardeeaan haan.
We work in London.

b ਮੇਰੀ ਬੇਟੀ ਸਕੂਲ ਵਿਚ ਪੜ੍ਹਦੀ ਹੈ।   meree betee sakool vich parhhdee hai.

c ਤੁਹਾਡਾ ਲੜਕਾ ਕਿੱਥੇ ਰਹਿੰਦਾ ਹੈ?   tuhaadaa larhkaa kiththe rahindaa hai?

d ਕੀ ਉਹ ਮੁੰਡਾ ਪੰਜਾਬੀ ਬੋਲਦਾ ਹੈ?   kee uh mundaa panjaabee boldaa hai?

05

ਕੀ ਗੱਲ ਸੀ ?

kee gall see?

what was the matter?

In this unit you will learn:
- how to describe
  continuous actions in the
  present and past
- how to form commands
  and requests
- how to express *was* and
  were

▶ 1 *What are you doing?*

ਗੱਲ ਬਾਤ ੧ ਤੂੰ ਕੀ ਕਰ ਰਹੀ ਹੈਂ?

gall baat 1 toon kee kar rahee hain?

Geeta and Sita are two women working in a garments factory. They are sitting next to one another as they are sewing and have the following conversation.

ਗੀਤਾ Geeta	ਨਮਸਤੇ ! ਤੂੰ ਕੀ ਕਰ ਰਹੀ ਹੈਂ? namaste! toon kee kar rahee hain? *Hello! What are you doing?*
ਸੀਤਾ Sita	ਨਮਸਤੇ। ਮੈਂ ਜੇਬਾਂ ਲਗਾ ਰਹੀ ਹਾਂ। ਮੇਰੀ ਮਸ਼ੀਨ ਕੰਮ ਨਹੀਂ ਕਰ ਰਹੀ। ਮੈਂ ਸੂਈ ਵਰਤ ਰਹੀ ਹਾਂ। namaste. main jebaan lagaa rahee haan. meree masheen kanm naheen kar rahee. main sooee vart rahee haan. *Hello. I am stitching pockets. My machine is not working so I am using a needle.*
ਗੀਤਾ Geeta	ਤੂੰ ਸਮਾਂ ਗਾਇਆ ਕਰ ਰਹੀ ਹੈਂ। ਸੁਣ! ਮੈਂ ਕੰਮ ਛੱਡ ਰਹੀ ਹਾਂ। toon samaan zaaiaa kar rahee hain. sunh! main kanm chadd rahee haan. *You are wasting your time. Listen! I am leaving work.*
ਸੀਤਾ Sita	ਤੂੰ ਕੰਮ ਕਿਉਂ ਛੱਡ ਰਹੀ ਹੈਂ? toon kanm kiun chadd rahee hain? *Why are you leaving work?*
ਗੀਤਾ Geeta	ਮੈਨੇਜਰ ਸਾਡੀ ਤਨਖ਼ਾਹ ਨਹੀਂ ਵਧਾ ਰਿਹਾ । ਉਹ ਸਾਡੀਆਂ ਮੰਗਾਂ ਪੂਰੀਆਂ ਨਹੀਂ ਕਰ ਰਿਹਾ ਹੈ। mainejar saadee tankhaah naheen vadhaa rihaa. uh saadeeaan mangaan pooreeaan naheen kar rihaa hai. *The manager is not increasing our pay. He is not fulfilling our demands.*
ਸੀਤਾ Sita	ਤੂੰ ਠੀਕ ਕਹਿ ਰਹੀ ਹੈਂ! toon theek kahi rahee hain! *You're right!* (lit. *You are saying it right.*)

ਸ਼ਬਦਾਵਲੀ   shabdaavalee   *Vocabulary*

ਕਰਨਾ	karnaa	*to do*
ਜੇਬਾਂ	jebaan	*pockets* (m. / f.)

ਲਗਾਉਣਾ	lagaaunhaa	*to stitch, to apply, to put on*
ਮਸ਼ੀਨ	masheen	*machine* (f.)
ਕੰਮ ਕਰਨਾ	ka<u>n</u>m karnaa	*to work*
ਸੂਈ	sooee	*needle* (f.)
ਵਰਤਣਾ	vara<u>t</u>nhaa	*to use*
ਸਮਾਂ	samaa<u>n</u>	*time* (m.)
ਜ਼ਾਇਆ ਕਰਨਾ	zaaiaa karnaa	*to waste time*
ਸੁਣਨਾ	sunhnaa	*to listen*
ਕੰਮ	ka<u>n</u>m	*work* (m.)
ਛੱਡਣਾ	<u>ch</u>addnhaa	*to leave, to quit*
ਮੈਨੇਜਰ	mainejar	*manager* (m. / f.)
ਤਨਖ਼ਾਹ	<u>t</u>an<u>kh</u>aah	*pay, salary* (f.)
ਵਧਾਉਣਾ	va<u>dh</u>aaunhaa	*to increase*
ਮੰਗਾਂ	mangaa<u>n</u>	*demands* (f.)
ਪੂਰੀਆਂ	pooreeaa<u>n</u>	*fulfilling*
ਠੀਕ	theek	*right, correct*
ਕਹਿਣਾ	kahinhaa	*to speak*

ਅਭਿਆਸ   abhiaas   *Exercises*

After reading the dialogue and / or listening to the recording, try to do the following exercises.

1 Arrange in correct word order.

a ਨਮਸਤੇ ਹੈਂ ਰਹੀ ਕਰ ਕੀ ਤੂੰ ?   namas<u>t</u>e-hai<u>n</u>-rahee-kar-kee-<u>t</u>oo<u>n</u>?
Hello. What are you doing?

b ਮੈਂ ਜੇਬਾਂ ਹਾਂ ਰਹੀ ਲਗਾ   mai<u>n</u>-jebaa<u>n</u>-haa<u>n</u>-rahee-lagaa
I am stitching pockets.

c ਨਹੀਂ ਵਧਾ ਰਿਹਾ ਤਨਖ਼ਾਹ ਮੈਨੇਜਰ ਸਾਡੀ   nahee<u>n</u>-va<u>dh</u>aa-rihaa <u>t</u>an<u>kh</u>aah-mainejar-saadee   *The manager is not increasing our pay.*

2 Crossword

Using the words given to you in Panjabi, complete the crossword with the English translations.

1 ਮਸ਼ੀਨ   masheen
2 ਕੰਮ   ka<u>n</u>m
3 ਤਨਖ਼ਾਹ   <u>t</u>an<u>kh</u>aah
4 ਜੇਬਾਂ   jebaa<u>n</u>
5 ਸਮਾਂ   samaa<u>n</u>
6 ਸੂਈ   sooee

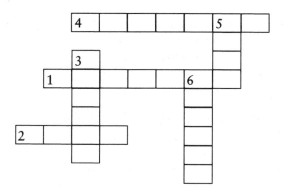

▶ 2 *What was the matter?*

ਗੱਲ ਬਾਤ ੨ ਕੀ ਗੱਲ ਸੀ?

gall baat 2 kee gall see?

Preet and Sumeet are close friends. They are meeting each other after the weekend.

ਪ੍ਰੀਤ **Preet**	ਤੁਸੀਂ ਕੱਲ੍ਹ ਕਿੱਥੇ ਸੀ? tuseen kallh kiththe see? *Where were you yesterday?*
ਸੁਮੀਤ **Sumeet**	ਅਸੀਂ ਘਰ ਸੀ। aseen ghar see. *We were at home.*
ਪ੍ਰੀਤ **Preet**	ਤੁਸੀਂ ਸਵੇਰੇ ਕੀ ਕਰ ਰਹੇ ਸੀ? tuseen savere kee kar rahe see? *What were you doing in the morning?*
ਸੁਮੀਤ **Sumeet**	ਮੈਂ ਫ਼ਿਲਮ ਦੇਖ ਰਹੀ ਸੀ। ਬੱਚੇ ਖੇਡ ਰਹੇ ਸਨ। main filam dekh rahee see. bachche khed rahe san. *I was watching a film. The children were playing.*
ਪ੍ਰੀਤ **Preet**	ਤੁਹਾਡੇ ਪਤੀ ਜੀ ਕੀ ਕਰ ਰਹੇ ਸਨ? tuhaade patee jee kee kar rahe san? *What was your husband doing?*
ਸੁਮੀਤ **Sumeet**	ਉਹ ਕਾਰ ਧੋ ਰਹੇ ਸਨ। uh kaar dho rahe san. *He was washing the car.*

ਪ੍ਰੀਤ		ਤੁਸੀਂ ਕਿਉਂ ਪੁੱਛ ਰਹੇ ਹੋ? ਕੀ ਗੱਲ ਸੀ?
Preet		tuseen kiun puchch rahe ho? kee gall see?
		Why are you asking? What was the matter?

ਸੁਮੀਤ

Sumeet

ਮੈਂ ਬੋਰ ਹੋ ਰਹੀ ਸੀ ਤੇ ਮੈਂ ਸਭ ਪਾਸੇ ਟੈਲੀਫ਼ੋਨ ਕਰ ਰਹੀ ਸੀ। ਮੈਂ ਤੁਹਾਡੇ ਬਾਰੇ ਸੋਚ ਰਹੀ ਸੀ।

main bor ho rahee see te main sabh paase taileefon kar rahee see. main tuhaade baare soch rahee see.

I was feeling bored and I called [was calling] everywhere. I was thinking of you.

ਪ੍ਰੀਤ
Preet

ਪਰ ਸਾਡਾ ਟੈਲੀਫ਼ੋਨ ਕੰਮ ਨਹੀਂ ਕਰ ਰਿਹਾ ਸੀ।

par saadaa taileefon kanm naheen kar rihaa see.

But our telephone was not working.

ਸ਼ਬਦਾਵਲੀ   **shabdaavalee**   *Vocabulary*

ਗੱਲ	gall	*matter* (f.) (lit. talk)
ਕੱਲ੍ਹ	kallh	*yesterday*
ਸਵੇਰੇ	savere	*morning*
ਫ਼ਿਲਮ	filam	*film* (f.)
ਦੇਖਣਾ	dekhnhaa	*to watch*
ਖੇਡਣਾ	khednhaa	*to play*
ਪਤੀ	patee	*husband* (m.)
ਕਾਰ	kaar	*car* (f.)
ਧੋਣਾ	dhonhaa	*to wash*
ਪੁੱਛਣਾ	puchchnhaa	*to ask*
ਬੋਰ ਹੋਣਾ	bor honhaa	*to be bored, to feel bored*
ਸਭ	sabh	*all, every*
ਸਭ ਪਾਸੇ	sabh paase	*everywhere*
ਪਾਸੇ	paase	*direction, way*
ਟੈਲੀਫ਼ੋਨ ਕਰਨਾ	taileefon karnaa	*to call by telephone*
ਤੁਹਾਡੇ ਬਾਰੇ	tuhaade baare	*about you*
ਸੋਚਣਾ	sochnhaa	*to think*

ਅਭਿਆਸ   **abhiaas**   *Exercises*

After reading the dialogue and / or listening to the recording, try to do the following exercises.

1 Word search

Four Panjabi words are hidden in the box. These words are **kaar, sumeet, kallh** and **ghar**. Find them by looking horizontally across each of the rows.

ੳ	ਸੁ	ਮੀ	ਤ
ਕੱ	ਲ੍ਹ	ਟ	ਤ
ਬ	ਭ	ਘ	ਰ
ਸ	ਕਾ	ਰ	ਮ

2 Answer the questions about the dialogue in Panjabi.

a ਸੁਮੀਤ ਕੀ ਕਰ ਰਹੀ ਸੀ?   sumeet kee kar rahee see?
b ਬੱਚੇ ਕੀ ਕਰ ਰਹੇ ਸਨ?   bachche kee kar rahe san?
c ਸੁਮੀਤ ਦਾ ਪਤੀ ਕੀ ਕਰ ਰਿਹਾ ਸੀ?   sumeet daa patee kee kar rihaa see?

ਬੋਲੀ ਬਾਰੇ bolee baare *Language points*

The present continuous tense (-*ing*)

The present continuous tense is generally used when an action is in progress. In English it is often signified by adding -*ing* to the end of a verb. In Panjabi, the stem, also known as the root, of the verb does not change its form. But the auxiliary verb and the progressive marker must agree with the subject. The progressive aspect of the verb, comparable with -*ing* in English, is expressed through ਰਹਿ **rahi** *the stem* of ਰਹਿਣਾ **rahinhaa**. It stands on its own as a separate word and should not be attached to either the main verb (*to . . .*) or the auxiliary verb. The progressive marker changes according to the gender and number of the subject.

For example: ਮੈਂ ਖਾ ਰਿਹਾ ਹਾਂ   main̲ khaa rihaa haan̲   *I am eating*

ਮੈਂ **main̲** *I* (subject) (1st person singular, masculine) + ਖਾ **khaa** (stem of the verb ਖਾਣਾ **khaanhaa** (*to eat*)) + ਰਿਹਾ **rihaa** (= -*ing*) (progressive marker) (masculine/singular) + ਹਾਂ **haan̲** (auxiliary verb (*am*)).

63

kee gall see?

05

The forms of **ਰਹਿ** rahi are as follows:

Masculine singular	Masculine plural	Feminine singular	Feminine plural
ਰਿਹਾ rihaa	ਰਹੇ rahe	ਰਹੀ rahee	ਰਹੀਆਂ raheeaan

The auxiliary verb also reflects the person, number and gender of the subject and takes on the present tense forms of **ਹੋਣਾ honhaa** as discussed in Unit 2.

1st person

Masculine singular	ਮੈਂ ਖਾ ਰਿਹਾ ਹਾਂ main khaa rihaa haan	*I am eating*
Feminine singular	ਮੈਂ ਖਾ ਰਹੀ ਹਾਂ main khaa rahee haan	*I am eating*
Masculine plural	ਅਸੀਂ ਖਾ ਰਹੇ ਹਾਂ aseen khaa rahe haan	*we are eating*
Feminine plural	ਅਸੀਂ ਖਾ ਰਹੀਆਂ ਹਾਂ aseen khaa raheeaan haan	*we are eating*

2nd person

Masculine singular	ਤੂੰ ਖਾ ਰਿਹਾਂ ਹੈਂ toon khaa rihaan hain	*you are eating*
Feminine singular	ਤੂੰ ਖਾ ਰਹੀ ਹੈਂ toon khaa rahee hain	*you are eating*
Masculine plural	ਤੁਸੀਂ ਖਾ ਰਹੇ ਹੋ tuseen khaa rahe ho	*you are eating*
Feminine plural	ਤੁਸੀਂ ਖਾ ਰਹੀਆਂ ਹੋ tuseen khaa raheeaan ho	*you are eating*

Masculine singular	ਉਹ / ਇਹ ਖਾ ਰਿਹਾ ਹੈ uh / ih khaa rihaa hai	*he is eating*
Feminine singular	ਉਹ / ਇਹ ਖਾ ਰਹੀ ਹੈ uh / ih khaa rahee hai	*she is eating*
Masculine plural	ਉਹ / ਇਹ ਖਾ ਰਹੇ ਹਨ uh / ih khaa rahe han	*they are eating*
Feminine plural	ਉਹ / ਇਹ ਖਾ ਰਹੀਆਂ ਹਨ uh / ih khaa raheeaa̱n han	*they are eating*

Uses of present continuous

Sometimes the simple present (see Unit 4) and present continuous tenses become interchangeable with one another when the action is on-going and habitual.

Simple present

ਮੈਂ ਸਕੂਲ ਵਿਚ ਕੰਮ ਕਰਦਾ ਹਾਂ   mai̱n sakool vich ka̱nm kar̲daa haa̱n   *I work in a school.*

Present continuous

ਮੈਂ ਸਕੂਲ ਵਿਚ ਕੰਮ ਕਰ ਰਿਹਾ ਹਾਂ   mai̱n sakool vich ka̱nm kar rihaa haa̱n   *I am working in a school.*

The present continuous tense may also be used in instances where an action in the immediate future is being denoted, though it may not be happening at the present time:

ਉਹ ਸ਼ਾਮ ਨੂੰ ਆ ਰਿਹਾ ਹੈ   uh shaam noo̱n aa rihaa hai   *He is coming in the evening.*

A less formal but more common manner of this use of the present continuous occurs if we drop the auxiliary verb. The meaning of the sentence does not change. However, because the sense becomes slightly less formal a change of **ਰਿਹਾ rihaa** to **ਰਿਹਾਂ rihaa̱n** by nasalizing the ending is required.

Examples:

ਉਹ ਜਾ ਰਿਹਾਂ   uh jaa rihaa̱n   *he's going*

ਮੈਂ ਪੜੂ ਰਿਹਾਂ   mai̱n parhh rihaa̱n   *I'm reading*

The imperative

The imperative is a form of the verb which expresses request, command or suggestion. The imperative has two forms: formal and informal. The formal imperative adds the vowel sound 'o' to the stem of the verb and the informal uses the stem on its own. Here are two examples which illustrate the formal and informal aspects of the imperative using the verb ਸੁਣਨਾ **sunhnaa**, *to listen*:

| (ਤੂੰ) ਸੁਣ | (<u>too</u><u>n</u>) sunh | *Listen!* (you, informal) |
| (ਤੁਸੀਂ) ਸੁਣੋ | (<u>t</u>usee<u>n</u>) sunho | *Listen!* (you, formal) |

ਤੂੰ <u>too</u><u>n</u> (*you*) is generally used with children, close relatives, equals and intimate relations while ਤੁਸੀਂ <u>t</u>usee<u>n</u> (*you*) is used as a respectful address with elders or formal acquaintances or in references to more than one person. The person and the tone of voice used to express imperative situations determine the nature of the order or request. For example, an imperative form in the 2nd person ਤੁਸੀਂ <u>t</u>usee<u>n</u> would denote a more polite, formal request while an imperative using the 2nd person ਤੂੰ <u>too</u><u>n</u> would reflect a more informal although authoritative order.

Was and *were*

The past tense of the verb *to be* ਹੋਣਾ **honhaa** is *was* and *were*. You have already learned that the auxiliary verb is formed with the verb *to be*. Just as the present tense of *to be* becomes *is*, *am* and *are*, the past tense of *to be* becomes *was* and *were*.

Here is the past tense of the verb **honhaa** ਹੋਣਾ *to be*:

Singular			**Plural**		
ਮੈਂ ਸੀ	mai<u>n</u> see	*I was*	ਅਸੀਂ ਸੀ	asee<u>n</u> see	*we were*
ਤੂੰ ਸੀ	<u>too</u><u>n</u> see	*you were*	ਤੁਸੀਂ ਸੀ	<u>t</u>usee<u>n</u> see	*you were*
ਇਹ ਸੀ	ih see	*he /she / it was*	ਇਹ ਸਨ / ਸੀ	ih san / see	*they were*
ਉਹ ਸੀ	uh see	*he / she / that was*	ਉਹ ਸਨ / ਸੀ	uh san / see	*they were*

Note that ਸੀ **see** can be used with any number, person or gender.

The past continuous tense

The past continuous tense describes actions which had continued to happen before and after a particular time (in English *was . . . -ing* and *were . . . -ing*). The past continuous tense follows the same pattern as the present continuous except that the auxiliary verb takes the past form. The progressive marker (*-ing*) is followed by the appropriate forms of *was* and *were*. ਸੀ **see** is the most commonly used past auxiliary, although ਸਨ **san** is also used for the plural. Both are neutral of gender and number.

Masculine singular	Masculine plural	Feminine singular	Feminine plural
ਰਿਹਾ ਸੀ rihaa see	ਰਹੇ ਸਨ rahe san	ਰਹੀ ਸੀ rahee see	ਰਹੀਆਂ ਸਨ raheeaa<u>n</u> san

ਮੈਂ **mai<u>n</u>** *I* (subject) (1st person singular, masculine) + ਖਾ **khaa** (stem of the verb ਖਾਣਾ (*to eat*)) + ਰਿਹਾ **rihaa** (= *-ing*) (progressive marker) (masculine singular) + ਸੀ **see** (auxiliary verb) (*was*) =

ਮੈਂ ਖਾ ਰਿਹਾ ਸੀ	mai<u>n</u> khaa rihaa see	*I was eating*

1st person

Masculine singular	ਮੈਂ ਜਾ ਰਿਹਾ ਸੀ mai<u>n</u> jaa rihaa see	*I was going*
Feminine singular	ਮੈਂ ਜਾ ਰਹੀ ਸੀ mai<u>n</u> jaa rahee see	*I was going*
Masculine plural	ਅਸੀਂ ਜਾ ਰਹੇ ਸੀ asee<u>n</u> jaa rahe see	*we were going*
Feminine plural	ਅਸੀਂ ਜਾ ਰਹੀਆਂ ਸੀ asee<u>n</u> jaa raheeaa<u>n</u> see	*we were going*

2nd person

Masculine singular	ਤੂੰ ਜਾ ਰਿਹਾ ਸੀ too<u>n</u> jaa rihaa see	*you were going*
Feminine singular	ਤੂੰ ਜਾ ਰਹੀ ਸੀ too<u>n</u> jaa rahee see	*you were going*

| Masculine plural | ਤੁਸੀਂ ਜਾ ਰਹੇ ਸੀ
<u>t</u>usee<u>n</u> jaa rahe see | *you were going* |
| Feminine plural | ਤੁਸੀਂ ਜਾ ਰਹੀਆਂ ਸੀ
<u>t</u>usee<u>n</u> jaa raheeaa<u>n</u> see | *you were going* |

3rd person

Masculine singular	ਉਹ / ਇਹ ਜਾ ਰਿਹਾ ਸੀ uh / ih jaa rihaa see	*he was going*
Feminine singular	ਉਹ / ਇਹ ਜਾ ਰਹੀ ਸੀ uh / ih jaa rahee see	*she was going*
Masculine plural	ਉਹ / ਇਹ ਜਾ ਰਹੇ ਸਨ / ਸੀ uh / ih jaa rahe san / see	*they were going*
Feminine plural	ਉਹ / ਇਹ ਜਾ ਰਹੀਆਂ ਸਨ / ਸੀ uh / ih jaa raheeaa<u>n</u> san / see	*they were going*

Negative sentences

Generally, sentences are made negative by inserting ਨਹੀਂ **nahee<u>n</u>** (*not*) between the verb stem and the progressive marker:

| Statement | ਮੈਂ ਖਾ ਰਿਹਾ ਹਾਂ | mai<u>n</u> khaa rihaa haa<u>n</u> | *I am eating* |
| Negative | ਮੈਂ ਖਾ ਨਹੀਂ ਰਿਹਾ ਹਾਂ | mai<u>n</u> khaa nahee<u>n</u> rihaa haa<u>n</u> | *I am not eating* |

In colloquial speech the auxiliary verb is often dropped in positive and negative statements. A native Panjabi speaker may instead say: ਮੈਂ ਖਾ ਨਹੀਂ ਰਿਹਾ **main khaa nahee<u>n</u> rihaa.**

Making interrogative sentences

An interrogative sentence is made simply by adding ਕੀ **kee** at the beginning of the sentence. The literal definition of ਕੀ **kee** is 'what' which can turn a statement into a question.

| Statement | ਤੂੰ ਖਾ ਰਿਹਾ ਹੈਂ | <u>t</u>oon khaa rihaa hai<u>n</u> | *you are eating* |
| Interrogative | ਕੀ ਤੂੰ ਖਾ ਰਿਹਾ ਹੈਂ? | kee <u>t</u>oon khaa rihaa hai<u>n</u>? | *Are you eating?* |

If ਕੀ **kee** is inserted between the subject and the verb, the meaning of the sentence will change. Note and compare the following sentences:

ਤੂੰ ਖਾ ਰਿਹਾ ਹੈਂ	<u>too</u>n khaa rihaa hai<u>n</u>	*You are eating.*
ਕੀ ਤੂੰ ਖਾ ਰਿਹਾ ਹੈਂ?	kee <u>too</u>n khaa rihaa hai<u>n</u>?	*Are you eating?*
ਤੂੰ ਕੀ ਖਾ ਰਿਹਾ ਹੈਂ?	<u>too</u>n kee khaa rihaa hai<u>n</u>?	*What are you eating?*

Similarly, other interrogative pronouns can be used in turning statements into questions such as ਕਿਉਂ **kiu<u>n</u>** (*why*), ਕਿਵੇਂ **kive<u>n</u>** (*how*) and ਕਿੱਥੇ **ki<u>thth</u>e** (*where*).

ਵਿਆਖਿਆ   viaakhiaa   *Commentary*

1 ਕੱਲ੍ਹ kallh (*yesterday* and *tomorrow*)

In Panjabi there is one word which means both *yesterday* and *tomorrow* ਕੱਲ੍ਹ **kallh**. This may at first seem quite confusing, but the sense in which ਕੱਲ੍ਹ **kallh** is used in a conversation can be gauged from the tense of the verbs and the sense of the context. For example:

| ਮੈਂ ਕੱਲ੍ਹ ਘਰ ਸੀ | mai<u>n</u> kallh ghar see | *I was (at) home yesterday.* |
| ਮੈਂ ਕੱਲ੍ਹ ਆ ਰਹੀ ਹਾਂ | mai<u>n</u> kallh aa rahee haa<u>n</u> | *I am coming tomorrow.* |

There is, however, a specific word for *tomorrow* – ਭਲਕ **bhalak** – but it is rarely used. The most common forms of signifying time are:

ਅੱਜ	ajj	*today*
ਕੱਲ੍ਹ	kallh	*yesterday/tomorrow*
ਭਲਕ / ਭਲਕੇ	bhalak / bhalke	*tomorrow*
ਪਰਸੋਂ	parso<u>n</u>	*day before yesterday/ day after tomorrow*

You will see all of these forms used in later units.

2 Panjabi women at work

In rural Panjab, women play a significant part in the contribution to the household economy. From helping in the fields to animal husbandry, women play a central role in the rural economy. This has continued in the diaspora, where Panjabi women have worked in factories in a similar way to their male counterparts. The factories of the Midlands in Britain and more recently

Silicon Valley in California have employed Panjabi women. In Britain these women have been at the forefront of industrial struggles, the most well known being 'Imperial Typewriters' and the more recent 'Burnsalls' Strike'. The contemporary concentration of Panjabi women in the textiles sector in sewing and stitching of garments is a continuity with the jobs they had on arrival. The daughters of these migrants are now forging new paths in a wide variety of occupations and businesses, a selection of which can be found in the book, *The Golden Thread*, by Zerbanoo Gifford.

ਅਭਿਆਸ   abhiaas   *Exercises*

1 Change the informal sentences into formal sentences.

Complete this exercise by replacing the subject pronoun ਤੂੰ (**toon**) with ਤੁਸੀਂ (**tuseen**).

a ਤੂੰ ਸਮਾਂ ਜਾਇਆ ਕਰ ਰਹੀ ਹੈਂ।   toon samaan zaaiaa kar rahee hain.
You are wasting your time.

b ਤੂੰ ਕੰਮ ਕਿਉਂ ਛੱਡ ਰਹੀ ਹੈਂ?   toon kanm kiun chadd rahee hain?
Why are you leaving work?

c ਤੂੰ ਠੀਕ ਕਹਿ ਰਹੀ ਹੈਂ।   toon theek kahi rahee hain.   *You are (saying) right.*

2 Complete the table.

ਪਤੀ		*husband*
ਘਰ	ghar	
	kallh	*yesterday*

▶ 3 Change present continuous to past continuous.

Listen to the recording. Phrases have been given to you in the present continuous (i.e. *am / is / are ___ -ing*). Change them to the past continuous (i.e. *was / were ___ -ing*). The first one has been done for you.

a ਮੈਂ ਕੰਮ ਕਰ ਰਹੀ ਹਾਂ।   main kanm kar rahee haan.   *I am working.*

ਮੈਂ ਕੰਮ ਕਰ ਰਹੀ ਸੀ।   main kanm kar rahee see.   *I was working.*

b ਤੁਸੀਂ ਕੀ ਪੁੱਛ ਰਹੇ ਹੋ?	<u>t</u>useen kee pu<u>chch</u> rahe ho?	*What are you asking?*
c ਉਹ ਕੀ ਕਰ ਹਹੇ ਹਨ?	uh kee kar rahe han?	*What are they doing?*
d ਉਹ ਕਾਰ ਧੋ ਰਿਹਾ ਹੈ।	uh kaar <u>dh</u>o rihaa hai.	*He is washing the car.*

4 Fill in the blanks.

Using the pictorial clues given, fill in the blanks with the main verb stem of the continuous actions being done.

a ਗੀਤਾ ਟੈਨਸ _____
gee<u>t</u>aa tainas (tennis) _____

b ਅਵਤਾਰ ਖਾਣਾ _____
av<u>t</u>aar khaanhaa _____

c ਸੀਤਾ ਤੇ ਗੀਤਾ ਪੰਜਾਬੀ _____
see<u>t</u>aa <u>t</u>e gee<u>t</u>aa pa<u>n</u>jaabee _____

d ਮੁੰਡਾ ਕਿਤਾਬ _____
mu<u>n</u>daa ki<u>t</u>aab _____

06

ਕੀ ਤੁਸੀਂ ਜਲੰਧਰ ਪੜ੍ਹੇ ਸੀ?

kee tuseen jalandhar parhhe see?

did you study in Jalandhar?

In this unit you will learn:
- how to express actions in the immediate past
- how to express habitual actions in the past
- about Sikh wedding customs
- about kinship and relations

▶ 1 *We went to London*

ਗੱਲ ਬਾਤ ੧ ਅਸੀਂ ਲੰਡਨ ਗਏ ਸੀ

gall baat 1 aseen landan gae see

Surjit Singh and Pavan Singh are friends and both belong to the Sikh religion. They are having a conversation on the phone.

ਸੁਰਜੀਤ ਸਿੰਘ	ਸਤਿ ਸ੍ਰੀ ਅਕਾਲ। ਤੁਸੀਂ ਐਤਵਾਰ ਕਿੱਥੇ ਸੀ ? ਮੈਂ ਤੁਹਾਡੇ ਘਰ ਆਇਆ ਸੀ।
Surjit Singh	sat sree akaal. tuseen aitvaar kiththe see? main tuhaade ghar aaiaa see.
	Hello. Where were you on Sunday? I came to your house.
ਪਵਨ ਸਿੰਘ	ਅਸੀਂ ਇੱਥੇ ਨਹੀਂ ਸੀ। ਅਸੀਂ ਹਫ਼ਤੇ ਦੇ ਅਖ਼ੀਰ ਲੰਡਨ ਗਏ ਸੀ।
Pavan Singh	aseen iththe naheen see. aseen hafte de akheer landan gae see.
	We were not here. We went to London over the weekend.
ਸੁਰਜੀਤ ਸਿੰਘ	ਕੀ ਕੋਈ ਖ਼ਾਸ ਮੌਕਾ ਸੀ ?
Surjit Singh	kee koee khaas maukaa see?
	Was there any special occasion?
ਪਵਨ ਸਿੰਘ	ਹਾਂ! ਮੇਰੀ ਭਤੀਜੀ ਦਾ ਵਿਆਹ ਸੀ।
Pavan Singh	haan! meree bhateejee daa viaah see.
	Yes! It was my niece's wedding.
ਸੁਰਜੀਤ ਸਿੰਘ	ਵਧਾਈਆਂ। ਕਿਹੜੇ ਸ਼ਹਿਰ ਤੋਂ ਬਰਾਤ ਆਈ ਸੀ ?
Surjit Singh	vadhaaeeaan. kihrhe shahir ton baraat aaee see?
	Congratulations. Which city did the marriage party come from?
ਪਵਨ ਸਿੰਘ	ਉਹ ਮਾਨਚੈਸਟਰ ਤੋਂ ਆਈ ਸੀ। ਤਕਰੀਬਨ ੧੦੦ ਬੰਦੇ ਸਨ।
Pavan Singh	uh maanchaistar ton aaee see. takreeban 100 bande san.
	They came from Manchester. There were about 100 people.
ਸੁਰਜੀਤ ਸਿੰਘ	ਵਿਆਹ ਕਿਵੇਂ ਰਿਹਾ ?
Surjit Singh	viaah kiven rihaa?
	How did the wedding go?

ਪਵਨ ਸਿੰਘ		
Pavan Singh	ਬਹੁਤ ਸੁਹਣਾ। ਤੁਸੀਂ ਕਦੀ ਆਓ ਤੇ ਵਿਆਹ ਦੀਆਂ ਫ਼ੋਟੇ ਦੇਖੇ।	

bahuṯ suhnhaa. ṯuseen kadee aao ṯe viaah deeaan foto dekho.

Excellent. Come over sometime and see the wedding photographs.

ਸ਼ਬਦਾਵਲੀ   shabdaavalee   *Vocabulary*

ਲੰਡਨ	landan	London (m.)
ਐਤਵਾਰ	aiṯvaar	Sunday (m.)
ਹਫ਼ਤੇ	hafṯe	week (m.)
ਅਖ਼ੀਰ	akheer	end
ਹਫ਼ਤੇ ਦੇ ਅਖ਼ੀਰ	hafṯe de akheer	weekend (m.)
ਕੋਈ	koee	any
ਖ਼ਾਸ	khaas	special
ਮੋਕਾ	maukaa	occasion (m.)
ਭਤੀਜੀ	bhaṯeejee	niece (f.)
ਵਿਆਹ	viaah	wedding (m.)
ਵਧਾਈਆਂ	vadhaaeeaan	congratulations
ਸ਼ਹਿਰ	shahir	city (m.)
ਮਾਨਚੈਸਟਰ	maanchaistar	Manchester (m.)
ਤਕਰੀਬਨ	ṯakreeban	about, approximately
ਬੰਦੇ	bande	people (m.)
ਕਿਵੇਂ ਰਿਹਾ	kiven rihaa	how did it go?
ਬਹੁਤ ਸੁਹਣਾ	bahuṯ suhnhaa	very nice, excellent (v.)
ਫ਼ੋਟੇ	foto	photograph (f.)
ਕਦੀ	kadee	sometime
ਆਓ	aao	come (formal)

ਅਭਿਆਸ   abhiaas   *Exercises*

After reading the dialogue and / or listening to the recording, try to do the following exercises.

1 Answer the following questions about Dialogue 1 in either short or long form.

a ਪਵਨ ਹਫ਼ਤੇ ਦੇ ਅਖ਼ੀਰ ਕਿੱਥੇ ਸੀ? pavan hafṯe de akheer kiththe see?

b ਖ਼ਾਸ ਮੋਕਾ ਕੀ ਸੀ? khaas maukaa kee see?

c ਕਿਹੜੇ ਸ਼ਹਿਰ ਤੋਂ ਬਰਾਤ ਆਈ ਸੀ? kihrhe shahir ṯon baraaṯ aaee see?

d ਵਿਆਹ ਤੇ ਤਕਰੀਬਨ ਕਿੰਨੇ ਬੰਦੇ ਸਨ? viaah ṯe ṯakreeban kinne bande san?

2 Translate the following into formal Panjabi.

a Where were you on Sunday?
b Where were you yesterday?
c Where were you over the weekend?

▶ 2 *Did you study in Jalandhar?*

ਗੱਲ ਬਾਤ ੨ ਕੀ ਤੁਸੀਂ ਜਲੰਧਰ ਪੜ੍ਹੇ ਸੀ ?

gall baaṯ 2 kee ṯuseeṉ jalanḏhar parhhe see?

Surjit Singh visits Pavan Singh in order to see the photographs of Pavan's niece's wedding.

ਸੁਰਜੀਤ ਸਿੰਘ	ਸਤਿ ਸ੍ਰੀ ਅਕਾਲ ਜੀ । ਕੀ ਹਾਲ ਹੈ ?
Surjit Singh	saṯ sree akaal jee. kee haal hai? *Hello. How are you?*
ਪਵਨ ਸਿੰਘ	ਸਤਿ ਸ੍ਰੀ ਅਕਾਲ । ਵਾਹਿਗੁਰੂ ਦੀ ਕਿਰਪਾ ਨਾਲ ਸਭ ਕੁਝ ਠੀਕ ਠਾਕ ਹੈ ।
Pavan Singh	saṯ sree akaal. vaahiguroo ḏee kirpaa naal sabh kujh theek thaak hai. *Hello. By the grace of God, everything is fine.*

(Pavan hands the wedding album over to Surjit.)

ਸੁਰਜੀਤ ਸਿੰਘ	(pointing to one of the photographs) ਇਹ ਪੁਰਸ਼ ਤੇ ਇਸਤਰੀ ਕੋਣ ਹਨ ?
Surjit Singh	ih pursh ṯe isṯaree kaunh han? *Who are this gentleman and lady?*
ਪਵਨ ਸਿੰਘ	ਇਹ ਮੇਰਾ ਭਰਾ ਹੈ ਅਤੇ ਇਹ ਮੇਰੀ ਭਾਬੀ ਹੈ । ਅਸੀਂ ਇੱਕੋ ਮਕਾਨ ਵਿਚ ਰਹਿੰਦੇ ਸੀ ।
Pavan Singh	ih meraa bharaa hai aṯe ih meree bhaabee hai. aseeṉ ikko makaan vich rahinḏe see. *He is my brother, and she is my sister-in-law. We used to live in one house.*
ਸੁਰਜੀਤ ਸਿੰਘ	(looking at another photograph) ਕੀ ਇਹ ਤੁਹਾਡੇ ਚਾਚਾ ਜੀ ਹਨ ?
Surjit Singh	kee ih ṯuhaade chaachaa jee han? *Is this your uncle?*

ਪਵਨ ਸਿੰਘ **Pavan Singh**	ਹਾਂ ਜੀ। ਅਸੀਂ ਕਾਲਜ ਵਿਚ ਹਾਕੀ ਇਕੱਠੇ ਖੇਡਦੇ ਸੀ। haa<u>n</u> jee. asee<u>n</u> kaalaj vich haakee ikaththe khed<u>d</u>e see. *Yes. We used to play hockey together in college.*
ਸੁਰਜੀਤ ਸਿੰਘ **Surjit Singh**	ਕੀ ਤੁਸੀਂ ਜਲੰਧਰ ਪੜ੍ਹੇ ਸੀ? kee <u>t</u>usee<u>n</u> jala<u>n</u>dhar parhhe see? *Did you study in Jalandhar?*
ਪਵਨ ਸਿੰਘ **Pavan Singh**	ਨਹੀਂ ਜੀ ਮੈਂ ਹੁਸ਼ਿਆਰਪੁਰ ਪੜ੍ਹਦਾ ਸੀ। nahee<u>n</u> jee. mai<u>n</u> hushiaarpur parhh<u>d</u>aa see. *No. I used to study in Hoshiarpur.*
ਸੁਰਜੀਤ ਸਿੰਘ **Surjit Singh**	ਕੀ ਵਿਆਹ ਵਿਚ ਬਹੁਤ ਪ੍ਰਾਹੁਣੇ ਸਨ? kee viaah vich bahu<u>t</u> praahunhe san? *Were there a lot of guests at the wedding?*
ਪਵਨ ਸਿੰਘ **Pavan Singh**	ਹਾਂ, ਇਹ ਇੱਕ ਚੰਗਾ ਇਕੱਠ ਸੀ। haa<u>n</u>, ih ikk cha<u>n</u>gaa ikathth see. *Yes, it was a good gathering.*

ਸ਼ਬਦਾਵਲੀ   shab<u>d</u>aavalee   *Vocabulary*

ਰਹਿਣਾ	rahinhaa	*to live, to stay*
ਕਿਰਪਾ	kirpaa	*blessings* (f.)
ਸਭ ਕੁਝ	sabh kujh	*everything*
ਠੀਕ ਠਾਕ	theek thaak	*OK, fine*
ਪੁਰਸ਼	purash	*gentleman* (m.)
ਇਸਤਰੀ	is<u>t</u>aree	*lady* (f.)
ਭਾਬੀ	bhaabee	*sister-in-law* (f.) (brother's wife)
ਚਾਚਾ ਜੀ	chaachaa jee	*uncle* (m.) (father's brother)
ਕਾਲਜ	kaalaj	*college* (m.)
ਖੇਡਣਾ	khednhaa	*to play*
ਪ੍ਰਾਹੁਣੇ	praahunhe	*guests* (m.)
ਇੱਕ	ikk	*one, a*
ਇਕੱਠ	ikathth	*gathering* (m.)

ਅਭਿਆਸ   abhiaas   *Exercises*

After reading the dialogue and / or listening to the recording, try to do the following exercises.

1 Complete the table.

The first one has been done for you.

ਪੁਰਸ਼	purash	*man*
	istaree	
ਇਕੱਠ		
		guests
	kaalaj	
		sister-in-law

2 Identify whether the statements are formal or informal.

Tick the appropriate box.

Formal   Informal

a ਇਹ ਮੇਰਾ ਭਰਾ ਹੈ।
ih meraa bharaa hai.
This is my brother.

b ਇਹ ਮੇਰੀ ਭਾਬੀ ਹੈ।
ih meree bhaabee hai.
This is my sister-in-law.

c ਇਹ ਮੇਰੇ ਚਾਚਾ ਜੀ ਹਨ।
ih mere chaachaa jee han.
This is my uncle.

ਬੋਲੀ ਬਾਰੇ bolee baare *Language points*

The past tense

The past tense in Panjabi describes actions or states of condition which have taken place at a particular time before the present one. Here we will discuss three different constructions of the past tense: the simple past, the remote past and the past habitual. As was shown in Unit 5, was and were in Panjabi are expressed through the past tense of the auxiliary verb *to be* ਹੋਣਾ honhaa. The more common forms for the past tense, however, are ਸੀ see and ਸਨ san. The appropriate form of the past of *to be* is determined by person, number and mode of address

kee tuseen jalandhar parhhe see?

06

(formal or informal). Here are some examples to refresh your memory:

| ਮੁੰਡਾ ਚੰਗਾ ਸੀ | muṉḏaa chaṉgaa see | *The boy was good.* |
| ਮੁੰਡੇ ਚੰਗੇ ਸਨ | muṉḏe chaṉge san | *The boys were good.* |

The simple past tense

The simple past tense is used when expressing actions or conditions completed in the past. The simple past is formed by adding appropriate endings to the stem of the main verb. The endings added to the stem reflect the gender and number of the subject. To determine if the subject is 1st/2nd or 3rd person, you need to refer to the subject pronoun. Here, the verb 'to speak' ਬੋਲਣਾ **bolnhaa**, will be used to illustrate the various past tenses:

Verb	Stem
ਬੋਲਣਾ bolnhaa (*to speak*)	ਬੋਲ - *bol*

Now note the endings added to the stem:

ਮੈਂ   main   *I* (subject) (1st person masculine)
ਬੋਲਿਆ   boliaa   *spoke* (simple past form of the verb *to speak* ਬੋਲਣਾ)

1st person

Masculine singular	ਮੈਂ ਬੋਲਿਆ	mai̱n boliaa	*I spoke*
Feminine singular	ਮੈਂ ਬੋਲੀ	mai̱n bolee	*I spoke*
Masculine plural	ਅਸੀਂ ਬੋਲੇ	aseen bole	*we spoke*
Feminine plural	ਅਸੀਂ ਬੋਲੀਆਂ	aseen boleeaan	*we spoke*

2nd person

Masculine singular informal	ਤੂੰ ਬੋਲਿਆ	toon boliaa	*you spoke*
Feminine singular informal	ਤੂੰ ਬੋਲੀ	toon bolee	*you spoke*
Masculine plural / formal	ਤੁਸੀਂ ਬੋਲੇ	ṯuseen bole	*you spoke*
Feminine plural	ਤੁਸੀਂ ਬੋਲੀਆਂ	ṯuseen boleeaan	*you spoke*

Masculine singular	ਉਹ / ਇਹ ਬੋਲਿਆ uh / ih boliaa	*he spoke*
Feminine singular	ਉਹ / ਇਹ ਬੋਲੀ uh / ih bolee	*she spoke*
Masc. plural / formal	ਉਹ / ਇਹ ਬੋਲੇ uh / ih bole	*they spoke*
Feminine plural	ਉਹ / ਇਹ ਬੋਲੀਆਂ uh / ih boleeaa<u>n</u>	*they spoke*

Some verbs change in a more irregular manner in the past tense. You will have to learn and watch out for them. Verbs such as ਜਾਣਾ jaanhaa *to go*, ਕਰਨਾ karnaa *to do* and ਦੇਣਾ <u>d</u>enhaa *to give* take on irregular forms in the past tense which do not derive from the root. Here we give the example of how ਜਾਣਾ jaanhaa *to go* is formed in the simple past tense. Note that the forms are not affected by person, only by gender and number.

ਜਾਣਾ jaanhaa – *to go* (*went*)

Masculine singular	Feminine singular	Masculine plural	Feminine plural
ਗਿਆ	ਗਈ	ਗਏ	ਗਈਆਂ
giaa	gaee	gae	gaeeaa<u>n</u>

The remote past
The remote past in Panjabi expresses actions which occurred prior to the present or the immediate past. The main verb used in the simple past is combined with the auxiliary verb in the past to form the remote past. The remote past tense is used when one is:

- being definitive in a statement
- emphasizing a particular point
- conveying the completion of an action
- referring to the remote past

The form of the main verb follows the pattern of the simple past just shown while the auxiliary verb reflects the appropriate forms of *was* and *were*. For example:

1st person

Masculine singular	ਮੈਂ ਬੋਲਿਆ ਸੀ	main boliaa see	*I spoke, had spoken*
Feminine singular	ਮੈਂ ਬੋਲੀ ਸੀ	main bolee see	*I spoke, had spoken*
Masculine plural	ਅਸੀਂ ਬੋਲੇ ਸੀ	aseen bole see	*we spoke, had spoken*
Feminine plural	ਅਸੀਂ ਬੋਲੀਆਂ ਸੀ	aseen boleeaan see	*we spoke, had spoken*

2nd person

Masculine singular informal	ਤੂੰ ਬੋਲਿਆ ਸੀ	toon boliaa see	*you spoke, had spoken*
Feminine singular informal	ਤੂੰ ਬੋਲੀ ਸੀ	toon bolee see	*you spoke, had spoken*
Masculine plural / formal	ਤੁਸੀਂ ਬੋਲੇ ਸੀ	tuseen bole see	*you spoke, had spoken*
Feminine plural	ਤੁਸੀਂ ਬੋਲੀਆਂ ਸੀ	tuseen boleeaan see	*you spoke, had spoken*

3rd person

Masculine singular	ਇਹ / ਉਹ ਬੋਲਿਆ ਸੀ	ih / uh boliaa see	*he spoke, had spoken*
Feminine singular	ਇਹ / ਉਹ ਬੋਲੀ ਸੀ	ih / uh bolee see	*she spoke, had spoken*
Masculine plural / formal	ਇਹ / ਉਹ ਬੋਲੇ ਸਨ / ਸੀ	ih / uh bolen san / see	*they spoke, had spoken*
Feminine plural	ਇਹ / ਉਹ ਬੋਲੀਆਂ ਸਨ / ਸੀ	ih / uh boleeaan san / see	*they spoke, had spoken*

The remote past of ਜਾਣਾ **jaanhaa** *to go* follows the same pattern using the simple past form with the appropriate form of *was* and *were*.

ਜਾਣਾ jaanhaa – *to go*

Masculine singular	Feminine singular	Masculine plural	Feminine plural
ਗਿਆ ਸੀ giaa see	ਗਈ ਸੀ gaee see	ਗਏ ਸੀ / ਸਨ gae see / san	ਗਈਆਂ ਸੀ / ਸਨ gaeeaan see / san

Past habitual tense – *used to*

In English *used to* expresses actions which occurred regularly in the past but which no longer exist in the present. In Panjabi the past habitual tense is used in the same manner. For example:

ਮੈਂ ਬੋਲਦਾ ਸੀ	main boldaa see	*I used to speak*

The components of this example can be broken down as follows:

ਮੈਂ	main	*I* (subject) (1st person masculine)
ਬੋਲਦਾ	boldaa	*speak* (simple present form of *to speak* ਬੋਲਣਾ bolnhaa)
ਸੀ	see	*was* (simple past of *to be* ਹੋਣਾ honhaa)

Note from the example that the past habitual tense is formed with the main verb, which takes on the same form as in the simple present tense, and the past tense of *to be* ਹੋਣਾ **honhaa**. Some examples follow.

1st person

Masculine singular	ਮੈਂ ਬੋਲਦਾ ਸੀ	main boldaa see	*I used to speak*
Feminine singular	ਮੈਂ ਬੋਲਦੀ ਸੀ	main boldee see	*I used to speak*
Masculine plural	ਅਸੀਂ ਬੋਲਦੇ ਸੀ	aseen bolde see	*we used to speak*
Feminine plural	ਅਸੀਂ ਬੋਲਦੀਆਂ ਸੀ	aseen boldeeaan see	*we used to speak*

2nd person

Masculine singular informal	ਤੂੰ ਬੋਲਦਾ ਸੀ	toon boldaa see	you used to speak
Feminine singular informal	ਤੂੰ ਬੋਲਦੀ ਸੀ	toon boldee see	you used to speak
Masculine plural / formal	ਤੁਸੀਂ ਬੋਲਦੇ ਸੀ	tuseen bolde see	you used to speak
Feminine plural	ਤੁਸੀਂ ਬੋਲਦੀਆਂ ਸੀ	tuseen boldeeaan see	you used to speak

3rd person

Masculine singular	ਇਹ / ਉਹ ਬੋਲਦਾ ਸੀ	ih / uh boldaa see	he used to speak
Feminine singular	ਇਹ / ਉਹ ਬੋਲਦੀ ਸੀ	ih / uh boldee see	she used to speak
Masculine plural / formal	ਇਹ / ਉਹ ਬੋਲਦੇ ਸਨ / ਸੀ	ih / uh bolde san / see	they used to speak
Feminine plural	ਇਹ / ਉਹ ਬੋਲਦੀਆਂ ਸਨ / ਸੀ	ih / uh boldeeaan san / see	they used to speak

Another form of the past habitual uses the verb expressing the action in the habitual and the habitual forms of ਹੋਣਾ **honhaa** with the past auxiliary. *I used to go* in this form is expressed in the following ways:

1st person

ਮੈਂ ਜਾਂਦਾ ਹੁੰਦਾ ਸੀ	main jaandaa hundaa see	I used to go
ਮੈਂ ਜਾਂਦੀ ਹੁੰਦੀ ਸੀ	main jaandee hundee see	I used to go
ਅਸੀਂ ਜਾਂਦੇ ਹੁੰਦੇ ਸੀ	aseen jaande hunde see	we used to go
ਅਸੀਂ ਜਾਂਦੀਆਂ ਹੁੰਦੀਆਂ ਸੀ	aseen jaandeeaan hundeeaan see	we used to go

2nd person

ਤੂੰ ਜਾਂਦਾ ਹੁੰਦਾ ਸੀ	<u>t</u>oo<u>n</u> jaa<u>nd</u>aa hu<u>nd</u>aa see	*you used to go*
ਤੂੰ ਜਾਂਦੀ ਹੁੰਦੀ ਸੀ	<u>t</u>oo<u>n</u> jaa<u>nd</u>ee hu<u>nd</u>ee see	*you used to go*
ਤੁਸੀਂ ਜਾਂਦੇ ਹੁੰਦੇ ਸੀ	<u>t</u>usee<u>n</u> jaa<u>nd</u>e hu<u>nd</u>e see	*you used to go*
ਤੁਸੀਂ ਜਾਂਦੀਆਂ ਹੁੰਦੀਆਂ ਸੀ	<u>t</u>usee<u>n</u> jaa<u>nd</u>eeaa<u>n</u> hu<u>nd</u>eeaa<u>n</u> see	*you used to go*

3rd person

ਇਹ / ਉਹ ਜਾਂਦਾ ਹੁੰਦਾ ਸੀ	ih / uh jaa<u>nd</u>aa hu<u>nd</u>aa see	*he used to go*
ਇਹ / ਉਹ ਜਾਂਦੀ ਹੁੰਦੀ ਸੀ	ih / uh jaa<u>nd</u>ee hu<u>nd</u>ee see	*she used to go*
ਇਹ / ਉਹ ਜਾਂਦੇ ਹੁੰਦੇ ਸੀ	ih / uh jaa<u>nd</u>e hu<u>nd</u>e san	*he / she / they used to go*
ਇਹ / ਉਹ ਜਾਂਦੀਆਂ ਹੁੰਦੀਆਂ ਸੀ	ih / uh jaa<u>nd</u>eeaa<u>n</u> hu<u>nd</u>eeaa<u>n</u> san	*they used to go*

You will come across these various forms of the past tense in subsequent units and there will therefore be plenty of opportunity to practise all of these constructions.

Negative sentences

Negative sentences in the various past tenses are formed by adding ਨਹੀਂ **nahee<u>n</u>** either before or after the main verb.

Simple past

ਮੈਂ ਬੋਲਿਆ	ਮੈਂ ਨਹੀਂ ਬੋਲਿਆ	ਮੈਂ ਬੋਲਿਆ ਨਹੀਂ
mai<u>n</u> boliaa	mai<u>n</u> nahee<u>n</u> boliaa	mai<u>n</u> boliaa nahee<u>n</u>
I spoke	*I did not speak*	*I did not speak*

Remote past

ਮੈਂ ਬੋਲਿਆ ਸੀ	ਮੈਂ ਨਹੀਂ ਬੋਲਿਆ ਸੀ	ਮੈਂ ਬੋਲਿਆ ਨਹੀਂ ਸੀ
mai<u>n</u> boliaa see	mai<u>n</u> nahee<u>n</u> boliaa see	mai<u>n</u> boliaa nahee<u>n</u> see
I spoke / had spoken	*I did not speak / had not spoken*	*I did not speak / had not spoken*

Habitual past

ਮੈਂ ਬੋਲਦਾ ਸੀ	ਮੈਂ ਨਹੀਂ ਬੋਲਦਾ ਸੀ	ਮੈਂ ਬੋਲਦਾ ਨਹੀਂ ਸੀ
main boldaa see	main naheen boldaa see	main boldaa naheen see
I used to speak	*I not used to speak*	*I used not to speak*

Interrogative sentences

As with the other verb tenses in Panjabi, interrogative sentences are formed in the past by adding the question word ਕੀ **kee** at the beginning of the sentence. Here are some examples of how questions are made out of statements in the past:

Simple past

Statement	Question
ਮੈਂ ਬੋਲਿਆ main boliaa *I spoke*	ਕੀ ਮੈਂ ਬੋਲਿਆ ? kee main boliaa? *Did I speak?*

Remote past

Statement	Question
ਮੈਂ ਬੋਲਿਆ ਸੀ main boliaa see *I spoke/had spoken*	ਕੀ ਮੈਂ ਬੋਲਿਆ ਸੀ ? kee main boliaa see? *Did I speak/Had I spoken?*

Habitual past

Statement	Question
ਮੈਂ ਬੋਲਦਾ ਸੀ main boldaa see *I used to speak*	ਕੀ ਮੈਂ ਬੋਲਦਾ ਸੀ ? kee main boldaa see? *Used I to speak?*

ਵਿਆਖਿਆ   viaakhiaa   *Commentary*

Panjabi families

Panjabi weddings are seen as social occasions and signify the coming together of two families rather than of two individuals, as is traditionally the case in modern western marriages. Kinship relations form a central part of Panjabi society. Often families live in extended units with three or more generations all living under one roof. In contrast to English-speaking cultures, Panjabi has very specific terms for members of the nuclear and extended family. Most kinship terms are determined by the paternal and maternal nature of the relationship and whether or not it is a relationship by marriage. Beware . . . these are only half of the possible kin names you may come across in conversation with Panjabis!

Paternal

ਦਾਦਾ	daadaa *father's father*
ਦਾਦੀ	daadee *father's mother*
ਪਿਤਾ	pitaa *father*
ਅੱਬਾ	abbaa *papa (father)*
ਪਤੀ	patee *husband*
ਭਰਾ	bharaa *brother*
ਜੀਜਾ	jeejaa *sister's husband*
ਚਾਚਾ	chaachaa *father's younger brother*
ਚਾਚੀ	chaachee *father's younger brother's wife*
ਤਾਇਆ	taaiaa *father's elder brother*
ਤਾਈ	taaee *father's elder brother's wife*
ਭੂਆ	bhooaa *father's sister*
ਫੁਫੜ	phupharh *father's sister's husband*

Maternal

ਨਾਨਾ	naanaa *mother's father*
ਨਾਨੀ	naanee *mother's mother*
ਮਾਤਾ	maataa *mother*
ਅੰਮੀ	ammee *mama (mother)*
ਪਤਨੀ	patnee *wife*
ਭੈਣ	bhainh *sister*
ਭਾਬੀ	bhaabee *brother's wife*
ਮਾਸੀ	maasee *mother's sister*
ਮਾਸੜ	maasarh *mother's sister's husband*
ਮਾਮਾ	maamaa *mother's brother*
ਮਾਮੀ	maamee *mother's brother's wife*
ਪੁੱਤਰੀ	puttaree *daughter*
ਭਾਂਜਾ	bhaanjaa *nephew (sister's son)*

ਪੁੱਤਰ	puṯṯar *son*	ਭਾਂਜੀ	bhaanjee *niece*
ਭਤੀਜਾ	bhaṯeejaa *nephew*		*(sister's daughter)*
	(brother's son)		
ਭਤੀਜੀ	bhaṯeejee *niece*		
	(brother's daughter)		

ਅਭਿਆਸ   abhiaas   *Exercises*

After reading the dialogue and / or listening to the recording, try to do the following exercises.

▶ 1 The family tree

Pavan is showing his family photos to Surjit. Read and / or listen to the following passage on the recording. Then try to complete Pavan's family tree (ਕੁਰਸੀ ਨਾਮਾ kursee naamaa).

ਇਹ ਹੈ ਮੇਰਾ ਕੁਰਸੀ ਨਾਮਾ:

ਮੇਰੇ ਪਿਤਾ ਜੀ ਦਾ ਨਾਮ ਜੋਗਿੰਦਰ ਸਿੰਘ ਹੈ ਅਤੇ ਮੇਰੇ ਮਾਤਾ ਜੀ ਦਾ ਨਾਮ ਗੁਰਮੀਤ ਕੌਰ ਹੈ। ਉਹਨਾਂ ਦੇ ਤਿੰਨ ਬੱਚੇ ਹਨ। ਮੈਂ, ਮੇਰਾ ਭਰਾ ਸੁਖਜੀਤ ਸਿੰਘ ਤੇ ਮੇਰੀ ਭੈਣ ਕੁਲਦੀਪ ਕੌਰ। ਮੇਰੀ ਭਾਬੀ ਦਾ ਨਾਮ ਜਗਜੀਤ ਕੌਰ ਹੈ ਤੇ ਮੇਰੇ ਭਤੀਜੇ ਦਾ ਨਾਮ ਗੁਰਤੇਜ ਸਿੰਘ ਹੈ। ਮੇਰੀ ਪਤਨੀ ਦਾ ਨਾਮ ਹਰਲੀਨ ਕੌਰ ਹੈ ਅਤੇ ਸਾਡੇ ਦੋ ਬੱਚੇ ਹਨ, ਇੱਕ ਪੁੱਤਰ, ਮਨਜੀਤ ਸਿੰਘ ਤੇ ਇੱਕ ਪੁੱਤਰੀ, ਬਲਦੇਵ ਕੌਰ।

ih hai meraa kursee naamaa:

mere piṯaa jee ḏaa naam joginḏar singh hai aṯe mere maaṯaa jee ḏaa naam gurmeeṯ kaur hai. uhnaan ḏe ṯinn bachche han. main, meraa bharaa sukhjeeṯ singh ṯe meree bhainh kulḏeep kaur. meree bhaabee ḏaa naam jagjeeṯ kaur hai ṯe mere bhaṯeeje ḏaa naam gurṯej singh hai. meree paṯnee ḏaa naam harleen kaur hai aṯe saade ḏo bachche han, ikk puṯṯar, manjeeṯ singh ṯe ikk puṯṯree, balḏev kaur.

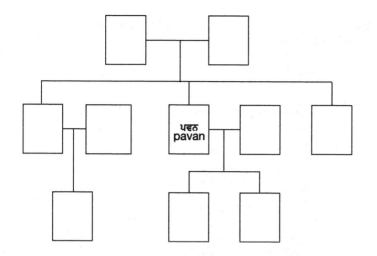

2 Matching

Match the questions with their correct responses.

a ਮੈਂ ਹਫ਼ਤੇ ਦੇ ਅਖ਼ੀਰ ਮਾਨਚੈਸਟਰ ਸੀ ।
main hafte de akheer maanchaistar see.

i ਤੁਸੀਂ ਕੱਲ੍ਹ ਕਿੱਥੇ ਸੀ ?
tuseen kallh kiththe see?

b ਮੈਂ ਐਤਵਾਰ ਘਰ ਸੀ ।
main aitvaar ghar see.

ii ਤੁਸੀਂ ਹਫ਼ਤੇ ਦੇ ਅਖ਼ੀਰ ਕਿੱਥੇ ਸੀ ?
tuseen hafte de akheer kiththe see?

c ਮੈਂ ਕੱਲ੍ਹ ਲੰਡਨ ਸੀ ।
main kallh landan see.

iii ਤੁਸੀਂ ਐਤਵਾਰ ਕਿੱਥੇ ਸੀ ?
tuseen aitvaar kiththe see?

3 True or false?

Indicate whether the following statements from the dialogues in the unit are true or false.

a ਪਵਨ ਸਿੰਘ ਹਾਕੀ ਖੇਡਦਾ ਸੀ । pavan singh haakee kheddaa see.
True / False

b ਪਵਨ ਸਿੰਘ ਜਲੰਧਰ ਪੜ੍ਹਦਾ ਸੀ । pavan singh jalandhar parhhdaa see. True / False

c ਵਿਆਹ ਵਿਚ ਬਹੁਤ ਪ੍ਰਾਹੁਣੇ ਸਨ । viaah vich bahut praahunhe san. True / False

4 Construct negative and interrogative sentences.

The first example is given.

1 ਰਾਮ ਲੰਡਨ ਰਹਿੰਦਾ ਸੀ।
Raam laṇdan rahinḏaa see.
Ram used to live in London.

> Negative: ਰਾਮ ਲੰਡਨ ਨਹੀਂ ਰਹਿੰਦਾ ਸੀ।
> raam laṇdan naheeṇ rahinḏaa see.
> *Ram used not to live in London.*

> Interrogative: ਕੀ ਰਾਮ ਲੰਡਨ ਰਹਿੰਦਾ ਸੀ?
> kee raam laṇdan rahinḏaa see?
> *Used Ram to live in London?*

2 ਉਹ ਹਫ਼ਤੇ ਦੇ ਅਖੀਰ ਲੰਡਨ ਗਏ ਸਨ।
uh hafṯe ḏe akheer laṇdan gae san.
They went to London over the weekend.

3 ਅਸੀਂ ਇੱਕਠੇ ਟੈਨਸ ਖੇਡਦੇ ਸੀ।
aseeṇ ikaththe tainas kheddde see.
We used to play tennis together.

4 ਉਹ ਪੰਜਾਬੀ ਬੋਲਦੀ ਹੁੰਦੀ ਸੀ।
uh panjaabee bolḏee hunḏee see.
She used to speak Panjabi.

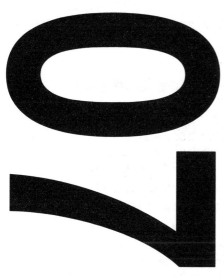

07

ਤੁਸੀਂ ਕੀ ਪੀਓ ਗੇ?

tuseen kee peeo ge?

what will you (have to) drink?

In this unit you will learn:
- how to express actions in the future
- days of the week
- how to tell the time
- about repetitive and rhyming words

▶ 1 *I'll wait*

ਗੱਲ ਬਾਤ ੧ ਮੈਂ ਉਡੀਕਾਂ ਗਾ

gall baat 1 main udeekaan gaa

Mr Ali and Mr Malik are old friends. Mr Ali is standing outside his house as Mr Malik happens to pass by.

ਮਿਸਟਰ ਅਲੀ **Mr Ali**	ਅੱਸਲਾਮ ਅਲੈਕਮ । ਕੀ ਹਾਲ ਚਾਲ ਏ ? asslaam alaikam. kee haal chaal e?
ਮਿਸਟਰ ਮਲਿਕ **Mr Malik**	ਵਾਲੈਕਮ ਅੱਸਲਾਮ । ਮੈਂ ਠੀਕ ਠਾਕ ਹਾਂ । vaalaikam asslaam. main theek thaak haan.
ਮਿਸਟਰ ਅਲੀ **Mr Ali**	ਅੰਦਰ ਆ ਜਾ । ਚਾਹ ਚੂ ਪੀ । andar aa jaa. chaah choo pee.
ਮਿਸਟਰ ਮਲਿਕ **Mr Malik**	ਅੱਜ ਮੈਂ ਨਹੀਂ ਠਹਿਰਾਂ ਗਾ । ਮੈਂ ਕਾਹਲ ਵਿਚ ਹਾਂ । ajj main naheen thahiraan gaa. main kaahal vich haan.
ਮਿਸਟਰ ਅਲੀ **Mr Ali**	ਕੀ ਤੂੰ ਕੱਲੂ ਆਵੇਂ ਗਾ ? kee toon kallh aaven gaa?
Mr Malik	ਇਨਸ਼ਾ ਅੱਲਾ । ਮੈਂ ਜ਼ਰੂਰ ਆਵਾਂ ਗਾ । ਕੱਲੂ ਐਤਵਾਰ ਹੈ । ਵਕਤ ਖੁੱਲ੍ਹਾ ਹੋਵੇ ਗਾ । inshaa alla. main zaroor aavaan gaa. kallh aitvaar hai. vakat khullhaa hove gaa.
ਮਿਸਟਰ ਅਲੀ **Mr Ali**	ਸੁਣ! ਤੂੰ ਕਿੰਨੇ ਵਜੇ ਆਵੇਂ ਗਾ ? sunh! toon kinne vaje aaven gaa?
ਮਿਸਟਰ ਮਲਿਕ **Mr Malik**	ਅਸੀਂ ਸਾਰੇ ਕੱਲੂ ਪੰਜ ਵਜੇ ਆਵਾਂ ਗੇ । aseen saare kallh panj vaje aavaan ge.
ਮਿਸਟਰ ਅਲੀ **Mr Ali**	ਚੰਗਾ ਫਿਰ । ਮੈਂ ਉਡੀਕਾਂ ਗਾ । changaa phir. main udeekaan gaa.

Mr Ali	*Hello! How are you?*
Mr Malik	*Hello! I'm fine.*
Mr Ali	*Come inside. Have some tea.*
Mr Malik	*I'm sorry. I won't stop today. I'm in a hurry.*
Mr Ali	*Will you come tomorrow?*
Mr Malik	*Hopefully [lit. If God wishes]. I'll definitely come. Tomorrow is Sunday. There will be plenty of time.*
Mr Ali	*Listen! What time will you come round?*
Mr Malik	*We'll all come tomorrow, at 5 o'clock.*
Mr Ali	*Fine then. I'll wait.*

ਸ਼ਬਦਾਵਲੀ shabḏaavalee *Vocabulary*

ਉਡੀਕਣਾ	udeeknhaa	to wait
ਅੰਦਰ	andar	inside
ਆ ਜਾ	aa jaa	come (informal request)
ਅੱਜ	ajj	today
ਠਹਿਰਨਾ	thahirnaa	to stay
ਕਾਹਲ ਵਿਚ	kaahal vich	in a hurry
ਇਨਸ਼ਾ ਅੱਲਾ	inshaa allaa	hopefully (lit. *if God wishes*)
ਜ਼ਰੂਰ	zaroor	definitely
ਵਕਤ	vakaṯ	time (m.)
ਖੁੱਲ੍ਹਾ	khullhaa	open, plenty (v.)
ਕਿੰਨੇ ਵਜੇ	kinne vaje	what time
ਅਸੀਂ ਸਾਰੇ	aseen saare	all of us, we all
ਪੰਜ ਵਜੇ	panj vaje	5 o'clock

ਅਭਿਆਸ abhiaas *Exercises*

After reading the dialogue and / or listening to the recording, try to do the following exercises.

1 Fill in the blanks.

Complete the sentences by filling in the blank with the correct Panjabi word.

a ਮੈਂ _____ ਆਵਾਂ ਗਾ । *I'll definitely come.*
b ਕੀ ਤੂੰ _____ ਆਵੇਂ ਗਾ ? *Will you come tomorrow?*
c ਤੂੰ _____ ਆਵੇਂ ਗਾ ? *What time will you come?*

2 Arrange the sentences in the correct order.

The order of the following sentences from the dialogue is mixed up. Can you unscramble them by numbering them in the correct order?

1 **ਮਿਸਟਰ ਮਲਿਕ** ਅਸੀਂ ਸਾਰੇ ਕੱਲ੍ਹ ਪੰਜ ਵਜੇ ਆਵਾਂ ਗੇ ।
   Mr Malik aseen saare kallh panj vaje aavaan ge.

2 **ਮਿਸਟਰ ਮਲਿਕ** ਵਾਲੈਕਮ ਅੱਸਲਾਮ, ਮੈਂ ਠੀਕ ਠਾਕ ਹਾਂ ।
   Mr Malik vaalaikam asslaam, main theek thaak haan.

3 **ਮਿਸਟਰ ਅਲੀ** ਸੁਣ! ਤੂੰ ਕਿੰਨੇ ਵਜੇ ਆਵੇਂ ਗਾ ?
   Mr Ali sunh! ṯoon kinne vaje aaven gaa?

4 **ਮਿਸਟਰ ਅਲੀ** ਅੱਸਲਾਮ ਅਲੈਕਮ । ਕੀ ਹਾਲ ਚਾਲ ਏ ?
   Mr Ali asslaam alaikam. kee haal chaal e?

▶ 2 *What will you (have to) drink?*

ਗੱਲ ਬਾਤ ੨ ਤੁਸੀਂ ਕੀ ਪੀਓ ਗੇ ?

gall baat 2 tuseen kee peeo ge?

Mr and Mrs Malik visit Mr Ali's home. Mr Malik knocks on the door and Mr Ali opens it.

ਮਿਸਟਰ ਅਲੀ	ਜੀ ਆਇਆਂ ਨੂੰ ਭਾਈ ਸਾਹਿਬ ਤੇ ਭਾਬੀ ਜੀ ।
Mr Ali	jee aaiaan noon bhaaee saahib te bhaabee jee.

(Mr and Mrs Ali exchange greetings with Mr and Mrs Malik.)

ਮਿਸਜ਼ ਅਲੀ	ਤਸ਼ਰੀਫ਼ ਰੱਖੋ ਜੀ । ਤੁਸੀਂ ਕੀ ਪੀਓ ਗੇ ?
Mrs Ali	tashreef rakhkho jee. tuseen kee peeo ge?

ਮਿਸਟਰ ਮਲਿਕ	ਸ਼ੁਕਰੀਆ । ਮੈਂ ਚਾਹ ਪੀਵਾਂ ਗਾ ।
Mr Malik	shukreeaa. main chaah peevaan gaa.

ਮਿਸਜ਼ ਮਲਿਕ	ਮੈਂ ਰਸ ਲਵਾਂ ਗੀ ।
Mrs Malik	main ras lavaan gee.

(Mrs Ali serves the drinks and then begins talking to Mrs Malik.)

ਮਿਸਜ਼ ਅਲੀ	ਬੱਚੇ ਕਦੋਂ ਆਉਣ ਗੇ ?
Mrs Ali	bachche kadon aaunh ge?

ਮਿਸਜ਼ ਮਲਿਕ	ਉਹ ੧੫ ਮਿੰਟਾਂ ਵਿਚ ਆਉਣ ਗੇ ।
Mrs Malik	uh 15 mintaan vich aaunh ge.

ਮਿਸਜ਼ ਅਲੀ	ਕੀ ਤੂੰ ਮੇਰੇ ਨਾਲ ਉਰਦੂ ਫ਼ਿਲਮ ਦੇਖੇਂ ਗੀ ?
Mrs Ali	kee toon mere naal urdoo filam dekhen gee?

ਮਿਸਜ਼ ਮਲਿਕ	ਕਿਹੜੀ ਫ਼ਿਲਮ ?
Mrs Malik	kihrhee filam?

ਮਿਸਜ਼ ਮਲਿਕ	'ਅਨਾਰਕਲੀ' ੮ ਵਜੇ ਟੀ ਵੀ ਤੇ ਆ ਰਹੀ ਹੈ ।
Mrs Ali	'anaarkalee' 8 vaje tee vee te aa rahee hai.

ਮਿਸਜ਼ ਮਲਿਕ	ਹਾਂ ਜੀ । ਮੈਂ ਜ਼ਰੂਰ ਦੇਖਾਂ ਗੀ!
Mrs Malik	haan jee. main zaroor dekhaan gee!

Mr Ali	*Welcome brother and sister-in-law.*

(Mr and Mrs Ali exchange greetings with Mr and Mrs Malik.)

Mrs Ali	*Please have a seat. What will you drink?*
Mr Malik	*I'll have [drink] tea.*
Mrs Malik	*I'll have juice.*

(Mrs Ali serves the drinks and then begins talking to Mrs Malik.)

Mrs Ali	*When will the children arrive?*
Mrs Malik	*They'll be here in 15 minutes.*
Mrs Ali	*Will you [would you like to] watch an Urdu film with me?*
Mrs Malik	*Which film?*
Mrs Ali	*Anarkali [name of a film] is on television at 8 o'clock.*
Mrs Malik	*Yes. I'll definitely watch it!*

ਸ਼ਬਦਾਵਲੀ   shab<u>d</u>aavalee   *Vocabulary*

ਜੀ ਅਇਆਂ ਨੂੰ	jee aaiaa<u>n</u> noo<u>n</u>	*welcome*
ਭਾਈ ਸਾਹਿਬ	bhaaee saahib	*brother (m.)*
ਭਾਬੀ ਜੀ	bhaabee jee	*sister-in-law (f.)*
ਤਸ਼ਰੀਫ਼ ਰੱਖੋ ਜੀ	<u>t</u>ashreef rakhkho jee	*please have a seat*
ਪੀਣਾ	peenhaa	*to drink*
ਰਸ	ras	*(fruit) juice (m.)*
ਲੈਣਾ	lainhaa	*to take, to have*
ਕਦੋਂ	ka<u>d</u>o<u>n</u>	*when*
ਮਿੰਟਾਂ	mi<u>n</u>taa<u>n</u>	*minutes (m.)*
ਮੇਰੇ ਨਾਲ	mere naal	*with me*
ਦੇਖਣਾ	<u>d</u>ekhnhaa	*to see, to watch*
ਉਰਦੂ	ur<u>d</u>oo	*Urdu (m. / f.)*
ਅਨਾਰਕਲੀ	anaarkalee	*name of a classic Urdu film (f.)*
੮ ਵਜੇ	8 vaje	*8 o'clock*
ਟੀ ਵੀ	tee vee	*TV (television) (m.)*

ਅਭਿਆਸ   abhiaas   *Exercises*

After reading the dialogue and / or listening to the recording, try to do the following exercises.

▶ 1 Questions to ask guests

Two guests, Mr and Mrs Malik, have come to your house for tea. Ask them the following questions.

a What will you have to drink?
b Would you like to watch television?
c Would you like to have juice or tea?

2 Word search

Three words *children, Urdu* and *sister-in-law* are hidden in Panjabi in the box. Find them by reading horizontally across each of the rows.

ਬੱ	ਚੇ	ਉ	ਪ	ਓ
ਸਾ	ਸ	ਕ	ਨ	ਹੀਂ
ਕਾ	ਕਿ	ਉ	ਰ	ਦੂ
ਸੇ	ਸਿ	ਕੁ	ਚ	ਨ
ਇ	ਭਾ	ਬੀ	ਹਾ	ਕੈ

ਬੋਲੀ ਬਾਰੇ bolee baare *Language points*

The future tense

In Panjabi, as in English, the future tense is used when one is making predictions about the future or referring to intentions, offers, or promises in the future. The Panjabi ending -ਗਾ **gaa** is used to denote actions or conditions in the future and means *will, shall* or *would*. As has been explained with other verb tenses in Panjabi, the form of the future tense varies according to the number and gender of the subject. Here are the ways in which -ਗਾ **gaa** is formed (notice that the forms of -ਗਾ **gaa** do not change according to the person of the subject):

-ਗਾ	gaa	masculine singular
-ਗੀ	gee	feminine singular
-ਗੇ	ge	masculine plural
-ਗੀਆਂ	geeaa<u>n</u>	feminine plural

The future tense therefore, as is also the case with the present tenses, is constructed by combining the main verb with the auxiliary ending, -ਗਾ **gaa**. The main verb in the future tense, however, does vary according to the person as well as the number of the subject. In the first dialogue in this unit, the verb ਉਡੀਕਣਾ **udeeknhaa** *to wait* was used in the future tense ਮੈਂ ਉਡੀਕਾਂ ਗਾ **mai<u>n</u> udeekaa<u>n</u> gaa** *I will wait*. The example of ਕਰਨਾ **karnaa** *to do* is now illustrated to show how verbs with stems ending in consonants are formed in the future.

ਕਰਨਾ – infinitive form of *to do* **ਕਰ** – stem

1st person

Masc. sing.	ਮੈਂ ਕਰਾਂ ਗਾ	main karaan gaa	*I shall / will do*
Fem. sing.	ਮੈਂ ਕਰਾਂ ਗੀ	main karaan gee	*I shall / will do*
Masc. pl.	ਅਸੀਂ ਕਰਾਂ ਗੇ	aseen karaan ge	*we shall / will do*
Fem. pl.	ਅਸੀਂ ਕਰਾਂ ਗੀਆਂ	aseen karaan geeaan	*we shall / will do*

2nd person

Masc. sing. informal	ਤੂੰ ਕਰੇਂ ਗਾ	toon karen gaa	*you will do*
Fem. sing. informal	ਤੂੰ ਕਰੇਂ ਗੀ	toon karen gee	*you will do*
Masc. pl. / formal	ਤੁਸੀਂ ਕਰੋ ਗੇ	tuseen karo ge	*you will do*
Fem. pl.	ਤੁਸੀਂ ਕਰੋ ਗੀਆਂ	tuseen karo geeaan	*you will do*

3rd person

Masc. sing.	ਉਹ / ਇਹ ਕਰੇ ਗਾ	uh / ih kare gaa	*he will do*
Fem. sing.	ਉਹ / ਇਹ ਕਰੇ ਗੀ	uh / ih kare gee	*she will do*
Masc. pl. / formal	ਉਹ / ਇਹ ਕਰਨ ਗੇ	uh / ih karan ge	*they will do*
Fem. pl.	ਉਹ / ਇਹ ਕਰਨ ਗੀਆਂ	uh / ih karan geeaan	*they will do*

Another construction of the future tense occurs when the stem of the main verb ends in a vowel such as ਜਾ-ਣਾ **jaa-nhaa** *to go*, ਆਉ-ਣਾ **aau-nhaa** *to come*, ਪੀ-ਣਾ **pee-nhaa** *to drink*, and ਲੈ-ਣਾ **lai-nhaa** *to have*. There are generally two acceptable ways of forming the future tense with such vowel-ending stems. The first manner follows the pattern as given for consonant-ending verb stems. The second manner in which the future tense is often formed is by inserting ਵ **vavvaa** after the vowel. There is no significant difference between the two, although the ਵ **vavvaa** forms often have a slightly more formal tone. Note these examples of the two commonly used main verb formations in the future tense:

ਮੈਂ main *I*	ਤੂੰ toon *you* (informal)	ਤੁਸੀਂ tuseen *you* (plural / formal)	ਇਹ ih ਉਹ uh	ਇਹ ih ਉਹ uh

ਅਸੀਂ aseen we			he / she / it (sing. informal)	(he / she) they (plural / formal)

ਜਾਣਾ jaanhaa – to go, ਜਾ – stem

1				
ਜਾਵਾਂ jaavaan	ਜਾਏਂ jaaen	ਜਾਓ jaao	ਜਾਏ jaae	ਜਾਣ jaanh
2				
ਜਾਵਾਂ jaavaan	ਜਾਵੇਂ jaaven	ਜਾਵੋ jaavo	ਜਾਵੇ jaave	ਜਾਵਣ jaavanh

ਆਉਣਾ aaunhaa – to come, ਆ – stem

1				
ਆਵਾਂ aavaan	ਆਏਂ aae	ਆਓ aao	ਆਏ aae	ਆਉਣ aaunh
2				
ਆਵਾਂ aavaan	ਆਵੇਂ aaven	ਆਵੋ aavo	ਆਵੇ aave	ਆਵਣ aavanh

ਪੀਣਾ peenhaa – to drink, ਪੀ – stem

1				
ਪੀਆਂ peeaan	ਪੀਏਂ pee-en	ਪੀਓ peeo	ਪੀਏ pee-e	ਪੀਣ peenh
2				
ਪੀਵਾਂ peevaan	ਪੀਵੇਂ peeven	ਪੀਵੋ peevo	ਪੀਵੇ peeve	ਪੀਵਣ peevanh

ਲੈਣਾ lainhaa – to have, to take, ਲੈ – stem

1				
ਲਵਾਂ lavaan	ਲਏਂ laen	ਲੋ lo	ਲਏ lae	ਲੈਣ lainh
2				
ਲਵਾਂ lavaan	ਲਵੇਂ laven	ਲਵੋ lavo	ਲਵੇ lave	ਲਵਣ lavanh

More forms of the imperative

In Unit 5 the imperative was briefly introduced as a means of expressing a request, order or command. The formal and informal uses of the imperative were illustrated through the verb ਸੁਣਨਾ sunhnaa *to listen*:

ਤੂੰ ਸੁਣ	toon sunh	*listen* (you, informal)
ਤੁਸੀਂ ਸੁਣੋ	tuseen sunho	*listen* (you, formal / plural)

The plural form of the imperative is used to denote a respectful tone when addressed to a single person. To make the request yet more formal and respectful, the English equivalent of *please* can also be added by use of the honorific particle ਜੀ jee.

| ਸੁਣੋ ਜੀ | sunho jee | *please listen* (you, formal) |

Please in Panjabi is expressed in the phrase ਕਿਰਪਾ ਕਰ ਕੇ kirpaa kar ke. By using this phrase, a formal request can be made more polite:

| ਅੰਦਰ ਆਓ | andar aao | *come in* |
| ਕਿਰਪਾ ਕਰ ਕੇ ਅੰਦਰ ਆਓ | kirpaa kar ke andar aao | *please come in* |

Politeness is also expressed by forming the imperative in the future tense:

| ਕੀ ਤੁਸੀਂ ਸੁਣੋ ਗੇ ਜੀ? | kee tuseen sunho ge jee? | *Will you please listen?* |

The tone of the request can be softened with the word ਜ਼ਰਾ zaraa, *just a little* used in combination with the infinitive form of the verb. The infinitive specifies the action of what is being requested. The colloquial sense of the earlier request becomes ਜ਼ਰਾ ਸੁਣਨਾ zaraa sunhnaa, *have a listen*. With ਦੇਖਣਾ dekhnhaa, *to look* the request becomes:

| ਜ਼ਰਾ ਦੇਖਣਾ | zaraa dekhnhaa | *have a look* |

Ordinal numbers

In Unit 3 you learned the cardinal numbers from 1 to 20. To expand your knowledge of numbers further here are some ordinal numbers.

ਪਹਿਲਾ	pahilaa	*first*
ਦੂਸਰਾ / ਦੂਜਾ	doosraa / doojaa	*second*
ਤੀਸਰਾ / ਤੀਜਾ	teesraa / teejaa	*third*
ਚੌਥਾ	chauthaa	*fourth*
ਪੰਜਵਾਂ	panjvaan	*fifth*

ਛੇਵਾਂ	<u>ch</u>evaa<u>n</u>	*sixth*
ਸੱਤਵਾਂ	sa<u>tt</u>vaa<u>n</u>	*seventh*
ਅੱਠਵਾਂ	a<u>thth</u>vaa<u>n</u>	*eighth*

As you can see, from *fifth* onwards ordinal numbers are formed with the ending -ਵਾਂ **vaaṇ**. Since ordinals are adjectives, they follow the same rules of agreement as other adjectives. The endings of ordinals will therefore agree with the nouns that they are describing.

| ਪਹਿਲੀ ਵਾਰੀ | pahilee vaaree | *first time* |
| ਦੂਜਾ ਦਿਨ | <u>d</u>oojaa <u>d</u>in | *second day* |

What time is it?

In English, time is expressed by the use of *o'clock* which refers specifically to the position of the hands on the clock when telling the time. Similarly in Panjabi, time is most commonly expressed through the use of the verb ਵੱਜਣਾ **vajjnhaa** which means *to chime, to strike*. When asking someone the time, the same rules apply as when transforming statements into interrogative sentences as shown in Unit 5. The word ਕੀ **kee** is simply placed at the beginning of the sentence. However, other words for time are also appropriate when asking someone the time in Panjabi. Here are a few commonly used phrases:

ਕੀ ਵਕਤ ਹੈ ?	kee vaka<u>t</u> hai?	*What time is it?*
ਕਿੰਨੇ ਵਜੇ ਹਨ ?	ki<u>n</u>ne vaje han?	*What time is it?* (lit. how many times has the clock struck?)
ਕੀ ਟਾਇਮ ਹੈ ?	kee taaim hai?	*What is the time?*

Therefore, when someone says that it is one o'clock, the expression in Panjabi would be:

| ਇੱਕ ਵਜਿਆ ਹੈ | ikk vajiaa hai | *It is one o'clock.* |

The verb ਵੱਜਣਾ vajjnhaa is formed in the present perfect tense here, literally meaning that *the clock has struck one*. Note that ਵਜਿਆ vajiaa is the singular form as it agrees with the number one. All other times which relate to the number one (such as quarter to one, quarter past one, half past one) also take on the singular form:

ਡੇਢ ਵਜਿਆ ਹੈ	dedh vajiaa hai	*It is half past one.*
ਪੌਣਾ ਇੱਕ ਵਜਿਆ ਹੈ	paunhaa ikk vajiaa hai	*It is a quarter to one.*
ਸਵਾ ਇੱਕ ਵਜਿਆ ਹੈ	savaa ikk vajiaa hai	*It is a quarter past one.*

As you will have noticed in the earlier examples there are terms in Panjabi for each 15-minute sequence of time on the clock. 1.30 and 2.30, however, have specific names while all other times use ਸਵਾ savaa, ਸਾਢੇ saadhe and ਪੌਣੇ paunhe:

half past one = ਡੇਢ dedh

half past two = ਢਾਈ dhaaee

quarter past the hour = ਸਵਾ savaa

30 minutes past the hour = ਸਾਢੇ saadhe

quarter to the hour = ਪੌਣਾ paunhaa, ਪੌਣੇ paunhe

All times relating to numbers greater than one use the plural form of ਵਜਿਆ. Here are some examples:

ਦੋ ਵਜੇ ਹਨ	do vaje han	*It is two o'clock.*
ਪੌਣੇ ਦੋ ਵਜੇ ਹਨ	paunhe do vaje han	*It is a quarter to two.*
ਤਿੰਨ ਵਜੇ ਹਨ	tinn vaje han	*It is three o'clock.*
ਸਾਢੇ ਤਿੰਨ ਵਜੇ ਹਨ	saadhe tinn vaje han	*It is three thirty.*
ਚਾਰ ਵਜੇ ਹਨ	chaar vaje han	*It is four o'clock.*
ਸਵਾ ਚਾਰ ਵਜੇ ਹਨ	savaa chaar vaje han	*It is a quarter past four.*
ਪੰਜ ਵਜੇ ਹਨ	panj vaje han	*It is five o'clock.*
ਛੇ ਵਜੇ ਹਨ	che vaje han	*It is six o'clock.*
ਪੌਣੇ ਛੇ ਵਜੇ ਹਨ	paunhe che vaje han	*It is a quarter to six.*
ਸੱਤ ਵਜੇ ਹਨ	satt vaje han	*It is seven o'clock.*
ਅੱਠ ਵਜੇ ਹਨ	athth vaje han	*It is eight o'clock.*
ਨੌਂ ਵਜੇ ਹਨ	naun vaje han	*It is nine o'clock.*

ਦਸ ਵਜੇ ਹਨ	das vaje han	It is ten o'clock.
ਸਾਢੇ ਗਿਆਰਾਂ ਵਜੇ ਹਨ	saadhe giaaraan vaje han	It is 11.30.
ਬਾਰ੍ਹਾਂ ਵਜੇ ਹਨ	baar-h-aan vaje han	It is 12 o'clock.

When the exact nature of the time is being expressed, it is also possible to use other forms of expression. Here are a few examples:

ਕਲਾਸ ਇੱਕ ਵਜੇ ਤੋਂ ਸ਼ੁਰੂ ਹੁੰਦੀ ਹੈ	kalaas ikk vaje ton shuroo hundee hai	The class starts at one o'clock.
ਤਿੰਨ ਵਜ ਰਹੇ ਹਨ	tinn vaj rahe han	It is just three o'clock.
ਨੌਂ ਵਜਣ ਵਾਲੇ ਹਨ	naun vajanh vaale han	It is nearly nine o'clock.

When the time of day needs to be specified, *morning* (ਸਵੇਰ saver), *afternoon* (ਦੁਪਹਿਰ dupahir), *day* (ਦਿਨ din), *evening* (ਸ਼ਾਮ shaam) and *night* (ਰਾਤ raat) can also be used:

ਛੇ ਵਜੇ ਸ਼ਾਮ ਨੂੰ	che vaje shaam noon	at six o'clock in the evening
ਸਵੇਰ ਦੇ ਅੱਠ ਵਜੇ	saver de athth vaje	at eight o'clock in the morning
ਦੁਪਹਿਰ ਦੇ ਡੇਢ ਵਜੇ	dupahir de dedh vaje	at 1.30 in the afternoon
ਦਿਨ ਦੇ ਦੋ ਵਜੇ	din de do vaje	at two o'clock in the afternoon (day)
ਬਾਰ੍ਹਾਂ ਵਜੇ ਰਾਤ ਨੂੰ	baar-h-aan vaje raat noon	at 12 o'clock at night

Further usages and expressions of time will be explained in subsequent units.

ਵਿਆਖਿਆ viaakhiaa *Commentary*

1 Repetitive and echo / rhyming words

The habitual use of repetitive and echo words is one of the many special characteristics of Panjabi which make it such an expressive language. Many words in Panjabi are repeated in the written and spoken forms to add emphasis. Repetition occurs when the same word is repeated while the echoing and rhyming of words occur through the use of two words which sound similar. Here are some examples:

ਹੌਲੀ ਹੌਲੀ ਚਲੋ	haulee haulee chalo	*walk slowly* (emphasizing slowly)
ਹਟ ਹਟ	hat hat	*get away* (showing intensity)
ਦੇਸ ਦੇਸ ਤੋਂ ਲੋਕ ਆਏ	<u>d</u>es <u>d</u>es <u>ton</u> lok aae	*people came from different countries* (emphasis on countries to signify the many different countries)
ਚਾਹ ਚੂ	chaah choo	*tea* [here the echo word ਚੂ has no specific meaning other than for emphasis]
ਦੁੱਖ ਸੁੱਖ	<u>d</u>ukhkh sukhkh	*miseries and comforts*
ਦਿਨ ਰਾਤ	<u>d</u>in raa<u>t</u>	*day and night* (all the time) [these words technically neither rhyme nor are echo words. However, their opposite meanings uttered together gives the idea of continuity.]
ਸੱਚ ਸੱਚ	sachch sachch	*the whole truth*
ਚੁੱਪ ਚਾਪ	chupp chaap	*(absolutely) quiet*

2 Days of the week

There are two words for *day* in Panjabi which are used to designate the days of the week: ਦਿਨ <u>d</u>in and ਵਾਰ vaar. If you want to ask someone what the day of the week is today, there are two ways to ask:

| ਅੱਜ ਕੀ ਦਿਨ ਹੈ ? | ajj kee <u>d</u>in hai? | *What day is it today?* |
| ਅੱਜ ਕੀ ਵਾਰ ਹੈ ? | ajj kee vaar hai? | *What day is it today?* |

The names of the days of the week are all masculine nouns. Some of the days of the week are different in West Panjab due to the influence of the Islamic calendar in Pakistan. The days of the week in Panjabi are as follows (* shows the Islamic calendar days):

Monday	ਸੋਮਵਾਰ	somvaar
	ਪੀਰ *	peer
Tuesday	ਮੰਗਲਵਾਰ	mangalvaar
Wednesday	ਬੁੱਧਵਾਰ	budhdhvaar
Thursday	ਵੀਰਵਾਰ	veervaar
	ਜੁਮੇਰਾਤ *	jumeraat
Friday	ਸ਼ੁੱਕਰਵਾਰ	shukkarvaar
	ਜੁਮਾ *	jumaa
Saturday	ਸਨਿਚਰਵਾਰ	sanicharvaar
	ਹਫ਼ਤਾ *	haftaa
Sunday	ਐਤਵਾਰ	aitvaar

Other useful calendar terms are:

ਹਫ਼ਤਾ	haftaa	*week* (m.)
ਸਪਤਾਹ	saptaah	*week* (m.)
ਮਹੀਨਾ	maheenaa	*month* (m.)
ਦਿਨ	din	*day* (m.)
ਸਾਲ	saal	*year* (m.)

3 Expressions of friendship

You will have noticed in Dialogue 2 that Mr Ali greets Mr Malik as ਭਾਈ ਸਾਹਿਬ **bhaaee saahib** (*brother*) and Mrs Malik as ਭਾਬੀ ਜੀ **bhaabee jee** (*sister-in-law*). It is not uncommon to address people with whom you wish to express closeness or affection with such terms ordinarily associated with kinship. In this example, it is quite clear that Mr Ali and Mr Malik are not brothers, but their friendship is the basis for Mr Ali referring to Mr Malik as *brother*. Since the relationship is primarily based upon the two men, Mrs Malik is referred to as ਭਾਬੀ ਜੀ **bhaabee jee** (as Mr Malik's wife) and not *sister*.

ਅਭਿਆਸ   abhiaas   *Exercises*

After reading the dialogue and / or listening to the recording, try to do the following exercises.

1 The imperative

You are trying to convey to someone that he or she should listen to you. How would you form the imperative of ਸੁਣਨਾ *sunhnaa* *to listen* in the following circumstances?

a to someone who is younger than you (informal)
b to someone who is older than you (formal)
c to someone to whom you wish to show respect (formal, polite)
d to someone with whom you wish to use a mild tone of request

2 What time is it?

Write the answers in Panjabi.

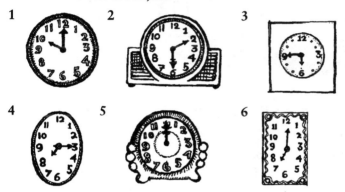

3 The future tense

After reviewing the future tense section in the unit, express the fact that you will have tea in the following gender and number situations:

a You are a singular male.
b You are a singular female.
c You are a plural male.
d You are a plural female.

4 Conversation

Suppose you have been asked to go to someone's house. Express the following conversational phrases in Panjabi.

a Yes, thank you.
b Yes, I'll come tomorrow.
c No, I'm in a hurry.
d Fine then. I'll wait.

08

ਮੈਨੂੰ ਸਿਤਾਰ ਵਜਾਉਣ
ਦਾ ਸ਼ੌਕ ਹੈ

mainoon sitaar vajaaunh daa shauk hai

I enjoy playing the sitar

In this unit you will learn:
- how to express your likes and dislikes
- how to express need, want, should, ought
- how to discuss visas
- how to negotiate a taxi ride

▶ 1 *I enjoy playing the sitar*

ਗੱਲ ਬਾਤ ੧ ਮੈਨੂੰ ਸਿਤਾਰ ਵਜਾਉਣ ਦਾ ਸ਼ੌਕ ਹੈ

gall baat 1 mainoon sitaar vajaaunh daa shauk hai

Jaspreet and Simran are two sisters living in Yuba City, California. They are planning a trip to India and are having a conversation with their father, Mr Sandhu.

ਮਿਸਟਰ ਸੰਧੂ **Mr Sandhu**	ਤੁਹਾਨੂੰ ਭਾਰਤ ਜਾਣ ਲਈ ਕਿੰਨੇ ਪੈਸੇ ਚਾਹੀਦੇ ਹਨ ? tuhaanoon bhaarat jaanh laee kinne paise chaaheede han?
ਜਸਪੀਤ ਤੇ ਸਿਮਰਨ **Jaspreet and Simran**	ਸਾਨੂੰ ਘੱਟੋ ਘੱਟ (੨੦੦੦) ਦੋ ਹਜ਼ਾਰ ਡਾਲਰ ਚਾਹੀਦੇ ਹਨ । saanoon ghatto ghatt (2000) do hazaar daalar chaaheede han.
ਮਿਸਟਰ ਸੰਧੂ **Mr Sandhu**	ਐਨੇ ਸਾਰੇ ਪੈਸੇ ? ਤੁਹਾਡਾ ਖ਼ਰਚਾ ਇੰਨਾ ਕਿਵੇਂ ਹੋਵੇ ਗਾ ? aine saare paise? tuhaadaa kharchaa innaa kiven hove gaa?
ਜਸਪੀਤ **Jaspreet**	ਪਿਤਾ ਜੀ ! ਤੁਹਾਨੂੰ ਪਤਾ ਹੈ ਕਿ ਮੈਨੂੰ ਸਿਤਾਰ ਵਜਾਉਣ ਦਾ ਸ਼ੌਕ ਹੈ । ਮੈਂ ਉੱਥੋਂ ਵਧੀਆ ਸਿਤਾਰ ਲਿਆਵਾਂ ਗੀ । pitaa jee! tuhaanoon pataa hai ki mainoon sitaar vajaaunh daa shauk hai. main uththon vadheeaa sitaar liaavaan gee.
ਸਿਮਰਨ **Simran**	. . . ਤੇ ਮੈਨੂੰ ਘੁੰਮਣਾ ਫਿਰਨਾ ਪਸੰਦ ਹੈ । . . . te mainoon ghunmnhaa phirnaa pasand hai.
ਮਿਸਟਰ ਸੰਧੂ **Mr Sandhu**	ਮੇਰੀਓ ਧੀਓ, ਮੈਨੂੰ ਅਫ਼ਸੋਸ ਹੈ ਕਿ ਤੁਹਾਨੂੰ ਦੇਣ ਲਈ ਮੇਰੇ ਕੋਲ ਐਨੇ ਪੈਸੇ ਨਹੀਂ ਹਨ । mereeo dheeo, mainoon afsos hai ki tuhaanoon denh laee mere kol aine paise naheen han.
ਜਸਪੀਤ ਤੇ ਸਿਮਰਨ **Jaspreet and Simran**	ਤੁਸੀਂ ਫ਼ਿਕਰ ਨਾ ਕਰੋ, ਪਿਤਾ ਜੀ । ਮਾਤਾ ਜੀ ਕੋਲ ਪੈਸੇ ਬਹੁਤ ਹਨ ! tuseen fikar naa karo, pitaa jee. maataa jee kol paise bahut han!
Mr Sandhu	*How much money do you need for going to India?*
Jaspreet and Simran	*We need at least $2000.*

Mr Sandhu	*So much money? Why will your expenses be so high?*
Jaspreet	*Father, you know that I am fond of playing the sitar. I'm going to bring a good quality sitar from there.*
Simran	*. . . and I like travelling around.*
Mr Sandhu	*My daughters, I am sorry that I don't have that much money to give you.*
Jaspreet and Simran	*Don't worry, Father. Mother has plenty of money!*

ਸ਼ਬਦਾਵਲੀ   shabḏaavalee   *Vocabulary*

ਲਈ	laee	*for, in order to*
ਕਿੰਨੇ	kinne	*how much, how many*
ਚਾਹੁਣਾ	chaahunhaa	*to need, to want*
ਖ਼ਰਚਾ	kharchaa	*expense, expenses (m.)*
ਘੱਟੋ ਘੱਟ	ghaṭṭo ghaṭṭ	*at least*
ਡਾਲਰ	daalar	*dollar (m.)*
ਐਨੇ ਸਾਰੇ	aine saare	*so much*
ਪਤਾ	paṭaa	*to know*
ਸਿਤਾਰ	siṭaar	*sitar (f.) (a stringed classical musical instrument)*
ਵਜਾਉਣਾ	vajaaunhaa	*to play (music)*
ਸ਼ੌਕ	shauk	*fondness, enjoyment*
ਵਜਾਉਣ ਦਾ ਸ਼ੌਕ	vajaaunh ḏaa shauk	*fond of playing, enjoy playing*
ਉੱਥੋਂ	uththon	*from there*
ਵਧੀਆ	vaḏheeaa	*good quality*
ਲਿਆਉਣਾ	liaaunhaa	*to bring*
ਘੁੰਮਣਾ	ghunmnhaa	*to go around*
ਫਿਰਨਾ	phirnaa	*to travel*
ਘੁੰਮਣਾ ਫਿਰਨਾ	ghunmnhaa phirnaa	*to travel around*
ਪਸੰਦ	pasanḏ	*like*
ਅਫ਼ਸੋਸ	afsos	*regret, sorry*
ਕੋਲ	kol	*with, next to, in possession*
ਮੇਰੇ ਕੋਲ ਨਹੀਂ	mere kol naheen	*not with me, not in my possession*
ਫ਼ਿਕਰ	fikar	*worry (m.)*
ਧੀਓ	ḏheeo	*daughters (f.) (vocative case: see Language points)*

ਅਭਿਆਸ   abhiaas   *Exercises*

After reading the dialogue and / or listening to the recording, try to do the following exercises.

1 Crossword

Complete the crossword in Gurmukhi script using the clues given.

1 a stringed classical instrument   **3** expense
2 US currency   **4** to travel

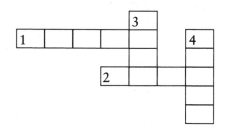

2 Match the statements.

a ਫ਼ਿਕਰ ਨਾ ਕਰੋ ।

b ਐਨੇ ਸਾਰੇ ਪੈਸੇ ?

c ਮੈਂ ਵਧੀਆ ਸਿਤਾਰ ਲਿਆਵਾਂ ਗੀ ।

i *I will bring a good quality sitar.*

ii *Don't worry.*

iii *So much money?*

▶ 2 *We want to go to Connaught Place*

ਗੱਲ ਬਾਤ ੨ ਅਸੀਂ ਕਨਾਟ ਪਲੇਸ ਜਾਣਾ ਚਾਹੁੰਦੀਆਂ ਹਾਂ

gall baat 2 aseen kanaat pales jaanhaa chaahundeeaan haan

Simran and Jaspreet have just arrived at the airport in Delhi. They have approached the immigration counter where they show their passports to the officer with whom they are having a conversation.

ਇਮੀਗ੍ਰੇਸ਼ਨ ਅਫ਼ਸਰ
Immigration officer

ਤੁਸੀਂ ਅਮਰੀਕਾ ਕਿੰਨਾ ਚਿਰ ਤੋਂ ਰਹਿ ਰਹੀਆਂ ਹੋ ?
tuseen amreekaa kinnaa chir ton rahi raheeaan ho?

ਸਿਮਰਨ Simran	ਅਸੀਂ ਅਮਰੀਕਾ ਵਿਚ ਜੰਮੀਆਂ ਸੀ। aseen amreekaa vich janmeeaan see.
ਇਮੀਗ੍ਰੇਸ਼ਨ ਅਫ਼ਸਰ Immigration officer	ਤੁਹਾਨੂੰ ਐਨੀ ਚੰਗੀ ਪੰਜਾਬੀ ਕਿਵੇਂ ਆਉਂਦੀ ਹੈ? tuhaanoon ainee changee panjaabee kiven aaundee hai?
ਜਸਪ੍ਰੀਤ Jaspreet	ਸਾਨੂੰ ਸਿਰਫ਼ ਥੋੜੀ ਬਹੁਤੀ ਆਉਂਦੀ ਹੈ। saanoon siraf thorhee bahutee aaundee hai.
ਸਿਮਰਨ Simran	ਇੱਕ ਬੇਨਤੀ ਹੈ, ਅਫ਼ਸਰ ਸਾਹਿਬ . . . ikk bentee hai, afsar saahib . . .
ਇਮੀਗ੍ਰੇਸ਼ਨ ਅਫ਼ਸਰ Immigration officer	ਉਹ ਕੀ ਹੈ? uh kee hai?
ਸਿਮਰਨ Simran	ਸਾਡੇ ਕੋਲ ਕੇਵਲ ਇੱਕ ਮਹੀਨੇ ਦਾ ਵੀਜ਼ਾ ਹੈ। ਜੀ ਕੀ ਤੁਸੀਂ ਸਾਨੂੰ ਦੋ ਮਹੀਨੇ ਰਹਿਣ ਦੀ ਆਗਿਆ ਦੇਵੋ ਗੇ? saade kol keval ikk maheene daa veezaa hai. jee kee tuseen saanoon do maheene rahinh dee aagiaa devo ge?
ਇਮੀਗ੍ਰੇਸ਼ਨ ਅਫ਼ਸਰ Immigration officer	ਇਹ ਮੇਰੇ ਵੱਸ ਵਿਚ ਨਹੀਂ ਹੈ। ਤੁਹਾਨੂੰ ਵੀਜ਼ਾ ਅਮਰੀਕਾ ਤੋਂ ਲੈਣਾ ਚਾਹੀਦਾ ਸੀ। ih mere vass vich naheen hai. tuhaanoon veezaa amreekaa ton lainhaa chaaheedaa see.
ਸਿਮਰਨ ਤੇ ਜਸਪ੍ਰੀਤ Simran and Jaspreet	ਫਿਰ ਸਾਨੂੰ ਇੱਕ ਮਹੀਨੇ ਵਿਚ ਸਾਰਾ ਕੁਝ ਦੇਖਣਾ ਪੈਣਾ। phir saanoon ikk maheene vich saaraa kujh dekhnhaa painhaa.
ਇਮੀਗ੍ਰੇਸ਼ਨ ਅਫ਼ਸਰ Immigration officer	ਦਿੱਲੀ ਦੇ ਆਸ ਪਾਸ ਕਾਫ਼ੀ ਕੁਝ ਦੇਖਣ ਵਾਲਾ ਹੈ। ਅਨੰਦ ਮਾਣੋ! dillee de aas paas kaafee kujh dekhanh vaalaa hai. anand maanho!

Immigration officer	*How long have you been living in America?*
Simran	*We were born in America.*
Immigration officer	*How do you know Panjabi so well?*
Jaspreet	*We only know a little.*
Simran	*Officer, one request . . .*
Immigration officer	*What is it?*
Simran	*We only have a one-month visa. Could you please give us permission to stay for two months?*

Immigration officer	*This is not within my authority. You should have obtained the visa from America.*
Simran and Jaspreet	*In that case, we'll have to see everything in a month.*
Immigration officer	*There are plenty of things to see around Delhi. Enjoy yourselves!*

Jaspreet and Simran have cleared customs with their luggage and exit from the airport. They approach a taxi driver about travelling into the centre of Delhi.

ਜਸਪ੍ਰੀਤ	ਅਸੀਂ ਕਨਾਟ ਪਲੇਸ ਜਾਣਾ ਚਾਹੁੰਦੀਆਂ ਹਾਂ। ਤੂੰ ਕਿੰਨੇ ਪੈਸੇ ਲਵੇਂ ਗਾ?
Jaspreet	aseen kanaat pales jaanhaa chaahundeeaan haan. toon kinne paise laven gaa?
ਟੈਕਸੀਵਾਲਾ	ਸਿਰਫ਼ ਸੌ ਰੁਪਇਆ।
Taxi driver	siraf sau rupaiaa.
ਸਿਮਰਨ	ਕਨਾਟ ਪਲੇਸ ਹਵਾਈ ਅੱਡੇ ਤੋਂ ਕਿੰਨੀ ਦੂਰ ਹੈ?
Simran	kanaat pales havaaee adde ton kinnee door hai?
ਟੈਕਸੀਵਾਲਾ	ਤਕਰੀਬਨ ਵੀਹ ਮੀਲ ਦੂਰ ਹੈ। ਤੁਸੀਂ ਠੀਕ ਕਿਹੜੀ ਜਗ੍ਹਾ ਜਾਣਾ ਹੈ?
Taxi driver	takreeban veeh meel door hai. tuseen theek kihrhee jag-h-aa jaanhaa hai?
ਸਿਮਰਨ	ਅਸੀਂ ਅੰਤਰ ਰਾਸ਼ਟਰੀ ਯੁਵਕ ਹੋਸਟਲ ਜਾਣਾ ਹੈ ਪਰ ਤੂੰ ਜ਼ਿਆਦਾ ਪੈਸੇ ਮੰਗ ਰਿਹਾ ਹੈਂ।
Simran	aseen antar raashtaree yuvak hostal jaanhaa hai par toon ziaadaa paise mang rihaa hain.
ਟੈਕਸੀਵਾਲਾ	ਨਹੀਂ ਨਹੀਂ। ਮੈਂ ਕਿਰਾਇਆ ਵਾਜਬੀ ਦੱਸਿਆ ਹੈ। ਤੁਸੀਂ ਦੋ ਸਵਾਰੀਆਂ ਹੋ ਤੇ ਸਮਾਨ ਵੀ ਬਹੁਤ ਹੈ। ਤੁਸੀਂ ਜਾਣਾ ਏ ਕਿ ਨਹੀਂ?
Taxi driver	naheen naheen. main kiraaiaa vaajbee dassiaa hai. tuseen do savaareeaan ho te samaan vee bahut hai. tuseen jaanhaa e ki naheen?
ਜਸਪ੍ਰੀਤ	ਅੱਛਾ, ਕਾਹਲਾ ਨ ਪਓ। ਸਮਾਨ ਰੱਖ ਗੱਡੀ ਵਿਚ।
Jaspreet	achchaa, kaahalaa na pao. samaan rakhkh gaddee vich.
Jaspreet	*We want to go to Connaught Place. How much will you charge?**

Taxi driver	*Only 100 rupees.*
Simran	*How far is Connaught Place from the airport?*
Taxi driver	*It's about 20 miles away. Exactly where are you going?*
Simran	*Take us [we want to go] to the International Youth Hostel, but you're asking for too much money.*
Taxi driver	*No, no. I've told you the reasonable fare. There are two of you travelling and there is a lot of luggage. Are you going or not?*
Jaspreet	*OK. Don't be impatient. Put the luggage in the car.*

*The language used in this dialogue with the taxi driver may seem a little informal (or even rude) in the English translation. This is because informal speech is generally used when haggling over the fare with taxi drivers in India and Pakistan (see Unit 2: Language points: Subject pronouns).

ਸ਼ਬਦਾਵਲੀ shabdaavalee *Vocabulary*

ਅਮਰੀਕਾ	amreekaa	*America (m.)*
ਚਿਰ	chir	*length of time*
ਕਿੰਨਾ ਚਿਰ ਤੋਂ	kinnaa chir ton	*since when, for how long*
ਜੰਮਣਾ	janmnhaa	*to be born*
ਥੋੜੀ ਬਹੁਤੀ	thorhee bahutee	*more or less, to some extent*
ਬੇਨਤੀ	bentee	*request (f.)*
ਕੇਵਲ	keval	*only*
ਵੀਜ਼ਾ	veezaa	*visa (m.)*
ਆਗਿਆ	aagiaa	*permission (f.)*
ਵੱਸ	vass	*authority, jurisdiction (m.)*

ਪਾਸਪੋਰਟ	paasport	passport (m.)
ਅਫ਼ਸਰ	afsar	officer (m. / f.)
ਸਾਹਿਬ	saahib	sir (m.)
ਆਸ ਪਾਸ	aas paas	around, around and about
ਕਾਫ਼ੀ ਕੁਝ	kaafee kujh	quite a lot, plenty
ਅਨੰਦ ਮਾਣੋ	anand maanho	enjoy yourselves
ਚਾਹੁਣਾ	chaahunhaa	to want, to need
ਸੌ (੧੦੦)	sau	100
ਰੁਪਇਆ	rupaiaa	rupees (m.)
ਹਵਾਈ ਅੱਡਾ	havaaee addaa	airport (m.)
ਕਿੰਨੀ ਦੂਰ	kinnee door	how far
ਦੂਰ	door	far, distant
ਵੀਹ (੨੦)	veeh	20
ਮੀਲ	meel	mile, miles (m.)
ਜਗ੍ਹਾ	jag-h-aa	place, location (f.)
ਅੰਤਰ ਰਾਸ਼ਟਰੀ	antar raashtaree	international
ਯੁਵਕ	yuvak	youth (m.)
ਹੋਸਟਲ	hostal	hostel (m.)
ਜ਼ਿਆਦਾ	ziaadaa	too much
ਮੰਗਣਾ	mangnhaa	to request, to ask, to charge
ਕਿਰਾਇਆ	kiraaiaa	rate, fare, rent (m.)
ਵਾਜਬੀ	vaajbee	reasonable, fair, right
ਸਵਾਰੀਆਂ	savaareeaan	passengers, travellers (f.)
ਸਮਾਨ	samaan	luggage, things (m.)
ਕਾਹਲਾ	kaahalaa	impatient, hasty (v.)
ਪੈਣਾ	painhaa	to act (to fall)
ਰੱਖਣਾ	rakhkhnhaa	to put
ਗੱਡੀ	gaddee	car, vehicle (f.)

ਅਭਿਆਸ   abhiaas   *Exercises*

After reading the dialogue and / or listening to the recording, try to do the following exercises.

1 Write in the correct word order.

a ਹੈ ਪੰਜਾਬੀ ਬਹੁਤੀ ਆਉਂਦੀ ਥੋੜੀ ਸਾਨੂੰ

hai-panjaabee-bahutee-aaundee-thorhee-saanoon

We only know a little Panjabi.

b ਪਲੇਸ ਅਸੀਂ ਹਾਂ ਜਾਣਾ ਚਾਹੁੰਦੀਆਂ ਕਨਾਟ

pales-aseen-haan-jaanhaa-chaahundeeaan-kanaat

We want to go to Connaught Place.

c ਤੁਸੀਂ ਜੀ ਦੋ ਦੀ ਦੇਵੋ ਗੇ ਮਹੀਨੇ ਰਹਿਣ ਕੀ ਆਗਿਆ

tuseen-jee-do-dee-devo-ge-maheene-rahinh-kee-aagiaa

Could you please give us permission to stay for two months?

2 Translate into Panjabi.

a There are two of you travelling and there is a lot of luggage.
b We only have a one-month visa.
c Enjoy yourselves!

ਬੋਲੀ ਬਾਰੇ bolee baare *Language points*

Pronouns in the oblique

In Unit 2 personal pronouns were introduced representing the English equivalents of *I*, *we*, *you*, *he*, *she* and *they*. As with nouns, personal pronouns also take on the oblique form when followed by postpositions. The most commonly used postposition with pronouns is ਨੂੰ **noon** *to* as is illustrated. Note that interrogative pronouns such as ਕੌਣ **kaunh,** *who* and ਕੀ **kee** *what* are also affected by postpositions.

Singular

Direct			Oblique		
I	ਮੈਂ	main	*to me*	ਮੈਨੂੰ	mainoon
you (inf.)	ਤੂੰ	toon	*to you* (inf.)	ਤੈਨੂੰ	tainoon
you (form.)	ਤੁਸੀਂ	tuseen	*to you* (form.)	ਤੁਹਾਨੂੰ	tuhaanoon
he / she / it	ਇਹ	ih	*to him / her / it*	ਇਹ ਨੂੰ,	ih noon
(near)				ਇਸ ਨੂੰ	is noon
he / she / it	ਉਹ	uh	*to him / her / it*	ਉਹ ਨੂੰ,	uh noon
(far)				ਉਸ ਨੂੰ	us noon

Interrogative pronouns					
who	ਕੌਣ	kaunh	*to whom*	ਕਿਸ ਨੂੰ	kis noon
what	ਕੀ	kee	*to what*	ਕਿਹਨੂੰ	kihnoon

Plural

Direct			Oblique		
we	ਅਸੀਂ	aseen	*to us*	ਸਾਨੂੰ	saanoon
you	ਤੁਸੀਂ	tuseen	*to you*	ਤੁਹਾਨੂੰ	tuhaanoon
they (near)	ਇਹ	ih	*to them*	ਇਹਨਾਂ ਨੂੰ	ihnaan noon
they (far)	ਉਹ	uh	*to them*	ਉਹਨਾਂ ਨੂੰ	uhnaan noon
Interrogative pronouns					
who	ਕੋਣ	kaunh	*to whom*	ਕਿਹਨਾਂ ਨੂੰ	kihnaan noon
what	ਕੀ	kee	*to what*	ਕਿਹਨਾਂ ਨੂੰ	kihnaan noon

The postposition ਨੂੰ **noon** is used in a number of ways. Generally, it directs an action, state or object towards the pronoun or noun after which it follows. Here are a few examples of how ਨੂੰ **noon** can be used with pronouns:

ਪੰਜਾਬੀ ਮੈਨੂੰ ਥੋੜੀ ਬਹੁਤੀ ਆਉਂਦੀ ਹੈ	panjaabee mainoon thorhee bahutee aaundee hai	*I know Panjabi to some extent.*
ਸਾਨੂੰ ਮਿਠਿਆਈ ਪਸੰਦ ਹੈ	saanoon mithiaaee pasand hai	*We like sweets.* (lit. sweets are liked by us)
ਤੂੰ ਕਿਹਨਾਂ ਨੂੰ ਦੱਸਿਆ ਸੀ ?	toon kihnaan noon dassiaa see?	*Whom did you tell?*

There are many other postpositions which are also used with pronouns. ਤੋਂ **ton**, ਨਾਲ **naal**, ਵਾਸਤੇ **vaaste**, ਕੋਲ **kol** and ਲਈ **laee** are some commonly used ones which were introduced in Unit 4. The manner in which the oblique is formed with these postpositions is noticeably different from pronouns followed by ਨੂੰ **noon**. The first and second person pronouns are changed to the appropriate possessive adjectives while the third person pronouns follow the same pattern of ਨੂੰ **noon** as already shown. Here are some examples using the postposition ਤੋਂ **ton** (*from*):

1st person

Direct			Oblique		
I	ਮੈਂ	main	*from me*	ਮੇਰੇ ਤੋਂ	mere <u>t</u>on
we	ਅਸੀਂ	asee<u>n</u>	*from us*	ਸਾਡੇ ਤੋਂ	saade <u>t</u>on

2nd person

Direct			Oblique		
you (inf.)	ਤੂੰ	<u>t</u>oo<u>n</u>	*from you* (inf.)	ਤੇਰੇ ਤੋਂ	<u>t</u>ere <u>t</u>on
you (form.)	ਤੁਸੀਂ	<u>t</u>usee<u>n</u>	*from you* (form.)	ਤੁਹਾਡੇ ਤੋਂ	<u>t</u>uhaade <u>t</u>on

3rd person

Direct			Oblique		
he / she / it (singular, near)	ਇਹ	ih	*from him / her / it*	ਇਸ ਤੋਂ	is <u>t</u>on
he / she / it (singular, far)	ਉਹ	ih	*from him / her / it*	ਉਸ ਤੋਂ	us <u>t</u>on
they (plural, near)	ਇਹ	ih	*from them*	ਇਹਨਾਂ ਤੋਂ	ihnaa<u>n</u> <u>t</u>on
they (plural, far)	ਉਹ	uh	*from them*	ਉਹਨਾਂ ਤੋਂ	uhnaa<u>n</u> <u>t</u>on

---

ਮੇਰੇ ਕੋਲ ਐਨੇ ਪੈਸੇ ਨਹੀਂ ਹਨ	mere kol aine paise nahee<u>n</u> han	*I don't have that much money.*
ਉਹਨਾਂ ਵਾਸਤੇ ਵੀ ਚਾਹ ਬਣਾਓ	uhnaa<u>n</u> vaas<u>t</u>e vee chaah banhaao	*Make tea for them too.*
ਕੀ ਤੁਸੀਂ ਸਾਡੇ ਨਾਲ ਆਵੋ ਗੇ ?	kee <u>t</u>usee<u>n</u> saade naal aavo ge?	*Will you come with us?*
ਅਸੀਂ ਕਪੜੇ ਇਹਨਾਂ ਤੋਂ ਖ਼ਰੀਦਾਂ ਗੇ	asee<u>n</u> kaprhe ihnaa<u>n</u> <u>t</u>on <u>kh</u>areedaan ge	*We will buy the clothes from them.*

Must, have to

In Panjabi, expressions of compulsion come in three forms: an intention to do something, a certainty about doing something and a strong sense of compulsion about doing something. In each of these cases, it is usually the infinitive of the verb which directs the action related to the situation. Often ਹੋਣਾ **honhaa** is used to give a sense of the present or past condition, depending on which tense of *to be* is used. The direct form of the pronoun is used in these cases:

| ਮੈਂ ਜਾਣਾ ਹੈ | **main jaanhaa hai** | *I am to go / I intend to go* |
| ਮੈਂ ਜਾਣਾ ਸੀ | **main jaanhaa see** | *I should have gone / I was to go / I had to go* |

Strong compulsion is indicated by the use of the verb ਪੈਣਾ **painhaa** (*to fall*). This gives a sense of habitual compulsion and is positioned after the infinitive. Note that the infinitive behaves as the subject in many of these expressions, and therefore the form of ਪੈਣਾ **painhaa** generally takes the singular masculine form (in agreement with the infinitive). For example:

| ਮੈਨੂੰ ਹਰ ਰੋਜ਼ ਜਾਣਾ ਪੈਂਦਾ ਹੈ | **mainoon har roz jaanhaa paindaa hai** | *I have to go every day.* |

Use of the verb ਚਾਹੁਣਾ 'chaahunhaa'

In Panjabi, expressions such as *should / ought* and *need / want* are generally formed with the verb ਚਾਹੁਣਾ **chaahunhaa** (*to want, to need*). These expressions use the infinitive followed by ਚਾਹੀਦਾ **chaaheedaa**, which is the passive form of the verb ਚਾਹੁਣਾ **chaahunhaa**. (The passive voice will be explained in a later unit.) ਚਾਹੀਦਾ **chaaheedaa** in the sentence ਮੈਨੂੰ ਚਾਹੀਦਾ ਹੈ **mainoon chaaheedaa hai** literally means *it is wanted by me*. However, the use of ਚਾਹੀਦਾ **chaaheedaa** can have two different meanings:

- should / ought
- need / want

Should, ought

ਚਾਹੀਦਾ **chaaheedaa**, as with all other verb formations, changes according to the subject. In the case of expressions of *should* and *ought*, pronouns followed by postpositions behave like objects (*to me, for me, with them*). Therefore, in the case of someone who has to go somewhere, the form of ਚਾਹੀਦਾ **chaaheedaa** must be in the singular masculine form in agreement with the infinitive. Similarly, if the object is feminine and / or plural, then the form of ਚਾਹੁਣਾ chaahunhaa, as well as the infinitive would reflect this:

| ਮੈਨੂੰ ਜਾਣਾ ਚਾਹੀਦਾ ਹੈ | mainoon jaanhaa chaaheedaa hai | *I should go* |
| ਮੈਨੂੰ ਜਾਣਾ ਚਾਹੀਦਾ ਸੀ | mainoon jaanhaa chaaheedaa see | *I should have gone* |

Care must be taken to identify the object in expressions of *ought* and *should*. In our earlier example, the pronoun served as the object, however in the following examples the infinitive and the form of ਚਾਹੀਦਾ chaaheedaa follow the gender and numerical nature of the *subject of obligation* which now becomes the object, in the first case tea and in the second books:

| ਮੈਨੂੰ ਚਾਹ ਨਹੀਂ ਪੀਣੀ ਚਾਹੀਦੀ | mainoon chaah naheen peenhee chaaheedee | *I should not drink tea.* |
| ਤੁਹਾਨੂੰ ਹੋਰ ਕਿਤਾਬਾਂ ਪੜ੍ਹਨੀਆਂ ਚਾਹੀਦੀਆਂ ਹਨ | tuhaanoon hor kitaabaan parhhneeaan chaaheedeeaan han | *You should read more books.* |

To want, to need
Expressions of desire or necessity are also formed with ਚਾਹੁਣਾ chaahunhaa. However, the verb is formed according to the subject of the sentence. For example, in Dialogue 2 Jaspreet and Simran say to the taxi driver, *We want to go to Connaught Place*. This is expressed as:

| ਅਸੀਂ ਕਨਾਟ ਪਲੇਸ ਜਾਣਾ ਚਾਹੁੰਦੀਆਂ ਹਾਂ | aseen kanaat pales jaanhaa chaahundeeaan haan | *We want to go to Connaught Place.* |

Notice in this example that ਅਸੀਂ aseen and ਚਾਹੁੰਦੀਆਂ ਹਾਂ chaahundeeaan haan are in agreement with each other. Therefore, the subject *we* dictates the form of *to want*. Here are some more examples of expressions of desire and necessity:

| ਕੀ ਤੁਸੀਂ ਅਮਰੀਕਾ ਜਾਣਾ ਚਾਹੁੰਦੇ ਹੋ ? | kee tuseen amreekaa jaanhaa chaahunde ho? | *Do you want to go to America?* |
| ਮੇਰਾ ਭਰਾ ਪੜ੍ਹਨਾ ਚਾਹੁੰਦਾ ਹੈ | meraa bharaa parhhnaa chaahundaa hai | *My brother wants to study.* |

As with constructions of *should* and *ought* the oblique form of pronouns with the postposition ਨੂੰ noon are also used in expressing *need* and *want* with the passive of ਚਾਹੁਣਾ chaahunhaa. This may seem confusing but you will be able to tell from the context of the sentence whether the speaker means that they need or want something, or that they should or ought to do something.

ਮੈਨੂੰ ਇੱਕ ਕਮੀਜ਼ ਚਾਹੀਦੀ ਹੈ	mainoo<u>n</u> ikk kameez chaahee<u>d</u>ee hai	*I need a shirt.*
ਮੈਨੂੰ ਦੋ ਕਮੀਜ਼ਾਂ ਚਾਹੀਦੀਆਂ ਹਨ	mainoo<u>n</u> <u>d</u>o kameezaa<u>n</u> chaahee<u>d</u>eeaa<u>n</u> han	*I need two shirts.*
ਉਹਨਾਂ ਨੂੰ ਪੈਸੇ ਚਾਹੀਦੇ ਹਨ	uhnaa<u>n</u> noo<u>n</u> paise chaahee<u>d</u>e han	*They need money.*

Infinitives in the oblique

The presence of postpositions after nouns, adjectives and pronouns has been discussed in previous units. You know by now that the forms of direct nouns, adjectives and pronouns are changed to the oblique when they are followed by a postposition. The same is true for infinitives. In the first dialogue, Mr Sandhu asks his daughters, *How much money do you need to go to India?* In this sentence *to go to India* is a phrase which contains an infinitive followed by a postposition:

| ਭਾਰਤ ਜਾਣ ਲਈ | bhaara<u>t</u> jaanh laee | *to go to India* |

The infinitive of the verb *to go* ਜਾਣਾ **jaanhaa** precedes the postposition ਲਈ **laee** requiring the infinitive to be in the oblique. The oblique of the infinitive is a shortened form which merely omits the vowel ending ਆ **aa**. Therefore, ਜਾਣਾ **jaanhaa** in the oblique becomes ਜਾਣ **jaanh**. The example given of ਜਾਣਾ **jaanhaa** is that of an infinitive with a vowel-ending stem. Other verbs such as ਖ਼ਰੀਦਣਾ <u>kh</u>aree<u>d</u>nhaa, ਲਿਖਣਾ **likhnhaa** and ਬੋਲਣਾ **bolnhaa** all have stems which end in consonants. These types of infinitives also have shortened forms which omit the ਆ **aa** ending making them ਖ਼ਰੀਦਣ <u>kh</u>aree<u>d</u>anh, ਲਿਖਣ **likhanh** and ਬੋਲਣ **bolanh**. Here are some examples of infinitives in the oblique and how they are formed:

ਉਹ ਸਾਨੂੰ ਪੈਸੇ ਦੇਣ ਨੂੰ ਤਿਆਰ ਨਹੀਂ	uh saanoo<u>n</u> paise <u>d</u>enh noo<u>n</u> <u>t</u>iaar nahee<u>n</u>	*He isn't ready* [willing] *to give us money.*
ਘੁੰਮਣ ਲਈ ਸਮਾਂ ਚਾਹੀਦਾ ਹੈ	ghu<u>n</u>manh laee samaa<u>n</u> chaahee<u>d</u>aa hai	*Time is needed for travelling.*
ਮੈਂ ਦੋਸਤ ਨੂੰ ਮਿਲਣ ਲਈ ਆਈ ਹਾਂ	mai<u>n</u> <u>d</u>ost noo<u>n</u> milanh laee aaee haa<u>n</u>	*I have come to meet a friend.*

Vocative case

The vocative case is used when addressing somebody directly or as an exclamation to someone. It can be used in both formal and informal situations. For example, in Dialogue 1, Mr Sandhu says ਧੀਓ! <u>dh</u>eeo! which means *daughters!* Another more formal setting might be in a meeting in which you wish to address the audience: ਭੈਣੋ ਤੇ ਭਰਾਵੋ bhainho <u>t</u>e bharaavo (*brothers and sisters*). The manner in which the vocative case is formed is quite similar to the plural oblique forms of nouns as shown in Unit 4, though the vocative case ends with ਓ o and not ਆਂ aa<u>n</u>. When the vocative case is used in reference to singular people, the noun takes on the ending ਏ e for feminine people and the ending ਆ aa for masculine people:

ਮੁੰਡਿਆ!	mu<u>n</u>diaa!	*boy!*
ਮੁੰਡਿਓ!	mu<u>n</u>dio!	*boys!*
ਬੱਚਿਓ!	bachchio!	*children!*
ਕੁੜੀਏ!	kurhee-e!	*girl!*
ਕੁੜੀਓ!	kurheeo!	*girls!*
ਦੋਸਤੋ!	<u>d</u>osto!	*friends!*

The ending -ਵਾਲਾ 'vaalaa'

ਵਾਲਾ vaalaa is added to nouns and verbs to give two main senses: *the one or ones* or *about to*. The use of -ਵਾਲਾ vaalaa with nouns expresses a relationship between the noun and the object or person being referred to. You will recall in the commentary in Unit 3 that the vegetable seller was called ਸਬਜ਼ੀਵਾਲਾ sabzeevaalaa and that earlier in this unit the taxi driver was referred to as ਟੈਕਸੀਵਾਲਾ taikseevaalaa. The ending -ਵਾਲਾ vaalaa in these examples has changed the role of the noun through the following pattern:

ਸਬਜ਼ੀ	+	-ਵਾਲਾ	=	ਸਬਜ਼ੀਵਾਲਾ
sabzee		-vaalaa		sabzeevaalaa
vegetable		*the one*		*vegetable seller*
ਟੈਕਸੀ	+	-ਵਾਲਾ	=	ਟੈਕਸੀਵਾਲਾ
taiksee		-vaalaa		taikseevaalaa
taxi		*the one*		*taxi driver*

Here are some more examples of this type of use of the ending -ਵਾਲਾ vaalaa with nouns:

ਲਾਹੌਰਵਾਲੀ ਔਰਤ	laahaurvaalee aura<u>t</u>	*the woman from Lahore*
ਪਿੰਡਵਾਲਾ	pi<u>n</u>dvaalaa	*villager*
ਪੈਸੇਵਾਲੇ	paisevaale	*wealthy people*
ਸਾੜ੍ਹੀਵਾਲੀ	saarhheevaalee	*the one wearing the sari*
ਘਰਵਾਲਾ	gharvaalaa	*husband*

Note that like other endings or adjectives, the ending -ਵਾਲਾ **vaalaa** changes according to the gender and number of the persons or objects being referred to.

The second meaning produced by the ending -ਵਾਲਾ **vaalaa** is *about to* or *on the point of doing*. This is created when -ਵਾਲਾ **vaalaa** is used with the oblique of the infinitive. The form resembles that of the oblique infinitive (or shortened form) used with postpositions presented earlier in this unit. Here are some examples of how this meaning is constructed:

ਉਹ ਭਾਰਤ ਜਾਣ ਵਾਲੇ ਹਨ	uh bhaarat jaanh vaale han	*They are about to go to India.*
ਮੈਂ ਤੁਹਾਨੂੰ ਚਿੱਠੀ ਲਿਖਣ ਵਾਲੀ ਸੀ	main tuhaanoon chiththee likhanh vaalee see	*I was about to write you a letter.*
ਕੁੜੀਆਂ ਆਉਣ ਵਾਲੀਆਂ ਸਨ	kurheeaan aaunh vaaleeaan san	*The girls were about to come.*
ਮੈਂ ਕਿਤਾਬ ਪੜ੍ਹਨ ਵਾਲਾ ਹਾਂ	main kitaab parhhanh vaalaa haan	*I am about to read the book.*

The ending -ਵਾਲਾ **vaalaa** used with oblique infinitives can also have the same meaning as that when used with nouns such as ਇੱਥੇ ਰਹਿਣ ਵਾਲਾ **iththe rahinh vaalaa** *the one who lives here* or ਕੰਮ ਕਰਨ ਵਾਲੇ **kanm karan vaale** *the ones who work* or *working people*. Once you understand how to use the ending -ਵਾਲਾ **vaalaa**, you will find it a very useful tool when referring to people and objects as well as to actions that are about to happen.

ਵਿਆਖਿਆ **viaakhiaa** *Commentary*

1 I like it!

Fondness is shown in Panjabi in a number of ways. Depending upon the degree of liking and context, fondness can be expressed through:

ਪਸੰਦ **pasand** means *pleasing* or *like*
ਸ਼ੌਕ **shauk** means *fondness* or *enjoyment*
ਲੱਗਣਾ **laggnhaa** means *seems* (e.g. *it seems nice / bad*)

Therefore, expressions of fondness generally require the use of ਨੂੰ **noon** in order to direct the feelings or emotions towards the person. A sentence such as *I like bananas* would translate directly into Panjabi as *Bananas are liked by me*: ਮੈਨੂੰ ਕੇਲੇ ਪਸੰਦ ਹਨ **mainoon** kele pasa<u>nd</u> han, thereby making *bananas* the subject and *me* the object. Another way of using ਪਸੰਦ pasa<u>nd</u> is in combination with ਕਰਨਾ karnaa. The use of ਕਰਨਾ karnaa gives an added sense of habituality, such as *I generally like bananas* or *I always like bananas* in ਮੈਂ ਕੇਲਿਆਂ ਨੂੰ ਪਸੰਦ ਕਰਦਾ ਹਾਂ mai<u>n</u> keliaa<u>n</u> noon pasa<u>nd</u> karda<u>a</u> haa<u>n</u>. ਲੱਗਣਾ laggnhaa (*to seem*) is a less specific word which requires the use of a qualifying adjective such as good, bad, tasty or ugly, in order to express how something seems. If you were to say *this food is good* one way in Panjabi to express this would be ਇਹ ਖਾਣਾ ਮੈਨੂੰ ਚੰਗਾ ਲੱਗਦਾ ਹੈ ih khaanhaa mainoo<u>n</u> changaa laggdaa hai (lit. *this food seems good to me*). Here are a few more examples:

ਮੈਨੂੰ ਸਿਤਾਰ ਵਜਾਉਣ ਦਾ ਸ਼ੌਕ ਹੈ	mainoo<u>n</u> si̱taar vajaaunh ḍaa shauk hai	*I enjoy playing the sitar.*
ਅਸੀਂ ਮਿਠਿਆਈ (ਨੂੰ) ਪਸੰਦ ਕਰਦੇ ਹਾਂ	aseen mithiaaee (noo<u>n</u>) pasa<u>nd</u> karde haa<u>n</u>	*We like sweets.*
ਤਸਵੀਰਾਂ ਉਹਨਾਂ ਨੂੰ ਚੰਗੀਆਂ ਲੱਗਦੀਆਂ ਹਨ	ṯasveeraa<u>n</u> uhnaa<u>n</u> noo<u>n</u> changeeaa<u>n</u> laggdeeaa<u>n</u> han	*They like the pictures.*

2 Usefulness of Panjabi in South Asia

Despite the fact that Hindi and Urdu are the national languages of India and Pakistan respectively, in practice once you leave the urban centres regional languages come to the fore. Panjabi has a unique position in the languages of North India and Pakistan, in that it has a large usage in the urban centres. In Lahore and throughout much of Pakistan, Panjabi is the language of the people and is spoken widely and understood almost universally. Furthermore, in Delhi many taxi drivers, rickshaw **vaalaas** and bus drivers tend to speak Panjabi (sometimes a few words may save the passenger from being overcharged!).

Taxi drivers are notorious in the sub-continent for overcharging and haggling with customers. Even though many main tourist resorts and public transport centres such as railway stations and airports now operate a prepayment system, there are still many occasions where unsuspecting travellers will be caught unaware. This has to be accepted as one of the many facets of travel to the sub-continent and should not cause frustration or anguish. On a more positive front, the fun of haggling, as you will see in the next unit, is a must when shopping.

3 Music in Panjab

Panjab is well known for folk music (as we shall see in Unit 16), however, there is a long tradition of classical music in Panjab. The world-renowned tabla player, Zakheer Hussain, comes from the tradition of the Panjabi gharana, which reflects a particular type of musical style and a particular rhythmic form known as ਕੈਰਵਾ **kairvaa**, which is an eight-beat cycle. One other musical form which crosses over the classical and popular is the **Qawaali**, made popular internationally by the late Nusrat Fateh Ali Khan. The Panjabi **Qawaals** sung by Khan are some of the most popular tunes throughout Panjab, and the elegant, poetic language is quite easy to understand.

ਅਭਿਆਸ   abhiaas   *Exercises*

After reading the dialogue and / or listening to the recording, try to do the following excercises.

1 Fill in the blanks.

a ਮੈਨੂੰ ਕਿਤਾਬ_____ਹੈ। mainoon kitaab _____ hai. *I want a book.*

b ਮੈਨੂੰ ਜਾਣਾ_____ਹੈ। mainoon jaanhaa _____ hai. *I should go.*

c ਮੈਨੂੰ ਸਿਤਾਰ ਦਾ _____ ਸ਼ੌਕ ਹੈ। mainoon sitaar _____ daa shauk hai. *I like playing the sitar.*

2 Translation

Say the following English sentences in Panjabi.

a What does he want?
b Daughters! What do you want?
c Whom did you tell?
d Should we go?

3 Use of 'vaalaa'

From the following equations work out what the words using the ending -ਵਾਲਾ are.

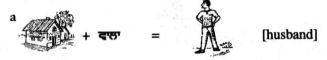

a [house] + ਵਾਲਾ = [man]   [husband]

b [taxi] + ਵਾਲਾ = [taxi]   [taxi driver]

c [vegetables] + ਵਾਲਾ = [vendor stall]   [vegetable vendor]

▶ 4 Listening comprehension

You are having a conversation with a taxi driver. Listen to the recording and then answer the following questions.

a How many passengers?
b Where are you travelling to?
c How much is the fare?
d How far is the hotel?
e How much luggage?
f Do you accept the taxi ride?

09

साडा कपड़ा सभ ते
वधीआ है।

saadaa kaprhaa sabh ton vadheeaa hai!

our cloth is the best!

In this unit you will learn:
- how to compare things
- how to talk about your health
- how to express actions which you can and cannot do
- how to express actions which have already occurred

▶ 1 *Our cloth is the best!*

ਗੱਲ ਬਾਤ ੧ ਸਾਡਾ ਕਪੜਾ ਸਭ ਤੋਂ ਵਧੀਆ ਹੈ!

gall baat 1 saadaa kaprhaa sabh ṯon vadheeaa hai!

Jaspreet and Simran have arrived in Delhi and are shopping in Karol Bagh, a popular place in Delhi to buy ready-made clothing as well as unstitched cloth. They are just entering a material shop where the shopkeeper greets them.

ਦੁਕਾਨਦਾਰ	ਅੰਦਰ ਆਓ, ਬੈਠ ਜੀ। ਸਾਰੀ ਦਿੱਲੀ ਵਿਚ ਸਾਡਾ ਕਪੜਾ ਸਭ ਤੋਂ ਵਧੀਆ ਹੈ!
Shopkeeper	andar aao, bhainh jee. saaree ḏillee vich saadaa kaprhaa sabh ṯon vadheeaa hai!
ਜਸਪ੍ਰੀਤ	ਸਾਨੂੰ ਛਪਾਈਵਾਲਾ ਕਪੜਾ ਚਾਹੀਦਾ ਹੈ ਜਿਸ ਦਾ ਅੱਜ ਕੱਲ੍ਹ ਰਵਾਜ ਹੈ।
Jaspreet	saanoon chapaaeevaalaa kaprhaa chaaheeḏaa hai jis ḏaa ajj kallh ravaaj hai.
ਦੁਕਾਨਦਾਰ	ਫ਼ਿਕਰ ਨਾ ਕਰੋ। ਮੈਂ ਤੁਹਾਨੂੰ ਉਹ ਕਪੜਾ ਦਿਖਾ ਰਿਹਾ ਹਾਂ ਜਿਹੜਾ ਵਧੇਰੇ ਹੰਢਣਸਾਰ ਹੈ ਅਤੇ ਸਭ ਤੋਂ ਵੱਧ ਵਿਕਦਾ ਹੈ।
Shopkeeper	fikar naa karo! main ṯuhaanoon uh kaprhaa ḏikhaa rihaa haan jihrhaa vaḏhere hanḏhanhsaar hai aṯe sabh ṯon vaḏhdh vikḏaa hai.

(The shopkeeper shows the girls some cloth pieces.)

ਸਿਮਰਨ	ਮੈਥੋਂ ਇਸ ਕਪੜੇ ਦਾ ਰੰਗ ਪਸੰਦ ਹੈ ਪਰ ਕਪੜਾ ਇਸ ਤੋਂ ਮੋਟਾ ਹੋਣਾ ਚਾਹੀਦਾ ਹੈ।
Simran	mainoon is kaprhe ḏaa rang pasanḏ hai par kaprhaa is ṯon motaa honhaa chaaheeḏaa hai.
ਦੁਕਾਨਦਾਰ	ਸਾਡੇ ਕੋਲ ਇਸ ਤੋਂ ਪਤਲਾ ਵੀ ਹੈ ਤੇ ਮੋਟਾ ਵੀ। ਤੁਸੀਂ ਛਾਪੇ ਦੀ ਚੋਣ ਕਰੋ।
Shopkeeper	saade kol is ṯon paṭlaa vee hai ṯe motaa vee. tuseen chaape ḏee chonh karo.
ਸਿਮਰਨ	ਜਸਪ੍ਰੀਤ, ਤੈਨੂੰ ਕਿਹੜਾ, ਵਧੇਰੇ ਚੰਗਾ ਲੱਗਦਾ ਹੈ, ਲਾਲ ਜਾਂ ਨੀਲਾ?
Simran	jaspreet, ṯainoon kihrhaa vaḏhere changaa laggḏaa hai, laal jaan neelaa?
ਜਸਪ੍ਰੀਤ	ਨੀਲਾ ਕਪੜਾ ਲਾਲ ਕਪੜੇ ਤੋਂ ਪਤਲਾ ਹੈ, ਪਰ ਫਿੱਕੇ ਰੰਗ ਵਾਲਾ ਸਭ ਤੋਂ ਸੁਹਣਾ ਹੈ।
Jaspreet	neelaa kaprhaa laal kaprhe ṯon paṭlaa hai, par phikke rang vaalaa sabh ṯon suhnhaa hai.

ਸਿਮਰਨ	ਇਹ ਕਪੜਾ ਕਿੰਨੇ ਦਾ ਮੀਟਰ ਹੈ?
Simran	ih kaprhaa kinne daa meetar hai?
ਦੁਕਾਨਦਾਰ	ਇੱਕ ਸੋ ਵੀਹ ਰੁਪਏ ਦਾ ਮੀਟਰ।
Shopkeeper	ikk sau veeh rupae daa meetar.
ਸਿਮਰਨ	ਇਹ ਕੀਮਤ ਬਹੁਤ ਜ਼ਿਆਦਾ ਹੈ। ਅਸੀਂ ਹੋਰ ਵੀ ਕਈ ਦੁਕਾਨਾਂ ਤੇ ਜਾ ਚੁਕੀਆਂ ਹਾਂ ਅਤੇ ਉਹਨਾਂ ਦੇ ਮੁਕਾਬਲੇ ਵਿਚ ਤੁਹਾਡੀਆਂ ਕੀਮਤਾਂ ਬਹੁਤ ਜ਼ਿਆਦਾ ਹਨ।
Simran	ih keemat bahut ziaadaa hai. aseen hor vee kaee dukaanaan te jaa chukeeaan haan ate uhnaan de mukaable vich tuhaadeeaan keemataan bahut ziaadaa han.
ਦੁਕਾਨਦਾਰ	ਮੈਨੂੰ ਅਫ਼ਸੋਸ ਹੈ ਕਿ ਮੈਂ ਕੀਮਤ ਹੋਰ ਘੱਟ ਨਹੀਂ ਕਰ ਸਕਦਾ।
Shopkeeper	mainoon afsos hai ki main keemat hor ghatt naheen kar sakdaa.

Shopkeeper	Come in, sisters! Our cloth is the best in all of Delhi!
Jaspreet	We want printed cloth that's in fashion these days.
Shopkeeper	Don't worry. What I'm showing you is cloth that is durable and sells a lot.
Simran	I like the colour, but the material should be thicker than this.
Shopkeeper	We have thinner and also thicker than this. Choose whatever print you like.
Simran	Jaspreet, which do you like better, red or blue?
Jaspreet	The blue is thinner than the red, but the light-coloured one is the nicest.
Simran	How much is this cloth per metre?
Shopkeeper	120 rupees per metre.
Simran	The price is too high. We've been to several other shops and in comparison with them, your prices are very high.
Shopkeeper	I'm sorry but (that) I can't lower the price any more.

ਸ਼ਬਦਾਵਲੀ   shabdaavalee   *Vocabulary*

ਦੁਕਾਨਦਾਰ	dukaandaar	*shopkeeper* (m.)
ਕਪੜਾ	kaprhaa	*cloth* (m.)
ਸਭ ਤੋਂ ਵਧੀਆ	sabh ton vadheeaa	*the best*
ਛਪਾਈਵਾਲਾ	chapaaeevaalaa	*the printed one* (m.)
ਜਿਸ	jis	*which* (oblique)
ਰਵਾਜ	ravaaj	*fashion* (m.)

ਅੱਜ ਕੱਲ੍ਹ	ajj kallh	these days
ਦਿਖਾਉਣਾ	dikhaaunhaa	to show
ਜਿਹੜਾ	jihrhaa	that, which
ਹੰਢਣਸਾਰ	handhanhsaar	durable, hardwearing
ਚਲਣਾ	chalnhaa	to go
ਵਿਕਣਾ	viknhaa	to be sold
ਰੰਗ	rang	colour (m.)
ਮੋਟਾ	motaa	fat, thick (v.)
ਪਤਲਾ	patlaa	thin (v.)
ਛਾਪੇ	chaape	print (m.)
ਚੋਣ	chonh	choice, selection (f.)
ਕਿਹੜਾ	kihrhaa	which
ਵਧੇਰੇ	vadhere	more
ਲਾਲ	laal	red
ਨੀਲਾ	neelaa	blue (v.)
ਜਾਂ	jaan	or
ਫਿੱਕਾ	phikkaa	light, pale (v.)
ਸੁਹਣਾ	suhnhaa	nice, pretty (v.)
ਕਿੰਨੇ ਦਾ ਮੀਟਰ ?	kinne daa meetar?	how much per metre?
ਇੱਕ ਸੋ ਵੀਹ	ikk sau veeh	120
ਕੀਮਤ	keemat	price (f.)
ਬਹੁਤ ਜ਼ਿਆਦਾ	bahut ziaadaa	far too much
ਕਈ	kaee	several
ਚੁਕਣਾ	chuknhaa	to be settled, finished
ਜਾ ਚੁਕਣਾ	jaa chuknhaa	have (already) been
ਮੁਕਾਬਲਾ	mukaablaa	competition
ਵੱਧ	vadhdh	high
ਘੱਟ	ghatt	less, lower
ਸਕਣਾ	saknhaa	can, to be able to

ਅਭਿਆਸ   **abhiaas**   *Exercises*

After reading the dialogue and / or listening to the recording, try to do the following exercises.

1 In the cloth shop

You are in a cloth shop telling the sales person exactly what you are looking for. Express the following in Panjabi:

a I want light-coloured cloth.
b I want material that is thick and also durable.
c The print should be in fashion.
d The price should not be too high.

2 Complete the table.

ਵਧੀਆ		
		better
	keemaṯ	
ਮੁਕਾਬਲਾ		
	sabh ṯon vadheeaa	

▶ 2 *What's the problem?*

ਗੱਲ ਬਾਤ ੨ ਕੀ ਤਕਲੀਫ਼ ਹੈ ?

gall baaṯ 2 kee ṯakleef hai?

On their way back from the market place in Delhi, Simran and Jaspreet had some snacks at a roadside restaurant, commonly known as a **dhaba**. On their way back to their hotel Simran begins to feel ill and has gone to visit the doctor.

ਡਾਕਟਰ **Doctor**	ਬੇਟੀ, ਕੀ ਤਕਲੀਫ਼ ਹੈ ? betee, kee ṯakleef hai?
ਸਿਮਰਨ **Simran**	ਮੇਰੀ ਤਬੀਅਤ ਖ਼ਰਾਬ ਹੈ । meree ṯabeeaṯ kharaab hai.
ਡਾਕਟਰ **Doctor**	ਕੀ ਤੈਨੂੰ ਬੁਖ਼ਾਰ ਹੈ ? kee ṯainoon bukhaar hai?
ਸਿਮਰਨ **Simran**	ਹਾਂ ਜੀ । ਮੈਨੂੰ ਠੰਡ ਲੱਗ ਰਹੀ ਹੈ, ਪੇਟ ਵਿਚ ਦਰਦ ਹੈ ਅਤੇ ਮੈਨੂੰ ਕਮਜ਼ੋਰੀ ਵੀ ਹੈ । haan jee. mainoon ṯhand lagg rahee hai, pet vich dard hai aṯe mainoon kamzoree vee hai.
ਡਾਕਟਰ **Doctor**	ਬਿਮਾਰ ਹੋਣ ਤੋਂ ਪਹਿਲੇ ਤੂੰ ਕੁਝ ਖਾਧਾ ਸੀ ? bimaar honh ṯon pahile ṯoon kee kujh khaadhaa see?
ਸਿਮਰਨ **Simran**	ਮੈਨੂੰ ਯਾਦ ਨਹੀਂ ਪਰ ਮੈਨੂੰ ਇੱਥੋਂ ਦੀਆਂ ਛੱਲੀਆਂ ਬਹੁਤ ਪਸੰਦ ਹਨ । mainoon yaad naheen par mainoon iththon deeaan challeeaan bahuṯ pasand han.

ਡਾਕਟਰ	ਹੁਣ ਮੈਂ ਸਮਝਿਆ। ਜਿਹੜੇ ਲੋਕ ਬਾਹਰੋਂ ਆਉਂਦੇ ਹਨ, ਉਹਨਾਂ ਨੂੰ ਦੇਸੀ ਖਾਣਾ ਹਜ਼ਮ ਨਹੀਂ ਹੁੰਦਾ। ਇਹ ਲਵੋ ਦਵਾਈ, ਅਰਾਮ ਕਰੋ ਤੇ ਛੱਲੀਆਂ ਤੋਂ ਦੂਰ ਰਵੋ!
Doctor	hunh main samajhiaa. jihrhe lok baahron aaunde han, uhnaan noon desee khaanhaa hazam naheen hundaa. ih lavo davaaee, araam karo, te challeeaan ton door ravo!
ਸਿਮਰਨ	ਧੰਨਵਾਦ।
Simran	dhannvaad.
Doctor	*Dear (daughter), what's the problem?*
Simran	*I'm not feeling well (lit. my health is bad).*
Doctor	*Do you have a fever?*
Simran	*Yes. I feel cold, I have a stomach ache and I'm also weak.*
Doctor	*Before falling ill, what did you eat?*
Simran	*I don't remember, but I like the corn on the cob here a lot.*
Doctor	*Now I understand. People who come from abroad can't digest the food here. Take this medicine, rest, and stay away from corn on the cob!*
Simran	*Thank you.*

ਸ਼ਬਦਾਵਲੀ   shabdaavalee   *Vocabulary*

ਤਕਲੀਫ਼	takleef	*trouble, irritation, bother (f.)*
ਤਬੀਅਤ	tabeeat	*state of health, condition (f.)*
ਬੁਖ਼ਾਰ	bukhaar	*fever / temperature (m.)*
ਠੰਡ	thand	*cold (f.)*
ਲੱਗਣਾ	laggnhaa	*to feel*
ਪੇਟ	pet	*stomach, belly (m.)*
ਦਰਦ	dard	*pain, hurt (f.)*
ਕਮਜ਼ੋਰੀ	kamzoree	*weakness (f.)*
ਬਿਮਾਰ	bimaar	*ill, sick*
ਬਿਮਾਰ ਹੋਣ ਤੋਂ ਪਹਿਲੇ	bimaar honh ton pahile	*before falling ill*
ਯਾਦ	yaad	*memory, remember (f.)*
ਛੱਲੀ	challee	*corn on the cob (f.)*
ਸਮਝਣਾ	samajhnhaa	*to understand / comprehend*
ਬਾਹਰੋਂ	baahron	*from outside / from abroad*
ਦੇਸੀ	desi	*Indian, Panjabi, home*
ਹਜ਼ਮ	hazam	*digest*
ਦੂਰ	door	*far / away*
ਅਰਾਮ	araam	*rest (m.)*
ਦਵਾਈ	davaaee	*medicine (f.)*

ਅਭਿਆਸ abhiaas *Exercises*

After reading the dialogue and / or listening to the recording, try to do the following exercises.

1 Write in the correct word order.

a ਹੈ ਤਕਲੀਫ਼ ਕੀ ?   hai ṭakleef kee?
b ਹੈ ਤੈਨੂੰ ਕੀ ਬੁਖ਼ਾਰ ?   hai ṭainoon kee buk̲h̲aar?
c ਸਮਝਿਆ ਹੁਣ ਮੈ   samajhiaa hunh main

2 Fill in the blanks.

Fill in the blanks with the correct terms from the dialogue. The English has been given in brackets, although not necessarily in the correct order.

You   ਮੇਰੀ _____ ਖ਼ਰਾਬ ਹੈ । (*health*)
      meree _____ k̲h̲arab hai.
Dr   ਕੀ _____ ਹੈ ? (*problem*)
      kee _____ hai?
You   ਮੇਰੇ _____ ਵਿਚ _____ ਹੈ ਤੇ ਮੈਨੂੰ _____ ਵੀ ਹੈ ।
      (*pain, fever, stomach*)
      mere _____ vich _____ hai ṭe mainoon _____ vee hai.
Dr   ਤੈਨੂੰ _____ ਹੈ ਤੇ _____ ਲੱਗ ਰਹੀ ਹੈ ? (*fever, cold*)
      ṭainoon _____ hai ṭe _____ lagg rahee hai?
You   ਹਾਂ ਜੀ _____ haan jee.
Dr   ਇਹ _____ ਲਵੋ ਤੇ _____ ਕਰੋ । (*rest, medicine*)
      ih _____ lavo ṭe _____ karo.

ਬੋਲੀ ਬਾਰੇ bolee baare *Language points*

Comparison of adjectives

When people or things are compared in Panjabi in terms of quality, size, number and price, there are no direct translations of the English expressions *good*, *better*, *best* or *big*, *bigger*, *biggest*. Instead the postpositions ਨਾਲੋਂ **naalon** (*than*) and ਤੋਂ **ṭon** (*from*) are commonly used to express comparison such as *more* _____ or _____ *than*. For example:

ਇਸ ਤੋਂ / ਨਾਲੋਂ ਮੋਟਾ   is ṭon / naalon motaa   *thicker than this*
ਉਸ ਤੋਂ / ਨਾਲੋਂ ਪਤਲਾ   us ṭon / naalon paṭlaa   *thinner that that*
ਰਾਮ ਸ਼ਾਮ ਤੋਂ ਲੰਬਾ ਹੈ   raam shaam ṭon   *Ram is taller than*
                          lanbaa hai   *Sham.*

ਵਧੇਰੇ va<u>dh</u>ere and ਜ਼ਿਆਦਾ ziaa<u>d</u>aa, which mean *much* or *more* are also used when making comparisons, especially when the object or objects being referred to are absent. The literal translations in Panjabi of *better* ਚੰਗੇਰਾ cha<u>n</u>geraa and *taller / longer* ਲੰਬੇਰਾ la<u>n</u>beraa are also occasionally used in a similar manner. Note in the following examples how adjectives such as *tall* are changed to comparisons such as *taller*:

ਰਾਮ ਲੰਬਾ ਹੈ	raam la<u>n</u>baa hai	*Ram is tall.*
ਰਾਮ ਜ਼ਿਆਦਾ ਲੰਬਾ ਹੈ	raam ziaa<u>d</u>aa la<u>n</u>baa hai	*Ram is taller.*
ਰਾਮ ਵਧੇਰੇ ਲੰਬਾ ਹੈ	raam va<u>dh</u>ere la<u>n</u>baa hai	*Ram is taller.*
ਇਹ ਕਪੜਾ ਚੰਗਾ ਹੈ	ih kaprhaa cha<u>n</u>gaa hai	*this cloth is good*
ਇਹ ਕਪੜਾ ਚੰਗੇਰਾ ਹੈ	ih kaprhaa cha<u>n</u>geraa hai	*this cloth is better*
ਉਹ ਕਮਰਾ ਲੰਬਾ ਹੈ	uh kamraa la<u>n</u>baa hai	*that room is long*
ਉਹ ਕਮਰਾ ਲੰਬੇਰਾ ਹੈ	uh kamraa la<u>n</u>beraa hai	*that room is longer*

In English the superlative degree is generally expressed with the ending *–est*, such as *tallest*, *biggest* and *nicest*. In Panjabi the superlative degree uses the words ਸਭ **sabh**, ਸਭਨਾਂ **sabhnaan**, and ਸਾਰੇ **saare** which mean *all* or *whole* with the postpositions ਨਾਲੋਂ **naalo<u>n</u>** and ਤੋਂ **<u>ton</u>**, to give the overall sense *out of all* or *of all*.

The superlative *the best* in Panjabi would literally translate as *out of all the best* in English:

ਸਭ ਤੋਂ ਚੰਗਾ ਕਪੜਾ	**sabh <u>ton</u> cha<u>n</u>gaa kaprhaa**	*the best cloth*

To say that something is even better or even taller, ਹੋਰ ਵੀ **hor vee**, meaning *more* and *also*, is used. Here are some examples of a variety of different uses of comparison and superlative degrees:

ਉਹ ਕੁੜੀ ਸਭ ਨਾਲੋਂ ਛੋਟੀ ਹੈ	uh kurhee sabh naalo<u>n</u> <u>ch</u>otee hai	*This girl is the smallest.*
ਰਮੇਸ਼ ਸਾਰੇ ਭਰਾਵਾਂ ਨਾਲੋਂ ਲੰਬਾ ਹੈ	ramesh saare bharaavaa<u>n</u> naalo<u>n</u> la<u>n</u>baa hai	*Ramesh is the tallest of the brothers.*
ਉਹਨਾਂ ਦਾ ਖਾਣਾ ਸਭ ਤੋਂ ਸੁਆਦ ਹੁੰਦਾ ਹੈ	uhnaa<u>n</u> <u>d</u>aa khaanhaa sabh <u>ton</u> suaa<u>d</u> hu<u>nd</u>aa hai	*Their food is the tastiest.*
ਉਹਨਾਂ ਦਾ ਖਾਣਾ ਹੋਰ ਵੀ ਸੁਆਦ ਹੁੰਦਾ ਹੈ	uhnaa<u>n</u> <u>d</u>aa khaanhaa hor vee suaa<u>d</u> hu<u>nd</u>aa hai	*Their food is even tastier.*

ਸਕਣਾ saknhaa *can* and *can't*

You will recall in the first dialogue that during the bargaining over the price of the cloth, the shopkeeper said to Simran and Jaspreet:

ਮੈਂ ਕੀਮਤ ਹੋਰ ਘੱਟ	main keemat hor ghatt	*I can't lower the*
ਨਹੀਂ ਕਰ ਸਕਦਾ	naheen kar sakdaa	*price any further.*

He expressed his inability (or unwillingness!) to lower the price by saying *I can't*. In Panjabi ਸਕਣਾ saknhaa is used in combination with the stem of the verb portraying the action which can or cannot be done. In this example, the shopkeeper is saying that he can't (i.e. is not able to) lower the price. Therefore, the stem of ਘਟਣਾ ghatnhaa (*to decrease*, *to lower*) is used with the negative ਨਹੀਂ naheen to give the expression *can't lower*. Alternatively, if he had wanted to say *I can lower the price*, the negative ਨਹੀਂ naheen would simply have been omitted. The form of ਸਕਣਾ saknhaa is always in agreement with the subject. Here are some more examples to illustrate how this construction is formed:

ਅਸੀਂ ਪੰਜਾਬੀ ਬੋਲ	aseen panjaabee bol	*We can speak*
ਸਕਦੀਆਂ ਹਾਂ	sakdeeaan haan	*Panjabi.*
ਕੀ ਤੁਸੀਂ ਕੱਲ੍ਹ ਨੂੰ	kee tuseen kallh	*Will you be able to*
ਆ ਸਕੋ ਗੇ ?	noon aa sako ge?	*come tomorrow?*
ਮੈਂ ਗਾ ਨਹੀਂ ਸਕਦੀ	main gaa naheen sakdee	*I cannot sing.*

You should remember that ਸਕਣਾ saknhaa never stands on its own and therefore always requires the stem, even when giving a reply to a question:

Question	ਕੀ ਤੁਸੀਂ ਕੱਲ੍ਹ ਨੂੰ	kee tuseen kallh	*Can you come*
	ਆ ਸਕਦੇ ਹੋ ?	noon aa sakde ho?	*tomorrow?*
Reply	ਹਾਂ ਜੀ, ਮੈਂ ਆ	haan jee, main aa	*Yes, I can*
	ਸਕਦੀ / ਸਕਦਾ ਹਾਂ	sakdee/sakdaa haan	*(come).*

ਚੁਕਣਾ 'chuknhaa' *already completed*

The stem of a verb followed by ਚੁਕਣਾ chuknhaa means *to have already done* or *to have finished doing*. This type of construction with ਚੁਕਣਾ chuknhaa is formed in a fashion similar to that of

सकਣਾ saknhaa as just described. चੁकਣਾ chuknhaa also cannot stand alone and requires a preceding stem to indicate the action that has already occurred.

ਮੈਂ ਖਾ ਚੁਕਾ ਹਾਂ	main khaa chukaa haan	I have (already) eaten.
ਜਸਬੀਰ ਜਾ ਚੁਕਾ ਸੀ	jasbeer jaa chukaa see	Jasbir had (already) gone.
ਕੁੜੀਆਂ ਸਾਰੀਆਂ ਕਿਤਾਬਾਂ ਪੜ੍ਹ ਚੁਕੀਆਂ ਹਨ	kurheeaan saareeaan ki<u>t</u>aabaan parhh chukeeaan han	The girls have (already) read all of the books.
ਅਸੀਂ ਉੱਥੇ ਜਾ ਚੁਕੇ ਹਾਂ	aseen u<u>th</u>the jaa chuke haan	We have (already) been there.

The relative pronouns ਜਿਹੜਾ 'jihrhaa' and ਜੋ 'jo'

The English relative pronouns *that* and *which* are used to form relative clauses following a pattern which relates the relative pronouns back to the subject, such as *The woman who came today teaches Urdu*. In Panjabi this sentence would be constructed in a rather different manner: *That woman who came today, she teaches Urdu*. In this example, *that* is the relative pronoun and *she* is the correlative pronoun. Another example of an English relative clause translated into Panjabi would be: *Go to the shop which (that) is closest*. In Panjabi this sentence would be expressed as: *Which shop is closest, go to that one*. In this example, *which* is the relative pronoun and *that one* is the correlative pronoun.

In Panjabi, the relative pronoun and adjective ਜਿਹੜਾ jihrhaa is used to represent words such as *that*, *which*, *those*, *he*, *she* and *who* and changes according to the gender and number of the objects being referred to. The relative pronoun ਜੋ jo means *whatever* or *whoever* and is used when referring to more abstract people and things. Often, the presence of the relative pronoun in the English translation is simply understood. Here are some examples of the ways in which relative clauses are formed with ਜਿਹੜਾ jihrhaa and ਜੋ jo:

ਜੋ ਕੁਝ ਤੁਸੀਂ ਕੀਤਾ ਹੈ ਮੈਨੂੰ ਠੀਕ ਲੱਗਦਾ ਹੈ	jo kujh <u>t</u>useen kee<u>t</u>aa hai, mainoon theek laggdaa hai	Whatever you've done looks fine to me.
ਜਿਹੜੇ ਲੋਕ ਬਾਹਰੋਂ ਆਉਂਦੇ ਹਨ, ਉਹਨਾਂ ਨੂੰ ਖਾਣਾ ਹਜ਼ਮ ਨਹੀਂ ਹੁੰਦਾ	jihrhe lok baahron aaun<u>d</u>e han, uhnaan noo<u>n</u> khaanhaa hazam naheen hun<u>d</u>aa	[Those] people who come from abroad can't digest the food.

ਜਿਹੜਾ ਆਦਮੀ ਅੱਜ ਆਇਆ ਸੀ, ਉਹ ਕੱਲ੍ਹ ਨਹੀਂ ਆ ਸਕੇਗਾ	jihrhaa aadmee ajj aaiaa see, uh kallh naheen aa sakegaa	*That man who came today will not be able to come tomorrow.*

Like other adjectives and pronouns in Panjabi, relative pronouns change their form in the oblique. In the singular ਜਿਹੜਾ jihrhaa takes the oblique form ਜਿਸ jis and in the plural it becomes ਜਿਹਨਾਂ jihnaan followed by the appropriate postposition. Here are some examples of the oblique forms of the relative pronoun ਜਿਹੜਾ jihrhaa:

ਅਸੀਂ ਜਿਹਨਾਂ ਦੇ ਘਰ ਗਏ ਸੀ, ਉਹ ਰਾਵਲਪਿੰਡੀ ਦੇ ਹਨ	aseen jinnaan de ghar ge see, uh raavalpindee de han	*(The people) whose house we went to are from Rawalpindi.*
ਜਿਸ ਜਨਾਨੀ ਨੂੰ ਪੰਜਾਬੀ ਆਉਂਦੀ ਹੈ, ਉਹ ਨੂੰ ਪੁੱਛੋ	jis janaanee noon panjaabee aaundee hai, uh noon puchcho	*Ask the lady who knows Panjabi.*
ਜਿਸ ਨੂੰ ਪਤਾ ਸੀ ਉਹ ਦਾ ਕਸੂਰ ਹੈ	jis noon pataa see uh daa kasoor hai	*He [who knew] was aware; it's his fault.*

More uses of ਨੂੰ 'noon'

By now you should be beginning to feel acquainted with the significance of postpositions in Panjabi. In Unit 4 simple postpositions were introduced as they affect nouns and adjectives in the oblique. In Unit 8 the two sisters Simran and Jaspreet illustrated in the dialogues some further uses of the postposition ਨੂੰ **noon** in expressing likes and dislikes, want, need, should and ought. In this unit more uses of ਨੂੰ **noon** have already been exemplified in the second dialogue, in which Simran and the doctor discuss health conditions. ਨੂੰ **noon** literally means *to* and directs the condition or state towards the person or pronoun it governs. It is used in a number of different senses ranging from awareness and health to feelings. Therefore, when the doctor asks Simran ਕੀ ਤੈਨੂੰ ਬੁਖ਼ਾਰ ਹੈ? **kee tainoon bukhaar hai?** he is literally asking *Is there a fever to you?* Here are some more examples of how ਨੂੰ **noon** can be used in this sense:

ਮੈਨੂੰ ਬੁਖ਼ਾਰ ਹੈ	mainoon bukhaar hai	*I have a fever.*
ਸਾਨੂੰ ਠੰਡ ਲੱਗ ਰਹੀ ਹੈ	saanoon thand lagg rahee hai	*We are feeling cold.*
ਮੈਨੂੰ ਅਫ਼ਸੋਸ ਹੈ	mainoon afsos hai	*I am sorry.*
ਉਹ ਨੂੰ ਉਮੀਦ ਹੈ	uh noon umeed hai	*He / she hopes.*
ਉਹਨਾਂ ਨੂੰ ਪਤਾ ਨਹੀਂ	uhnaan noon pataa naheen	*They do not know.*

ਮੈਨੂੰ ਜ਼ੁਕਾਮ ਹੈ	mainoon zukaam hai	*I have a cold.*
ਤੁਹਾਨੂੰ ਕੋਈ ਪਤਾ ਹੈ ਕਿ ਇਕਬਾਲ ਕਿੱਥੇ ਹੈ?	tuhaanoon koee paṭaa hai ki ikbaal kiththe hai?	*Do you have any idea where Iqbal is?*
ਸਾਨੂੰ ਬਹੁਤ ਖ਼ੁਸ਼ੀ ਹੈ	saanoon bahuṭ khushee hai	*We are very happy.*

ਵਿਆਖਿਆ   viaakhiaa   *Commentary*

1 Parts of the body

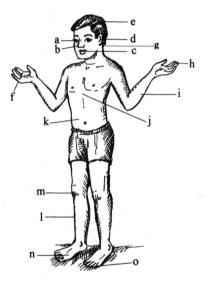

a	– ਅੱਖ
b	– ਨੱਕ
c	– ਮੂੰਹ
d	– ਕੰਨ
e	– ਸਿਰ
f	– ਹੱਥ
g	– ਗਰਦਨ
h	– ਉੱਂਗਲ
i	– ਬਾਂਹ
j	– ਛਾਤੀ
k	– ਪੇਟ
l	– ਲੱਤ
m	– ਗੋਡਾ
n	– ਪੈਰ
o	– ਪੱਬ

2 Clothes people wear

There are various forms of dress worn by Panjabis. Perhaps the most popular form is the **salwaar kameez** (**shalwaar kameez** in West Panjab). This form of dress is now ubiquitous in almost all of South Asia, but it is most popular in Pakistan Panjab, where both men and women wear it. Traditionally, women in rural Panjab would wear a flowing skirt – **ghagra** – and a blouse, although this is a rare sight in contemporary Panjab. Women may wear a **sari** for special occasions and Christian women often wear dresses as a way of distinguishing themselves. Male dress was traditionally a turban with a flowing top shirt and a wrap called a **lungi** or **dhoti** around the legs. However, western dress is increasingly popular. The following pictures illustrate the various forms of dress.

ਅਭਿਆਸ   abhiaas   *Exercises*

After reading the dialogue and / or listening to the recording, try to do the following exercises.

1 Word search

The following words are hidden in the word search boxes below. In the first box they are hidden horizontally and in the second they are hidden vertically.

ਬੁਖ਼ਾਰ, ਭੈਣਜੀ, ਕਪੜਾ, ਦੁਕਾਨਦਾਰ, ਬਿਮਾਰ, ਛਾਪੇ, ਦਰਦ, ਕਮਜ਼ੋਰੀ, ਕੀਮਤ, ਹੱਢਣਸਾਰ

ਭੈ	ਣ	ਜੀ	ਜਾ	ਭ
ਜੋ	ਕ	ਪ	ੜਾ	ਕੀ
ਦੁ	ਕਾ	ਨ	ਦਾ	ਰ
ਉ	ਉ	ਛਾ	ਪੇ	ਸ਼
ਤਾ	ਕੀ	ਮ	ਤ	ਭ

ਨ	ਮੇ	ਰ	ਕ	ਹੰ
ਮਾ	ਬਿ	ਬੁ	ਮ	ਛ
ਦ	ਮਾ	ਖ਼ਾ	ਝੋ	ਣ
ਰ	ਰ	ਰ	ਰੀ	ਸਾ
ਦ	ਦ	ਰੀ	ਗੋ	ਰ

2 Talking to the doctor

Look at the pictures and tell how each person would respond in Panjabi to the doctor's question: ਕੀ ਤਕਲੀਫ਼ ਹੈ? What's the problem?

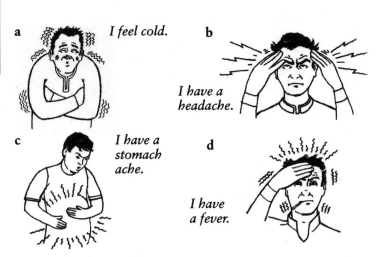

a *I feel cold.*

b *I have a headache.*

c *I have a stomach ache.*

d *I have a fever.*

3 Write sentences in Panjabi.

Express the following sentences in Panjabi using either ਚੁਕਣਾ chuknhaa or ਸਕਣਾ saknhaa:

a I can't come tomorrow.
b Can you speak Panjabi?
c We've already been there.
d They have already eaten.

4 Relative pronouns

Insert the correct forms of the relative pronouns ਜੋ jo, ਜਿਹੜਾ jihrhaa and ਜਿਸ jis:

a _____ ਆਦਮੀ ਅੱਜ ਪਾਕਿਸਤਾਨ ਗਿਆ ਹੈ, ਉਹ ਮੇਰਾ ਚਾਚਾ ਹੈ।
_____ aadmee ajj paakistaan giaa hai, uh meraa
chaachaa hai.
The man who went to Pakistan today is my uncle.

b _____ ਨੂੰ ਪਤਾ ਹੈ, ਉਹ ਨੂੰ ਪੁੱਛੋ।
_____ noon pataa hai, uh noon puchcho.
Ask the person who knows.

c _____ ਲੋਕ ਪਿੰਡ ਵਿਚ ਰਹਿੰਦੇ ਹਨ ਉਹਨਾਂ ਨੂੰ ਸ਼ਹਿਰ ਪਸੰਦ ਨਹੀਂ।
_____ lok pind vich rahinde han uhnaan noon shahir
pasand naheen.
People who live in the village don't like the city.

d _____ ਕੁਝ ਤੁਸੀਂ ਚਾਹੁੰਦੇ ਹੋ ਉਹ ਮੇਰੇ ਲਈ ਠੀਕ ਹੈ।
_____ kujh tuseen chaahunde ho uh mere laee theek hai.
Whatever you want is fine with me.

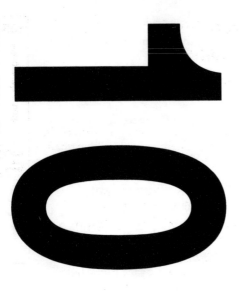

10

ਇੱਕ ਦਿਨ ਪਿੰਡ ਵਿੱਚ
ikk din pind vich

a day in the village

In this unit you will learn:
- about Panjabi village life
- how to talk about things you've done and seen

▶ *What else did you buy?*

ਗੱਲ ਬਾਤ ਤੂੰ ਹੋਰ ਕੀ ਕੁਝ ਖ਼ਰੀਦਿਆ?

gall baat toon hor kee kujh khareediaa?

Jaspreet and Simran have arrived at their relatives' house in Jalandhar after their tour of Delhi. Their aunt is asking them about their stay in Delhi.

ਚਾਚੀ **Aunt (chaachee)**	ਤੁਹਾਡੀ ਦਿੱਲੀ ਦੀ ਸੈਰ ਕਿਵੇਂ ਰਹੀ? tuhaadee dillee dee sair kiven rahee?
ਜਸਪ੍ਰੀਤ **Jaspreet**	ਬਹੁਤ ਸੁਹਣੀ ਰਹੀ। ਇੱਕ ਦਿਨ ਮੈਂ ਪੁਰਾਣੀ ਦਿੱਲੀ ਵਿਚ ਘੁੰਮੀ। ਲਾਲ ਕਿਲ੍ਹਾ ਅਤੇ ਸੀਸ ਗੰਜ ਗੁਰਦਵਾਰਾ ਦੇਖਿਆ। ਉਹ ਦਿਨ ਸਭ ਤੋਂ ਚੰਗਾ ਗੁਜ਼ਰਿਆ। ਮੈਂ ਚਾਂਦਨੀ ਚੌਕ ਬਜ਼ਾਰ ਤੋਂ ਸਿਤਾਰ ਵੀ ਖ਼ਰੀਦੀ। bahut suhnhee rahee. ikk din main puraanhee dillee vich ghunmee. laal kilhaa ate sees ganj gurdavaaraa dekhiaa. uh din sabh ton changaa guzriaa. main chaandnee chaunk bazaar ton sitaar vee khareedee.
ਚਾਚੀ **Aunt**	ਤੂੰ ਹੋਰ ਕੀ ਕੁਝ ਖ਼ਰੀਦਿਆ? toon hor kee kujh khareediaa?
ਜਸਪ੍ਰੀਤ **Jaspreet**	ਚਾਚੀ ਜੀ, ਮੈਂ ਕਪੜੇ ਖ਼ਰੀਦੇ ਤੇ ਜੁੱਤੀ ਵੀ ਖ਼ਰੀਦੀ। chaachee jee, main kaprhe khareede te juttee vee khareedee.
ਚਾਚੀ **Aunt**	ਸਿਮਰਨ, ਤੂੰ ਕੀ ਕੀਤਾ? simran, toon kee keetaa?
ਸਿਮਰਨ **Simran**	ਮੈਂ ਹਰ ਕਿਸਮ ਦੇ ਖਾਣੇ ਖਾਧੇ, ਪਰ ਮੈਂ ਬਿਮਾਰ ਹੋ ਗਈ ਸੀ। ਫਿਰ ਮੈਂ ਡਾਕਟਰ ਕੋਲ ਗਈ ਅਤੇ ਉਸ ਨੇ ਮੈਨੂੰ ਦਵਾਈ ਦਿੱਤੀ। main har kisam de khaanhe khaadhe par main bimaar ho gaee see. phir main daaktar kol gaee ate us ne mainoon davaaee dittee.
ਚਾਚੀ **Aunt**	ਉਮੀਦ ਹੈ ਕਿ ਹੁਣ ਤੂੰ ਠੀਕ ਹੈਂ ਕਿਉਂ ਕਿ ਅਸੀਂ ਅੱਜ ਸਰ੍ਹੋਂ ਦਾ ਸਾਗ ਤੇ ਮੱਕੀ ਦੀ ਰੋਟੀ ਬਣਾਈ ਹੈ। ਇਹ ਪੰਜਾਬ ਦੀ ਖ਼ਾਸ ਸੁਗਾਤ ਹੈ! umeed hai ki hunh toon theek hain kion ki aseen ajj sar-h-on daa saag te makkee dee rotee banhaaee hai. ih panjaab dee khaas sugaat hai!

Aunt	How was your tour of Delhi?
Jaspreet	It was very nice. One day I went around Old Delhi. I saw the Red Fort and Sees Ganj Gurdwara. That was the best day I had. I also bought a sitar from Chandni Chowk market.
Aunt	What else did you buy?
Jaspreet	Aunty Ji, I bought clothes and shoes too!
Aunt	Simran, what did you do?
Simran	I ate every type of food, but I fell ill. Then I went to the doctor and he gave me some medicine.
Aunt	I hope you're fine now since today we've made sarhon daa saag and makkee dee rotee. This is a speciality of Panjab!

ਸ਼ਬਦਾਵਲੀ   shabdaavalee   *Vocabulary*

ਸੈਰ	sair	*tour, trip* (f.)
ਸੁਹਣੀ	suhnhee	*nice, pretty* (v.)
ਪੁਰਾਣੀ	puraanhee	*old* (v.)
ਪੁਰਾਣੀ ਦਿੱਲੀ	puraanhee dillee	*Old Delhi* (f.)
ਕਿਲ੍ਹਾ	kilhaa	*fort* (m.)
ਚੰਗਾ	changaa	*good* (v.)
ਗੁਜ਼ਰਨਾ	guzarnhaa	*to be spent, to go by*
ਚਾਂਦਨੀ	chaandanee	*moonlight*
ਚੌਂਕ	chaunk	*roundabout, circle, centre* (m.)
ਬਜ਼ਾਰ	bazaar	*bazaar* (m.)
ਖ਼ਰੀਦਨਾ	khareednhaa	*to buy*
ਕੀ ਕੁਝ	kee kujh	*what else*
ਕਪੜੇ	kaprhe	*clothes* (m.)
ਜੁੱਤੀ	juttee	*shoes* (f.)
ਹਰ	har	*each, every*
ਕਿਸਮ	kisam	*type*
ਹਰ ਕਿਸਮ ਦੇ ਖਾਣੇ	har kisam de khaanhe	*every type of food*
ਪਰ	par	*but*
ਉਮੀਦ	umeed	*hope, wish* (f.)
ਕਿਉਂ ਕਿ	kion ki	*because, since*
ਸਰ੍ਹੋਂ ਦਾ ਸਾਗ	sarhon daa saag	*mustard leaves* (m.)
ਮੱਕੀ ਦੀ ਰੋਟੀ	makkee dee rotee	*unleavened corn bread* (f.)

ਬਣਾਉਣਾ	banhaaunhaa	*to make*
ਖ਼ਾਸ	khaas	*special*
ਸੁਗਾਤ	sugaat	*gift* (f.)
ਖ਼ਾਸ ਸੁਗਾਤ	khaas sugaat	*speciality* (f.)

ਅਭਿਆਸ   abhiaas   *Exercises*

After reading the dialogue and / or listening to the recording, try to do the following exercises.

1 True or false?

a ਚਾਚੀ ਜਸਪ੍ਰੀਤ ਤੇ ਸਿਮਰਨ ਨੂੰ ਦਿੱਲੀ ਦੀ ਸੈਰ ਬਾਰੇ   True / False
ਪੁੱਛ ਰਹੀ ਸੀ ।
chaachee jaspreet te simran noon dillee dee
sair baare puchch rahee see.

b ਚਾਚੀ ਨੇ ਕੁੜੀਆਂ ਨੂੰ ਕਿਹਾ ਕਿ ਜ਼ਿਆਦਾ ਪੈਸਾ ਨਹੀਂ   True / False
ਖ਼ਰਚਣਾ ਚਾਹੀਦਾ ।
chaachee ne kurheeaan noon kihaa ki ziaadaa
paisaa naheen kharchnhaa chaaheedaa.

c ਸਿਮਰਨ ਮੌਸਮ ਕਰ ਕੇ ਬਿਮਾਰ ਹੋ ਗਈ ਸੀ ।   True / False
simran mausam kar ke bimaar ho gaee see.

2 Match the responses appropriate to the questions

a ਤੂੰ ਹੋਰ ਕੀ ਕੁਝ ਖ਼ਰੀਦਿਆ ?   i   ਬਹੁਤ ਸੁਹਣੀ ਰਹੀ ।
toon hor kee kujh khareediaa?   bahut suhnhee rahee.

b ਤੂੰ ਬਿਮਾਰ ਕਿਉਂ ਹੋ ਗਈ ਸੀ ?   ii   ਮੈਂ ਹਰ ਕਿਸਮ ਦੇ ਖਾਣੇ ਖਾਧੇ ।
toon bimaar kiun ho gaee see?   main har kisam de
         khaanhe khadhe.

c ਦਿੱਲੀ ਦੀ ਸੈਰ ਕਿਵੇਂ ਰਹੀ ?   iii   ਮੈਂ ਕਪੜੇ ਖ਼ਰੀਦੇ ਤੇ ਜੁੱਤੀ ਵੀ
dillee dee sair kiven rahee?   ਖ਼ਰੀਦੀ ।
         main kaprhe khareede te
         juttee vee khareedee.

d ਦਿੱਲੀ ਵਿਚ ਤੁਸੀਂ ਕੀ ਕੁਝ ਦੇਖਿਆ ?   iv   ਮੈਂ ਲਾਲ ਕਿਲ੍ਹਾ ਅਤੇ ਸੀਸ
dillee vich tuseen kee kujh   ਗੰਜ ਗੁਰਦਵਾਰਾ ਦੇਖਿਆ ।
dekhiaa?   main laal kilhaa ate sees
         ganj gurdavaaraa dekhiaa.

Passage: A day in the village

ਪੈਰਾ: ਇੱਕ ਦਿਨ ਪਿੰਡ ਵਿਚ

pairaa: ikk din pind vich

Jaspreet and Simran have gone to their mother's family's village after having seen their father's relatives in Jalandhar. The following passage is a page from Jaspreet's diary. She has written about the day that she and her sister spent in the village.

17 ਜਨਵਰੀ

ਅਸੀਂ ਅੱਜ ਜਲੰਧਰ ਤੋਂ ਕੇ ਨਾਨਕੇ ਪਿੰਡ ਗਈਆਂ।
ਸਾਰੇ ਸਾਨੂੰ ਪਿਆਰ ਨਾਲ ਮਿਲੇ। ਸਾਡੇ ਮਾਮਾ
ਜੀ, ਨਾਨਾ ਜੀ ਤੇ ਨਾਨੀ ਜੀ ਦੇ ਕੋਲ ਰਹਿੰਦੇ
ਹਾਂ। ਉਹਨਾਂ ਨੇ ਸਾਨੂੰ ਸਾਰਾ ਪਿੰਡ ਦਿਖਾਇਆ।
ਅਸੀਂ ਟਰੈਕਟਰ ਤੇ ਚੜ੍ਹੀਆਂ ਅਤੇ ਖੇਤਾਂ ਵਿਚ ਘੁੰਮੀ-
ਆਂ। ਅਸੀਂ ਖੂਹ ਤੇ ਗਏ। ਮੈਂ ਖੂਹ ਪਹਿਲੀ ਵਾਰੀ
ਦੇਖਿਆ ਸੀ। ਸ਼ਿਮਰਨ ਅੰਬ ਨੂੰ ਦੇਖ ਕੇ ਡਰ
ਗਈ ਤੇ ਇੱਕ ਦਮ ਦੌੜ ਗਈ। ਖੂਹ ਦੇ ਨਾਲ
ਇੱਕ ਘੰਟਾ ਗੀਡੇ ਦੇ ਰਮ ਤੋਂ ਰਾਖ ਚੜ੍ਹਾ
ਰਿਹਾ ਸੀ। ਸ਼ਾਮ ਨੂੰ ਜਦੋਂ ਅਸੀਂ ਵਾਪਸ
ਆਏ ਤਾਂ ਮਾਮੀ ਜੀ ਨੇ ਸਾਨੂੰ ਰੋਟੀ ਖੁਆਈ।
ਉਸ ਤੋਂ ਬਾਅਦ ਵਿਹੜੇ ਵਿਚ ਅਸੀਂ ਨਾਨੀ ਜੀ
ਕੋਲੋਂ ਪੁਰਾਣੀਆਂ ਕਹਾਣੀਆਂ ਸੁਣੀਆਂ। ਰਾਤ ਨੂੰ
ਸਾਰਿਆਂ ਨੇ ਰਾਬਰ ਦੁੱਧ ਪੀਤਾ ਅਤੇ ਫਿਰ ਸੌਂ
ਗਏ। ਪਿੰਡ ਦਾ ਮਾਹੌਲ ਮੈਨੂੰ ਬਹੁਤ ਪਸੰਦ ਹੈ।

17 Janvaree

aseen ajj jalandhar ho ke naanke pind gaeeaan. saare saanoon
piaar naal mile. saade maamaa jee naanaa jee te naanee jee de
kol rahinde han. uhnaan ne saanoon saaraa pind dikhaaiaa.
aseen taraiktar te charh-h-eeaan ate khetaan vich ghunmeeaan.
aseen khooh te ruke. main khooh pahilee vaaree vekhiaa see.
simran majhjh noon dekh ke dar gaee te ikk dam daurh gaee.
khooh de naal ikk bandaa ganne de ras ton gurh banhaa rihaa
see. shaam noon jadon aseen vaapas aae taan maamee jee ne
saanoon rotee khuaaee. us ton baa-a-d vihrhe vich aseen naanee
jee kolon puraanheeaan kahaanheeaan sunheeaan. raat noon
saariaa ne garam dudhdh peetaa ate phir saun gae. pind daa
maahaul mainoon bahut pasand hai.

17 January

*Today, after having been to Jalandhar, we went to our mother's
family's village. Everyone met us with affection. Our mother's
brother lives with grandfather and grandmother. He showed us
the entire village. We rode on a tractor and went around the
fields. We stopped at the well. It was the first time that I had seen
a well. Simran saw buffalo, got scared and immediately ran
away. Next to the well there was a man who was making Gurh
(a sweet delicacy) from the juice of the sugarcane. In the evening
when we arrived, mami ji fed us. After that we all sat in the
courtyard and heard old stories from grandmother. At night
everyone drank hot milk and then went to sleep. I like the atmosphere of the village a lot.*

ਸ਼ਬਦਾਵਲੀ shabdaavalee *Vocabulary*

ਨਾਨਕੇ ਪਿੰਡ	naanke pind	*mother's family's village*
ਪਿਆਰ	piaar	*love, affection* (m.)
ਮਿਲਣਾ	milnhaa	*to meet*
ਟਰੈਕਟਰ	taraiktar	*tractor* (m.)
ਚੜੂਣਾ	charhhnhaa	*to climb, to ride*
ਖੇਤ	khet	*land, field* (m.)
ਖੂਹ	khooh	*water well* (m.)
ਪਹਿਲੀ ਵਾਰੀ	pahilee vaaree	*first time*
ਮੱਝ	majhjh	*buffalo* (f.)
ਡਰਨਾ	darnaa	*to be scared*
ਇੱਕ ਦਮ	ikk dam	*immediately, at once*
ਦੌੜ	daurh	*to run*
ਬੰਦਾ	bandaa	*man* (m.)

ਗੰਨਾ	gannaa	sugarcane (m.)
ਗੁੜ	gurh	brown sugar cake (m.)
ਵਾਪਸ	vaapas	return, back to
ਤਾਂ	taan	then
ਰੋਟੀ	rotee	food (lit. unleavened bread which is part of the staple diet of Panjab) (f.)
ਖੁਆਈ	khuaaee	to feed
ਉਸ ਤੋਂ ਬਾਅਦ	us ton baa-a-d	after that
ਵਿਹੜਾ	vihrhaa	courtyard (m.)
ਕਹਾਣੀ	kahaanhee	story (f.)
ਗਰਮ	garam	warm, hot
ਦੁੱਧ	dudhdh	milk (m.)
ਸੌਣਾ	saunhaa	to sleep
ਮਾਹੌਲ	maahaul	atmosphere, environment (m.)

ਅਭਿਆਸ   abhiaas   *Exercises*

After reading the passage and / or listening to the recording, try to do the following exercises.

1 Answer the following questions about the passage.

a ਜਸਪ੍ਰੀਤ ਤੇ ਸਿਮਰਨ ਦੇ ਮਾਮਾ ਜੀ ਕਿਹਨਾਂ ਕੋਲ ਰਹਿੰਦੇ ਹਨ?
jaspreet te simran de maamaa jee kihnaan kol rahinde han?

b ਜਿਹੜਾ ਬੰਦਾ ਖੂਹ ਦੇ ਕੋਲ ਸੀ, ਉਹ ਕੀ ਬਣਾ ਰਿਹਾ ਸੀ?
jihrhaa bandaa khooh de kol see, uh kee banhaa rihaa see?

c ਰੋਟੀ ਖਾਣ ਤੋਂ ਬਾਅਦ ਕੁੜੀਆਂ ਨੇ ਕੀ ਕੀਤਾ?
rotee khaanh ton baa-a-d kurheeaan ne kee keetaa?

d ਸੌਣ ਤੋਂ ਪਹਿਲੇ ਸਾਰਿਆਂ ਨੇ ਕੀ ਪੀਤਾ?
saunh ton pahile saariaan ne kee peetaa?

2 Complete the table.

ਪਿੰਡ		
	khooh	
ਵਿਹੜਾ		
		fields
	gannaa	

ਬੋਲੀ ਬਾਰੇ bolee baare *Language points*

The past tense

You have already been introduced to the simple past tense in Unit 6. Verbs in the simple past tense were shown to agree with the number and gender of the subject. To help you remember, here are examples of the verbs ਆਉਣਾ aaunhaa (*to come*), ਰੋਣਾ ronhaa (*to cry*), ਬੋਲਣਾ bolnhaa (*to speak*), ਹੋਣਾ honhaa (*to be*) and ਦੱਸਣਾ <u>d</u>assnhaa (*to tell*) in their past perfect forms:

Masculine singular	Masculine plural	Feminine singular	Feminine plural	
ਆਇਆ aaiaa	ਆਏ aae	ਆਈ aaee	ਆਈਆਂ aaeeaa<u>n</u>	*came*
ਰੋਇਆ roiaa	ਰੋਏ roe	ਰੋਈ roee	ਰੋਈਆਂ roeeaa<u>n</u>	*cried*
ਬੋਲਿਆ boliaa	ਬੋਲੇ bole	ਬੋਲੀ bolee	ਬੋਲੀਆਂ boleeaa<u>n</u>	*spoke*
ਦੱਸਿਆ <u>d</u>assiaa	ਦੱਸੇ <u>d</u>asse	ਦੱਸੀ <u>d</u>assee	ਦੱਸੀਆਂ <u>d</u>asseeaa<u>n</u>	*told*
ਹੋਇਆ hoiaa	ਹੋਏ hoe	ਹੋਈ hoee	ਹੋਈਆਂ hoeeaa<u>n</u>	*happened*

In the past perfect tenses in Panjabi, all verbs can be categorized into two groups: intransitive and transitive. Intransitive verbs do not rely upon an object to dictate the form of the verb. This literally means that the form of the verb is unchanging except, of course, in relation to the subject of the sentence. Intransitive verbs generally do not take a direct object. Transitive verbs, are those verbs which do take a direct object, and are more flexible. In such cases where an object is present, the ending of the verb will agree with the object. In the examples given above, *cried* and *spoke* are both intransitive verbs, meaning that the act of crying and speaking can stand alone without the requirement of an object. *Told*, on the other hand, can require the presence of an object such as *he told me a story* with *story* being the direct object. The following examples illustrate how the transitive verb is affected by the presence of a direct object:

ਮੈਂ ਕੇਲਾ ਖਾਧਾ	mai<u>n</u> kelaa khaa<u>dh</u>aa	*I ate a banana.*
ਮੈਂ ਕੇਲੇ ਖਾਧੇ	mai<u>n</u> kele khaa<u>dh</u>e	*I ate bananas.*

| ਮੈਂ ਨਾਸ਼ਪਾਤੀ ਖਾਧੀ | main naashpaatee khaa<u>dh</u>ee | *I ate a pear.* |
| ਮੈਂ ਨਾਸ਼ਪਾਤੀਆਂ ਖਾਧੀਆਂ | main naashpaateeaa<u>n</u> khaa<u>dh</u>eeaa<u>n</u> | *I ate pears.* |

You will notice that the first two examples both have the same object, except that the first is singular and the second is plural. Therefore, ਖਾਧਾ khaa<u>dh</u>aa in the first example reflects the singular masculine nature of *banana* and ਖਾਧੇ khaa<u>dh</u>e refers to the plural masculine nature of *bananas*. The third and fourth examples show a similar pattern for the feminine object *pear* with ਖਾਧੀ khaa<u>dh</u>ee and ਖਾਧੀਆਂ khaa<u>dh</u>eeaa<u>n</u> corresponding to the respective singular and plural forms.

The main point to remember when using verbs in the past tense is that some verbs are subject inflected (meaning that they change according to the subject), while others are object inflected (i.e. change according to the object of the sentence). However, some verbs can be in either category. There are transitive verbs which behave like intransitive verbs when there is no direct object present, such as ਸਮਝਨਾ samajhnhaa (*to understand*) and ਪੜੂਨਾ parhhnaa (*to read*). There are also intransitive verbs which can behave as transitive verbs, such as ਕਹਿਣਾ kahinhaa (*to say*), ਪੁੱਛਣਾ pu<u>chchh</u>nhaa (*to ask*), and ਥੁੱਕਣਾ <u>th</u>ukknhaa (*to spit*). However, there is no convention for knowing when a verb is intransitive or transitive apart from the nature of the verb and the presence of an object.

The agentive postposition ਨੇ 'ne'

Nearly all transitive verbs in the past tenses are affected by the postposition **ne** ਨੇ which directs the action of the verb towards the subject. In usual circumstances ਨੇ follows the subject of the sentence. However, in the example ਮੈਂ ਨਾਸ਼ਪਾਤੀ ਖਾਧੀ **main naashpaatee khaa<u>dh</u>ee**, ਨੇ **ne** is implicit and does not appear. The use of ਨੇ **ne** is illustrated in the table. Note that for some pronouns in the third person, the use of ਨੇ **ne** is optional as is indicated in parentheses.

Pronouns in the ਨੇ construction

Direct pronouns			In the ਨੇ (ne) construction	
1st person	ਮੈਂ	mai<u>n</u>	ਮੈਂ	*no change*
	ਅਸੀਂ	asee<u>n</u>	ਅਸੀਂ	*no change*
2nd person	ਤੁਸੀਂ	<u>t</u>usee<u>n</u>	ਤੁਸੀਂ	*no change*
	ਤੂੰ	<u>t</u>oo<u>n</u>	ਤੂੰ	*no change*

3rd person	ਇਹ (sing.)	ih	ਇਹ ਨੇ	ਨੇ ne *required*
	ਇਸ (sing.)	is	ਇਸ (ਨੇ)	ਨੇ ne *optional*
	ਉਹ (sing.)	uh	ਉਹ ਨੇ	ਨੇ ne *required*
	ਉਸ (sing.)	us	ਉਸ (ਨੇ)	ਨੇ ne *optional*
	ਇਹ (formal, plural)	ih	ਇਹਨਾਂ ihnaan (ਨੇ)	ਨੇ ne *optional*
	ਉਹ (formal, plural)	uh	ਉਹਨਾਂ uhnaan (ਨੇ)	ਨੇ ne *optional*
	ਕੋਣ (sing.)	kaunh	ਕਿਸ kis (ਨੇ)	ਨੇ ne *optional*
	ਕੋਣ (formal, plural)	kaunh	ਕਿਹਨਾਂ kihnaan (ਨੇ)	ਨੇ ne *optional*

In cases where no direct object is present or the direct object is already followed by a postposition, the verb is made 'neutral'. The neutral verb is always in the singular masculine form. Most commonly, the postposition ਨੂੰ **noon** follows the object of the sentence, thus making the verb neutral. Here are some examples of transitive verbs in the ਨੇ, **ne** construction as well as with the postposition ਨੂੰ **noon**:

ਮੈਂ ਦਰਖ਼ਤ* ਨੂੰ ਕਟਿਆ	main darakhat noon katiaa	*I cut the tree.*
ਮੈਂ ਟਾਹਣੀ* ਨੂੰ ਕਟਿਆ	main taahanhee noon katiaa	*I cut the branch.*
ਮੈਂ ਦਰਖ਼ਤਾਂ* ਨੂੰ ਕਟਿਆ	main darakhataan noon katiaa	*I cut the trees.*
ਮੈਂ ਟਾਹਣੀਆਂ* ਨੂੰ ਕਟਿਆ	main taahanheeaan noon katiaa	*I cut the branches.*

*ਦਰਖ਼ਤ is grammatically masculine
*ਟਾਹਣੀ is grammatically feminine

Here are more examples of the use of transitive verbs:

ਅਮਰ ਨੇ ਕਹਾਣੀ ਸੁਣੀ	amar ne kahaanhee sunhee	*Amar heard the story.*
ਅਮਰ ਨੇ ਤਿੰਨ ਕਹਾਣੀਆਂ ਸੁਣੀਆਂ	amar ne tinn kahaanheeaan sunheeaan	*Amar heard three stories.*
ਅਮਰ ਨੇ ਸੁਣਿਆ	amar ne sunhiaa	*Amar heard.*

ਅਮਰ ਨੇ ਇਸ ਕਹਾਣੀ ਨੂੰ ਸੁਣਿਆ	amar ne is kahaanhee noon sunhiaa	*Amar heard this story.*
ਅਮਰ ਨੇ ਇਹਨਾਂ ਕਹਾਣੀਆਂ ਨੂੰ ਸੁਣਿਆ	amar ne ihnaan kahaanheeaan noon sunhiaa	*Amar heard these stories.*

You will recall from Unit 8 that pronouns and nouns change to their oblique forms when followed by postpositions. Taking the same examples: ਇਹ ਕਹਾਣੀ **ih kahaanhee** *this story* changes to ਇਸ ਕਹਾਣੀ **is kahaanhee** in the sentence:

ਅਮਰ ਨੇ ਇਸ ਕਹਾਣੀ ਨੂੰ ਸੁਣਿਆ	**amar ne is kahaanhee noon sunhiaa**	*Amar heard this story.*

This story in the English is identical in both examples. In Panjabi, however, *this story* in the first example is in the direct form while *this story* in the second example is in the oblique form.

Many verbs can fall within either category of transitive or intransitive making the past tense in Panjabi less straightforward than, say, the present or future tenses which are not reliant upon the object's relationship with the verb. For instance, the verb ਕਰਨਾ **karnaa** *to do* and ਸਮਝਣਾ **samjhnhaa** *to understand* can act as intransitive verbs when not followed by an object or can behave as transitive verbs when an object is present. The same is true for ਪੜ੍ਹਨਾ **parhhnaa** which can take the ਨੇ **ne** construction when used in the sense *to read* or can stand alone when meaning *to study*. Often, ਨੇ **ne** can be invisible, meaning that the sentence may be dictated by the ਨੇ **ne** construction but that it is simply understood. This, however, occurs with only a few verbs, so you should be cautious when applying these rules. The best way of illustrating transitive verbs with ਨੇ **ne** is through examples:

ਅਸੀਂ ਕਿਰਨ ਨੂੰ ਅੰਮ੍ਰਿਤਸਰ ਵੇਖਿਆ	**aseen kiran (f.) noon amritsar vekhiaa**	*We saw Kiran in Amritsar.*
ਅਸੀਂ ਤਾਰਿਕ ਨੂੰ ਲੰਡਨ ਵੇਖਿਆ	**aseen taarik (m.) noon landan vekhiaa**	*We saw Tariq in London.*

Note that the verb did not change in these examples even though the gender of the object does because of the presence of ਨੂੰ **noon**. In the following examples you will see how the ending of the verb in the past tense corresponds with the gender and number of the objects:

ਉਹਨਾਂ (ਨੇ) ਬਹੁਤ ਕੇਲੇ ਖਾਧੇ	uhnaa<u>n</u> ne bahu<u>t</u> kele khaa<u>dh</u>e	*They ate many bananas.*
ਤੁਸੀਂ ਇਹ ਕਮੀਜ਼ਾਂ ਕਿਉਂ ਖ਼ਰੀਦੀਆਂ ?	<u>t</u>useen ih kameezaa<u>n</u> kiu<u>n</u> <u>kh</u>areedeeaa<u>n</u>?	*Why did you buy these shirts?*
ਕਿਸ ਨੇ ਗੱਡੀ ਨੂੰ ਸਾਫ਼ ਕੀਤਾ ਸੀ ?	kis ne gaddee noo<u>n</u> saaf kee<u>t</u>aa see?	*Who cleaned the car?*
ਰਾਮ ਨੇ ਮੇਰੀ ਗੱਲ ਸਮਝੀ	raam ne meree gall samajhee	*Ram understood what I said.*

Compound verbs

Compound verbs are formed when the stem of a main verb is followed by an auxiliary verb. These constructions are very common in Panjabi and are the equivalent of two verbs coming together in English such as in the expression *to go to sleep*. In Unit 9 you learned how to express *can* and *already* through the uses of ਸਕਣਾ **saknhaa** and ਚੁਕਣਾ **chuknhaa** which, when combined with other verb stems, form compound verb constructions. In a similar way, other verbs are used as auxiliary verbs to emphasize or give an added meaning to the verb stem. Whereas ਸਕਣਾ **saknhaa** and ਚੁਕਣਾ **chuknhaa** have very specific meanings, this is not the case for most other compound constructions which are less simple to define. A helpful hint regarding compound verbs, however, is that the auxiliary verb loses its own meaning when it accompanies the stem of another verb. Often it is the context of the sentence and the meaning of the main verb that will tell you about the emphasis that the auxiliary verb has added.

The most common auxiliary verbs are ਜਾਣਾ **jaanhaa** (*to go*), ਦੇਣਾ <u>d</u>enhaa (*to give*) and ਲੈਣਾ **lainhaa** (*to take*). When an intransitive verb is the main verb, ਜਾਣਾ **janhaa** (*to go*) is generally used to give the sense of completeness or change. To show how the meaning of the main verb is affected by the auxiliary ending, here are a few examples:

ਆਉਣਾ	aaunhaa	*to come*	ਆ ਜਾਣਾ	aa jaanhaa	*to arrive*
ਸੌਣਾ	saunhaa	*to sleep*	ਸੌਣ ਜਾਣਾ	saunh jaanhaa	*to go to sleep*
ਖਾਣਾ	khaanhaa	*to eat*	ਖਾ ਜਾਣਾ	khaa jaanhaa	*to eat up*
ਪੀਣਾ	peenhaa	*to drink*	ਪੀ ਜਾਣਾ	pee jaanhaa	*to drink up*

The following sentences illustrate how these compound verbs with **jaanhaa** (*to go*) can be used in sentences:

ਚਾਚੀ ਪਿੰਡ ਤੋਂ ਆ ਗਈ ਸੀ	chaachee pind ton aa gaee see	*Aunt had come from the village.*
ਮੈਂ ਬਾਰ੍ਹਾਂ ਵਜੇ ਸੌਂ ਜਾਵਾਂ ਗੀ	main baar-h-aan vaje saunh jaavaan gee	*I will go to sleep at 12 o'clock.*
ਉਹ ਐਨਾ ਭੁੱਖਾ ਸੀ ਕਿ ਉਹ ਸਭ ਕੁਝ ਖਾ ਗਿਆ!	uh ainaa bhukhkhaa see ki uh sabh kujh khaa giaa!	*He was so hungry that he ate everything up!*
ਬਿੱਲੀ ਸਾਰਾ ਦੁੱਧ ਪੀ ਗਈ	billee saaraa dudhdh pee gaee	*The cat drank (up) all the milk.*

Of the transitive verbs, the auxiliaries of **ਲੈਣਾ lainhaa** (*to take*) and **ਦੇਣਾ denhaa** (*to give*) are the most common. The effects of each upon the main verb can be best described in terms of the direction of the action. **ਲੈਣਾ lainhaa** tends to give the sense that the action is being done towards or for the benefit of the performer while **ਦੇਣਾ denhaa** indicates that the action is being directed away from the performer. The difference between the two can often be quite subtle:

ਇਹ ਕਿਤਾਬ ਰੱਖ ਲੈ	ih kitaab rakhkh lai	*Keep this book (with you).*
ਇਹ ਕਿਤਾਬ ਮੇਜ਼ ਤੇ ਰੱਖ ਦੇ	ih kitaab mez te rakhkh de	*Put this book on the table.*
ਉਹ ਪੰਜਾਬੀ ਪੜ੍ਹ ਲੈਂਦੀ ਹੈ	uh panjaabee parhh laindee hai	*She reads Panjabi.*
ਉਹ ਚਿੱਠੀ ਪੜ੍ਹ ਦੇਂਦੀ ਹੈ	uh chiththee parhh dendee hai	*She reads out the letter.*

ਲੈਣਾ lainhaa and **ਦੇਣਾ denhaa**, in addition to directing the action, also add a feeling of completeness:

ਮੈਂ ਕੰਮ ਜਲਦੀ ਕਰ ਲਿਆ ਸੀ	main kanm jaldee kar liaa see	*I [had] finished the job quickly.*
ਸਿਮਰਨ ਨੇ ਜੁੱਤੀ ਖ਼ਰੀਦ ਲਈ	simran ne juttee khareed laee	*Simran bought shoes.*
ਡਾਕਟਰ ਨੇ ਸਿਮਰਨ ਨੂੰ ਦਵਾਈ ਦੇ ਦਿੱਤੀ	daaktar ne simran noon davaaee de dittee	*The doctor gave Simran medicine.*
ਟੈਕਸੀ ਵਾਲੇ ਨੇ ਸਾਮਾਨ ਗੱਡੀ ਵਿਚ ਰੱਖ ਦਿੱਤਾ	taiksee vaale ne samaan gaddee vich rakhkh dittaa	*The taxi driver put the luggage in the car.*

The particle -ਕੇ 'ke'

The particle -ਕੇ ke resembles the conjunction *and* in English. In English two verbs can be joined by *and* such as in the case *he came (home) and ate*. In Panjabi the first verb is followed by -ਕੇ ke to denote that the first action occurred first. In this example, the literal meaning would be *having come (home), he ate*. Therefore, the literal meaning of -ਕੇ ke is *having*. In the passage from Jaspreet's diary, you will recall that she says *Simran saw a buffalo and ran away*. In Panjabi this would be translated as: *Having seen a buffalo, Simran ran away*. Here are a few more examples of how -ਕੇ ke is used:

ਰਾਜਿੰਦਰ ਨੂੰ ਬੁਲਾ ਕੇ ਉਹ ਨੂੰ ਦੱਸੋ	raajindar noon bulaa ke uh noon dasso	*Call Rajinder and tell him.*
ਕੰਮ ਖ਼ਤਮ ਕਰ ਕੇ ਤੂੰ ਘਰ ਨੂੰ ਚਲੇ ਜਾ	kanm khatam kar ke toon ghar noon chale jaa	*After finishing work, go home.*
ਦੁਕਾਨ ਤੇ ਜਾ ਕੇ ਮੱਖਣ ਲਿਆਓ	dukaan te jaa ke makhkhanh liaao	*Go to the shop and bring some butter.*

-ਕੇ ke can be used with more idiomatic expressions as well, which are often not easily translated into English but which are useful ways of expressing what might otherwise be lengthy sentences. Here are some examples of the usage of -ਕੇ ke in idiomatic phrases as well as in adverbial expressions (i.e. expressions which describe actions) which will help you to understand its functions better.

Adverbial phrases

ਅੱਗੇ ਚਲ ਕੇ	agge chal ke	*from now on, in the future*
ਸੋਚ ਕੇ	soch ke	*after thinking*
ਹੱਸ ਕੇ	hass ke	*laughingly*
ਡਰ ਕੇ	dar ke	*being scared*

Idiomatic uses of -ਕੇ

ਚੰਡੀਗੜ੍ਹ ਤੋਂ ਹੋ ਕੇ ਜਾਣਾ	chandeegarh ton hoke jaanhaa	*Go via Chandigarh.*
ਪਿਤਾ ਜੀ ਨੇ ਮੈਨੂੰ ਜਾਣ ਕੇ ਨਹੀਂ ਦੱਸਿਆ	pitaa jee ne mainoon jaanh ke naheen dassiaa	*Father purposely didn't tell me.*
ਇੱਕ ਘਰ ਛੱਡ ਕੇ ਸਾਡਾ ਹੈ	ikk ghar chadd ke saadaa hai	*The house after the next one is ours.*

The particle -ਕੇ ke is also used when expressing the time of the day. You will recall from Unit 7 that the verb ਵੱਜਣਾ vajjnhaa (to strike, to chime) is used to tell the time. The times of quarter past, half past, quarter to, and times on the hour which are regularly used were illustrated to you in this unit. When you wish to show that the time is a few minutes before or after the hour, then the particle -ਕੇ ke is combined with ਵੱਜਣਾ vajjnhaa. Therefore, ਵਜ ਕੇ vaj ke means having struck. ਵਜਣ ਵਿਚ vajnh vich means before the hour. The following examples illustrate how -ਕੇ ke and ਵਿਚ vich are used to express such times:

ਪੰਜ ਵਜਣ ਵਿਚ ਦੋ ਮਿੰਟ ਹਨ	panj vajanh vich do mint han	It is two minutes to five.
ਪੰਜ ਵਜ ਕੇ ਦੋ ਮਿੰਟ ਹਨ	panj vaj ke do mint han	It is two minutes past five.
ਬਾਰ੍ਹਾਂ ਵਜਣ ਵਿਚ ਅਠਾਰ੍ਹਾਂ ਮਿੰਟ ਹਨ	baar-haan vajanh vich athaar-haan mint han	It is 18 minutes to 12.
ਬਾਰ੍ਹਾਂ ਵਜ ਕੇ ਅਠਾਰ੍ਹਾਂ ਮਿੰਟ ਹਨ	baar-haan vaj ke athaar-haan mint han	It is 18 minutes past 12.

ਵਿਆਖਿਆ   viaakhiaa   *Commentary*

Rural Panjab

Panjab's predominantly rural society has had a profound impact on the development of the Panjabi language. On the one hand there is a great deal of local diversity, such that dialects and pronunciations can change over small distances. On the other, there is a richness in the language which comes from rural idioms. Conversations in Panjabi are often peppered with these sayings and it is difficult to relate them without some knowledge of village life. As with all rural settings, day-to-day life in a village is dominated by the agricultural economy which is in turn related to the changing seasons.

Panjab is renowned in the whole of India as the 'bread basket' of the country. In the 1970s the region benefited enormously from the introduction of genetically engineered wheat seeds which resulted in much larger crop returns. This phenomenon has been called the 'Green Revolution' and resulted in Panjab having the greatest per capita income of all the states in the Indian Union.

ਅਭਿਆਸ   abhiaas   *Exercises*

After reading the dialogue and / or listening to the recording, try to do the following exercises.

1 Use the particle -ਕੇ 'ke' to express the sentences in Panjabi.

a Having eaten, we all went to sleep.
b Go to the shop and bring some milk.
c After completing the task, go home.
d Go to Amritsar via Jalandhar.

2 Insert the appropriate past tense forms.

Write the appropriate past form of the verbs given to you in parentheses. Remember the rules about transitive and intransitive verbs!

a ਮੈਂ ਦੋ ਕੇਲੇ _____ (ਖਾਣਾ)
  main do kele _____ (khaanhaa)

b ਬੱਚੀ _____ (ਰੋਣਾ)
  bachchee _____ (ronhaa)

c ਨਾਨੀ ਜੀ ਨੇ ਸਾਨੂੰ ਕਹਾਣੀ _____ (ਸੁਣਾਉਣਾ)
  naanee jee ne saanoon kahaanhee _____ (sunhaaunhaa)

d ਮੈਂ ਦਰਖ਼ਤ ਨੂੰ _____ (ਕਟਣਾ)
  main darakhat noon _____ (katnhaa)

▶ 3 Responses in Panjabi

The following is a conversation between you and your aunt. You are visiting her in London and she is asking you about your trip to central London today. Respond to her questions in Panjabi with the answers given to you in English.

Aunt	ਤੁਹਾਡੀ ਲੰਡਨ ਦੀ ਸੈਰ ਕਿਵੇਂ ਰਹੀ ? tuhaadee landan dee sair kiven rahee?
You	**It was very nice. I went to Trafalgar Square and saw Nelson's Column. I also went to Buckingham Palace.**
Aunt	ਤੁਸੀਂ ਹੋਰ ਕੀ ਕੀਤਾ ? tuseen hor kee keetaa?
You	**I went to Oxford Circus and bought some clothes.**
Aunt	ਤੁਸੀਂ ਕੀ ਕੁਝ ਖਾਧਾ ? tuseen kee kujh khaadhaa?

You	I only ate some pizza.
Aunt	ਉਮੀਦ ਹੈ ਕਿ ਤੁਹਾਨੂੰ ਭੁੱਖ ਲੱਗੀ ਹੈ ਕਿਉਂ ਕਿ ਅੱਜ ਅਸੀਂ ਮੱਛੀ ਤੇ ਚਿਪਸ ਬਣਾਏ ਹਨ। ਇਹ ਹੈ ਇੰਗਲੈਂਡ ਦੀ ਖ਼ਾਸ ਸੁਗਾਤ!
	umeed hai ki tuhaanoon bhukhkh laggee hai kiun ki ajj aseen machchee te chips banhaae han. ih hai inglaind dee khaas sugaat!

4 Name the numbered objects in Panjabi.

1 water well   2 buffalo   3 sugarcane   4 house   5 fields

ਹਰਿਮੰਦਰ ਸਾਹਿਬ
harmandar saahib
the Golden Temple

In this unit you will learn:
- how to make enquiries and collect information
- how to buy train tickets
- about the Golden Temple

▶ 1 *Shan-e-Panjab*

ਗੱਲ ਬਾਤ ੧ ਸ਼ਾਨੇ ਪੰਜਾਬ

gall baat 1 shaane panjaab

Both sisters are at Jalandhar railway station early in the morning. After visiting their relatives, they are now on their way to pay homage to Harmandar Sahib, the Golden Temple in Amritsar.

ਜਸਪ੍ਰੀਤ	ਅੰਮ੍ਰਿਤਸਰ ਜਾਣ ਲਈ ਸਭ ਤੋਂ ਚੰਗੀ ਗੱਡੀ ਕਿਹੜੀ ਹੈ ?
ਟਿਕਟ ਬਾਬੂ	ਸ਼ਾਨੇ ਪੰਜਾਬ। ਬਹੁਤ ਸਾਰੇ ਸੈਲਾਨੀ ਇਸ ਗੱਡੀ ਵਿਚ ਸਫਰ ਕਰਦੇ ਹਨ।
ਜਸਪ੍ਰੀਤ	ਅਸੀਂ ਦੋਨੋਂ ਅੱਜ ਜਾਣਾ ਚਾਹੁੰਦੀਆਂ ਹਾਂ। ਕੀ ਸਾਨੂੰ ਫਰਸਟ ਕਲਾਸ ਵਿਚ ਸੀਟ ਮਿਲ ਜਾਏ ਗੀ ?
ਟਿਕਟ ਬਾਬੂ	ਕੀ ਤੁਹਾਨੂੰ ਵਾਪਸੀ ਟਿਕਟ ਚਾਹੀਦੀ ਹੈ ਜਾਂ ਇੱਕ ਪਾਸੇ ਦੀ ?
ਸਿਮਰਨ	ਇੱਕ ਪਾਸੇ ਦੀ। ਗੱਡੀ ਕਿੰਨੇ ਵਜੇ ਚਲਦੀ ਹੈ ?
ਟਿਕਟ ਬਾਬੂ	ਗੱਡੀ ਗਿਆਰਾਂ ਵਜੇ ਸਵੇਰੇ ਚਲਦੀ ਹੈ, ਅਤੇ ਢਾਈ ਵਜੇ ਬਾਅਦ ਦੁਪਹਿਰ ਨੂੰ ਤੁਹਾਨੂੰ ਅੰਮ੍ਰਿਤਸਰ ਪਹੁੰਚਾ ਦੇਂਦੀ ਹੈ।
ਸਿਮਰਨ	ਅੱਛਾ, ਸਾਨੂੰ ਦੋ ਟਿਕਟਾਂ ਦੇ ਦੇਵੋ।
ਟਿਕਟ ਬਾਬੂ	ਨਵੀਆਂ ਥਾਂਵਾਂ ਦੇਖਣਾ ਚੰਗੀ ਗੱਲ ਹੈ। ਇਹ ਹਨ ਤੁਹਾਡੀਆਂ ਦੋ ਟਿਕਟਾਂ।
ਜਸਪ੍ਰੀਤ	ਧੰਨਵਾਦ।
ਟਿਕਟ ਬਾਬੂ	ਸੁਰੱਖਿਅਤ ਸਫ਼ਰ ਲਈ ਸ਼ੁਭ ਇਛਾਵਾਂ।

Jaspreet	*Which is the best train to Amritsar?*
Booking clerk	*The Shan-e-Panjab [the pride of Panjab]. A lot of tourists travel on this train.*
Jaspreet	*The two of us want to go today. Will we be able to get a seat in first class?*
Booking clerk	*Do you want return or single?*
Simran	*Single. What time does the train leave?*
Booking clerk	*The train leaves at eleven in the morning and gets you to Amritsar at 2.30 in the afternoon.*
Simran	*Okay, can we have [lit. give us] two tickets.*
Booking clerk	*It is good to see new places. Here are your two tickets.*
Jaspreet	*Thanks.*
Booking clerk	*Best wishes for a safe journey.*

ਸ਼ਬਦਾਵਲੀ   **shabdaavalee**   *Vocabulary*

ਗੱਡੀ	gaddee	automobile, train (f.)
ਬਹੁਤ ਸਾਰੇ	bahut saare	a lot, many
ਸੈਲਾਨੀ	sailaanee	tourists (m. / f.)
ਸਫ਼ਰ ਕਰਨਾ	safar karnaa	to travel
ਮਿਲ ਜਾਣਾ	mil jaanhaa	to get, to receive
ਬਾਅਦ ਦੁਪਹਿਰ	baa-a-d dupahlr	afternoon
ਪਹੁੰਚਾ ਦੇਣਾ	pahunchaa denhaa	to deliver, to cause to arrive
ਸੁਰੱਖਿਅਤ ਸਫ਼ਰ	surakhkhiat safar	safe journey
ਸ਼ੁਭ ਇਛਾਵਾਂ	shubh ichaavaan	best wishes

ਅਭਿਆਸ   **abhiaas**   *Exercises*

After reading the dialogue and / or listening to the recording, try to do the following exercises.

1 Identify the speaker.

The following phrases have been taken from the dialogue. Identify who said each of the phrases.

a ਬਹੁਤ ਸਾਰੇ ਸੈਲਾਨੀ ਇਸ ਗੱਡੀ ਵਿਚ ਸਫ਼ਰ ਕਰਦੇ ਹਨ।   _____

b ਅੰਮ੍ਰਿਤਸਰ ਜਾਣ ਲਈ ਸਭ ਤੋਂ ਚੰਗੀ ਗੱਡੀ ਕਿਹੜੀ ਹੈ ?   _____

c ਨਵੀਆਂ ਥਾਂਵਾਂ ਦੇਖਣਾ ਚੰਗੀ ਗੱਲ ਹੈ।   _____

d ਗੱਡੀ ਕਿੰਨੇ ਵਜੇ ਚਲਦੀ ਹੈ ?   _____

e ਕੀ ਸਾਨੂੰ ਫ਼ਰਸਟ ਕਲਾਸ ਵਿਚ ਸੀਟ ਮਿਲ ਜਾਏ ਗੀ ?   _____

2 Rewrite in the correct word order.

a ਅਸੀਂ ਹਾਂ ਜਾਣਾ ਅੱਜ ਚਾਹੁੰਦੀਆਂ

b ਹੈ ਗੱਲ ਚੰਗੀ ਦੇਖਣਾ ਥਾਂਵਾਂ ਨਵੀਆਂ

c ਇਹ ਟਿਕਟਾਂ ਦੋ ਹਨ ਤੁਹਾਡੀਆਂ

▶ 2 *The Golden Temple*

ਗੱਲ ਬਾਤ ੨ ਹਰਿਮੰਦਰ ਸਾਹਿਬ

gall baat 2 harmandar saahib

Simran and Jaspreet are visiting the Golden Temple in Amritsar. They are accompanied by a guide provided by the temple management committee.

ਗਾਇਡ	ਸਿੱਖਾਂ ਦੇ ਚੌਥੇ ਗੁਰੂ, ਰਾਮਦਾਸ ਜੀ ਨੇ ਅੰਮ੍ਰਿਤਸਰ ਸ਼ਹਿਰ ਵਸਾਇਆ ਸੀ ਅਤੇ ਪੰਜਵੇਂ ਗੁਰੂ, ਅਰਜਨ ਦੇਵ ਜੀ ਨੇ ਹਰਿਮੰਦਰ ਸਾਹਿਬ ਬਣਵਾਇਆ ਸੀ ।
ਸਿਮਰਨ	ਅੰਮ੍ਰਿਤਸਰ ਦਾ ਅਰਥ ਕੀ ਹੈ ?
ਗਾਇਡ	ਇਸ ਦਾ ਲਫ਼ਜ਼ੀ ਅਰਥ ਹੈ: ਅੰਮ੍ਰਿਤ ਦਾ ਸਰੋਵਰ ।
ਜਸਪ੍ਰੀਤ	ਹਰਿਮੰਦਰ ਸਾਹਿਬ ਨੂੰ ਸੁਨਹਿਰੀ ਮੰਦਰ ਕਿਉਂ ਕਿਹਾ ਜਾਂਦਾ ਹੈ ?
ਗਾਇਡ	ਕਿਉਂ ਕਿ ਗੁੰਬਦਾਂ ਤੇ ਬਹੁਤ ਸਾਰਾ ਸੋਨਾ ਲੱਗਾ ਹੋਇਆ ਹੈ । ਇਹ ਮਹਾਰਾਜਾ ਰਣਜੀਤ ਸਿੰਘ ਨੇ ਲੱਗਵਾਇਆ ਸੀ ।
ਸਿਮਰਨ	ਲਗਾਤਾਰ ਹੋ ਰਿਹਾ ਕੀਰਤਨ ਮਨ ਨੂੰ ਸ਼ਾਂਤੀ ਦੇਂਦਾ ਹੈ ਅਤੇ ਸਾਰਾ ਮਾਹੌਲ ਸਵਰਗ ਵਰਗਾ ਹੈ ।
ਗਾਇਡ	ਇਸ ਕਰ ਕੇ ਦਰਸ਼ਕ ਨਾ ਕੇਵਲ ਭਾਰਤ ਤੋਂ ਇੱਥੇ ਆਉਂਦੇ ਹਨ ਬਲਕਿ ਸਾਰੀ ਦੁਨੀਆਂ ਤੋਂ ਆਉਂਦੇ ਹਨ ।

Guide	*The town of Amritsar was founded by the fourth Guru of the Sikhs, Ram Das, and the fifth Guru Arjan Dev had Harmandar Sahib built.*
Simran	*What does the word Amritsar mean?*
Guide	*The literal meaning is 'a pool of nectar'.*
Jaspreet	*Why is the Harmandar Sahib called the Golden Temple?*
Guide	*Because the domes are covered in a lot of gold. This gold was put on by Maharaja Ranjit Singh.*
Simran	*The continuous recitation of religious hymns gives peace of mind and the entire atmosphere is heavenly.*
Guide	*That is why visitors come here not only from India but from all over the world.*

ਸ਼ਬਦਾਵਲੀ　　**shabdaavalee**　　*Vocabulary*

ਸਿੱਖਾਂ ਦੇ ਚੌਥੇ ਗੁਰੂ	sikhkhaan de chauthe guroo	*of the Sikhs fourth Guru* (m.)

ਸ਼ਹਿਰ	shahir	*city* (m.)
ਵਸਾਉਣਾ	vasaaunhaa	*to establish, to found*
ਪੰਜਵਾਂ	panjvaan	*fifth*
ਬਣਵਾਉਣਾ	banhvaaunhaa	*to get built*
ਅਰਥ	arth	*meaning*
ਲਫ਼ਜ਼ੀ	lafzee	*literal*
ਅੰਮ੍ਰਿਤ	anmrit	*nectar, holy water* (m.)
ਸਰੋਵਰ	sarovar	*pool* (m.)
ਹਰਿਮੰਦਰ ਸਾਹਿਬ	harmandar saahib	*Golden Temple* (m.)
ਸੁਨਹਿਰੀ	sunahiree	*golden*
ਕਿਉਂ	kiun	*why*
ਕਿਹਾ ਜਾਂਦਾ ਹੈ ।	kihaa jaandaa hai	*is said, is called*
ਕਿਉਂ ਕਿ	kiun ki	*because*
ਗੁੰਬਦ	gunbad	*dome* (m.)
ਸੋਨਾ	sonaa	*gold* (m.)
ਲੱਗਣਾ	laggnhaa	*to be covered, laden*
ਲੱਗਵਾਉਣਾ	laggvaaunhaa	*to get covered*
ਲਗਾਤਾਰ	lagaataar	*continuously*
ਕੀਰਤਨ	keertan	*singing of hymns* (m.)
ਮਨ	man	*mind* (m.)
ਸ਼ਾਂਤੀ	shaantee	*peace* (f.)
ਦੇਣਾ	denhaa	*to give*
ਸਾਰਾ ਮਾਹੌਲ	saaraa maahaul	*whole atmosphere* (m.)
ਸਵਰਗ	savarag	*heaven* (m.)
ਵਰਗਾ	vargaa	*like* (v.)
ਇਸ ਕਰ ਕੇ	is kar ke	*that's why*
ਦਰਸ਼ਕ	darshak	*visitors* (m. / f.)
ਨਾ ਕੇਵਲ	naa keval	*not only*
ਬਲਕਿ	balki	*but also*
ਦੁਨੀਆਂ	duneeaan	*world* (f.)

ਅਭਿਆਸ   abhiaas   *Exercises*

After reading the dialogue and / or listening to the recording, try to do the following exercises.

1 Matching

Match the questions with the appropriate answers.

ਸਵਾਲ **savaal** *question*   ਜਵਾਬ **javaab** *answer*

a ਅੰਮ੍ਰਿਤਸਰ ਦਾ ਅਰਥ ਕੀ ਹੈ ?   i ਛੇਵੇ ਗੁਰੂ ਜੀ ਨੇ ।

b ਹਰਿਮੰਦਰ ਸਾਹਿਬ ਕਿਸ ਨੇ   ii ਅੰਮ੍ਰਿਤ ਦਾ ਸਰੋਵਰ ।
    ਬਣਵਾਇਆ ਸੀ ?

c ਅੰਮ੍ਰਿਤਸਰ ਸ਼ਹਿਰ ਕਿਸ ਨੇ
ਵਸਾਇਆ ਸੀ ?

iii ਮਹਾਰਾਜਾ ਰਣਜੀਤ ਸਿੰਘ ਨੇ ।

d ਗੁੰਬਦਾਂ ਤੇ ਕਿਸ ਨੇ ਸੋਨਾ
ਲਗਵਾਇਆ ਸੀ ?

iv ਪੰਜਵੇਂ ਗੁਰੂ ਜੀ ਨੇ ।

2 Crossword

Complete the crossword in English using the clues given in Panjabi.
Can you figure out what the 'mystery word' is in the shaded boxes?

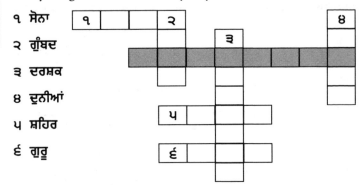

੧ ਸੋਨਾ

੨ ਗੁੰਬਦ

੩ ਦਰਸ਼ਕ

੪ ਦੁਨੀਆਂ

੫ ਸ਼ਹਿਰ

੬ ਗੁਰੂ

ਬੋਲੀ ਬਾਰੇ bolee baare *Language points*

Conjunct verbs

Conjunct verbs have meanings which are specified by the nouns
or adjectives that they include. Conjunct verbs are formed by
combining a noun or adjective with an infinitive (either in its
simple form or as a verb tense). For example, *to clean* in English
merely requires the infinitive. In Panjabi *to clean* would require
two words: ਸਾਫ਼ (*clean*, adjective) and ਕਰਨਾ (*to do*, infinitive).
The adjective specifies the type or nature of the action while the
infinitive directs the action. The most common infinitives used in
conjunct constructions are ਕਰਨਾ (*to do*) and ਹੋਣਾ (*to be*). Here
are some examples of common conjunct verbs using both adjectives and nouns.

With nouns

ਪਿਆਰ ਕਰਨਾ	*to love*
ਪਸੰਦ ਕਰਨਾ	*to like, to prefer*
ਕੰਮ ਕਰਨਾ	*to work*
ਸ਼ੁਰੂ ਕਰਨਾ	*to begin, to commence*
ਮੱਦਦ ਕਰਨਾ	*to help*
ਕੋਸ਼ਿਸ਼ ਕਰਨਾ	*to try*

With adjectives

ਸਾਫ਼ ਕਰਨਾ	to clean
ਖ਼ਤਮ ਕਰਨਾ	to finish, to complete
ਠੀਕ ਕਰਨਾ	to fix, to correct
ਬੰਦ ਕਰਨਾ	to close
ਘੱਟ ਕਰਨਾ	to reduce, to lessen

Here are a few examples to illustrate how conjunct verbs are used:

1 ਕੰਮ ਸਵੇਰੇ ਸ਼ੁਰੂ ਹੁੰਦਾ ਹੈ *Work begins in the morning.*

[ਸ਼ੁਰੂ ਹੋਣਾ *to begin* is an intransitive verb formed with the noun ਕੰਮ.]

2 ਮੈਂ ਤੁਹਾਡੀ ਉਡੀਕ ਕਰਾਂ ਗੀ *I will wait for you.*

[Here ਉਡੀਕ ਕਰਨਾ *to wait* is a transitive verb with ਉਡੀਕ as a noun. This is an example of a verbal expression which is formed exactly as a conjunct verb. However, the noun retains its own meaning and sense.]

3 ਮੇਰਾ ਵਿਆਹ ੧੯੬੪ ਵਿਚ ਹੋਇਆ ਸੀ *I got married in 1964.*

There are some conjunct verbs in which neither ਕਰਨਾ nor ਹੋਣਾ is involved.

ਦਿਖਾਈ ਦੇਣਾ *to be visible*

ਯਾਦ ਆਉਣਾ *to come, to mind*

ਯਾਦ ਰੱਖਣਾ *to bear in mind, to remember*

Causative verbs

Causative verbs are groups of related verbs which share a similar meaning, but which differ in terms of who is carrying out the action. You have already come across such related verbs in Unit 10, in the first dialogue when Simran says to Chaachee:

ਮੈਂ ਹਰ ਕਿਸਮ ਦੇ ਖਾਣੇ ਖਾਧੇ *I ate every type of food.*

In the diary passage in Unit 10, Jaspreet writes:

ਮਾਮੀ ਜੀ ਨੇ ਸਾਨੂੰ ਰੋਟੀ ਖੁਆਈ *Aunt fed us.*

As you can see from these examples, ਖੁਆਣਾ *to feed* and ਖਾਣਾ *to eat* are clearly related to one another. However, the difference lies in who the agent or 'doer' of the action is. Not all verbs are grouped into causative pairs. However, there are a large number of verbs which can be placed into such groups. Causative pairs and groupings are formed by a pattern of adding a suffix (or ending) to the stem of the verb as the action moves further away from the subject:

ਕਰਨਾ	*to do*
ਕਰਾਉਣਾ	*to cause to be done*
ਕਰਵਾਉਣਾ	*to cause to be done by someone else*
ਦੇਖਣਾ	*to see*
ਦਿਖਾਣਾ	*to be shown, to appear*
ਦਿਖਾਉਣਾ	*to show*
ਬਣਨਾ	*to make, to build*
ਬਣਾਉਣਾ	*to be made, to be built*
ਬਣਵਾਉਣਾ	*to have made or built (from/by someone else)*
ਪਕਾਉਣਾ	*to cook*
ਪਕਣਾ	*to be cooked*
ਪਕਵਾਉਣਾ	*to have cooked (by someone else), to cause to be cooked*
ਜਾਗਣਾ	*to wake*
ਜਗਾਉਣਾ	*to awaken*
ਜਗਵਾਉਣਾ	*to cause to wake*

The infinitive as a verbal noun

The simple verb, or infinitive, was explained in Unit 3 as the base of all Panjabi verbs. To refresh your memory, the infinitive of Panjabi verbs is formed by the root of the verb plus the ending -ਣਾ or -ਨਾ. By now you should be familiar with the various tenses of the Panjabi verb. In addition to being the base of all verb tenses, the infinitive can also be used as a noun. You will recall in the first dialogue that the booking clerk says to Jaspreet and Simran:

ਨਵੀਆਂ ਥਾਂਵਾਂ ਦੇਖਣਾ ਚੰਗੀ ਗੱਲ ਹੈ   *It's good seeing [to see] new places.*

Notice that the infinitive **ਦੇਖਣਾ** is not the verb of the sentence (ਹੋਣਾ is the verb) but that it is a verbal noun indicating an action (which behaves as a noun) within the sentence. Here are a few more examples of the infinitive as a verbal noun:

ਜਲਦੀ ਉਠਣਾ ਜ਼ਰੂਰੀ ਹੈ   *Waking up [to wake up] early is necessary.*

ਜ਼ਿਆਦਾ ਬੋਲਣਾ ਚੰਗਾ ਨਹੀਂ ਲੱਗਦਾ   *Talking [to talk] too much doesn't look good.*

ਪੜ੍ਹਨਾ ਸੌਖਾ ਹੈ. ਲਿਖਣਾ ਮੁਸ਼ਕਲ *Reading [to read] is easy, writing [to write] is difficult.*

When the infinitive has an object, it will correspond to the gender and number of that noun. Since the infinitive already has a masculine / singular appearance with the -ਆ ending, it does not change when the object is masculine and singular. However, when the object is masculine / plural it will take the ending -ਏ and when the object is feminine, then the ending changes to -ਈ, -ਈਆਂ if plural. Note the following examples:

ਨੌਕਰੀ ਕਰਨੀ	*working* (to work, to have a job)
ਕਿਤਾਬਾਂ ਪੜ੍ਹਨੀਆਂ	*reading* (to read) *books*
ਖਾਣਾ ਬਣਾਉਣਾ	*cooking* (to cook, to make food)
ਦਰਵਾਜ਼ੇ ਖੋਲ੍ਹਣੇ	*opening* (to open) *the doors*

Like other nouns, the infinitive is also affected by postpositions. The ending of the infinitive in the oblique, therefore, changes to the shortened form as discussed in Unit 8. Here are some examples of verbal nouns in the oblique:

ਮੈਂ ਹਾਲੇ ਬਾਹਰ ਜਾਣ ਨੂੰ ਤਿਆਰ ਨਹੀਂ ਹਾਂ	*I am not ready to go out yet.*
ਉਹਨਾਂ ਦੇ ਇੱਥੇ ਆਉਣ ਨਾਲ ਮੇਰਾ ਸਮਾਂ ਜ਼ਾਇਆ ਹੋ ਗਿਆ	*Their coming here wasted my time.*
ਚਾਹ ਪੀਣ ਦਾ ਮੌਕਾ ਨਹੀਂ ਮਿਲਿਆ	*There wasn't an opportunity to drink tea.*

The passive voice

In English *I said* is in the active voice (i.e. the subject of the verb is directly carrying out the action) and *it was said* is in the passive voice (i.e. the subject is on the receiving end of the action). The same distinction is also true in Panjabi. The passive voice can be formed in two ways. In the first form the passive verb (the participle [see Unit 12] and the form of ਜਾਣਾ) agrees with the subject:

ਲੁਧਿਆਣੇ ਵਿਚ ਪੰਜਾਬੀ ਬੋਲੀ ਜਾਂਦੀ ਹੈ	*Panjabi is spoken in Ludhiana.*
ਕਿਹਾ ਜਾਂਦਾ ਹੈ ਕਿ ਅੰਮ੍ਰਿਤਸਰ ਸਿੱਖਾਂ ਦਾ ਸ਼ਹਿਰ ਹੈ	*It is said that Amritsar is the city of the Sikhs.*
ਕੱਲ੍ਹ ਤਕ ਸਾਰਾ ਕੰਮ ਕਰ ਲਿਆ ਜਾਏਗਾ	*By tomorrow all of the work will be done.*

The passive voice can also be expressed by using the postpositions ਤੋਂ and ਕੋਲੋਂ to indicate by whom the action was done. In this form the verb of the sentence agrees with the object. Note the following examples:

ਕਪ ਮੇਰੇ ਤੋਂ ਟੁੱਟ ਗਿਆ	*The cup was broken by me.*
ਕੁਰਸੀ ਮੇਰੇ ਤੋਂ ਟੁੱਟ ਗਈ	*The chair was broken by me.*
ਗ਼ਲਤੀ ਪਿਤਾ ਜੀ ਕੋਲੋਂ ਹੋਈ	*The mistake was made by father.*

You will recall from earlier in this unit that causative verbs are groups of related verbs. Active intransitive verbs and passive transitive verbs (see Unit 10) can both be used to express the passive voice. For example, the verb ਬਣਨਾ *to be made* and ਬਣਾਉਣਾ *to make* can both be used to give the sense *is / are made.*

ਜੁੱਤੀਆਂ ਇੱਥੇ ਬਣਦੀਆਂ ਹਨ	*Shoes are made here.*
ਜੁੱਤੀਆਂ ਇੱਥੇ ਬਣਾਈਆਂ ਜਾਂਦੀਆਂ ਹਨ	*Shoes are made here.*

ਵਰਗਾ 'vargaa' *like*

The postposition ਵਰਗਾ is used when comparing objects or people with one another in terms of quality, size, colour, etc. You will recall in Dialogue 2 that the guide described the atmosphere of the Golden Temple: ਮਾਹੌਲ ਸਵਰਗ ਵਰਗਾ ਹੈ (*the atmosphere is heavenly* (lit. like heaven)). ਵਰਗਾ is affected by the gender and number of the person or object being likened to, so that the ending of ਵਰਗਾ is masculine, in this example, since *heaven* is a masculine noun. Note in the following examples how the ending of ਵਰਗਾ changes accordingly:

ਇਹ ਕੁੜੀ ਪਰੀ ਵਰਗੀ ਹੈ	*This girl is like a fairy.*
ਇਹ ਕੁੜੀਆਂ ਪਰੀਆਂ ਵਰਗੀਆਂ ਹਨ	*The girls are like fairies.*
ਉਸ ਦਾ ਮਕਾਨ ਮਹੱਲ ਵਰਗਾ ਵੱਡਾ ਹੈ	*His house is big like a palace.*
ਉਹ ਮੁੰਡੇ ਦੈਂਤਾਂ ਵਰਗੇ ਹਨ	*Those boys are like giants.*
ਉਹ ਦਵਾਈ ਖੰਡ ਵਰਗੀ ਮਿੱਠੀ ਹੈ	*That medicine is sweet like sugar.*

There are also other words for describing likeness in Panjabi: ਜਿਹਾ (jihaa), ਵਾਂਗੂੰ (vaangoon) and ਤਰ੍ਹਾਂ (tar-h-aan). These words all appear in this book.

1 Railways

India has one of the largest railway networks in the world. Trains may be both the most luxurious and most uncomfortable way to travel in India, but they are always entertaining. The fastest trains to Panjab from Delhi are the Shan-e-Panjab and the Shatabdi. However, almost all trains heading north from Delhi will pass through Panjab. There is also a train called the Samjota Express which crosses the India–Pakistan border from East to West Panjab at Attari.

2 The city of Amritsar

The city of Amritsar is one of the central towns in the corridor to India for those travelling by land to and from Central Asia. Amritsar is a cultural and religious centre not only in the state of Panjab but also in South Asia. Founded over 400 years ago, Amritsar has become the political and cultural centre of the region and is the religious centre for the Sikh faith. At the time of the annexation of Panjab by the British in 1849, Amritsar was the largest city in Panjab. However, other larger cities such as Lahore and Ludhiana have now surpassed Amritsar in terms of size and economic dynamism since the partition in 1947. Today Amritsar is still the most significant religious centre for the Sikhs, being the home of the Golden Temple, and continues to be regarded as one of the main tourist attractions of Panjab.

ਅਭਿਆਸ   abhiaas   *Exercises*

After reading the dialogue and / or listening to the recording, try to do the following exercises.

1 Fill in the blanks.

a ਜਿਹੜੀ ਗੱਡੀ ਜਲੰਧਰ ਤੋਂ ਅੰਮ੍ਰਿਤਸਰ ਜਾਂਦੀ ਹੈ ਉਸ ਦਾ ਨਾਮ _____ ਹੈ।

b ਬਹੁਤ ਸਾਰੇ _____ ਉਸ ਗੱਡੀ ਵਿਚ _____ ਹਨ।

c ਅੰਮ੍ਰਿਤਸਰ ਦਾ _____ ਅਰਥ ਹੈ: '_____' ।

d ਲਗਾਤਾਰ _____ ਮਨ ਨੂੰ _____ ਦੇਂਦਾ ਹੈ ਅਤੇ ਸਾਰਾ
  ਮਾਹੌਲ_____ਵਰਗਾ ਹੈ।

▶ 2 Answer the following questions in Panjabi.

a Who was the founder of the city of Amritsar?
b What is the meaning of Amritsar?
c Why is Harmandar Sahib known as the Golden Temple?

▶ 3 Listening

You are standing at the ticket counter at Amritsar railway station speaking with the booking clerk about your planned journey to Delhi. Listen to the recording and converse with the ticket master by translating the English sentences given to you.

| You | **I want to go to Delhi today. Which is the best train to Delhi?** |
| **Ticket master** | ਸ਼ੇਤਾਬਦੀ ਐਕਸਪ੍ਰੈਸ ਸਭ ਤੋਂ ਚੰਗੀ ਹੈ। ਬਹੁਤ ਲੋਕ ਉਸ ਵਿਚ ਸਫ਼ਰ ਕਰਦੇ ਹਨ। |

You	Will I be able to get a seat in second class?
Ticket master	ਹਾਂ ਜੀ ਕੀ ਤੁਹਾਨੂੰ ਸਿਰਫ਼ ਇੱਕ ਪਾਸੇ ਦੀ ਟਿਕਟ ਚਾਹੀਦੀ ਹੈ ?
You	No, I want a return ticket. What time does the train leave from Amritsar?
Ticket master	ਗੱਡੀ ਅੰਮ੍ਰਿਤਸਰ ਤੋਂ ਢਾਈ ਵਜੇ ਚਲਦੀ ਹੈ ਅਤੇ ਦਿੱਲੀ ਅੱਠ ਵਜੇ ਰਾਤ ਨੂੰ ਪਹੁੰਚਦੀ ਹੈ।
You	OK, give me one second-class ticket.
Ticket master	ਸੁਰੱਖਿਅਤ ਸਫ਼ਰ ਲਈ ਸ਼ੁਭ ਇਛਾਵਾਂ।

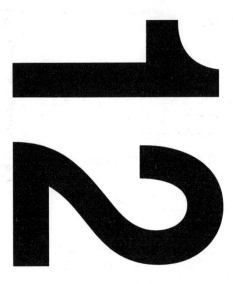

12

ਘਰ ਨੂੰ ਚਿੱਠੀ
ghar noon chiththee

a letter home

In this unit you will learn:
- how to write a letter
- how to express *how did it go?*
- how to talk about where you've visited
- how to construct sentences beginning with *if*

▶ 1 *Changing money*

ਗੱਲ ਬਾਤ ੧ ਪੈਸੇ ਬਦਲਣਾ

gall baat 1 paise badalnhaa

Simran and Jaspreet are in the Air India office in Chandigarh waiting to get their tickets confirmed. While they are there a German tourist, Paul, strikes up a conversation with them.

ਪੋਲ	ਮੇਰਾ ਨਾਮ ਪੋਲ ਹੈ। ਮੈਂ ਜਰਮਨ ਹਾਂ। ਮੈਨੂੰ ਅੰਗਰੇਜ਼ੀ ਨਹੀਂ ਆਉਂਦੀ ਪਰ ਮੈਂ ਪੰਜਾਬੀ ਬੋਲ ਸਕਦਾ ਹਾਂ।
ਸਿਮਰਨ	ਅਸੀਂ ਅਮਰੀਕਨ ਹਾਂ। ਅਸੀਂ ਵੀ ਪੰਜਾਬੀ ਬੋਲ ਸਕਦੀਆਂ ਹਾਂ। ਅਸੀਂ ਤਿੰਨ ਹਫ਼ਤਿਆਂ ਲਈ ਭਾਰਤ ਆਈਆਂ ਹਾਂ। ਸਾਨੂੰ ਬਹੁਤ ਹੀ ਚੰਗਾ ਲੱਗਾ ਹੈ।
ਪੋਲ	ਮੈਂ ਅੱਜ ਹੀ ਅੰਮ੍ਰਿਤਸਰ ਤੋਂ ਵਾਪਸ ਆਇਆ ਹਾਂ। ਜੇ ਅਸੀਂ ਪਹਿਲੇ ਮਿਲਦੇ ਤਾਂ ਅਸੀਂ ਇਕੱਠੇ ਘੁੰਮਦੇ। ਤੁਸੀਂ ਕਿੱਥੇ ਕਿੱਥੇ ਗਾਈਆਂ?
ਜਸਪ੍ਰੀਤ	ਅਸੀਂ ਬਹੁਤ ਜਗ੍ਹਾ ਦੇਖੀਆਂ ਹਨ। ਤੁਹਾਨੂੰ ਕਿਹੜੀ ਜਗ੍ਹਾ ਸਭ ਤੋਂ ਚੰਗੀ ਲੱਗੀ?
ਪੋਲ	ਤਾਜ ਮੱਹਲ ਮੈਂ ਪਹਿਲੇ ਦੇਖ ਚੁਕਾ ਸੀ। ਹੁਣ ਮੈਂ ਹਰਿਮੰਦਰ ਸਾਹਿਬ ਦੇਖਿਆ ਹੈ। ਹਰਿਮੰਦਰ ਸਾਹਿਬ ਦਾ ਕੋਈ ਮੁਕਾਬਲਾ ਨਹੀਂ।
ਜਸਪ੍ਰੀਤ ਤੇ ਸਿਮਰਨ	ਅਸੀਂ ਤੁਹਾਡੇ ਨਾਲ ਸਹਿਮਤ ਹਾਂ।
ਪੋਲ	ਮੈਂ ਪੈਸੇ ਬਦਲਣਾ ਚਾਹੁੰਦਾ ਹਾਂ। ਮੇਰੇ ਕੋਲ ਯੂ.ਐਸ. ਡਾਲਰ ਹਨ। ਮੈਨੂੰ ਕੀ ਕਰਨਾ ਚਾਹੀਦਾ ਹੈ?
ਸਿਮਰਨ	ਤੁਸੀਂ ਕਿਸੇ ਬੈਂਕ ਜਾਓ। ਡਾਲਰ ਦੇ ਕੇ ਰੁਪਏ ਲੈ ਲਵੋ। ਇਹ ਕੰਮ ਸੌਖਾ ਹੈ।
ਪੋਲ	ਜੇ ਮੈਂ ਬੈਂਕ ਦੇ ਰੇਟ ਤੋਂ ਜ਼ਿਆਦਾ ਲੈਣਾ ਚਾਹਵਾਂ?
ਜਸਪ੍ਰੀਤ	. . . ਤਾਂ ਤੁਹਾਨੂੰ ਕਿਸੇ ਦੁਕਾਨਦਾਰ ਨੂੰ ਪੁੱਛਣਾ ਚਾਹੀਦਾ ਹੈ।
ਪੋਲ	ਧੰਨਵਾਦ। ਮੇਰੀ ਵਾਰੀ ਆ ਗਈ ਹੈ। ਉਮੀਦ ਹੈ ਕਿ ਫਿਰ ਮਿਲਾਂ ਗੇ।

Paul	*My name is Paul. I'm German. I don't know any English but I can speak Panjabi.*
Simran	*We are American. We can also speak Panjabi. We've come to India for three weeks. We like it very much.*
Paul	*I have just come from Amritsar today. Had we met before, we could have travelled together. Where have you been?*

Jaspreet	We have seen many places. Which one did you like the most?
Paul	I had already seen the Taj Mahal. Now I have seen Harmandar Sahib. There is no comparison with Harmandar Sahib.
Jaspreet and Simran	We agree with you.
Paul	I want to change some money. I have US dollars. What should I do?
Simran	Go to any bank. Get rupees by giving dollars. This is not difficult to do [lit. an easy task].
Paul	And if I want a higher rate than the bank?
Jaspreet	. . . then you should ask any shopkeeper.
Paul	Thanks. My turn has come now. Hope we'll meet again.

ਸ਼ਬਦਾਵਲੀ **shab_daavalee** *Vocabulary*

ਵਾਪਸ	vaapas	*return, back*
ਜੇ	je	*if*
ਮਿਲਣਾ	milnhaa	*to meet*
ਪਹਿਲੇ	pahile	*before*
ਇਕੱਠੇ	ikaththe	*together* (v.)
ਤਾਂ	_taan_	*then*
ਜਗ੍ਹਾ	jag-h-aa	*place* (f.)
ਦੇਖਣਾ	_dekhnhaa_	*to see*
ਮੁਕਾਬਲਾ	mukaablaa	*comparison, competition* (m.)
ਸਹਿਮਤ	sahima_t_	*agree*
ਬਦਲਣਾ	ba_d_alnhaa	*to change, exchange*
ਕੰਮ	ka_n_m	*job, work, task* (m.)
ਸੌਖਾ	saukhaa	*easy, simple* (v.)
ਉਮੀਦ	umee_d_	*hope* (f.)
ਫਿਰ	phir	*again*

ਅਭਿਆਸ **abhiaas** *Exercises*

After reading the dialogue and / or listening to the recording, try to do the following exercises.

1 True or false?

a ਜਸਪ੍ਰੀਤ ਤੇ ਸਿਮਰਨ ਅਮਰੀਕਨ ਹਨ ਪਰ ਉਹਨਾਂ ਨੂੰ ਪੰਜਾਬੀ ਨਹੀਂ ਆਉਂਦੀ ।   True / False

b ਪੌਲ ਨੇ ਕਿਹਾ ਕਿ ਜੇ ਉਹ ਪਹਿਲੇ ਮਿਲਦੇ ਤਾਂ ਉਹ   True / False
  ਇਕੱਠੇ ਘੁੰਮਦੇ।

c ਜਦੋਂ ਪੌਲ ਨੇ ਦੋਨਾਂ ਭੈਣਾਂ ਨੂੰ ਪੈਸੇ ਬਦਲਣ ਬਾਰੇ   True / False
  ਪੁੱਛਿਆ ਤਾਂ ਉਹਨਾਂ ਨੇ ਜਵਾਬ ਦਿੱਤਾ ਕਿ ਇਹ ਕੰਮ
  ਬਹੁਤ ਮੁਸ਼ਕਲ ਹੈ।

d ਜਸਪ੍ਰੀਤ ਤੇ ਸਿਮਰਨ ਨੇ ਪੌਲ ਨੂੰ ਕਿਹਾ ਕਿ ਜੇ ਉਹ ਬੈਂਕ   True / False
  ਦੇ ਰੇਟ ਤੋਂ ਜ਼ਿਆਦਾ ਲੈਣਾ ਚਾਹੁੰਦਾ ਹੈ ਤਾਂ ਫਿਰ ਕਿਸੇ
  ਦੁਕਾਨਦਾਰ ਨੂੰ ਪੁੱਛਣਾ ਚਾਹੀਦਾ ਹੈ।

2 Fill in the blanks.

a ਪੌਲ _____ ਹੈ ਤੇ ਉਸ ਨੂੰ _____ ਨਹੀਂ ਆਉਂਦੀ ਪਰ ਉਹ
  _____ ਬੋਲ ਸਕਦਾ ਹੈ।

b ਪੌਲ _____ ਪਹਿਲੇ ਦੇਖ ਚੁੱਕਾ ਸੀ।

c ਜਸਪ੍ਰੀਤ, ਸਿਮਰਨ ਤੇ ਪੌਲ _____ ਹਨ ਕਿ ਹਰਿਮੰਦਰ ਸਾਹਿਬ ਦਾ ਕੋਈ
  _____ ਨਹੀਂ।

d ਪੌਲ ਅੱਜ ਹੀ _____ ਤੋਂ ਵਾਪਸ ਆਇਆ ਹੈ।

A letter home   ਘਰ ਨੂੰ ਚਿੱਠੀ   ghar noo<u>n</u> chiththee

ਪਿਆਰੇ ਪਿਤਾ ਤੇ ਮਾਤਾ ਜੀ,   ੪ ਜੁਲਾਈ

ਸਤਿ ਸ੍ਰੀ ਅਕਾਲ

ਸਾਨੂੰ ਉਮੀਦ ਹੈ ਕਿ ਤੁਸੀਂ ਠੀਕ ਠਾਕ ਹੋ। ਅਸੀਂ ਇੱਥੇ ਖੁਸ਼ ਹਾਂ। ਅਸੀਂ ਪਿੰਡ
ਗਈਆਂ ਸੀ ਤੇ ਉਹ ਮਕਾਨ ਦੇਖਿਆ ਜਿੱਥੇ ਤੁਸੀਂ ਰਹਿੰਦੇ ਹੁੰਦੇ ਸੀ। ਪਿੰਡ ਦੇ ਲੋਕਾਂ
ਨੇ ਸਾਨੂੰ ਬਹੁਤ ਪਿਆਰ ਦਿਖਾਇਆ, ਪਰ ਗਰਮੀ ਬਹੁਤ ਸੀ। ਇੱਕ ਵਾਰੀ ਤਿੰਨ
ਦਿਨ ਲਗਾਤਾਰ ਬਾਰਸ਼ ਹੁੰਦੀ ਰਹੀ ਸੀ। ਇੱਥੇ ਆ ਕੇ ਸਾਡੀ ਪੰਜਾਬੀ ਦੀ
ਸ਼ਬਦਾਵਲੀ ਬਹੁਤ ਵੱਧ ਗਈ ਹੈ। ਅਸੀਂ ਹੈਰਾਨ ਹੋਈਆਂ ਹਾਂ ਕਿ ਇੱਥੇ ਐਨੀ
ਅਬਾਦੀ ਤੇ ਟਰੈਫ਼ਿਕ ਹੈ। ਅਸੀਂ ਤੁਹਾਡੇ ਲਈ ਬਹੁਤ ਸੁਗਾਤਾਂ ਖ਼ਰੀਦੀਆਂ ਹਨ।
ਅਸੀਂ ਚਾਹੁੰਦੀਆਂ ਸੀ ਕਿ ਤੁਸੀਂ ਸਾਡੇ ਨਾਲ ਹੁੰਦੇ।

ਸ਼ੁਭ ਇੱਛਾਵਾਂ ਨਾਲ

ਤੁਹਾਡੀਆਂ ਪਿਆਰੀਆਂ ਬੇਟੀਆਂ

ਜਸਪ੍ਰੀਤ ਤੇ ਸਿਮਰਨ

Dear Dad and Mum,   4 July

Sat sri akal.

We hope that you are fine. We are happy here. We went to the village and saw the house where you used to live. The people of the village have shown us tremendous affection but it was very hot. Once, it rained for three days without stopping. Our Panjabi vocabulary has increased a lot by coming here. We are astonished to see so many people and so much traffic. We have bought many presents for you. We wish you were here with us.

With best wishes,

Your loving daughters,

Jaspreet and Simran

ਸ਼ਬਦਾਵਲੀ   shab<u>d</u>aavalee *Vocabulary*

ਪਿਆਰੇ	piaare	*dear, beloved* (v.)
ਕਿ	ki	*that*
ਖ਼ੁਸ਼	<u>kh</u>ush	*happy*
ਮਕਾਨ	makaan	*house* (m.)
ਜਿੱਥੇ	ji<u>thth</u>e	*where*
ਲੋਕ	lok	*people* (m.)
ਪਿਆਰ	piaar	*love, affection* (m.)
ਦਿਖਾਉਣਾ	<u>d</u>ikhaaunhaa	*to show*
ਗਰਮੀ	garmee	*heat, warmth (hot, warm)* (f.)
ਵਾਰੀ	vaaree	*turn, instance* (f.)
ਅਬਾਦੀ	abaa<u>d</u>ee	*population* (f.)
ਲਗਾਤਾਰ	lagaa<u>t</u>aar	*continuously, on-going*
ਬਾਰਸ਼	baarash	*rain* (f.)

ਅਭਿਆਸ   abhiaas   *Exercises*

After reading the dialogue and / or listening to the recording, try to do the following exercises.

1 Complete the box.

ਲਗਾਤਾਰ		
	piaare	
ਖ਼ੁਸ਼		
		warmth
	vaaree	

2 Answer the questions about Jaspreet and Simran's letter home.

a ਜਸਪ੍ਰੀਤ ਤੇ ਸਿਮਰਨ ਨੇ ਪਿੰਡ ਵਿਚ ਕੀ ਦੇਖਿਆ ?

b ਇੱਕ ਵਾਰੀ ਤਿੰਨ ਦਿਨ ਲਗਾਤਾਰ ਕੀ ਹੁੰਦੀ ਰਹੀ ਸੀ ?

c ਜਸਪ੍ਰੀਤ ਤੇ ਸਿਮਰਨ ਕਿਉਂ ਹੈਰਾਨ ਹੋਈਆਂ ਹਨ ?

d ਜਸਪ੍ਰੀਤ ਤੇ ਸਿਮਰਨ ਨੇ ਆਪਣੇ ਮਾਤਾ ਜੀ ਤੇ ਪਿਤਾ ਜੀ ਲਈ ਕੀ ਖ਼ਰੀਦਿਆ ?

▶ 2 Simran at the post office

ਗੱਲ ਬਾਤ ੨ ਸਿਮਰਨ ਡਾਕਖ਼ਾਨੇ ਤੇ

gall baaṯ 2 simran daakkhaane ṯe

ਸਿਮਰਨ	ਮੈਂ ਇਹ ਚਿੱਠੀ ਅਮਰੀਕਾ ਭੇਜਣੀ ਹੈ ।
ਡਾਕਬਾਬੂ	ਕੀ ਤੁਸੀਂ ਸਮੁੰਦਰੀ ਡਾਕ ਰਾਹੀਂ ਭੇਜਣੀ ਹੈ ਜਾਂ ਹਵਾਈ ਡਾਕ ਰਾਹੀਂ ?
ਸਿਮਰਨ	ਹਵਾਈ ਡਾਕ ਰਾਹੀਂ ।
ਡਾਕਬਾਬੂ	ਇਸ ਤੇ ੧੨ ਰੁਪਏ ਦੀਆਂ ਟਿਕਟਾਂ ਲਾਓ ।
ਸਿਮਰਨ	ਅੱਛਾ ਜੀ । ਧੰਨਵਾਦ ।

Simran	*I want to send this letter to America.*
Postal worker	*Do you want to send the letter by sea or by air mail?*
Simran	*By air mail.*
Postal worker	*Put 12 rupees worth of stamps on it [the letter].*
Simran	*OK. Thanks.*

ਸ਼ਬਦਾਵਲੀ   **shabdaavalee**   *Vocabulary*

ਚਿੱਠੀ	chiththee	*letter* (f.)
ਭੇਜਣਾ	bhejnhaa	*to send, to post*
ਸਮੁੰਦਰ	samundar	*sea* (m.)
ਡਾਕ	daak	*mail, post* (f.)
ਸਮੁੰਦਰੀ ਡਾਕ	samundaree daak	*sea mail* (f.)
ਰਾਹੀਂ	raaheen	*via, by*
ਹਵਾਈ	havaaee	*by air*
ਹਵਾਈ ਡਾਕ	havaaee daak	*air mail* (f.)
ਟਿਕਟ	tikat	*stamp* (f.)

ਬੋਲੀ ਬਾਰੇ   **bolee baare**   *Language points*

The perfect tenses

The perfect tenses describe actions which have been completed.

Present perfect

The present perfect tense in Panjabi refers to those actions which have just occurred, such as *I have eaten*. It is generally used when one is concerned with the present effects of something which happened in the recent past. You will recall from Unit 9 that the verb ਚੁਕਣਾ is used to express *to have already done* or *to have finished doing*. The stem that is used with ਚੁਕਣਾ represents the action in the present perfect tense that has already occurred. The present perfect of ਖਾਣਾ *to eat* is as follows:

Masculine singular	ਮੈਂ ਖਾ ਚੁਕਾ / ਚੁਕਿਆ ਹਾਂ	*I have eaten*
Feminine singular	ਮੈਂ ਖਾ ਚੁਕੀ ਹਾਂ	*I have eaten*
Masculine plural	ਅਸੀਂ ਖਾ ਚੁਕੇ ਹਾਂ	*we have eaten*
Feminine plural	ਅਸੀਂ ਖਾ ਚੁਕੀਆਂ ਹਾਂ	*we have eaten*
Masculine informal singular	ਤੂੰ ਖਾ ਚੁਕਾ / ਚੁਕਿਆ ਹੈਂ	*you have eaten*
Feminine informal singular	ਤੂੰ ਖਾ ਚੁਕੀ ਹੈਂ	*you have eaten*
Formal / masculine plural	ਤੁਸੀਂ ਖਾ ਚੁਕੇ ਹੋ	*you have eaten*
Masculine singular	ਇਹ / ਉਹ ਖਾ ਚੁਕਾ / ਚੁਕਿਆ ਹੈ	*he has eaten*
Feminine singular	ਇਹ / ਉਹ ਖਾ ਚੁਕੀ ਹੈ	*she has eaten*
Formal / masculine plural	ਇਹ / ਉਹ ਖਾ ਚੁਕੇ ਹਨ	*(he has) / they have eaten*
Feminine plural	ਇਹ / ਉਹ ਖਾ ਚੁਕੀਆਂ ਹਨ	*they have eaten*

Past perfect

The past perfect tense is used when the effects of an action in the remote past is being referred to in the more recent past. In English *to eat* in the past perfect would be expressed as *had eaten*. The past perfect tense in Panjabi is formed similarly to the present perfect tense as just shown, except that the present auxiliary verbs are used in the present perfect while the past perfect tense is formed with the past form of the auxiliary verbs. The following examples show *to eat* ਖਾਣਾ in the past perfect tense:

Masculine singular	ਮੈਂ ਖਾ ਚੁਕਾ / ਚੁਕਿਆ ਸੀ	*I had eaten*
Feminine singular	ਮੈਂ ਖਾ ਚੁਕੀ ਸੀ	*I had eaten*
Masculine plural	ਅਸੀਂ ਖਾ ਚੁਕੇ ਸੀ	*we had eaten*
Feminine plural	ਅਸੀਂ ਖਾ ਚੁਕੀਆਂ ਸੀ	*we had eaten*
Masculine informal singular	ਤੂੰ ਖਾ ਚੁਕਾ / ਚੁਕਿਆ ਸੀ	*you had eaten*
Feminine informal singular	ਤੂੰ ਖਾ ਚੁਕੀ ਸੀ	*you had eaten*
Formal / masculine plural	ਤੁਸੀਂ ਖਾ ਚੁਕੇ ਸੀ	*you had eaten*
Masculine singular	ਇਹ / ਉਹ ਖਾ ਚੁਕਾ / ਚੁਕਿਆ ਸੀ	*he had eaten*
Feminine singular	ਇਹ / ਉਹ ਖਾ ਚੁਕੀ ਸੀ	*she had eaten*
Formal / masculine plural	ਇਹ / ਉਹ ਖਾ ਚੁਕੇ ਸਨ	*he / they had eaten*
Feminine plural	ਇਹ / ਉਹ ਖਾ ਚੁਕੀਆਂ ਸਨ	*they had eaten*

Compound constructions with ਲੈਣਾ, ਦੇਣਾ and ਜਾਣਾ can also be used to express the present and past perfect, most commonly when there is an object present. Notice the following examples:

| ਮੈਂ ਖਾਣਾ ਖਾ ਲਿਆ ਹੈ | *I have eaten food.* |
| ਉਸ ਨੇ ਸਾਨੂੰ ਸੁਗਾਤ ਦੇ ਦਿੱਤੀ ਹੈ | *He has given us a gift.* |

The present perfect continuous and the past perfect continuous are expressed in the same manner as the present and past continuous tenses except that an indication of time is used to denote whether or not the action is in the perfect tense:

present continuous	ਬਾਰਸ਼ ਹੋ ਰਹੀ ਹੈ	*It is raining.*
present perfect continuous	ਬਾਰਸ਼ ਦੋ ਦਿਨ ਤੋਂ ਹੋ ਰਹੀ ਹੈ	*It has been raining for two days.*
past continuous	ਬਾਰਸ਼ ਹੋ ਰਹੀ ਸੀ	*It was raining.*
past perfect continuous	ਬਾਰਸ਼ ਦੋ ਦਿਨ ਤੋਂ ਹੋ ਰਹੀ ਸੀ	*It had been raining for two days.*

How did it go?

In Panjabi, *how did it go?* is expressed through the use of the continuous form of ਰਹਿਣਾ. You have already been introduced to ਰਹੀ / ਰਿਹਾ as the continuous tense form of ਰਹਿਣਾ *to stay, to live* equivalent to the English *-ing*. In Unit 5 Geeta asks Sita: ਤੂੰ ਕੀ ਕਰ ਰਹੀ ਹੈਂ? literally meaning *What are you doing?* The continuous form of ਰਹਿਣਾ can have another quite different sense as *how did it go?*. Although the form of ਰਹਿਣਾ is in the continuous, the sense of the sentence refers to the past:

| ਤੁਹਾਡੀ ਇੰਡੀਆ ਦੀ ਫੇਰੀ ਕਿਵੇਂ ਰਹੀ? | *How was your tour of India?* |
| ਤੁਹਾਡਾ ਦਿਨ ਕਿਵੇਂ ਰਿਹਾ? | *How was your day?* |

ਰਹੀ / ਰਿਹਾ in these examples means outcome or conclusion. Therefore, this sentence has the sense *How did your trip to India go?* and *How did your day go?* Notice that the form of ਰਹਿਣਾ corresponds with the gender / number character of the object being described, in this case ਫੇਰੀ (*trip, tour*) which is feminine. *How did it go?* is a colloquial phrase which you will find useful when informally asking someone about their day or trip.

The subjunctive

The subjunctive mood (set of verb tenses) is commonly used when there is a sense of possibility, vagueness or indefiniteness.

When the exact time or state of an action is uncertain, the subjunctive is used. The present subjunctive is formed in a way similar to the future tense, except that the -ਗਾ / -ਗੀ / -ਗੇ / -ਗੀਆਂ endings are left out. In English we rarely use the subjunctive mood, but learners of other European languages will be aware of this system of verbal constructions:

ਮੈਂ ਕਰਾਂ
ਅਸੀਂ ਬੋਲੀਏ
ਤੂੰ ਕਰੇਂ
ਤੁਸੀਂ ਬੋਲੋ
ਇਹ / ਉਹ ਬੋਲੇ
ਇਹ / ਉਹ ਬੋਲਣ

The range of situations in which the present subjunctive is used can be best compared with the future tense, as in the following examples:

Future

ਉਹ ਕਿੱਥੇ ਜਾਏਗੀ ?	*Where will she go?*
ਮੈਂ ਕੁਝ ਕਵਾਂਗੀ	*I will say something.*
ਅਸੀਂ ਕੀ ਕਰਾਂਗੇ ?	*What will we do?*

Present subjunctive

ਉਹ ਕਿੱਥੇ ਜਾਏ ?	*Where shall he / she go?*
ਮੈਂ ਕੁਝ ਕਵਾਂ ?	*Shall / may I say something?*
ਅਸੀਂ ਕੀ ਕਰੀਏ ?	*What might we do?*

The examples of the future tense show that an action is to occur sometime in the future while the present subjunctive gives a sense that an action *may* happen.

Past subjunctive

The past subjunctive expresses that an action might have happened in the past, but that it did not occur. It is formed in exactly the same way as the present imperfect tense which you learned in Unit 4, and, unlike the present subjunctive, is affected by gender:

ਮੈਂ ਕਰਦਾ / ਕਰਦੀ
ਅਸੀਂ ਕਰਦੇ / ਕਰਦੀਆਂ
ਤੂੰ ਕਰਦਾ / ਕਰਦੀ
ਤੁਸੀਂ ਕਰਦੇ
ਇਹ / ਉਹ ਕਰਦਾ / ਕਰਦੀ
ਇਹ / ਉਹ ਕਰਦੇ / ਕਰਦੀਆਂ

The past subjunctive will be illustrated in the following section where conditional sentences will be introduced. The subjunctive is also used when there is a feeling of possibility, commonly expressed through perhaps **ਸ਼ਾਇਦ** or it is possible **ਹੋ ਸਕਦਾ ਹੈ**:

ਸ਼ਾਇਦ ਉਹ ਆਵੇ, ਸ਼ਾਇਦ ਨਾ ਆਵੇ	*Perhaps he'll come, perhaps he won't come.*
ਹੋ ਸਕਦਾ ਹੈ ਕਿ ਬੱਚੇ ਬਾਹਰ ਹੋਣ	*It is possible that the children are outside.*

More complex sentences can be constructed by combining the present tense or present continuous tense to express the nature of the action in question such as *perhaps he might be coming* in which *coming* is in the continuous tense while the sense of possibility is expressed through the subjunctive form of **ਹੋਣਾ** which is **ਹੋਣ**:

ਸ਼ਾਇਦ ਮੁੰਡੇ ਗੁਜਰਾਤੀ ਸਿੱਖ ਰਹੇ ਹੋਣ	*Perhaps the boys are learning Gujarati.*
ਸ਼ਾਇਦ ਪਿਤਾ ਜੀ ਆਉਂਦੇ ਹੋਣ	*Perhaps father might be coming.*

The subjunctive is also used in a number of other situations in which necessity, command or obligation are being expressed. Notice such instances in the following examples:

ਜ਼ਰੂਰੀ ਹੈ ਕਿ ਅਸੀਂ ਠੀਕ ਸਮੇਂ ਤੇ ਨਿਕਲੀਏ	*It is necessary that we leave on time.*
ਉਹ ਨੂੰ ਦੱਸ ਕਿ ਚੁੱਪ ਰਵੇ!	*Tell him to be quiet!*

Conditional sentences

Conditional sentences (i.e. where an action is dependent on a *condition*) in Panjabi are formed by using a sequence of **ਜੇ** *if* and **ਤਾਂ** *then*. In English conditional sentences also follow a similar pattern: *if he comes, then I won't go*. In Panjabi this sentence would be **ਜੇ ਉਹ ਆਏ ਗਾ ਤਾਂ ਮੈਂ ਨਹੀਂ ਜਾਵਾਂ ਗਾ।** If the conditional action being referred to is in the future. such as in this example, the verb tense of the *if* clause will be in the future. However, when the action in an *if* clause is not definite or certain, it must be expressed in the subjunctive mood. In the following examples both the future tense and the subjunctive mood are used:

Future

| ਜੇ ਉਹ ਆਏ ਗਾ ਤਾਂ ਮੈਂ ਸੌਵਾਂ ਗਾ | *If he comes (will come), then I'll sleep.* |

Subjunctive

| ਜੇ ਅਸੀਂ ਸੱਤ ਵਜੇ ਨਿਕਲੀਏ ਤਾਂ ਕਿੰਨੇ ਵਜੇ ਘਰ ਪਹੁੰਚਾਂ ਗੇ ? | *If we leave at 7 o'clock, (then) what time will we reach home?* |
| ਜੇ ਟੈਕਸੀ ਨਾ ਮਿਲੇ ਤਾਂ ਬਸ ਫੜੋ | *If you don't get a taxi, then catch a bus.* |

The present tense can be used in the *if* clause when the action being referred to is in the past. In the first dialogue in this unit, Paul says to Jaspreet and Simran: ਜੇ ਅਸੀਂ ਪਹਿਲੇ ਮਿਲਦੇ ਤਾਂ ਅਸੀਂ ਇਕੱਠੇ ਘੁੰਮਦੇ meaning *If we had met before, then we would have travelled together*:

| ਜੇ ਉਹ ਆਉਂਦਾ ਤਾਂ ਮੈਂ ਸੌਂਦਾ | *If he had come, I would have slept.* |
| ਜੇ ਤੁਸੀਂ ਸਾਡੇ ਨਾਲ ਹੁੰਦੇ ਤਾਂ ਜ਼ਿਆਦਾ ਮਜ਼ਾ ਆਉਂਦਾ | *If you had been with us, we would have enjoyed it more.* |

ਵਿਆਖਿਆ   viaakhiaa   *Commentary*

Letter writing

Letter writing in Panjabi is similar to English. As *Dear* in English is used, in Panjabi ਪਿਆਰੇ (which translates literally as *dear* or *beloved*) is generally used to address people who are relatively familiar to the writer. For more formal letters ਪਿਆਰੇ is often too intimate an address, so ਮਾਨਯੋਗ (*respected*) followed by the name of the person or ਸ੍ਰੀਮਾਨ ਜੀ (*Dear Sir*) are often more appropriate when writing to someone not known to you.

Greetings (see Unit 1) such as ਸਤਿ ਸ੍ਰੀ ਅਕਾਲ, ਨਮਸਕਾਰ and ਅੱਸਲਾਮ ਅਲੈਕਮ are commonly placed after the initial address on the line below, according to the religion of the addressee. The body of the letter follows no specific rules. However, a letter is generally concluded with the equivalent of the appropriate endings such as ਪਿਆਰ ਨਾਲ *with affection,* ਤੁਹਾਡਾ ਦੋਸਤ *your friend,* ਤੁਹਾਡੀਆਂ ਬੇਟੀਆਂ *your daughters* (as Jaspreet and Simran finish their letter to their parents), or whichever ending is fitting.

Doaba

Jaspreet and Simrans's trip to Jalandhar is no surprise when considering the pattern of migration from Panjab. The Doaba region, of which Jalandhar is a central town, is the main area in India from which migration has taken place. People from this region can be found in the four corners of the world. In fact the 'Doaba' dialect is what you are most likely to encounter if you are learning and using Panjabi in the west. It is often said that there is no family in the Doaba without a relative in the USA, UK, Far East or the Gulf.

ਅਭਿਆਸ   abhiaas   *Exercises*

After reading the dialogue and / or listening to the recording, try to do the following exercises.

1 Write the following in Panjabi.

Make the following statements in Panjabi according to the directions in parentheses:

a I have eaten. (singular/male)
b I have eaten. (singular/female)
c They had spoken. (plural/male)
d He had been speaking for ten minutes. (singular/masculine)

▶ 2 Listening

Paul is at the bank changing some money. Listen to the dialogue between Paul and the bank teller on the recording. Answer the following questions about the dialogue:

ਪੋਲ ਕੋਲ ਕਿਹੜੇ ਦੇਸ਼ ਦੇ ਪੈਸੇ ਹਨ ?
ਪੋਲ ਕਿੰਨੇ ਪੈਸੇ ਬਦਲਣਾ ਚਾਹੁੰਦਾ ਹੈ ?
ਅੱਜ ਦਾ ਰੇਟ ਕੀ ਹੈ ?
ਕੀ ਰੁਪਇਆਂ ਦਾ ਰੇਟ ਕੱਲ੍ਹ ਤੋਂ ਘੱਟ ਹੈ ਜਾਂ ਵੱਧ ?
ਪੋਲ ਕੋਲ ਕਿਹੜਾ ਪਾਸਪੋਰਟ ਹੈ ?

3 Writing a postcard

You are writing a postcard to your friend Sonia about your stay in Panjab. Some words are missing. Select the appropriate words from the list to complete the postcard.

_____ਸੋਨੀਆ ਜੀ

ਸਤਿ ਸ੍ਰੀ ਅਕਾਲ। ਮੇਰੀ ਪੰਜਾਬ ਦੀ _____ਅੱਛੀ

ਰਹੀ ਹੈ। ਮੈਂ ਬਹੁਤ _____ ਦੇਖੀਆਂ ਹਨ ਪਰ

_____ ਮੈਨੂੰ ਸਭ ਤੋਂ ਚੰਗਾ ਲੱਗਾ। ਉਸ ਦਾ ਕੋਈ

_____ ਨਹੀਂ। ਇੱਥੇ ਆ ਕੇ ਮੇਰੀ ਪੰਜਾਬੀ ਦੀ_____

ਵੱਧ ਗਈ ਹੈ। ਜੇ ਤੁਸੀਂ ਮੇਰੇ ਨਾਲ _____, __

ਜ਼ਿਆਦਾ ਮਜ਼ਾ_____ .

To

Sonia Kaur

222 Carl Road

Apt 31

Marion, Ohio

43302 U.S.A

- ਤਾਂ   - ਜਗ੍ਹਾ   - ਪਿਆਰੇ   - ਹੁੰਦੇ   - ਫੇਰੀ   - ਮੁਕਾਬਲਾ

- ਸ਼ਬਦਾਵਲੀ   - ਆਉਂਦਾ   - ਹਰਿਮੰਦਰ ਸਾਹਿਬ

13

ਵਿਆਹ ਦੀਆਂ ਰਸਮਾਂ

viaah deeaan
rasmaan

marriage customs

In this unit you will learn:
- more about Panjabi marriage customs
- how to tell the date and month of year
- how to express *sort of, rather*

Matrimonial advertisement

ਵਿਆਹ ਸਬੰਧੀ

viaah sabandhee

The following paragraph is a matrimonial advertisement taken from a widely read Panjabi newspaper in Britain called *Des Pardes* (*Home and Abroad*). The parents of a young man have placed the advertisement in order to find a partner for their son.

ਲੁਧਿਆਣੇ ਤੋਂ ਪਤਵੰਤੇ ਹਿੰਦੂ ਖਤਰੀ ਮਾਪਿਆਂ ਦੇ ਲੜਕੇ ਲਈ ਯੋਗ ਰਿਸ਼ਤੇ ਦੀ ਲੋੜ ਹੈ। ਲੜਕਾ ਪੜ੍ਹਿਆ ਲਿਖਿਆ, ਪੇਸ਼ਵਾਰ, ਸੱਚੀ ਮੁੱਚੀ ਸੁਹਣਾ ਤੇ ਨਰਮ ਸੁਭਾ ਦਾ ਹੈ। ਲੜਕੇ ਦਾ ਕੱਦ ੫ ਫੁੱਟ ੮ ਇੰਚ ਤੇ ਉਮਰ ੨੮ ਸਾਲ ਹੈ। ਲੜਕੀ ਪਤਲੀ, ਗੋਰੀ, ਸੁਹਣੀ, ਬ੍ਰਿਟਿਸ਼ ਸ਼ਹਿਰੀਅਤ ਵਾਲੀ, ਪੜ੍ਹੀ ਲਿਖੀ, ਵਿਹਾਰੀ ਨੌਕਰੀ ਤੇ ਲੱਗੀ ਹੋਈ ਚਾਹੀਦੀ ਹੈ। ਪੂਰਬ ਤੇ ਪੱਛਮ ਦੀਆਂ ਕਦਰਾਂ ਨੂੰ ਸਮਝਣ ਵਾਲੀ ਹੋਣੀ ਚਾਹੀਦੀ ਹੈ। ਲੜਕੀ ਦੀ ਉਮਰ ੨੫ ਸਾਲ ਤੋਂ ਵੱਧ ਨਾ ਹੋਵੇ। ਛੋਟੇ ਵਾਪਸ ਭੇਜ ਦਿੱਤੀ ਜਾਏ ਗੀ। ਤਲਾਕ ਸ਼ੁਦਾ ਕੁੜੀਆਂ ਨੂੰ ਲਿਖਣ ਦੀ ਲੋੜ ਨਹੀਂ। ਸੰਪਰਕ ਕਰੋ: Box number 2961 c/o ਦੇਸ ਪਰਦੇਸ।

Respectable Hindu Khatri parents from Ludhiana seek suitable match for their son. The boy is educated, a professional, genuinely handsome and kind natured. The boy is 5 ft 8 inches tall and he is 28 years old. The girl should be slim, fair, beautiful, a British citizen, educated and professionally employed. Should understand eastern and western values and be not more than 25 years of age. Photo returnable. Divorcees need not apply. Contact: Box number 2961 c/o Des Pardes.

ਸ਼ਬਦਾਵਲੀ   shabdaavalee   *Vocabulary*

ਪਤਵੰਤੇ	patvante	*respectable* (v.)
ਖਤਰੀ	khatree	*Khatri* (m. / f.) (*caste*)
ਮਾਪਿਆਂ	maapiaan	*parents* (m.)
ਰਿਸ਼ਤਾ	rishtaa	*(marriage) relation* (m.)
ਯੋਗ	yog	*suitable*
ਲੋੜ	lorh	*require, necessity, wanted*

ਪੜ੍ਹਿਆ ਲਿਖਿਆ	parhhiaa likhiaa	*educated* (v.)
ਪੇਸ਼ਵਾਰ	peshaavar	*professional* (m. / f.)
ਸੱਚੀ ਮੁੱਚੀ	sachchee muchchee	*genuinely*
ਸੁਹਣਾ	suhnhaa	*handsome* (v.)
ਨਰਮ ਸੁਭਾ	naram subhaa	*kind natured* (m.)
ਕੱਦ	kadd	*height* (m.)
ਉਮਰ	umar	*age* (f.)
ਪਤਲੀ	patlee	*thin, slim* (v.)
ਗੋਰੀ	goree	*fair, white* (v.)
ਸ਼ਹਿਰੀਅਤ	shahireeat	*citizen* (f.)
ਵਿਹਾਰੀ ਨੌਕਰੀ	vihaaree naukaree	*professionally employed* (f.)
ਨੌਕਰੀ	naukaree	*job, employment* (f.)
ਪੂਰਬ	poorab	*east* (m.)
ਪੱਛਮ	pachcham	*west* (m.)
ਕਦਰਾਂ	kadraan	*values* (f.)
ਵਾਪਸ	vaapas	*return*
ਭੇਜਣਾ	bhejnhaa	*to send*
ਤਲਾਕ	talaak	*divorce* (m.)
ਸੰਪਰਕ	sanparak	*contact* (m.)

ਅਭਿਆਸ   abhiaas   *Exercises*

After reading the passage and / or listening to the recording, try to do the following exercises.

1 Answer the questions about the passage.

a ਕੀ ਲੜਕੇ ਦੇ ਮਾਪੇ ਹਿੰਦੂ ਹਨ ?
b ਕੀ ਲੜਕਾ ਪੜ੍ਹਿਆ ਲਿਖਿਆ ਹੈ ?
c ਕੀ ਲੜਕੀ ੨੦ ਸਾਲ ਤੋਂ ਘੱਟ ਹੋਵੇ ?

2 Reply to matrimonial advertisement

The following is a reply to the matrimonial advertisement. From the personal information given, decide whether or not the couple are a suitable match (i.e. they have at least five of the qualities that were specified in the advertisement). It's up to you to decide!

Box number 2961 c/o ਦੇਸ ਪਰਦੇਸ:

ਦਿੱਲੀ ਤੋਂ ਮਾਪੇ ਆਪਣੀ ਲੜਕੀ ਲਈ ਰਿਸ਼ਤਾ ਲੱਭ ਰਹੇ ਹਨ। ਲੜਕੀ ਸੁਹਣੀ ਤੇ ਪਤਲੀ ਹੈ। ਪੜ੍ਹੀ ਲਿਖੀ ਹੈ ਪਰ ਨੌਕਰੀ ਨਹੀਂ ਕਰਦੀ ਹੈ। ਭਾਰਤੀ ਸ਼ਹਿਰੀਅਤ ਵਾਲੀ ਹੈ। ਪੂਰਬ ਤੇ ਪੱਛਮ ਦੀਆਂ ਕਦਰਾਂ ਸਮਝਣ ਵਾਲੀ ਹੈ ਅਤੇ ਉਸ ਦੀ ਉਮਰ ੨੮ ਸਾਲਾਂ ਦੀ ਹੈ। ਵਿਆਹ ਇੱਕ ਵਾਰੀ ਹੋ ਚੁਕਾ ਹੈ।

3 Say or write in the correct word order.

a ਵਿਹਾਰੀ ਨੌਕਰੀ ਹੈ ਲੜਕੀ ਚਾਹੀਦੀ ਤੇ ਹੋਣੀ ਲੱਗੀ

b ਤਲਾਕ ਸ਼ੁਦਾ ਲਿਖਣ ਨੂੰ ਲੜਕੀਆਂ ਲੋੜ ਦੀ ਨਹੀਂ

c ਉਮਰ ਦੀ ਲੜਕੀ ੨੫ ਸਾਲ ਹੋਵੇ ਵੱਧ ਨਾ ਤੋਂ

d ਲੜਕਾ ਸੁਹਣਾ ਸੱਚੀ ਮੁੱਚੀ ਹੈ

▶ *A wedding invitation*

ਗੱਲ ਬਾਤ ਸੱਦਾ ਪੱਤਰ

gall baa<u>t</u> sa<u>dd</u>aa pa<u>tt</u>ar

Debra has received an invitation to attend a Panjabi wedding. Since she has never been to a Panjabi wedding, she has gone to her friend Darshana to ask her what the ceremonies will be like.

ਡੇਬਰਾ	ਮੇਰੀ ਸਹੇਲੀ ਜੀਤੀ ਦੇ ਵਿਆਹ ਦਾ ਸੱਦਾ ਪੱਤਰ ਆਇਆ ਹੈ। ਵਿਆਹ ੨੮ ਜਨਵਰੀ ਨੂੰ ਹੈ। ਮੈਨੂੰ ਮਹਿੰਦੀ ਬਾਰੇ ਕੁਝ ਦੱਸ।
ਦਰਸ਼ਨਾ	ਮਹਿੰਦੀ ਪਰਵਾਰਕ ਰਸਮ ਹੈ। ਕੁੜੀਆਂ ਆਪਣੇ ਹੱਥਾਂ ਤੇ ਮਹਿੰਦੀ ਲਗਾਉਂਦੀਆਂ ਹਨ। ਕਈ ਤਰ੍ਹਾਂ ਦੇ ਨਮੂਨੇ ਬਣਾਦੀਆਂ ਹਨ ਅਤੇ ਵਿਆਹ ਦੇ ਗੀਤ ਵੀ ਗਾਏ ਜਾਂਦੇ ਹਨ।
ਡੇਬਰਾ	ਕੀ ਆਦਮੀ ਇਸ ਰਸਮ ਵਿਚ ਸ਼ਾਮਲ ਹੁੰਦੇ ਹਨ?
ਦਰਸ਼ਨਾ	ਨਹੀਂ, ਇਹ ਕੇਵਲ ਔਰਤਾਂ ਲਈ ਹੈ। ਆਦਮੀ ਬਰਾਤ ਵਿਚ ਸ਼ਾਮਲ ਹੁੰਦੇ ਹਨ।
ਡੇਬਰਾ	ਬਰਾਤ ਦਾ ਕੀ ਮਤਲਬ ਹੈ?
ਦਰਸ਼ਨਾ	ਬਰਾਤ ਵਿਚ ਲਾੜੇ ਦੇ ਰਿਸ਼ਤੇਦਾਰ ਅਤੇ ਦੋਸਤ ਸ਼ਾਮਲ ਹੁੰਦੇ ਹਨ। ਇਹ ਛੋਟਾ ਜੇਹਾ ਜਲੂਸ ਹੁੰਦਾ ਹੈ। ਮੁੰਡਾ ਘੋੜੀ ਤੇ ਚੜ੍ਹਿਆ ਹੁੰਦਾ ਹੈ ਅਤੇ ਅੱਗੇ ਅੱਗੇ ਵਾਜੇ ਵਾਲੇ ਹੁੰਦੇ ਹਨ। ਜਾਂਝੀ ਭੰਗੜਾ ਪਾਉਂਦੇ ਹਨ।
ਡੇਬਰਾ	ਸੱਦਾ ਪੱਤਰ ਤੇ ਲਿਖਿਆ ਹੋਇਆ ਹੈ ਕਿ ਡੋਲੀ ਚਾਰ ਵਜੇ ਤੁਰੇਗੀ। ਇਹ ਕੀ ਰਸਮ ਹੈ?
ਦਰਸ਼ਨਾ	ਡੋਲੀ ਦਾ ਮਤਲਬ ਹੈ ਕਿ ਕੁੜੀ ਦਾ ਪੇਕੇ ਛੱਡ ਕੇ ਸੁਹਰੇ ਜਾਣਾ। ਇਹ ਮੋਕਾ ਖ਼ੁਸ਼ੀ ਤੇ ਗ਼ਾਮੀ ਦਾ ਮੇਲ ਹੈ।
ਡੇਬਰਾ	ਇਹ ਗੱਲ ਬੜੀ ਦਿਲਚਸਪ ਲੱਗਦੀ ਹੈ। ਮੈਂ ਵਿਆਹ ਤੇ ਜਾਣ ਲਈ ਉਤਸੁਕ ਹਾਂ।

Debra	*My friend Jeeti's wedding invitation has come. The wedding is on the 28th of January. Tell me something about* mehndi.
Darshana	*Mehndi is a family custom. Girls put henna on their hands. They draw different designs and wedding songs are sung.*
Debra	*Are men present during this ritual?*

Darshana		*No. This is just for the women. Men are present at the* baraat.
Debra		*What is the meaning of* baraat?
Darshana		*At the* baraat *the groom's relatives and friends are present. This is a sort of small procession. The boy is on a mare and in front are some musicians. The wedding party performs* bhangra *(a folk dance of Panjab).*
Debra		*It's written on the invitation that the* doli *will leave at 4 o'clock. What is this custom?*
Darshana		Doli *means that the girl leaves her family's home to go her in-laws. This time is a happy and sad occasion.*
Debra		*This seems interesting. I look forward to going to the wedding!*

ਸ਼ਬਦਾਵਲੀ **shabdaavalee** *Vocabulary*

ਸਹੇਲੀ	sahelee	*friend (f.)*
ਸੱਦਾ ਪੱਤਰ	saddaa pattar	*invitation (m.)*
ਮਹਿੰਦੀ	mahindee	*henna (f.)*
ਜਾਣਨਾ	jaanhnaa	*to know*
ਆਪਣਾ	aapnhaa	*one's own*
ਪਰਵਾਰਕ	parvaarak	*family (relating to family)*
ਰਸਮ	rasam	*custom, ritual (f.)*
ਕਈ ਤਰ੍ਹਾਂ	kaee tar-h-aan	*different types*
ਨਮੂਨਾ	namoonaa	*pattern, design (m.)*
ਗੀਤ	geet	*song (m.)*
ਗਾਣਾ	gaanhaa	*to sing*
ਸ਼ਾਮਲ	shaamal	*to be present, to join or participate*
ਬਰਾਤ	baraat	*procession of the groom's relatives and friends (f.)*
ਮਤਲਬ	matlab	*meaning, definition (m.)*
ਲਾੜਾ	laarhaa	*groom (m.)*
ਰਿਸ਼ਤੇਦਾਰ	rishtedaar	*relatives (m. / f.)*
ਜਿਹਾ	jihaa	*sort of, rather*
ਜਲੂਸ	jaloos	*procession, parade (m.)*
ਘੋੜੀ	ghorhee	*mare (f.)*
ਚੜ੍ਹਨਾ	charhhnaa	*to be upon, to ride*
ਵਾਜੇ ਵਾਲੇ	vaaje vaale	*band of musicians (m.)*
ਜਾਂਞੀ	jaannjee	*members of groom's wedding party (m. / f.)*

ਭੰਗੜਾ	bha<u>n</u>grhaa	*bhangra* (m.) (style of Panjabi dance) (see Commentary, Unit 16)
ਡੋਲੀ	dolee	*ceremony* (f.) *bidding farewell to the bride* (see Commentary)
ਤੁਰਨਾ	<u>t</u>urnaa	*to walk, to depart, to leave*
ਪੇਕੇ	peke	*bride's family, bride's parents* (m.)
ਛੱਡਨਾ	<u>ch</u>addnaa	*to leave*
ਸਹੁਰੇ	sahure	*in-laws* (m.)
ਮੋਕਾ	maukaa	*opportunity, occasion* (m.)
ਖ਼ੁਸ਼ੀ	<u>kh</u>ushee	*happiness* (f.)
ਗ਼ਮੀ	<u>gh</u>amee	*sadness* (f.)
ਮੇਲ	mel	*meeting, combination* (m.)
ਦਿਲਚਸਪ	<u>d</u>ilchasp	*interesting*
ਉਤਸੁਕ	u<u>t</u>suk	*anxious, awaiting*

ਅਭਿਆਸ   abhiaas   *Exercises*

After reading the dialogue and / or listening to the recording, try to do the following exercises.

1 Match the questions with the correct answer.

1 ਮਹਿੰਦੀ ਦੀ ਰਸਮ ਕੀ ਹੈ?

2 ਵਿਆਹ ਕਿਸ ਤਾਰੀਖ਼ ਨੂੰ ਹੈ?

3 ਬਰਾਤ ਵਿਚ ਕੌਣ ਸ਼ਾਮਲ ਹੁੰਦਾ ਹੈ?

4 ਡੋਲੀ ਕੀ ਹੁੰਦੀ ਹੈ?

a ਵਿਆਹ ੨੮ ਜਨਵਰੀ ਨੂੰ ਹੈ।

b ਕੁੜੀਆਂ ਆਪਣੇ ਹੱਥਾਂ ਤੇ ਮਹਿੰਦੀ ਲਗਾਉਂਦੀਆਂ ਹਨ।

c ਕੁੜੀ ਦਾ ਪੇਕੇ ਛੱਡ ਕੇ ਸੁਹਰੇ ਜਾਣ ਨੂੰ ਡੋਲੀ ਕਿਹਾ ਜਾਂਦਾ ਹੈ।

d ਲੜਕੇ ਦੇ ਦੋਸਤ ਅਤੇ ਰਿਸ਼ਤੇਦਾਰ ਸ਼ਾਮਲ ਹੁੰਦੇ ਹਨ।

Bhupinder Singh and Harjinder Kaur Panesar

cordially request your company at the wedding of their son

Manjit Singh   to   Kanwaljit Kaur

daughter of Gurbax Singh and Jasvir Kaur Kalsi, Ilford

on May 23 at the Sikh Gurdwara of North London

Baraat: 9:30 a.m. Anand Karaj: 10 a.m. Guru ka langar: 12:00

RSVP

The Panesar Family

23 Old Road, Edinburgh, Scotland

2 Answer the questions about the wedding invitation.

a ਮੁੰਡੇ ਦੇ ਮਾਪੇ ਕਿੱਥੇ ਰਹਿੰਦੇ ਹਨ ?

b ਕੁੜੀ ਦੇ ਮਾਪੇ ਕਿੱਥੋਂ ਦੇ ਹਨ ?

c ਮੁੰਡੇ ਦਾ ਨਾਮ ਕੀ ਹੈ ?

d ਕੁੜੀ ਦਾ ਨਾਮ ਕੀ ਹੈ ?

e ਕੁੜੀ ਦੇ ਮਾਪਿਆਂ ਦੇ ਨਾਮ ਕੀ ਹਨ ?

f ਵਿਆਹ ਕਿਹੜੇ ਸ਼ਹਿਰ ਵਿਚ ਹੋ ਰਿਹਾ ਹੈ ?

g ਵਿਆਹ ਕਿਹੜੀ ਤਾਰੀਖ਼ ਨੂੰ ਹੈ ?

h ਬਰਾਤ ਕਿੰਨੇ ਵਜੇ ਤੁਰੇਗੀ ?

i ਅਨੰਦ ਕਾਰਜ ਕਦੋਂ ਸ਼ੁਰੂ ਹੋਣਾ ਹੈ ?

j ਗੁਰੂ ਦਾ ਲੰਗਰ ਕਿੰਨੇ ਵਜੇ ਵਰਤੇ ਗਾ ?

ਬੋਲੀ ਬਾਰੇ bolee baare *Language points*

Participial uses

A participle is a verb which is used to describe an object or an action. Therefore, participle constructions in Panjabi can either be used adjectively to describe nouns or adverbially to describe actions. You will remember from the matrimonial advertisement that the boy is described as *educated*. In Panjabi this was expressed as ਪੜ੍ਹਿਆ ਲਿਖਿਆ. Both verbs ਪੜ੍ਹਨਾ and ਲਿਖਣਾ are combined in their perfect forms in agreement with ਲੜਕਾ. Similarly, the prospective girl was said to be *educated*, expressed as ਪੜ੍ਹੀ ਲਿਖੀ, also showing agreement with the object being described. Often, the perfect forms of ਹੋਣਾ can also be used to strengthen the participial expression. Here are some more examples of how the participle can be used in Panjabi:

Adjective participles

ਮੈਂ ਉਬਲੇ ਹੋਏ ਅੰਡੇ ਨਹੀਂ ਖਾਂਦਾ	*I don't eat boiled eggs.*
ਉਹ ਬੈਠਾ ਹੋਇਆ ਆਦਮੀ ਕੋਣ ਹੈ ?	*Who is that man sitting down (i.e. seated)?*
ਮਾਤਾ ਜੀ ਨੇ ਡਰੀ ਹੋਈ ਕੁੜੀ ਨੂੰ ਚੁੱਕ ਲਿਆ	*Mum picked up the scared girl.*

Adverbial participles

ਉਹ ਮੁਸਕਰਾਂਦਾ ਹੋਇਆ ਲਤੀਫ਼ਾ ਸੁਣਾ ਰਿਹਾ ਸੀ	*He was telling a joke smilingly.*

Another use of the participle is in order to emphasize the ongoing nature or repetitiveness of the action being described. This can be done in two ways: by repeating the verb in the simple present tense or by using the past participle with a form of ਜਾਣਾ, both forms agreeing with the subject:

ਪੜ੍ਹਦੇ ਪੜ੍ਹਦੇ ਅਸੀਂ ਥੱਕ ਗਏ ਹਾਂ	*We are tired from constantly studying.*
ਰਸਤੇ ਵਿਚ ਜਾਂਦੇ ਜਾਂਦੇ ਮੈਨੂੰ ਮਿਲਣਾ	*As you go (along) the way, come and see me.*
ਛੋਟੀ ਲੜਕੀ ਬੋਲੀ ਜਾਂਦੀ ਹੈ	*The little girl keeps on talking.*

The particle ਜਿਹਾ 'jihaa'

ਜਿਹਾ is a particle which is added after an adjective in order to give it a modest or diluted sense. In English the sense of a description is diluted in a number of different ways, most commonly by using such words as rather, sort of, quite, and the suffix -ish. The form of ਜਿਹਾ is affected by the gender and number of the noun being described and can therefore also appear in the following forms: ਜਿਹੀ, ਜਿਹੇ and ਜਿਹੀਆਂ:

ਛੋਟਾ ਜਿਹਾ ਘਰ	*rather a small house*
ਥੋੜਾ ਜਿਹਾ	*quite a small (amount)*
ਪੁਰਾਣੀ ਜਿਹੀ ਗੱਡੀ	*an old-ish car*

The opposite of ਜਿਹਾ, in this sense, is ਸਾਰਾ. This is used to exaggerate rather than dilute a description, such as in Unit 11 when the booking clerk is telling the girls how popular the train to Amritsar, Shan-e-Panjab, is: ਬਹੁਤ ਸਾਰੇ ਸੈਲਾਨੀ ਇਸ ਗੱਡੀ ਵਿਚ ਸਫ਼ਰ ਕਰਦੇ ਹਨ *A lot of tourists travel on this train.*

The particle -ਜਿਹਾ can also follow a noun in order to give the sense *like*. Therefore, the noun preceding -ਜਿਹਾ represents what the description is being likened to. For example:

ਪਟਾਕਾ -ਜਿਹਾ	*like a firecracker*

When asking the question *what sort of?* or *what is it like?* then ਕਿਹੋ is combined with ਜਿਹਾ.

ਕਿਹੋ ਜਿਹਾ ਮਕਾਨ ?	*what sort of house?*
ਕਿਹੋ ਜਿਹੇ ਕਪੜੇ ?	*what sort of clothes?*

Reflexive adjectives and pronouns

In English *myself* and *themselves* are reflexive pronouns indicating that the action is directed towards or belongs to the subject of the sentence. In Panjabi the reflexive adjective ਆਪਣਾ means *one's own* and is defined by the noun or pronoun being affected by the reflexive nature of the sentence. Like other adjectives, it also changes according to the gender and number of the object that it is describing as well as in the oblique form.

ਉਹ ਆਪਣੇ ਘਰ ਵਿਚ ਰਹਿੰਦਾ ਹੈ	*He lives in his own house.*
ਉਹ ਆਪਣੇ ਭਰਾ ਨਾਲ ਆਇਆ ਹੈ	*He has come with his (own) brother.*
ਹਰ ਚੀਜ਼ ਆਪਣੀ ਜਗ੍ਹਾ ਤੇ ਹੋਣੀ ਚਾਹੀਦੀ ਹੈ	*Everything should be in its proper place.*
ਆਪਣੀਆਂ ਲੜਕੀਆਂ ਕੀ ਕਰਦੀਆਂ ਹਨ ?	*What do your (own) daughters do?*

Reflexive pronouns, unlike reflexive adjectives, do not rely upon another noun or adjective to be defined. If you recall from Unit 2, pronouns were introduced as naming words. The reflexive pronouns, in a similar way, are also naming words which are used to represent a person. The most common reflexive pronoun is ਆਪ which translates as *by oneself*. ਖ਼ੁਦ which is borrowed from Persian, can also be used to give the same sense. Note the following examples:

ਮੈਂ ਇਹ ਕੰਮ ਆਪ ਕਰਾਂ ਗਾ	*I will do this work myself.*
ਮੈਂ ਸਾਰਾ ਖਾਣਾ ਖ਼ੁਦ ਬਣਾਇਆ ਹੈ	*I have made all the food myself.*
ਉਹ ਨੇ ਆਪ ਜਾ ਕੇ ਫਲ ਖ਼ਰੀਦਿਆ	*She went and bought fruit herself.*

The reflexive adjective ਆਪਣਾ and the reflexive pronoun ਆਪ can be combined to give another meaning: *on one's own* or *without anyone's help* ਆਪਣੇ ਆਪ.

ਕਿਰਨ ਆਪਣੇ ਆਪ ਪੰਜਾਬੀ ਪੜ੍ਹਦੀ ਹੈ	*Kiran studies Panjabi on her own (without anyone else's help).*
ਸੰਜੀਵ ਆਪਣੇ ਆਪ ਨੂੰ ਬਹੁਤ ਸਮਝਦਾ ਹੈ	*Sanjeev thinks highly of himself.*

ਆਪਸ, meaning *fraternity*, is used to express situations of mutuality or reciprocity with the postposition ਵਿਚ to form *among* or *between*.

ਅਸੀਂ ਆਪਸ ਵਿਚ ਗੱਲ ਕਰ ਰਹੇ ਸੀ	*We were talking among ourselves.*
ਬੱਚੇ ਆਪਸ ਵਿਚ ਖੇਡ ਰਹੇ ਸਨ	*The children were playing among themselves.*

Finally, ਆਪਾਂ is used specifically with a group of people otherwise referred to as ਅਸੀਂ *us*. Therefore, the new meaning given by the reflexive pronoun is *let's* or *all of us*:

ਆਪਾਂ ਚਲੀਏ   *let's go*

ਵਿਆਖਿਆ viaakhiaa *Commentary*

1 What's the date today?

When asking someone today's date in Panjabi, you would say ਅੱਜ ਕੀ ਤਾਰੀਖ਼ ਹੈ? This is different from asking someone the day or day of the week, as explained in Unit 7 with the words ਦਿਨ *day* and ਵਾਰ *day of the week*. ਤਾਰੀਖ਼ literally means *date* and the reply to your question would be a numerical figure of the date accompanied by the month of the year: ਅੱਜ ਅਠਾਰ੍ਵਾਂ ਜੂਨ ਹੈ *Today is the 18th of June*. It is also not uncommon to use ordinal numbers for the first three or four days of the month: ਅੱਜ ਮਹੀਨੇ ਦੀ ਤੀਜੀ ਤਾਰੀਖ਼ ਹੈ *It is the third day of the month*.

Months of the year

ਜਨਵਰੀ	janvaree	*January*
ਫ਼ਰਵਰੀ	farvaree	*February*
ਮਾਰਚ	maarch	*March*
ਅਪਰੈਲ	aprail	*April*
ਮਈ	maee	*May*
ਜੂਨ	joon	*June*
ਜੁਲਾਈ	julaaee	*July*
ਅਗਸਤ	agas̲t	*August*
ਸਤੰਬਰ	satan̲bar	*September*
ਅਕਤੂਬਰ	akt̲oobar	*October*
ਨਵੰਬਰ	navan̲bar	*November*
ਦਸੰਬਰ	d̲asan̲bar	*December*

The four seasons of the year in English are spring, autumn, winter and summer which describe the weather of the period. In Panjabi there are terms less influenced by English (as the months of the year) to denote the seasons which, in Pakistan and North India, are quite distinctive.

ਬਸੰਤ	basan̲t	*spring*
ਗਰਮੀ	garmee	*summer*
ਬਰਸਾਤ	barsaat̲	*rainy season*
ਪੱਤਝੜ	pat̲tjharh	*autumn*
ਸਰਦੀ	sard̲ee	*winter*

2 Marriage customs

Panjabi weddings are lavish affairs with numbers of guests usually in the hundreds, sometimes in the thousands, and large amounts of food and decoration. Weddings are seen as social occasions and signify the coming together of two families rather than of two individuals, as is traditionally the case in western marriages. It is this aspect of Panjabi – and most other South Asian – weddings that leads to them often being labelled as 'arranged'. Usually the families arrange the weddings of their offspring, in that families are present at the meeting of the man and woman. There is a huge variety in the process of arranging marriages from one extreme where the man and woman do not meet until the wedding day (which is rare in the diaspora) to a situation where the man and woman see each other and make their own decision about whether they wish to marry or not. It is this latter version that is more usual in the diaspora.

When families are involved in the selection of the partner, they take into account a range of factors, such as those outlined in the advert at the beginning of this unit. Alongside education and other social aspects, the advert specifies a particular caste group, in this case **Khatri**. Caste is a form of social grouping and organization which is based upon occupational traditions as well as kinship ties. Even in the diaspora, caste affiliations are still adhered to and most advertisements of this kind carry some sort of caste affiliation. Some common castes are **Jat, Ramgharia** and **Brahmin**.

The wedding ceremonies that we described in this unit are religion-neutral in the Panjabi context and most Sikh, Hindu and Muslim weddings share these customs. The actual wedding vows, however, are of a religious nature and for Sikhs this is called the **Anand Karaj,** for Hindus it is the **Vivaah** and for Muslims the **Nikah**. For all Panjabis, however, weddings are major social events and involve spectacles of emotion, family participation and financial expenditure.

A common Panjabi wedding will involve a **mehndi** ritual, where the bride is adorned on her hands and feet with exquisite patterns in dye. The groom arrives on horseback with his relatives at the bride's house and the wedding ceremony takes place here. The ceremony is followed by a feast. The saddest occasion is when the bride is seen off at the end of the ceremony. This is called the **doli** and often involves protracted crying and sadness. Each of the events of the Panjabi wedding is accompanied by music.

ਅਭਿਆਸ   abhiaas   *Exercises*

After reading the dialogue and / or listening to the recording, try to do the following exercises.

1 Write a matrimonial advertisement.

Prepare a matrimonial advertisement in Panjabi on behalf of the parents of a girl giving the following information:

a The parents are Sikhs living in London.
b The girl is beautiful, educated and working in a bank.
c The girl is 25 years of age and is 5' 3" tall.
d The boy should be from a respectable family, be a British citizen and professionally employed.

2 Complete the sentences.

Use the appropriate forms of ਆਪਣਾ and ਜਿਹਾ.

a ਥੋੜਾ _____ ਹੋਰ ਦੁੱਧ ਦੇਵੋ।   *Give me a little more milk.*

b ਮੈਂ _____ ਪਿਤਾ ਜੀ ਨਾਲ ਆਇਆ ਹਾਂ।   *I have come with my father.*

c ਮੇਰੀਆਂ _____ ਭੈਣਾਂ ਵਿਆਹ ਤੇ ਨਹੀਂ ਗਈਆਂ।   *My own sisters didn't go to the wedding.*

d ਉਹ ਕਿਹੋ _____ ਲੋਕ ਸਨ?   *What sort of people were they?*

3 Fill in the blanks.

Use the appropriate participle expressions.

a _____ _____ ਅੰਡੇ   *boiled eggs*

b _____ _____ ਮੁੰਡਾ   *scared boy*

c _____ _____ ਲੜਕਾ   *educated boy*

▶ 4 Listening

The following passage has been recorded. Listen to it and then answer the questions in Panjabi.

ਡੇਬਰਾ ਨੂੰ ਜੀਤੀ ਦੇ ਵਿਆਹ ਦਾ ਸੱਦਾ ਪੱਤਰ ਆਇਆ ਹੈ। ਵਿਆਹ ੨੮ ਜਨਵਰੀ ਨੂੰ ਹੈ। ਡੇਬਰਾ ਪਹਿਲੇ ਕਦੇ ਕਿਸੇ ਪੰਜਾਬੀ ਵਿਆਹ ਤੇ ਨਹੀਂ ਗਈ। ਉਹ ਵਿਆਹ ਦੀਆਂ ਰਸਮਾਂ ਬਾਰੇ ਜਾਣਨਾ ਚਾਹੁੰਦੀ ਹੈ। ਇਸ ਲਈ ਉਹ ਆਪਣੀ ਸਹੇਲੀ ਦਰਸ਼ਨਾ ਕੋਲ ਗਈ ਹੈ।

a ਵਿਆਹ ਦਾ ਸੱਦਾ ਪੱਤਰ ਕਿਸ ਨੂੰ ਆਇਆ ਹੈ?

b ਵਿਆਹ ਕਿਸ ਦਾ ਹੈ?

c ਕੀ ਡੇਬਰਾ ਕਦੀ ਪੰਜਾਬੀ ਵਿਆਹ ਤੇ ਗਈ ਹੈ?

d ਵਿਆਹ ਕਿਹੜੀ ਤਾਰੀਖ਼ ਹੈ?

e ਡੇਬਰਾ ਦਰਸ਼ਨਾ ਕੋਲ ਕਿਉਂ ਗਈ ਹੈ?

14

ਉਹਨਾਂ ਨੇ ਮੇਰੇ ਬਾਰੇ
ਕੀ ਕਿਹਾ ਸੀ ?

uhnaan ne
mere baare
kee kihaa see?

what did they say about me?

In this unit you will learn:
- how to have a conversation about school
- how to speak with a police officer and a social worker
- how to use purpose clauses with *so that*

▶ 1 *Did you meet my class teacher?*

ਗੱਲ ਬਾਤ ੧ ਕੀ ਤੁਸੀਂ ਮੇਰੇ ਸ਼੍ਰੇਣੀ ਅਧਿਆਪਕ ਨੂੰ ਮਿਲੇ ਸੀ ?

gall baat 1 kee tuseen mere shrenhee adhiaapak noon mile see?

Mr Lall has just attended his son Ramesh's parents' evening at his school. Mr Lall has come home and is talking to Ramesh.

ਰਮੇਸ਼	ਪਾਪਾ ਜੀ! ਕੀ ਤੁਸੀਂ ਮੇਰੇ ਸ਼੍ਰੇਣੀ ਅਧਿਆਪਕ ਨੂੰ ਮਿਲੇ ਸੀ ?
ਮਿਸਟਰ ਲਾਲ	ਹਾਂ, ਮੈਂ ਉਸ ਤੋਂ ਇਲਾਵਾ ਤੇਰੇ ਦੂਜੇ ਮਜ਼੍ਮੂਨਾਂ ਦੇ ਅਧਿਆਪਕਾਂ ਨੂੰ ਵੀ ਮਿਲਿਆ ਸੀ ।
ਰਮੇਸ਼	ਉਹਨਾਂ ਨੇ ਮੇਰੇ ਬਾਰੇ ਕੀ ਕਿਹਾ ਸੀ ?
ਮਿਸਟਰ ਲਾਲ	ਹਿਸਾਬ ਦੇ ਅਧਿਆਪਕ ਨੇ ਕਿਹਾ ਕਿ ਤੂੰ ਘਰ ਦਾ ਕੰਮ ਕਰਨ ਵਿਚ ਲਾ ਪਰਵਾਹ ਹੈਂ ਅਤੇ ਕਾਲਜ ਵਿਚ ਗਾਲੜੀ ਹੈਂ ।
ਰਮੇਸ਼	ਉਹ ਮੈਥੋਂ ਪਸੰਦ ਨਹੀ ਕਰਦਾ। ਅੰਗਰੇਜ਼ੀ ਦੇ ਅਧਿਆਪਕ ਨੇ ਕੀ ਕਿਹਾ ?
ਮਿਸਟਰ ਲਾਲ	ਉਸ ਨੇ ਕਿਹਾ ਕਿ ਰਮੇਸ਼ ਵਿਚ ਲਿਆਕਤ ਹੈ ਪਰ ਉਹ ਵਰਤਦਾ ਨਹੀਂ ।
ਰਮੇਸ਼	ਉਹ ਸਾਨੂੰ ਚੰਗੀ ਤਰ੍ਹਾਂ ਪੜ੍ਹਾਂਦਾ ਨਹੀਂ।
ਮਿਸਟਰ ਲਾਲ	ਖ਼ੈਰ! ਤੈਨੂੰ ਪੜ੍ਹਾਈ ਵਿਚ ਮਿਹਨਤ ਕਰਨੀ ਚਾਹੀਦੀ ਹੈ ਤਾਂ ਕਿ ਤੂੰ ਚੰਗੇ ਗਰੇਡ ਲੈ ਕੇ ਡਾਕਟਰ ਬਣ ਸਕੇਂ।

Ramesh	*Dad! Did you meet my class teacher?*
Mr Lall	*Yes and apart from him I also met your other subject teachers.*
Ramesh	*What did they say about me?*
Mr Lall	*The maths teacher said that you were careless in doing your homework and talkative in class.*
Ramesh	*He doesn't like me. What did the English teacher say?*
Mr Lall	*He said that Ramesh has the ability but does not use it.*
Ramesh	*He does not teach us properly.*
Mr Lall	*Anyway! You should study hard so that you get good grades and can become a doctor.*

ਸ਼ਬਦਾਵਲੀ shabdaavalee *Vocabulary*

ਸ਼ੇਣੀ	shrenhee	*class* (f.)
ਅਧਿਆਪਕ	adhiaapak	*teacher* (m. / f.)
ਤੋਂ ਇਲਾਵਾ	ton ilaavaa	*apart from, besides*
ਦੂਜੇ	dooje	*others*
ਮਜ਼ਮੂਨਾਂ	mazmoonaan	*subjects* (m.)
ਹਿਸਾਬ	hisaab	*maths* (m.)
ਘਰ ਦਾ ਕੰਮ	ghar daa kanm	*homework* (m.)
ਲਾ ਪਰਵਾਹ	laa parvaah	*careless*
ਗਾਲੜੀ	gaalrhee	*talkative*
ਲਿਆਕਤ	liaakat	*ability* (f.)
ਵਰਤਣਾ	vartnhaa	*to use*
ਤਰ੍ਹਾਂ	tar-h-aan	*way, style*
ਪੜ੍ਹਾਉਣਾ	parhhaaunhaa	*to teach*
ਖ਼ੈਰ	khair	*anyway*
ਪੜ੍ਹਾਈ	parhhaaee	*studies* (f.)
ਤਾਂ ਕਿ	taan ki	*so that*
ਗਰੇਡ	gared	*grade* (m.)
ਬਣਨਾ	banhnaa	*to become*

ਅਭਿਆਸ abhiaas *Exercises*

After reading the dialogue and / or listening to the recording, try to do the following exercises.

1 Insert the missing vowels.

The vowel signs in the following sentences are missing. Rewrite them after inserting the vowels and joining the letters.

a ਪ ਪ ਜ ! ਕ / ਤ ਸ / ਮ ਰ / ਸ਼ ਣ / ਅ ਧ ਅ ਪ ਕ / ਨੰ / ਮ ਲ / ਸ ?
b ਉ ਹ / ਸ ਨੰ / ਚੰ ਗ / ਤ ਰੰ / ਪੜੰ ਦ / ਨ ਹਂ ।
c ਤ ਨੰ / ਪੜੁ ਏ / ਵ ਚ / ਮ ਹ ਨ ਤ / ਕ ਰ ਨ / ਚ ਹ ਦ / ਹ ।

2 Crossword

Complete the crossword in English using the clues given in Panjabi.

੧ ਅਧਿਆਪਕ

੨ ਰਮੇਸ਼

੩ ਘਰ ਦਾ ਕੰਮ

੪ ਹਿਸਾਬ

੫ ਲਾ ਪਰਵਾਹ

▶ 2 *Yes, officer*

ਗੱਲ ਬਾਤ ੨ ਹਾਂ ਜੀ, ਅਫ਼ਸਰ ਸਾਹਿਬ

gall baat 2 haan jee, afsar saahib

Sheela has been stopped by a police officer for using her mobile phone while driving her car.

ਪੁਲਿਸ ਅਫ਼ਸਰ	ਬੀਬੀ ਜੀ, ਕਾਰ ਇੱਕ ਪਾਸੇ ਖੜ੍ਹੀ ਕਰੋ ਅਤੇ ਮੋਬਾਇਲ ਫ਼ੋਨ ਬੰਦ ਕਰੋ ਤਾਂ ਕਿ ਤੁਸੀਂ ਮੈਥੋਂ ਸੁਣ ਕਰੋ।
ਸ਼ੀਲਾ	ਹਾਂ ਜੀ, ਅਫ਼ਸਰ ਸਾਹਿਬ।
ਪੁਲਿਸ ਅਫ਼ਸਰ	ਤੁਸੀਂ ਅਪਰਾਧ ਕਰ ਰਹੇ ਹੋ। ਤੁਹਾਡੇ ਤੇ ਕਾਰ ਚਲਾਦਿਆਂ ਮੋਬਾਇਲ ਫ਼ੋਨ ਦੀ ਵਰਤੋਂ ਕਰਨ ਦਾ ਦੋਸ਼ ਲਗਾਇਆ ਜਾਂਦਾ ਹੈ।
ਸ਼ੀਲਾ	ਮੈਂ ਕੇਵਲ ਇੱਕ ਮਿੰਟ ਲਈ ਫ਼ੋਨ ਵਰਤ ਰਹੀ ਸੀ।
ਪੁਲਿਸ ਅਫ਼ਸਰ	ਤੁਸੀਂ ਪਿਛਲੇ ਦਸ ਮਿੰਟ ਤੋਂ ਗੱਲਾਂ ਕਰ ਰਹੇ ਸੀ। ਤੁਸੀਂ ਕਾਰ ਤੋਂ ਬਾਹਰ ਆਓ ਅਤੇ ਆਪਣਾ ਲਾਇਸੈਂਸ ਦਿਖਾਓ।
ਸ਼ੀਲਾ	ਅਫ਼ਸਰ ਸਾਹਿਬ, ਕਿਰਪਾ ਕਰ ਕੇ ਇਸ ਵਾਰੀ ਮੈਥੋਂ ਮਾਫ਼ ਕਰ ਦੇਵੋ।
ਪੁਲਿਸ ਅਫ਼ਸਰ	ਤੁਸੀਂ ਕਾਨੂੰਨ ਦੀ ਉਲੰਘਣਾ ਕੀਤੀ ਹੈ। ਇਹ ਤੁਹਾਡੀ ਟਿਕਟ ਹੈ। ਹਫ਼ਤੇ ਅੰਦਰ ਆਪਣੇ ਕਾਰ ਦੇ ਕਾਗ਼ਜ਼ਾਤ ਪੇਸ਼ ਕਰੋ।

Police officer	*Madam, please pull the car over to one side and stop using the telephone so that you can listen to me.*
Sheela	*Yes, officer.*
Police officer	*You are committing an offence. I am charging you [lit. you are charged] for using a mobile phone while driving.*
Sheela	*I was only using the phone for one minute.*
Police officer	*You've been talking for the last ten minutes. Please get out of the car and show me your licence.*
Sheela	*Officer, please let me off this time.*
Police officer	*You have broken the law. Here is your ticket. Please produce your car documents within one week.*

ਸ਼ਬਦਾਵਲੀ   shabdaavalee   *Vocabulary*

ਬੀਬੀ	beebee	*madam* (f.)
ਇੱਕ ਪਾਸੇ	ikk paase	*one side*
ਖੜ੍ਹਨਾ	kharh-h-naa	*to stand, to park*

ਬੰਦ	band	closed, off
ਅਪਰਾਧ	apraadh	offence (m.)
ਦੋਸ਼	dosh	charge (m.)
ਗੱਲਾਂ	gallaan	speech, conversation (f.)
ਲਾਇਸੈਂਸ	laaisains	licence (m.)
ਇਸ ਵਾਰੀ	is vaaree	this time
ਮਾਫ਼	maaf	pardon, excuse
ਕਾਨੂੰਨ	kaanoonn	law (m.)
ਉਲੰਘਣਾ	ulanghnhaa	to disobey, to break
ਕਾਗਜ਼ਾਤ	kaaghzaat	papers, documents (m.)
ਪੇਸ਼ ਕਰਨਾ	pesh karnaa	to present, to produce

ਅਭਿਆਸ   abhiaas   *Exercises*

After reading the dialogue and / or listening to the recording, try to do the following exercises.

1 Complete the table.

ਕਾਨੂੰਨ		law
	beebee	
		documents
ਮਾਫ਼		
	ulanghnhaa	

2 Loan words

Make a list of five words borrowed from English used in Dialogue 2.

▶ 3 *I am a social worker*

ਗੱਲ ਬਾਤ ੩ ਮੈਂ ਸਮਾਜ ਸੇਵਕ ਹਾਂ

gall baat 3 main samaaj sevak haan

A social worker, Mrs Kaur, visits Kuldeep's house. She is following a complaint that under-aged children have been left unattended for long periods in the house.

ਸਮਾਜ ਸੇਵਕ   ਹੈਲੋ। ਮੈਂ ਸਮਾਜ ਸੇਵਕ ਹਾਂ ਅਤੇ ਮੇਰਾ ਨਾਮ ਮਿਸਜ਼ ਕੌਰ ਹੈ। ਇਹ ਮੇਰਾ ਸ਼ਨਾਖ਼ਤੀ ਕਾਰਡ ਹੈ। ਮੈਂ ਤੁਹਾਡੇ ਨਾਲ ਗੱਲ ਕਰਨ ਆਈ ਹਾਂ।

ਕੁਲਦੀਪ	ਅੰਦਰ ਆ ਜਾਓ । ਕੀ ਗੱਲ ਹੈ ?
ਸਮਾਜ ਸੇਵਕ	ਤੁਹਾਡੇ ਖ਼ਿਲਾਫ਼ ਸਾਡੇ ਦਫ਼ਤਰ ਵਿਚ ਇੱਕ ਸ਼ਿਕਾਇਤ ਪਹੁੰਚੀ ਹੈ ।
ਕੁਲਦੀਪ	ਕੀ ਹੋ ਗਿਆ ਹੈ ? ਕੀ ਮੈਂ ਕੋਈ ਗ਼ਲਤ ਕੰਮ ਕਰ ਬੈਠੀ ਹਾਂ ?
ਸਮਾਜ ਸੇਵਕ	ਤੁਸੀਂ ਆਪਣੇ ਦੋਨਾਂ ਬੱਚਿਆਂ ਨੂੰ ਇਕੱਲੇ ਘਰ ਦੇ ਅੰਦਰ ਛੱਡ ਕੇ, ਕੰਮ ਤੇ ਚਲੇ ਜਾਂਦੇ ਹੋ । ਇਹ ਇੱਕ ਖ਼ਤਰਨਾਕ ਸਥਿਤੀ ਬਣ ਸਕਦੀ ਹੈ ।
ਕੁਲਦੀਪ	ਮੈਂ ੫ ਵਜੇ ਜਾਂਦੀ ਹਾਂ । ਮੇਰੇ ਪਤੀ ੭ ਵਜੇ ਆਉਂਦੇ ਹਨ । ਸਿਰਫ਼ ਦੋ ਘੰਟੇ ਦੀ ਗੱਲ ਹੈ ।
ਸਮਾਜ ਸੇਵਕ	ਇਹਨਾਂ ਦੋ ਘੰਟਿਆ ਵਿਚ ਕੁਝ ਵੀ ਹੋ ਸਕਦਾ ਹੈ । ਕੰਮ ਦੇ ਘੰਟੇ ਬਦਲੋ ਜਾਂ ਕੋਈ ਹੋਰ ਇੰਤਜ਼ਾਮ ਕਰੋ ।
ਕੁਲਦੀਪ	ਇਹ ਮੇਰੇ ਲਈ ਮੁਸ਼ਕਲ ਹੈ । ਮੈਂ ਕੰਮ ਨਹੀਂ ਛੱਡ ਸਕਦੀ ।
ਸਮਾਜ ਸੇਵਕ	ਕੋਈ ਬੇਬੀ ਸਿਟਰ ਲੱਭੋ ।
ਕੁਲਦੀਪ	ਮੈਂ ਪੂਰੀ ਕੋਸ਼ਿਸ਼ ਕਰਾਂ ਗੀ ।

Social worker	*Hello, I am a social worker and my name is Mrs Kaur. Here is my identity card. I have come to talk to you.*
Kuldeep	*Please come in. What is the matter?*
Social worker	*We have received a complaint in our office against you.*
Kuldeep	*What has happened? Have I done anything wrong?*
Social worker	*You leave both of your children alone in the house and go to work. This is a potentially dangerous situation.*
Kuldeep	*I leave at 5 o'clock. My husband comes home at 7 o'clock. It is only a matter of two hours.*
Social worker	*Anything can happen in those two hours. Either change your hours of work or make alternative arrangements.*
Kuldeep	*This is difficult for me. I can't leave work.*
Social worker	*Find a baby sitter.*
Kuldeep	*I will try my best.*

ਸ਼ਬਦਾਵਲੀ   shab<u>d</u>aavalee   *Vocabulary*

ਸਮਾਜ ਸੇਵਕ	samaaj sevak	*social worker (m. / f.)*
ਸ਼ਨਾਖ਼ਤੀ ਕਾਰਡ	shanaa<u>kh</u>tee kaard	*identity card (m.)*
ਖ਼ਿਲਾਫ਼	<u>kh</u>ilaaf	*against*
ਦਫ਼ਤਰ	<u>d</u>af<u>t</u>ar	*office (m.)*
ਸ਼ਿਕਾਇਤ	shikaai<u>t</u>	*complaint (f.)*

ਗਲਤ	ghalat	wrong
ਖ਼ਤਰਨਾਕ	khaṭarnaak	dangerous
ਸਥਿਤੀ	saṭhitee	situation (f.)
ਇੰਤਜ਼ਾਮ	intzaam	arrangements (m.)
ਬੇਬੀ ਸਿਟਰ	bebee sitar	baby sitter (m. / f.)
ਲੱਭਣਾ	labhbhṇhaa	to find

ਅਭਿਆਸ abhiaas *Exercises*

After reading the dialogue and / or listening to the recording, try to do the following exercises.

1 Write or say in the correct word order.

a ਹਾਂ ਸੇਵਕ ਸਮਾਜ ਮੈਂ

b ਹੈ ਕੀ ਗੱਲ ?

c ਜਾਓ ਆ ਅੰਦਰ

d ਹੈ ਲਈ ਮੇਰੇ ਇਹ ਮੁਸ਼ਕਲ

2 Complete the sentences.

Choose the correct word from the bracket to complete the sentence according to the specifications of gender and number. Remember that the verb changes according to the subject.

a ਮੈਂ ਤੁਹਾਡੇ ਨਾਲ ਗੱਲ ਕਰਨ   [masculine singular]
   (ਆਈ / ਆਇਆ) ਹਾਂ ।
   I have come to talk to you.

b ਮੈਂ ਕੰਮ ਨਹੀਂ ਛੱਡ (ਸਕਦੀ / ਸਕਦਾ) ।   [feminine singular]
   I can't leave work.

c ਤੁਸੀਂ ਕੰਮ ਤੇ (ਚਲੇ ਜਾਂਦੇ /   [formal singular]
   ਚਲੀ ਜਾਂਦੇ) ਹੋ ।
   You go to work.

d ਮੈਂ ਪੂਰੀ ਕੋਸ਼ਿਸ਼ (ਕਰਾਂ ਗੇ / ਕਰਾਂ ਗੀ)   [feminine singular]
   I will try my best.

ਬੋਲੀ ਬਾਰੇ bolee baare *Language points*

Purpose clauses

In Unit 7 infinitives in the oblique were shown to express purpose such as ਮੈਂ ਦੋਸਤ ਨੂੰ ਮਿਲਣ ਆਇਆ ਹਾਂ, *I have come to meet a friend*. Another way of expressing purpose is through the use of ਤਾਂ ਕਿ, *so that*, *in order to*. The verb in the purpose clause is normally in the subjunctive (since the action is often indefinite or uncertain):

ਸਿਮਰਨ ਨੇ ਦਵਾਈ ਲੈ ਲਈ ਤਾਂ
ਕਿ ਬੁਖ਼ਾਰ ਉਤਰ ਜਾਏ

Simran took medicine so that her fever would come down.

ਮੈਂ ਦਰਵਾਜ਼ਾ ਬੰਦ ਕੀਤਾ ਸੀ ਤਾਂ
ਕਿ ਬਿੱਲੀ ਅੰਦਰ ਨਾ ਆ ਸਕੇ

I closed the door so that the cat couldn't come inside.

ਇਮਰਾਨ ਉਰਦੂ ਪੜ੍ਹ ਰਿਹਾ ਹੈ ਤਾਂ ਕਿ
ਉਹ ਪਾਕਿਸਤਾਨ ਵਿਚ ਆਪਣੇ
ਰਿਸ਼ਤੇਦਾਰਾਂ ਨਾਲ ਗੱਲ ਕਰ ਸਕੇ

Imran is studying Urdu so that he can speak with his relatives in Pakistan.

Compound postpositions

In Unit 4 simple postpositions such as **ਵਿਚ** *in*, **ਤੋਂ** *from* and **ਨੂੰ** *to* were introduced. Postpositions having more than one word are called compound postpositions, most commonly using the postposition **ਦੇ** *of*. Compound postpositions behave in the same way as simple postpositions by requiring the words preceding them to be in the oblique case. Here are some commonly used compound postpositions:

ਦੇ ਅੰਦਰ	*inside*	ਦੇ ਵਾਸਤੇ	*for*
ਦੇ ਉੱਪਰ	*above, upon*	ਦੇ ਲਈ	*for*
ਦੇ ਪਿੱਛੇ	*behind*	ਦੀ ਜਗ੍ਹਾ	*in place of*
ਦੇ ਥੱਲੇ	*below*	ਦੇ ਸਾਹਮਣੇ	*opposite, facing*
ਤੋਂ ਪਹਿਲੇ	*before*	ਦੇ ਬਾਹਰ	*outside*
ਤੋਂ ਬਾਅਦ	*after*	ਤੋਂ ਇਲਾਵਾ	*apart from*
ਦੇ ਨੇੜੇ	*near*	ਤੋਂ ਬਿਨਾਂ / ਬ.ਗ਼ੈਰ	*without*
ਦੇ ਬਾਰੇ	*about, concerning*	ਦੇ ਬਾਵਜੂਦ	*in spite of*

Indirect speech

So far in this book we have focused on direct speech, when sentences and phrases have been directly spoken or reproduced. Indirect speech occurs when another action or speech is being reported or conveyed, such as in English: *She told me to call him*, ਉਸ ਨੇ ਮੈਨੂੰ ਕਿਹਾ ਕਿ ਉਹ ਨੂੰ ਬੁਲਾਓ. Indirect speech in Panjabi is expressed with the particle **ਕਿ** *that* to denote what was actually said or done.

Indirect speech is used when the verb of thought or speech occurred before the thought or speech being conveyed:

ਮੈਂ ਆਪਣੇ ਆਪ ਵਿਚ ਸੋਚਿਆ
ਕਿ ਮੈਂ ਜ਼ਰੂਰ ਜਿੱਤਾਂ ਗੀ

I thought to myself that I would definitely win.

ਜਗਜੀਤ ਨੇ ਕਿਹਾ ਕਿ ਇਹ
ਕਿਤਾਬ ਪੜ੍ਹਨ ਵਾਲੀ ਹੈ

Jagjit said that this book is worth reading.

ਕਿਸੇ ਨੇ ਮੈਨੂੰ ਦੱਸਿਆ ਕਿ ਮਿਸਜ਼ ਸ਼ਰਮਾ ਭਾਰਤ ਚਲੀ ਗਈ ਹੈ	*Someone told me that Mrs Sharma has gone to India.*

When the speech being conveyed is a command:

ਉਸ ਨੇ ਬੱਚਿਆਂ ਨੂੰ ਕਿਹਾ ਕਿ ਚੁੱਪ ਰਹੋ	*He told the children to be quiet.*
ਮੈਂ ਸਾਰਿਆਂ ਨੂੰ ਕਿਹਾ ਕਿ ਘਰ ਵਾਪਸ ਚਲੇ ਜਾਓ	*I told everyone to go back home.*

ਅਭਿਆਸ   abhiaas   *Exercises*

After reading the dialogue and / or listening to the recording, try to do the following exercises.

1 Fill in the blanks with the appropriate compound postpositions.

a ਸਾਡਾ ਘਰ ਸਕੂਲ _____ ਹੈ। *Our house is near the school.*

b ਬਿੱਲੀ ਡੱਬੇ _____ ਹੈ। *The cat is inside the box.*

c ਉਹ ਰੋਟੀ ਖਾਣ _____ ਆਵੇ ਗਾ। *He will come after eating.*

d ਤਸਵੀਰ _____ ਕੁਝ ਹੋਰ ਚਾਹੀਦਾ ਹੈ। *There should be something else in place of the picture.*

2 Match the pairs.

The following eight sentences need to be joined with ਤਾਂ ਕਿ. Match the correct pairs of sentences with one another.

a ਮੈਂ ਦਰਵਾਜ਼ਾ ਬੰਦ ਕੀਤਾ		i ... ਸਵੇਰੇ ਜਲਦੀ ਉਠ ਸਕੇ
b ਅਸੀਂ ਪੰਜਾਬੀ ਬੋਲਾਂ ਗੇ	ਤਾਂ ਕਿ	ii ... ਕੁੱਤਾ ਅੰਦਰ ਨਾ ਆ ਸਕੇ
c ਤੈਨੂੰ ਜਲਦੀ ਆਉਣਾ ਚਾਹੀਦਾ ਹੈ		iii ... ਸਾਰੇ ਸਮਝ ਜਾਣ
d ਤੁਸੀਂ ਜਲਦੀ ਸੌਂ ਜਾਓ		iv ... ਅਸੀਂ ਬਸ ਫੜ ਸਕੀਏ

▶ 3 Listening

Sheela is telling her story to her friend Meena about how she was stopped by the police officer for using her mobile phone while driving. Listen to the recording and answer the following questions. You may answer the questions with short or full answers.

a ਸ਼ੀਲਾ ਆਪਣੀ ਕਾਰ ਵਿਚ ਕਿੱਥੇ ਜਾ ਰਹੀ ਸੀ?

b ਉਹ ਕਿੰਨੀ ਦੇਰ ਤੋਂ ਮੋਬਾਈਲ ਤੇ ਗੱਲਾਂ ਕਰ ਰਹੀ ਸੀ?

c ਕੀ ਸ਼ੀਲਾ ਨੇ ਅਫ਼ਸਰ ਅੱਗੇ ਸੱਚ ਬੋਲਿਆ?
d ਇੱਕ ਹਫ਼ਤੇ ਦੇ ਅੰਦਰ ਸ਼ੀਲਾ ਨੂੰ ਕੀ ਕਰਨਾ ਪੈਣਾ ਹੈ?

4 Alphabetical order

Rearrange the following words into alphabetical order, considering only the first letter of each word.

ਪਾਪਾ	ਵਰਤਣਾ	ਡਾਕਟਰ	ਅਧਿਆਪਕ	ਬਾਰੇ
ਪੜ੍ਹਾਉਣਾ	ਮਜ਼ਮੂਨਾਂ	ਦੂਜੇ	ਹਿਸਾਬ	ਕਲਾਸ
ਲਿਆਕਤ	ਕੰਮ	ਮਿਹਨਤ	ਸ਼੍ਰੇਣੀ	ਇਲਾਵਾ

15

ਵੈਸਾਖੀ **vaisaakhee**

Vaisakhi

In this unit you will learn:
- about the *Vaisakhi* festival
- about Panjabi poetry and music
- how to express *to allow*

▶ *The Vaisakhi fair*

ਵੈਸਾਖੀ ਦਾ ਮੇਲਾ

vaisaakhee ḏaa melaa

The following extract is a news report from the BBC Asian Network reporting on the events of the **Vaisakhi** festival in Birmingham, UK.

ਨੀਲੂ	ਮੈਂ ਨੀਲੂ ਹਾਂ ਤੇ ਮੈਂ ਬੀ. ਬੀ. ਸੀ. ਰੇਡੀਓ ਲਈ ਹੈਂਡਜ਼ਵਰਥ ਪਾਰਕ ਤੋਂ ਰਿਪੋਰਟ ਪੇਸ਼ ਕਰ ਰਹੀ ਹਾਂ। ਇਸ ਸਾਲ ਵੈਸਾਖੀ ਦਾ ਤਿਉਹਾਰ ਬੜੀ ਧੂਮ ਧਾਮ ਨਾਲ ਮਨਾਇਆ ਜਾ ਰਿਹਾ ਹੈ। ਅੱਜ ਲੱਗਦਾ ਹੈ ਜਿਵੇਂ ਸਾਰੇ ਸ਼ਹਿਰ ਦੇ ਪੰਜਾਬੀ ਲੋਕ ਪਹੁੰਚੇ ਹੋਏ ਹਨ। ਹੁਣੇ ਮੈਂ ਅੰਕਲ ਜੀ ਨੂੰ ਪੁੱਛਿਆ ਹੈ ਕਿ ਉਹਨਾਂ ਨੂੰ ਮੇਲਾ ਕਿਵੇਂ ਲੱਗ ਰਿਹਾ ਹੈ।
ਅੰਕਲ	ਮੈਨੂੰ ਆਪਣਾ ਪੇਂਡੂ ਜੀਵਨ ਯਾਦ ਆ ਰਿਹਾ ਹੈ। ਸਾਡੇ ਲਈ ਇਹ ਫ਼ਸਲਾਂ ਕਟਣ ਦੀ ਖੁਸ਼ੀ ਦਾ ਤਿਉਹਾਰ ਹੈ।
ਨੀਲੂ	. . . ਨਾਲੇ ਵੈਸਾਖ ਪੰਜਾਬੀ ਸਾਲ ਦਾ ਪਹਿਲਾ ਮਹੀਨਾ ਵੀ ਹੈ। ਅੱਛਾ ਆਂਟੀ ਜੀ, ਤੁਸੀਂ ਇੱਥੇ ਅੱਜ ਕਿਉਂ ਆਏ ਹੋ ?
ਆਂਟੀ	ਬੇਟੀ, ਵੈਸਾਖੀ ਸਿੱਖ ਕੌਮ ਦਾ ਜਨਮ ਦਿਨ ਹੈ। ਜਿੱਥੇ ਅਸੀਂ ਖਲੋਤੇ ਹਾਂ, ਉੱਥੇ ਨਗਰ ਕੀਰਤਨ ਆਉਣ ਵਾਲਾ ਹੈ। ਅੱਗੋ ਅੱਗੇ ਨੌਜੁਆਨ ਗਤਕਾ ਖੇਡ ਰਹੇ ਹਨ। ਪਿੱਛੇ ਗੁਰੂ ਗਰੰਥ ਸਾਹਿਬ ਦੀ ਸਵਾਰੀ ਹੈ।
ਨੀਲੂ	ਮੈਂ ਹੁਣ ਲੰਗਰ ਹਾਲ ਵੱਲ ਜਾ ਰਹੀ ਹਾਂ। ਦੇਖੋ! ਜਲੇਬੀਆਂ, ਪਕੌੜੇ ਅਤੇ ਹੋਰ ਕਈ ਚੀਜ਼ਾ ਸੇਵਾਦਾਰ ਮੁਫ਼ਤ ਵਰਤਾ ਰਹੇ ਹਨ। ਬੱਚਿਆਂ ਨੂੰ ਲੰਗਰ ਪਹਿਲੇ ਲੈਣ ਦੇਵੋ।
ਕਾਕਾ	ਨੀਲੂ ਆਂਟੀ! ਮੈਂ ਲੰਗਰ ਛਕਣ ਤੋ ਬਾਅਦ ਝੂਟੇ ਲਵਾਂ ਗਾ। ਬੱਚਿਆਂ ਦੇ ਮਨਪਰਚਾਵੇ ਲਈ ਬਹੁਤ ਕੁਝ ਹੈ।
ਨੀਲੂ	ਅੱਛਾ ਬੇਟਾ। ਝੂਟਿਆਂ ਤੋਂ ਇਲਾਵਾ ਨੁਮਾਇਸ਼ ਵੀ ਲੱਗੀ ਹੋਈ ਹੈ। ਭੰਗੜਾ ਸ਼ੁਰੂ ਹੋਣ ਲੱਗਾ ਹੈ। ਹੁਣ ਮੈਨੂੰ ਇਜਾਜ਼ਤ ਦੇਵੋ। ਸਾਰਿਆਂ ਨੂੰ ਬੀ. ਬੀ. ਸੀ. ਵੱਲੋਂ ਵੈਸਾਖੀ ਦੀ ਵਧਾਈ!

Neelu	*I'm Neelu and I'm reporting for BBC Radio from Handsworth Park. The* Vaisakhi *festival this year is being celebrated with a 'bang'. It seems today that all the Panjabi people of the city have come here. I have just asked Uncle how he feels about the fair.*
Uncle	*I am remembering my village life. For us this is a happy festival of harvest.*
Neelu	Vaisakh *is also the first month of the Panjabi calendar. Well, Auntie, why have you come here?*
Auntie	Vaisakhi *is the birthday of the Sikh nation. The religious procession is due to arrive where we are standing. In*

front of the procession young people are playing
gatka. *It is followed by the installation of the*
Guru Granth Sahib.

Neelu   *I am going towards the* langar *hall. Look.* Jalebeeaan,
pakaurhe *and many other things are being served by
volunteers free of charge. Please allow the children to
have* langar *first.*

Young *Auntie Neelu! I will go on the rides after I've had* langar.
boy   *There is a lot of entertainment for the children.*

Neelu   *OK, son. Apart from the rides, there is also an exhibition.*
Bhangra *is about to begin. Now, please excuse me. To
everyone from BBC Radio, happy* Vaisakhi!

ਸ਼ਬਦਾਵਲੀ   shab<u>d</u>aavalee   *Vocabulary*

ਪੇਸ਼	pesh	*to present*
ਵੈਸਾਖੀ	vaisaakhee	Vaisakhi, one of the Sikh festivals (f.)
ਮੇਲਾ	melaa	*fair* (m.)
ਧੂਮ ਧਾਮ	<u>dh</u>oom <u>dh</u>aam	*bang, pomp and show* (f.)
ਮਨਾਉਣਾ	manaaunhaa	*to celebrate*
ਦਰਸ਼ਕ	<u>d</u>arshak	*participant, visitor* (m. / f.)
ਪੁੱਛਣਾ	pu<u>chch</u>nhaa	*to ask*
ਪੇਂਡੂ	pe<u>n</u>doo	*of the village, village-like*
ਜੀਵਨ	jeevan	*life* (m.)
ਫ਼ਸਲਾਂ	fasalaa<u>n</u>	*crops* (f.)
ਕਟਣ	katanh	*to cut*
ਤਿਉਹਾਰ	<u>t</u>iuhaar	*celebration, festival* (m.)
ਵੈਸਾਖ	vaisaakh	one of the Indian months (m.)
ਕੌਮ	kaum	*nation, community* (f.)
ਜਨਮ ਦਿਨ	janam <u>d</u>in	*birthday* (m.)
ਖਲੋਣਾ	khalonhaa	*to be stood, to stand*
ਨਗਰ ਕੀਰਤਨ	nagar keer<u>t</u>an	*religious procession* (m.)
ਗਾਤਕਾ	ga<u>t</u>kaa	a Sikh martial art like fencing (m.)
ਖੇਡਣਾ	khednhaa	*to play*
ਗੁਰੂ ਗਰੰਥ	guroo gara<u>nth</u>	*Guru Granth; holy book of the Sikhs* (m.)
ਸਵਾਰੀ	savaaree	*installation* (f.)
ਲੰਗਰ	la<u>n</u>gar	*community kitchen* (m.)
ਸੇਵਾਦਾਰ	sevaa<u>d</u>aar	*volunteer* (m. / f.)
ਮੁਫ਼ਤ	mufa<u>t</u>	*free*

ਵਰਤਾਉਣਾ	vartaaunhaa	to serve
ਛਕਣਾ	chaknhaa	to take, to consume
ਝੂਟੇ	jhoote	rides (m.)
ਮਨਪਰਚਾਵੇ	manparchaave	entertainment, enjoyment (m.)
ਨੁਮਾਇਸ਼	numaaish	exhibition (f.)
ਵੱਲੋਂ	vallon	on behalf of
ਵਧਾਈ	vadhaaee	congratulations (f.)

ਅਭਿਆਸ   abhiaas   *Exercises*

After reading the dialogue and / or listening to the recording, try to do the following exercises.

1 Answer in Panjabi.

Answer the questions in Panjabi in either full sentences or in short form answers. The answers to the questions can be found in the dialogue. The first one has been done for you.

a What is the name of the radio presenter?
  ਪੇਸ਼ ਕਰਤਾ ਦਾ ਨਾਮ ਨੀਲੂ ਹੈ l (full sentence) or ਨੀਲੂ (short answer)
b What is the report about?
c Name two main things associated with the Vaisakhi festival.
d What is being served in the community kitchen?
e What is the name of the game being played in front of the procession?
f Name two main activities taking place at the Vaisakhi fair.

2 Identify the appropriate answers.

The *Vaisakhi* festival is associated with:

- village people
- candles
- harvest season
- the new year
- Sikh religion

3 True or false?

Langar means *community kitchen*.	True / False
Guru Granth is the holy book of the Sikhs.	True / False
Gatka is a group dance.	True / False
Nagar kirtan is singing.	True / False

▶ *Folk song: My spinning wheel is of many colours*

ਲੋਕ ਗੀਤ: ਚਰਖਾ ਮੇਰਾ ਰੰਗਲਾ

lok geet̲: charkhaa meraa ranglaa

The following is a traditional Panjabi folk song. Listen to the song on the recording while reading the verses of the song:

ਚਰਖਾ ਮੇਰਾ ਰੰਗਲਾ ਵਿਚ ਸੋਨੇ ਦੀਆਂ ਮੇਖਾਂ
ਵੇ ਮੈਂ ਤੈਨੂੰ ਯਾਦ ਕਰਾਂ ਜਦ ਚਰਖੇ ਵੱਲ ਵੇਖਾਂ

ਚਰਖੇ ਦੇ ਸ਼ੀਸ਼ਿਆਂ 'ਚ ਦਿਸੇ ਤੇਰਾ ਮੁੱਖ ਵੇ
ਵੇਖ ਵੇਖ ਮਿਟ ਦੀ ਨਾ ਅੱਖੀਆਂ ਦੀ ਭੁੱਖ ਵੇ
ਸੀਨੇ ਵਿਚ ਨੇ ਰੜਕ ਦੀਆਂ ਇਹ ਚਰਖੇ ਦੀਆਂ ਮੇਖਾਂ

ਦਿਨ ਰਾਤ ਤੇਰੀਆਂ ਰਾਹਾਂ ਵੱਲ ਜਾਵਾਂ ਝਾਕੀ ਵੇ
ਤੇਰੇ ਬਿਨ ਅਸੀਂ ਕੀ ਮਨਾਊਣੀ ਏ ਵੈਸਾਖੀ ਵੇ
ਸੌ ਸੌ ਪੀਰ ਮਨਾਵਾਂ ਨਾਲੇ ਥਾਂ ਥਾਂ ਮੱਥੇ ਟੇਕਾਂ
ਵੇ ਮੈਂ ਤੈਨੂੰ ਯਾਦ ਕਰਾਂ ਜਦ ਚਰਖੇ ਵੱਲ ਵੇਖਾਂ

My spinning wheel is of many colours, studded with gold nails
Oh! I remember you, when I look at the spinning wheel

I see your face in the mirror work of the spinning wheel
Continuously looking does not satisfy my eyes' desire
The studded nails of this spinning wheel prick my heart

Day and night I keep watch on the road for your return
Without you, what kind of Vaisakhi *am I to celebrate?*
For your return I pray to a hundred holy men
and bow my head at many holy places
Oh! I remember you, when I look at the spinning wheel

ਸ਼ਬਦਾਵਲੀ   shab<u>d</u>aavalee   *Vocabulary*

ਚਰਖਾ	charkhaa	*spinning wheel* (m.)
ਰੰਗਲਾ	ra<u>ng</u>laa	*colourful* (v.)
ਸੋਨਾ	sonaa	*gold* (m.)
ਮੇਖ	mekh	*nail* (f.)
ਵੇ	ve	subjunctive particle
ਵੱਲ	vall	*towards*
ਵੇਖਣਾ	vekhnhaa	*to see*
ਸ਼ੀਸ਼ਾ	sheeshaa	*mirror* (m.)
ਦਿਸਣਾ	<u>d</u>isnhaa	*to be visible, to be seen*
ਮੁੱਖ	mukhkh	*face* (m.)
ਮਿਟਣਾ	mitnhaa	*to finish, to vanish*
ਭੁੱਖ	bhukhkh	*hunger* (f.)
ਸੀਨਾ	seenaa	*bosom, heart* (m.)
ਰੜਕਣਾ	rarhkanhaa	*to prick, to rub against*
ਰਾਹਾਂ	raahaa<u>n</u>	*roads, routes* (f.)
ਝਾਕਣਾ	jhaaknhaa	*to stare, to look at*
ਪੀਰ	peer	*holy man* (m.)
ਮਨਾਉਣਾ	manaaunhaa	*to pray, to believe*
ਟੇਕਣਾ	teknhaa	*to bow down*

ਅਭਿਆਸ   abhiaas   *Exercise*

After reading the folk song and / or listening to the recording, try to do the following exercise.

Answer the questions (yes or no)

My spinning wheel is many-coloured.
It is studded with nails of gold.
I remember you whenever I look at it.
These nails make me suffer in love.

ਮੇਰਾ ਚਰਖਾ ਕਈ ਰੰਗਾਂ ਵਾਲਾ ਹੈ।
ਇਸ ਵਿਚ ਸੋਨੇ ਦੀਆਂ ਮੇਖਾਂ ਲੱਗੀਆਂ ਹੋਈਆਂ ਹਨ।
ਜਦੋਂ ਮੈਂ ਇਸ ਵੱਲ ਦੇਖਦੀ ਹਾਂ, ਉਦੋਂ ਤੈਨੂੰ ਯਾਦ ਕਰਦੀ ਹਾਂ।
ਇਹ ਮੇਖਾਂ ਮੈਨੂੰ ਪਿਆਰ ਵਿਚ ਤੜਫਾਂਦੀਆਂ ਹਨ।

a ਕੀ ਇਹ ਗੀਤ ਪਿਆਰ ਬਾਰੇ ਕੁਝ ਦੱਸ ਰਿਹਾ ਹੈ?
b ਕੀ ਚਰਖੇ ਵਿਚ ਲੋਹੇ (iron) ਦੀਆਂ ਮੇਖਾਂ ਹਨ?
c ਜਦੋਂ ਔਰਤ ਚਰਖੇ ਵੱਲ ਵੇਖਦੀ ਹੈ ਕੀ ਉਦੋਂ ਆਪਣੇ ਪਿਆਰ ਨੂੰ ਭੁੱਲ ਜਾਂਦੀ ਹੈ?
d ਕੀ ਚਰਖੇ ਦਾ ਸਿਰਫ਼ ਇੱਕ ਰੰਗ ਹੈ?

ਬੋਲੀ ਬਾਰੇ   bolee baare   *Language points*

Relative–correlatives

You have already been introduced to the most common relative pronoun, **ਜਿਹੜਾ** which means *that* (see Unit 9 for a review of how sentences with relative pronouns are formed). Relative–correlatives are relative pronouns which are paired with their correlating counterparts. The correlating counterpart of the relative pronoun **ਜਿਹੜਾ** can be either **ਇਹ** or **ਉਹ** (*that . . . which*). In English, the sentence *I will go when he comes* contains only one relative pronoun *when*. However, the same sentence would be expressed in Panjabi as *when he comes, then I will go* with the relative pronoun *when* and its correlative *then*. There are a number of such pairings, that can be used to indicate place, time, quantity and likeness. For example:

Relative		Correlative	
ਜਿਹੜਾ	*who, which*	ਉਹ	*he, she, it, that*
ਜਿਹੜਾ	*who, which*	ਇਹ	*he, she, it, this*
ਜਦੋਂ	*when*	ਉਦੋਂ	*then*
ਜੱਦ ਤਕ	*as long as*	ਤੱਦ ਤਕ	*until then*
ਜਿਵੇਂ	*in such a way*	ਉਵੇਂ	*in that way*
ਜਿੰਨਾਂ	*as many, however much*	ਓਨਾਂ	*that much, that many*
ਜਿੰਨਾਂ	*as many, however much*	ਇੰਨਾਂ	*this much, this many*
ਜਿੱਥੇ	*where*	ਉੱਥੇ	*there*

ਜਿੱਥੇ ਅਸੀਂ ਰਹਿੰਦੇ ਹਾਂ ਉੱਥੇ ਪੰਜਾਬੀ ਬੋਲੀ ਜਾਂਦੀ ਹੈ	*Panjabi is spoken where we live.* (lit. *Where we live, Panjabi is spoken there.*)
ਜਿਵੇਂ ਤੁਸੀਂ ਚਾਹੁੰਦੇ ਹੋ ਉਵੇਂ ਅਸੀਂ ਕਰਾਂ ਗੇ	*We'll do as you like.* (lit. *As you like, that is the way we will do.*)
ਜਿਹੜਾ ਬੰਦਾ ਲਾਹੌਰ ਜਾ ਚੁਕਾ ਹੈ ਉਹ ਨੂੰ ਰਸਤਾ ਪੁੱਛੋ	*Ask directions from the man who has been to Lahore.* (lit. *The man who has been to Lahore, ask the way from him.*)
ਜੱਦ ਤਕ ਤੂੰ ਪੰਜਾਬ ਨਹੀਂ ਜਾਂਦਾ ਤੱਦ ਤਕ ਤੈਨੂੰ ਚੰਗੀ ਪੰਜਾਬੀ ਨਹੀਂ ਆਏ ਗੀ	*You won't learn good Panjabi until you go to Panjab.* (lit. *As long as you don't go to Panjab, until then you won't learn good Panjabi.*)
ਜਿੰਨਾਂ ਜ਼ਿਆਦਾ ਕੰਮ ਕਰੋ ਗੇ ਓਨੇ ਜ਼ਿਆਦਾ ਪੈਸੇ ਕਮਾ ਸਕੋ ਗੇ	*The more you work, the more money you can earn.* (lit. *As much work as you will do, that much more money you will earn.*)

The subjunctive particle ਵੇ 've'

You will recall from Unit 12 that the subjunctive mood is used to indicate uncertainty or indefiniteness. The particle ਵੇ is associated with the endings of the subjunctive mood. It is not, however, uncommon to see the particle ਵੇ on its own, particularly in poetic language and songs. It can appear as part of the verb in the subjunctive or on its own in the phrase or sentence. In the passage of the song ਚਰਖਾ ਮੇਰਾ ਰੰਗਲਾ the particle ਵੇ occurs at the beginning of the second line:

ਵੇ ਮੈਂ ਤੈਨੂੰ ਯਾਦ ਕਰਾਂ   *(Oh!) I remember you.*

The vocative case, as you learned in Unit 8, is a projection of an address to someone similar to the English *oh!* or *hey!*. ਵੇ is a colloquial form of address in friendly and informal situations.

The verb ਲੱਗਣਾ 'laggnhaa'

The verb ਲੱਗਣਾ has occured a number of times throughout the units so far. In Unit 9 Simran asks Jaspreet about the cloth: ਤੈਨੂੰ ਕਿਹੜਾ ਵਧੇਰੇ ਚੰਗਾ ਲੱਗਦਾ ਹੈ?, *Which one do you like better?* In the second dialogue of Unit 9 Simran says to the doctor: ਮੈਨੂੰ ਠੰਡ ਲੱਗ ਰਹੀ ਹੈ, *I am feeling cold.* The basic definition of ਲੱਗਣਾ is *to be applied to*, however it can also carry slightly different meanings. In the first example it means *to seem* or *to appear* and in the second example it has the sense *to be struck*. In fact ਲੱਗਣਾ is used in a wide range of situations and it is therefore always necessary to take the context of the sentence into account. Here are some examples of these different, yet related, senses of the verb ਲੱਗਣਾ:

ਲੱਗਣਾ meaning *to seem, to like, to be struck*

ਨਿਆਣੇ ਨੂੰ ਠੰਡ ਲੱਗੇ ਗੀ	*The child will feel cold.*
ਅਮਰੀਕਾ ਰਹਿਣਾ ਮੈਨੂੰ ਅੱਛਾ ਲੱਗਦਾ ਹੈ	*I like living in America.* (lit. *Living in America seems good to me.*)
ਘਰ ਨੂੰ ਅੱਗ ਲੱਗੀ ਹੋਈ ਸੀ	*The house was on* (lit. *struck by*) *fire.*

ਲੱਗਣਾ to mean *time taken* or *to cost*

ਅੰਮ੍ਰਿਤਸਰ ਪਹੁੰਚਣ ਨੂੰ ਕਿੰਨਾ ਚਿਰ ਲੱਗੇ ਗਾ ?	*How long will it take to get to Amritsar?*
ਮੈਨੂੰ ਸਿਰਫ਼ ਦਸ ਮਿੰਟ ਲੱਗੇ	*It only took me ten minutes.*
ਇੱਕ ਟਿਕਟ ਲਈ ਕਿੰਨੇ ਪੈਸੇ ਲੱਗਦੇ ਹਨ ?	*How much money does one ticket cost?* (lit. *it take*)

ਲੱਗਣਾ following an oblique infinitive

In this case, its meaning changes to give the sense *to begin*:

ਬਾਰਸ਼ ਹੋਣ ਲੱਗੀ	*It began to rain.*
ਮੈਂ ਕੰਮ ਸ਼ੁਰੂ ਕਰਨ ਲੱਗਾ ਸੀ	*I was about to begin work.*
ਉਹ ਸੋਚਣ ਲੱਗਾ ਕਿ ਸਾਰੇ ਚਲੇ ਗਏ ਹਨ	*He began to think that everyone had left.*

Oblique infinitives with ਦੇਣਾ '*denhaa*'

The general use of ਦੇਣਾ in compound constructions was discussed in Unit 9. ਦੇਣਾ can also be used with oblique infinitives to give the meaning of *to allow to* or *to permit*. Similar to the way in which ਲੱਗਣਾ changes its meaning to *to begin* when following oblique infinitives, ਦੇਣਾ with the oblique infinitive also changes its meaning.

ਕੁੱਤੇ ਨੂੰ ਅੰਦਰ ਆਉਣ ਦੇ	*Let the dog come inside.*
ਪਿਤਾ ਜੀ ਨੇ ਮੈਨੂੰ ਗੱਡੀ ਚਲਾਉਣ ਨਹੀਂ ਦਿੱਤੀ	*Father did not allow me to drive the car.*
ਉਹ ਆਪਣੇ ਬੱਚੇ ਨੂੰ ਬਾਹਰ ਖੇਡਣ ਦੇਂਦੇ ਹਨ	*They allow their child to play outside.*

ਵਿਆਖਿਆ viaakhiaa *Commentary*

1 Media

There are many opportunities, living in the west, to interact with Panjabi speakers and to hear the language being spoken. In particular there has been a growth in media output. In most big towns and cities in England, and the major cities in North America, there are radio stations which either produce programming totally in Panjabi or have specific Panjabi language programmes. In Toronto, Canada, a mainstream cable television channel broadcasts six hours of Panjabi programming every day. Generally, most satellite and cable TV channels catering for a South Asian audience will have some Panjabi programmes in addition to Hindi / Urdu, Gujarati and Bengali programming.

Much of the programming on these TV channels is taken up with films. The Indian sub-continent produces more films every year than Hollywood. Bombay (Mumbai) is the centre of the Indian film industry and to mark this fact it is affectionately called 'Bollywood'. However, regional film makers are also very significant in the overall production and consumption of cinema in South Asia. In fact the Telegu film industry matches – in terms of number of films produced – that of Mumbai. Despite the presence of large numbers of Panjabi actors and directors – in fact the Kapoor family has dominated Indian films over the last 40 years – the Panjabi-language film industry is not well developed in East Panjab. The majority of Panjabi-language films are produced in Lahore (also called 'Lollywood') and are high in action but low in quality, both cinematically and in terms of language use. However, there are a few films to be recommended which are useful to watch in order to pick up the language. These films are available in any South Asian area in England, Canada and beyond. Wherever a South Asian community is settled, there is always an outlet for videos and, more recently, cinema halls showing films from the sub-continent.

2 Poetry

Panjab is renowned for folk poetry, particularly for the tradition of Sufi-inspired poems. Poetry flourished in medieval times with poets such as Bulleh Shah and Warish Shah making indelible implants on the social consciousness of the Panjabi *literati*. In the modern period, Bhai Vir Singh and Amrita Pritam are two poets worthy of mention. Poetry is popular primarily because of its sung form. The folk song given earlier in this unit is a good example of a form of poetic verse. Much of this music has become professionalized and Panjab is the foremost producer of folk music in India and Pakistan.

ਅਭਿਆਸ   abhiaas   *Exercises*

After reading the dialogue and / or listening to the recording, try to do the following exercises.

1 Fill in the blanks.

In this unit you have learned about relative–correlatives in the language points section. Fill in the blanks with the appropriate relative–correlative pairs.

a _____ ਦੋੜੇ ਗਾ, _____ ਇਨਾਮ ਜਿਤੇ ਗਾ ।
The person who runs will win the prize.
b _____ ਤੁਸੀਂ ਚਾਹੁੰਦੇ ਹੋ, _____ ਅਸੀਂ ਕਰਾਂ ਗੇ ।
We will do as you like.
c _____ ਤੁਸੀਂ ਰਹਿੰਦੇ ਹੋ, _____ ਪੰਜਾਬੀ ਬੋਲੀ ਜਾਂਦੀ ਹੈ ।
Panjabi is spoken where you live.
d _____ ਮੈਂ ਦਵਾਈ ਖਾਧੀ, _____ ਹੀ ਆਰਾਮ ਆ ਗਿਆ ।
When I took the medicine I felt relief immediately.

2 Complete the sentences.

Complete the sentences in Panjabi with the appropriate expressions of *to allow to*. The first one has been done for you.

a ਉਸ ਨੂੰ ਅੰਦਰ (ਆਉਣ ਦੇ)   *Let him come inside.*
b ਕੁੱਤੇ ਨੂੰ _____   *Let the dog go out.*
c ਮੈਨੂੰ ਜੂਸ _____   *Let me drink juice.*
d ਬੀਬੀ ਜੀ ਨੂੰ ਟੀ ਵੀ _____   *Allow the lady to watch TV.*

3 Write sentences using the verb ਲੱਗਣਾ.

a It takes 15 minutes to get to work.
b How much does one first-class ticket cost?
c I am feeling hot.
d It started to rain.
e We were about to go out.

16

ਪੰਜਾਬ ਦੇ ਲੋਕ ਨਾਚ

panjaab de lok naach

folk dances of Panjab

In this unit you will learn:
- about the folk dances of Panjab
- about experiences of the Panjabi diaspora
- phrases of choice

▶ 1 *Folk dances of Panjab*
ਗੱਲ ਬਾਤ ੧ ਪੰਜਾਬ ਦੇ ਲੋਕ ਨਾਚ
gall baat 1 panjaab de lok naach

It is the end of Mr Singh's Panjabi class. He has taken all the students to a cultural programme in the Southall Community Centre to see a range of folk dances. As they enter the hall they hear the sound of drums and see the dancers.

ਮਿਸਟਰ ਸਿੰਘ	ਉਹ ਮੁੰਡੇ ਸਟੇਜ ਤੇ ਪੰਜਾਬ ਦਾ ਲੋਕ ਨਾਚ ਭੰਗੜਾ ਪਾ ਰਹੇ ਹਨ। ਉਹਨਾਂ ਨੇ ਚਮਕੀਲੇ ਰੰਗਦਾਰ ਕਪੜੇ ਪਾਏ ਹੋਏ ਹਨ। ਉਹਨਾਂ ਦੇ ਹੱਥਾਂ ਵਿਚ ਡਾਂਗਾਂ ਹਨ।
ਡੇਵਿਡ	ਇੱਕ ਬੰਦੇ ਨੇ ਢੋਲ ਚੁੱਕਿਆ ਹੋਇਆ ਹੈ।
ਮਿਸਟਰ ਸਿੰਘ	ਢੋਲ ਦੇ ਵੱਜਣ ਨਾਲ ਸਿਰਫ਼ ਪੈਰ ਨਹੀਂ ਸਗੋਂ ਦਿਲ ਵੀ ਨੱਚਣ ਲੱਗ ਪੈਂਦਾ ਹੈ।
ਜੇਨ	ਭੰਗੜੇ ਵਾਲਿਆਂ ਦੀਆਂ ਬੋਲੀਆਂ ਪੁਰਾਣੀਆਂ ਹਨ। ਮੈਨੂੰ ਨਵੇਂ ਤੇ ਅਜੋਕੇ ਗੀਤ ਚੰਗੇ ਲੱਗਦੇ ਹਨ ਜਿਹੜੇ ਇੱਥੋਂ ਦੇ ਜੰਮਪਲ ਨੌਜੁਆਨਾਂ ਨੇ ਰਚੇ ਹਨ।
ਮਿਸਟਰ ਸਿੰਘ	ਮੰਨੋ ਜਾਂ ਨਾ ਮੰਨੋ, ਭੰਗੜਾ ਅੰਤਰ ਰਾਸ਼ਟਰੀ ਨਾਚ ਬਣ ਗਿਆ ਹੈ। ਭਾਵੇਂ ਤੁਸੀਂ ਪੰਜਾਬ ਜਾਂ ਬਾਹਰ ਹੋ, ਭੰਗੜਾ ਦੇਖ ਸਕਦੇ ਹੋ।
ਜੇਨ	ਕੀ ਸਿਰਫ਼ ਮੁੰਡੇ ਭੰਗੜਾ ਪਾਉਂਦੇ ਹਨ ?
ਮਿਸਟਰ ਸਿੰਘ	ਪੁਰਾਣੇ ਜ਼ਮਾਨੇ ਵਿਚ ਭੰਗੜਾ ਮੁੰਡਿਆਂ ਲਈ ਸੀ ਤੇ ਗਿੱਧਾ ਕੁੜੀਆਂ ਲਈ ਸੀ। ਹੁਣ ਸਭ ਕੁਝ ਰਲ ਮਿਲ ਗਿਆ ਹੈ। ਦੇਖੋ! ਗਿੱਧਾ ਸ਼ੁਰੂ ਹੋ ਗਿਆ ਹੈ।
ਡੇਵਿਡ	ਉਹਨਾਂ ਵਿੱਚੋਂ ਇੱਕ ਕੁੜੀ ਢੋਲਕੀ ਵਜਾ ਰਹੀ ਹੈ ਅਤੇ ਦੂਜੀ ਢੋਲਕੀ ਤੇ ਚਮਚਾ ਮਾਰ ਰਹੀ ਹੈ।
ਜੇਨ	ਹਰ ਕੋਈ ਚੜ੍ਹਦੀ ਕਲਾ ਵਿਚ ਹੈ। ਆਓ, ਆਪਾਂ ਨੱਚੀਏ।
Mr Singh	*Those boys on the stage are performing* bhangra, *a folk dance of Panjab. They are wearing sparkling, colourful clothes. They are carrying long wooden poles in their hands.*
David	*One man is carrying a big drum.*
Mr Singh	*With the beat of the drum, it is not only the feet but also the heart that starts dancing.*
Jane	*The verses of* bhangra *are old fashioned. I like the new, modern songs which are composed by young people born and raised here.*
Mr Singh	*Believe it or not,* bhangra *has become an international dance. Whether you are in Panjab or abroad, you can always see* bhangra.

Jane	*Do only boys perform* bhangra?
Mr Singh	*In the old times,* bhangra *was for the boys and* gidha *was for the girls. Now everything is mixed up. Look! The* gidha *has started.*
David	*One of the girls is playing a small drum and the other girl is tapping the small drum with a spoon.*
Jane	*Everyone is in high spirits. Come on, let's dance!*

ਸ਼ਬਦਾਵਲੀ   shab<u>d</u>aavalee   *Vocabulary*

ਲੋਕ ਨਾਚ	lok naach	*folk dance* (m.)
ਚਮਕੀਲਾ	chamkeelaa	*glittering, shining, sparkling* (v.)
ਰੰਗਦਾਰ	ran<u>g</u>daar	*colourful*
ਡਾਂਗ	daa<u>ng</u>	*long wooden pole* (f.)
ਢੋਲ	dhol	*big drum* (m.)
ਵੱਜਣਾ	vajjnhaa	*to be played, to be beaten*
ਪੈਰ	pair	*feet* (m.)
ਸਗੋਂ	sago<u>n</u>	*but also*
ਦਿਲ	<u>d</u>il	*heart* (m.)
ਨੱਚਣਾ	nachchnhaa	*to dance*
ਬੋਲੀਆਂ	boleeaa<u>n</u>	*folk verse couplets* (f.)
ਅਜੋਕਾ	ajokaa	*modern*
ਜੰਮਪਲ	ja<u>n</u>mpal	*raised, born and bred*
ਨੌਜੁਆਨ	naujuaan	*youth* (m.)
ਰਚਨਾ	rachnaa	*composition* (f.)
ਮੰਨੋ ਜਾਂ ਨਾ ਮੰਨੋ	ma<u>n</u>no jaa<u>n</u> naa ma<u>n</u>no	*believe it or not*
ਅੰਤਰ ਰਾਸ਼ਟਰੀ	a<u>n</u>tar raashtaree	*international*
ਜ਼ਮਾਨਾ	zamaanaa	*times* (m.)

ਗਿੱਧਾ	gidhdhaa	*women's folk dance* (m.)
ਰਲ ਮਿਲਣਾ	ral milnhaa	*to be mixed*
ਵਿੱਚੋਂ	vichchon	*from within*
ਢੋਲਕੀ	dholkee	*small drum* (f.)
ਵਜਾਉਣਾ	vajaaunhaa	*to play (music), to beat*
ਚਮਚਾ	chamchaa	*spoon* (m.)
ਮਾਰਨਾ	maarnaa	*to hit, to tap*
ਚੜ੍ਹਦੀ ਕਲਾ	charhhdee kalaa	*high spirits*

ਅਭਿਆਸ   abhiaas   *Exercises*

After reading the dialogue and / or listening to the recording, try
to do the following exercises.

1 True or false?

a ਪੁਰਾਣੇ ਜ਼ਮਾਨੇ ਵਿਚ ਭੰਗੜਾ ਸਿਰਫ਼ ਮੁੰਡਿਆਂ ਲਈ ਸੀ ।   True / False

b ਜੈਨ ਨੂੰ ਉਹ ਗੀਤ ਚੰਗੇ ਲੱਗਦੇ ਹਨ ਜਿਹੜੇ ਪੁਰਾਣੇ ਤੇ
ਪੰਜਾਬ ਦੇ ਹਨ ।   True / False

c ਢੋਲਕੀ ਤੇ ਕੁੜੀਆਂ ਡਾਂਗਾਂ ਮਾਰਦੀਆਂ ਹਨ ।   True / False

d ਭੰਗੜਾ ਅੰਤਰ ਰਾਸ਼ਟਰੀ ਨਾਚ ਬਣ ਗਿਆ ਹੈ ।   True / False

2 Write or say the sentences in Panjabi.

a I like bhangra.
b I like bhangra more than gidha.
c Whether you're in Panjab or abroad, you can see bhangra.
d Come on, let's dance!

3 Try to identify the items from the descriptions given in the dialogue.

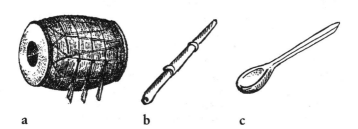

a   b   c

▶ 2 *Avtar's life story*

ਗੱਲ ਬਾਤ ੨ ਅਵਤਾਰ ਦੀ ਜੀਵਨ ਕਹਾਣੀ

gall baat̲ 2 avt̲aar d̲ee jeevan kahaanhee

Two men, Avtar and Tarlok, are sitting on a park bench in Vancouver enjoying the sunny day. Avtar is reminiscing about his family's history and how he came to settle in Vancouver.

ਅਵਤਾਰ	ਕੀ ਸਾਨੂੰ ਆਪਣੇ ਬਚਪਨ ਵਿਚ ਕਦੀ ਖ਼ਿਆਲ ਸੀ ਕਿ ਅਸੀਂ ਇਸ ਉਮਰ ਵਿਚ ਕੈਨੇਡਾ ਰਹਿ ਰਹੇ ਹੋਵਾਂ ਗੇ? ਮੇਰਾ ਪੜਦਾਦਾ ਅੰਗਰੇਜ਼ਾਂ ਦੇ ਰਾਜ ਵੇਲੇ ਫ਼ੌਜ ਵਿਚ ਭਰਤੀ ਹੋ ਗਿਆ ਤੇ ਉਸ ਨੂੰ ਮਲੇਸ਼ੀਆ ਭੇਜ ਦਿੱਤਾ ਗਿਆ। ਮੇਰੇ ਦਾਦੇ ਦਾ ਜਨਮ ਉੱਥੇ ਹੋਇਆ। ਜਦੋਂ ਉਹ ਵਾਪਸ ਪਰਤਿਆ ਤਾਂ ਆਜ਼ਾਦੀ ਲਈ ਜਦੋ ਜਹਿਦ ਸ਼ੁਰੂ ਹੋ ਗਈ ਸੀ। ਮੇਰਾ ਦਾਦਾ ਗ਼ਦਰ ਪਾਰਟੀ ਵਿਚ ਸ਼ਾਮਲ ਹੋ ਕੇ ਵੈਨਕੂਵਰ ਆ ਗਿਆ।
ਤਰਲੋਕ	ਕੀ ਤੇਰਾ ਜਨਮ ਕੈਨੇਡਾ ਹੋਇਆ ਸੀ?
ਅਵਤਾਰ	ਕਹਾਣੀ ਲੰਬੀ ਹੈ। ਸਾਡੇ ਵਡੱਕਿਆਂ ਨੇ ਥਾਂ ਥਾਂ ਦਾ ਪਾਣੀ ਪੀਤਾ ਹੈ। ਸਮਾਂ ਪਾ ਕੇ ਮੇਰਾ ਦਾਦਾ ਪੰਜਾਬ ਮੁੜ ਗਿਆ। ਫਿਰ ੧੯੪੭ ਵਿਚ ਪੰਜਾਬ ਦਾ ਬਟਵਾਰਾ ਹੋ ਗਿਆ। ਉਦੋਂ ਮੇਰੇ ਪਿਤਾ ਜੀ ਲਾਇਲਪੁਰ ਸਨ ਤੇ ਸਾਰੇ ਪਰਵਾਰ ਨੂੰ ਜਲੰਧਰ ਜਾਣਾ ਪਿਆ। ਮੇਰਾ ਜਨਮ ਜਲੰਧਰ ਹੋਇਆ ਸੀ।
ਤਰਲੋਕ	ਮੇਰੇ ਦਾਦਾ ਜੀ ਈਸਟ ਅਫ਼ਰੀਕਾ ਰੇਲਵੇ ਬਣਾਉਣ ਚਲੇ ਗਏ। ਮੇਰਾ ਜਨਮ ਅਸਥਾਨ ਯੂਗੰਡਾ ਹੈ। ੧੯੭੧ ਵਿਚ ਛੱਡ ਛੱਡਾ ਕੇ ਅਸੀਂ ਪਹਿਲੇ ਇੰਗਲੈਂਡ ਗਏ ਤੇ ਫਿਰ ਕੈਨੇਡਾ ਆ ਗਏ।
ਅਵਤਾਰ	ਇਸ ਦਾ ਮਤਲਬ ਇਹ ਹੈ ਕਿ ਤੁਸੀਂ ਪੰਜਾਬ ਤੋਂ ਕਾਫ਼ੀ ਦੇਰ ਤੋਂ ਉਖੜੇ ਹੋਏ ਹੋ।
ਤਰਲੋਕ	ਹਾਂ। ਪਰ ਹੁਣ ਮੇਰਾ ਦਿਲ ਲੱਗ ਗਿਆ ਹੈ, ਭਾਵੇਂ ਅਸੀਂ ਪੰਜਾਬ ਤੋਂ ਦੂਰ ਹਾਂ। ਇੱਥੇ ਆਪਣੀ ਅਬਾਦੀ ਕਾਫ਼ੀ ਹੈ। ਮਾਹੌਲ ਪੰਜਾਬ ਵਾਂਗੂੰ ਹੈ।
ਅਵਤਾਰ	ਦੁਨੀਆਂ ਵਿਚ ਕਿਸੇ ਵੀ ਜਗ੍ਹਾ ਚਲੇ ਜਾਓ, ਭਾਵੇਂ ਕੈਨੇਡਾ ਭਾਵੇਂ ਇੰਗਲੈਂਡ ਜਾਂ ਅਮਰੀਕਾ, ਕੋਈ ਨਾ ਕੋਈ ਆਪਣਾ ਪੰਜਾਬੀ ਬੰਦਾ ਤੈਨੂੰ ਮਿਲ ਜਾਏ ਗਾ।
ਤਰਲੋਕ	ਪਰ ਸਿਆਣੇ ਲੋਕ ਕਹਿੰਦੇ ਹਨ ਕਿ ਧੋਬੀ ਦਾ ਕੁੱਤਾ ਨਾ ਘਰ ਦਾ ਨਾ ਘਾਟ ਦਾ!
ਅਵਤਾਰ	ਇਹ ਅਖਾਣ ਪੁਰਾਣਾ ਹੈ। ਹੁਣ ਸਾਰੀ ਦੁਨੀਆਂ ਤੁਹਾਡੀ ਹੈ। ਵਾਹਿਗੁਰੂ ਭਲੀ ਕਰੇ ਗਾ।

Avtar	Did we ever dream in our childhood that at this age we would be living in Canada? My great grandfather joined the army during the time of British rule and he was sent to Malaysia. My grandfather was born there. When he returned home, the struggle for independence had started. My grandfather joined the Gadar Party and came to Vancouver.
Tarlok	So, were you born in Canada?
Avtar	It's a long story. Our forefathers have been to many places [lit. our forefathers drank water from many different places]. After a while, my grandfather returned to Panjab. Then in 1947 Panjab was partitioned. At that time my father was in Lyallpur and the whole family had to go to Jalandhar. I was born in Jalandhar.
Tarlok	My grandfather went to East Africa to build the railways. My birthplace is Uganda. In 1971 we left everything and went first to England and then came to Canada.
Avtar	This means that you have been uprooted from Panjab for a long time.
Tarlok	Yes. But even though we are far away from Panjab, I am now happily settled [lit. my heart has been applied or fixed]. There are quite a lot of our own people here. The atmosphere is just like Panjab.
Avtar	Go anywhere in the world, whether it's Canada, England or America, and you will meet a Panjabi person.
Tarlok	But wise men say that immigrants belong to no one place. [Proverb: the dog of a washerman belongs neither at home nor at the washing place.]
Avtar	This is an old proverb. Now the whole world belongs to you. God will watch over you.

ਸ਼ਬਦਾਵਲੀ   shabdaavalee   *Vocabulary*

ਜੀਵਨ	jeevan	*life* (m.)
ਬਚਪਨ	bachpan	*childhood* (m.)
ਪੜਦਾਦਾ	parhdaadaa	*great grandfather* (m.)

ਰਾਜ	raaj	*rulership, kingdom* (m.)
ਵੇਲ	vele	*period, time* (m.)
ਫੌਜ	fauj	*military* (f.)
ਭਰਤੀ	bhartee	*join*
ਜਨਮ	janam	*birth* (m.)
ਪਰਤਨਾ	partnhaa	*to return*
ਅਜ਼ਾਦੀ	azaadee	*freedom, independence* (f.)
ਜਦੋ ਜਹਿਦ	jado jahid	*struggle* (f.)
ਅਜ਼ਾਦੀ ਲਈ ਜਦੋ ਜਹਿਦ	azaadee laee jado jahid	*struggle for independence*
ਗਦਰ	ghadar	*mutiny* (m.)
ਗਦਰ ਪਾਰਟੀ	ghadar paartee	*Gadar Party* (f.) (an anti-colonial political movement in Panjab in the early twentieth century which had strong connections with Vancouver because of the large number of exiles from Panjab who went there)
ਲੰਬਾ	lanbaa	*long, lengthy* (v.)
ਵਡੱਕਿਆਂ	vadkkiaan	*ancestors, forefathers* (m.)
ਥਾਂ ਥਾਂ	thaan thaan	*each and every place* (m.)
ਸਮਾਂ ਪਾ ਕੇ	samaan paa ke	*after a while, after some time*
ਮੁੜਨਾ	murhnaa	*to turn around, to return*
ਬਟਵਾਰਾ	batvaaraa	*division, partition* (m.)
ਈਸਟ ਅਫ਼ਰੀਕਾ	eest afreekaa	*East Africa* (m.)
ਯੂਗੰਡਾ	yoogandaa	*Uganda* (m.)
ਜਨਮ ਅਸਥਾਨ	janam asthaan	*birthplace* (m.)
ਉਖੜਨਾ	ukharhnaa	*to be displaced, to be uprooted*
ਦਿਲ ਲੱਗਣਾ	dil laggnhaa	*to feel at home, to be settled, to live happily*
ਕੋਈ ਨਾ ਕੋਈ	koee na koee	*some one or another*
ਸਿਆਣਾ	siaanhaa	*wise, mature* (v.)
ਧੋਬੀ	dhobee	*washerman* (m.)
ਕੁੱਤਾ	kuttaa	*dog* (m.)
ਘਾਟ	ghaat	*place where clothes are washed on the bank of the river or canal* (m.)
ਅਖਾਣ	akhaanh	*proverb, saying* (m.)
ਭਲੀ	bhalee	*look after, watch over*

ਅਭਿਆਸ   abhiaas   *Exercises*

After reading the dialogue and / or listening to the recording, try to do the following exercises.

1 Name four countries mentioned in the dialogue.

2 Answer the questions.

Answer the following questions in Panjabi either in short form or in full sentences. You may lift the answers from the dialogue.

a ਜਿਹੜੇ ਦੋਨੋਂ ਦੋਸਤ ਆਪਸ ਵਿਚ ਗੱਲਾਂ ਕਰ ਰਹੇ ਹਨ, ਉਹਨਾਂ ਦੇ ਨਾਮ ਕੀ ਹਨ ?
b ਅਵਤਾਰ ਦੇ ਦਾਦੇ ਦਾ ਜਨਮ ਕਿੱਥੇ ਹੋਇਆ ਸੀ ?
c ਜਦੋਂ ਪੰਜਾਬ ਦਾ ਬਟਵਾਰਾ ਹੋ ਗਿਆ, ਅਵਤਾਰ ਦਾ ਪਿਤਾ ਕਿੱਥੇ ਸੀ ?
d ਤਰਲੋਕ ਦਾ ਜਨਮ ਅਸਥਾਨ ਕਿੱਥੇ ਹੈ ?
e ਸਿਆਣੇ ਬੰਦੇ ਕੀ ਕਹਿੰਦੇ ਹਨ ?

3 Give the reasons why Avtar and Tarlok's families migrated to each place.

a ਅਵਤਾਰ ਦੇ ਪੜਦਾਦਾ ਜੀ ਮਲੇਸ਼ੀਆ ਕਿਉਂ ਗਏ ਸੀ ?
b ਅਵਤਾਰ ਦੇ ਦਾਦਾ ਜੀ ਵੈਨਕੂਵਰ ਕਿਉਂ ਗਏ ਸੀ ?
c ੧੯੪੭ ਵਿਚ ਅਵਤਾਰ ਦੇ ਸਾਰੇ ਪਰਵਾਰ ਨੂੰ ਜਲੰਧਰ ਕਿਉਂ ਜਾਣਾ ਪਿਆ ?
d ਤਰਲੋਕ ਦੇ ਦਾਦਾ ਜੀ ਈਸਟ ਅਫ਼ਰੀਕਾ ਕਿਉਂ ਗਏ ਸੀ ?

ਬੋਲੀ ਬਾਰੇ bolee baare *Language points*

Future continuous

The future continuous is used when an ongoing action in the future is being described, similar to the usage in the English sentence *I will be going*. This would be expressed in Panjabi as ਮੈਂ ਜਾ ਰਿਹਾ ਹੋਵਾਂ ਗਾ. The future continuous can also be used in situations when the on-going action in the future was not certain at the time of contemplation. For example, at the beginning of the second dialogue, when Avtar says to Tarlok ਕੀ ਸਾਨੂੰ ਕਦੀ ਖ਼ਿਆਲ ਸੀ ਕਿ ਅਸੀਂ ਕੈਨੇਡਾ ਰਹਿ ਰਹੇ ਹੋਵਾਂ ਗੇ ? *Did we ever dream that we would be living in Canada?* In English the uncertainty of the sentence would be expressed through the use of *would* rather than *will*. In Panjabi the future continuous tense can be used for both types of situations.

In previous units you were introduced to both the present continuous tense and the future tense. The future continuous tense can be most simply understood as a combination of the present continuous and the future tenses. Notice in the following examples how the future continuous combines the two tenses:

Future tense	ਮੈਂ ਜਾਵਾਂ ਗਾ	I will go
Present continuous	ਮੈਂ ਜਾ ਰਿਹਾ ਹਾਂ	I am going
Future continuous	ਮੈਂ ਜਾ ਰਿਹਾ ਹੋਵਾਂ ਗਾ	I will / would be going
Future tense	ਅਸੀਂ ਖਾਵਾਂ ਗੇ।	We will eat
Present continuous	ਅਸੀਂ ਖਾ ਰਹੇ ਹਾਂ	We are eating
Future continuous	ਅਸੀਂ ਖਾ ਰਹੇ ਹੋਵਾਂ ਗੇ	We will / would be eating

The continuous action in the sentence takes the present continuous form such as in these examples with *going* represented through the stem ਜਾ and *eating* with the stem ਖਾ and with the appropriate forms of ਰਿਹਾ. You should have noticed that the auxiliary verb that comes at the end of the present continuous tense does not appear in the future continuous. Instead, the verb ਹੋਣਾ is in the future form with the respective -ਗਾ endings.

Phrases of choice

In English, phrases of choice are expressed through such words as *either . . . or, neither . . . nor* and *not only . . . but also*. In Panjabi there are similar types of constructions to express choice most commonly using the following:

ਭਾਵੇਂ . . . ਭਾਵੇਂ	either . . . or, whether or not
ਚਾਹੇ . . . ਚਾਹੇ	either . . . or, whether or not
ਨਾ . . . ਨਾ	neither . . . nor
ਨਾ ਸਿਰਫ਼ . . . ਸਗੋਂ	not only . . . but
ਜਾਂ . . . ਨਾ	may or not

Some examples of these words in use:

ਭਾਵੇਂ ਤੁਸੀਂ ਜਾਓ ਭਾਵੇਂ ਨਾ ਜਾਓ, ਮੈਂ ਇੱਥੇ ਰਹਾਂਗੀ।	Whether you go or not, I will stay here. (lit. Whether you go or whether you do not go, I will stay here.)
ਚਾਹੇ ਸਾਡੇ ਨਾਲ ਆਓ ਚਾਹੇ ਉਹਨਾਂ ਨਾਲ ਜਾਓ, ਤੁਹਾਨੂੰ ਜਲਦੀ ਨਿਕਲਣਾ ਪੈਣਾ	Whether you come with us or (whether you) go with them, you'll have to get out quickly.
ਸਾਡੇ ਕੋਲ ਨਾ ਕਿਤਾਬਾਂ ਹਨ ਨਾ ਕਾਗ਼ਜ਼ ਹੈ	We have neither books nor paper.
ਲੋਕ ਨਾ ਸਿਰਫ਼ ਭਾਰਤ ਤੋਂ ਆਉਂਦੇ ਹਨ ਸਗੋਂ ਸਾਰੀ ਦੁਨੀਆਂ ਤੋਂ ਆਉਂਦੇ ਹਨ	People come not only from India, but from all over the world.
ਮੰਨੋ ਜਾਂ ਨਾਂ ਮੰਨੋ ਇਹ ਜਗ੍ਹਾ ਸਭ ਤੋਂ ਸੁਹਣੀ ਹੈ।	You may or may not agree but this is the nicest place.

ਹੈ ਗਾ 'hai gaa' and ਸੀ ਗਾ 'see gaa'

In colloquial Panjabi, the verb ਹੋਣਾ is often expressed with the ending -ਗਾ when there is an added emphasis. The ending -ਗਾ merely indicates definiteness or confirmation, and must agree with the number and gender of the subject that it is referring to followed by the appropriate present form of ਹੋਣਾ. In Unit 3 Jane and Henry went to the sweet shop with Mr Singh. Jane asked the shopkeeper ਕੀ ਕੋਈ ਨਮਕੀਨ ਚੀਜ਼ ਹੈ? *Is there anything salty?* This question is general in nature. If Jane had wished to put further emphasis on the definite availability of something salty, she could have said: ਕੀ ਕੋਈ ਨਮਕੀਨ ਚੀਜ਼ ਹੈ ਗੀ ਏ? *Is there anything salty (available)?* The shopkeeper could have then replied ਹਾਂ ਜੀ, ਹੈ ਗੀ ਏ *Yes, there (definitely) is.* Note that the feminine singular form is used (-ਗੀ) in agreement with ਚੀਜ਼, although in the shopkeeper's response the subject is omitted as it is simply understood. Since ਹੈ ਗਾ is only used in informal speech, the auxiliary verb ਹੋਣਾ also appears in its informal form, hence ਏ instead of ਹੈ.

When one wants to express the same type of definiteness in the past, then ਸੀ (was) is followed by the ending -ਗਾ. Again, the number and gender of the subject will determine the ending of -ਗਾ. Some examples are as follows:

ਜਸਪ੍ਰੀਤ ਤੇ ਸਿਮਰਨ ਘਰ ਸੀ ਗੀਆਂ	*Jaspreet and Simran were (definitely) at home.*
ਤੁਸੀਂ ਚੁੱਪ ਚਾਪ ਸੀ ਗੇ	*You (certainly) were quiet.*

You will come across ਹੈ ਗਾ and ਸੀ ਗਾ frequently in spoken colloquial conversation, though rarely in the written form.

ਵਿਆਖਿਆ viaakhiaa *Commentary*

Folk music

Folk music is an integral part of cultural expression not only in Panjab, but in the three Panjabs: East Panjab in India, West Panjab in Pakistan and the Panjabi diaspora all over the world. In fact, music is one of the main factors that links Panjabis across religious, national and caste divisions. **Bhangra** music, in particular, has come to prominence in the last 20 years in the west. The following illustration shows the traditional costume of **bhangra** dancers. This active and incessant dance music form is a vital part of a global expression of youth culture as well as a particular link between **des** (*home*) and **pardes** (*abroad*) for many Panjabis.

As we saw in the previous unit, there are many other musical forms from Panjab which focus on the relationship between music and poetry which are less related to the robust dance style of **bhangra** and more to the film music and **ghazal** (*ballad*) form. A wide range of Panjabi music from westernized dance music to slow ballads is widely available in the South Asian shopping centres of London, New York, Toronto and Melbourne.

ਅਭਿਆਸ   abhiaas   *Exercises*

After reading the dialogue and / or listening to the recording, try to do the following exercises.

1 Complete the sentences.

Complete the sentences (verbally or in written form) with the help of the vocabulary given. The first one has been done for you.

a ਸਾਡੇ ਕੋਲ ਨਾ ਕਿਤਾਬਾਂ ਹਨ, ਨਾ ਕਾਗ਼ਜ਼ ਹੈ ।

  We have neither books nor paper.

b ਸਾਡੇ ਕੋਲ ਨਾ —— ਹਨ, ਨਾ —— ਹੈ ।

c ਸਾਡੇ ਕੋਲ ਨਾ —— ਹਨ, ਨਾ —— ਹੈ।
d ਸਾਡੇ ਕੋਲ ਨਾ —— ਹਨ, ਨਾ —— ਹੈ।

ਪੈਂਸਲਾਂ *pencils* ਕਾਪੀ *exercise book* ਘੜੀਆਂ *watches*
ਰੇਡੀਓ *radio* ਬੋਤਲਾਂ *bottles* ਪਾਣੀ *water*

2 Say or write the sentences in Panjabi.

a ਮੰਨੋ ਜਾਂ ਨਾ ਮੰਨੋ, ਇਹ ਜਗ੍ਹਾ ਸੋਹਣੀ ਹੈ।
   Believe it or not, this place is beautiful.
b Not only is this book long, but it is also difficult.
c Not only do we like **bhangra**, but we also like **gidha**.
d Whether you live in Panjab or abroad, you can see **bhangra**.
e You may or may not agree, but Vancouver's atmosphere is just like Panjab.

3 Tick the boxes which correspond with Tarlok and Avtar's respective life histories.

	ਇੰਗਲੈਂਡ	ਮਲੇਸ਼ੀਆ	ਕੈਨੇਡਾ	ਲਾਇਲਪੁਰ	ਯੂਗੰਡਾ	ਜਲੰਧਰ
ਤਰਲੋਕ						
ਅਵਤਾਰ						

Appendix 1

Consonants			Velar	Palatal	Retroflex	Dental	Labi
Plosives	Voiceless	Unaspirated	ਕ	ਚ	ਟ	ਤ	ਪ
		Aspirated	ਖ	ਛ	ਠ	ਥ	ਫ
	Voiced	Unaspirated	ਗ	ਜ	ਡ	ਦ	ਬ
		Aspirated	ਘ	ਝ	ਢ	ਧ	ਭ
Nasals			ਙ	ਞ	ਣ	ਨ	ਮ
Fricatives	Voiceless		ਖ਼	ਸ਼		ਸ	ਫ਼
	Voiced		ਗ਼			ਜ਼	
Flapped and tapped sounds					ੜ	ਰ	
Aspirate, semi-vowel and liquid				ਹ	ਯ		ਲ	ਵ

Appendix 2

Comparison of tongue positions

a   b   c

a Pronunciation of t and d in English. Tongue against the teeth ridge.
b Pronunciation of ਤ t̪ and ਦ d̪. Tongue against the base of upper incisors.
c Pronunciation of ਟ t and ਡ d. Tongue against the back hard palate.

Reading and writing

Lesson 4 Exercise 2 a ਰਿੱਛ   b ਕਿੱਲ   c ਹਿਰਨ Lesson 5 Exercise 2 a ਸੀਟੀ   b ਬਿੱਲੀ   c ਵਾਲੀ Lesson 6 Exercise 2 a ਢੱਕਣ b ਜ਼ਬਾਨ   c ਉੱਨ Lesson 7 Exercise 2 a ਉਠ   b ਸੁਰ   c ਝਾੜੂ Lesson 8 Exercise 2 a ਲੇਲੇ   b ਭੇੜ   c ਸੇਬ Lesson 9 Exercise 2 a ਭੈਣ   b ਐਤਵਾਰ   c ਐਨਕ Lesson 10 Exercise 2 a ਖੋਤਾ   b ਮੋਟਾ c ਘੋੜਾ Lesson 11 Exercise 2 a ਚੌਲ   b ਖਿਡੌਣੇ   c ਫੌਜੀ Lesson 12 Exercise 2 a ਜੰਘ   b ਲੰਡਾ   c ਵਟਾਊਂ

Unit 1

Dialogue 1 exercises

1 a True   b True   c False 2 a ਮੇਰਾ ਨਾਂ ਡੇਵਿਡ ਹੈ। meraa naan devid hai. b ਤੁਹਾਡਾ ਕੀ ਨਾਮ ਹੈ? tuhaadaa kee naam hai? c ਤੇਰਾ ਕੀ ਨਾਂ ਏ? teraa kee naan e?

Dialogue 2 exercises

1 a ਅੱਸਲਾਮ ਅਲੈਕਮ। asslaam alaikam. b ਤੁਹਾਡਾ ਕੀ ਹਾਲ ਹੈ? tuhaadaa kee haal hai? c ਕੀ ਪਰਵਾਰ ਠੀਕ ਹੈ? kee parvaar theek hai? 2 a 2   b 3   c 1

End exercises

1 1st line, 2nd letter; 3rd line, 1st letter; 5th line, 4th letter 2 a ਨਮਸਤੇ namaste b ਵਾਲੈਕਮ ਅੱਸਲਾਮ vaalaikam asslaam c ਸਤਿ ਸ੍ਰੀ ਅਕਾਲ sat sree akaal 3 a ਤੁਹਾਡਾ tuhaadaa b ਤੇਰਾ teraa c ਤੇਰਾ teraa 4 You: ਸਤਿ ਸ੍ਰੀ ਅਕਾਲ। ਮੇਰਾ ਨਾਮ_____ਹੈ। ਤੁਹਾਡਾ ਕੀ ਨਾਮ ਹੈ? sat sree akaal. meraa naam_____hai. tuhaadaa kee naam hai? You: ਮੈਂ ਠੀਕ ਹਾਂ। ਤੁਸੀਂ ਕਿਵੇਂ ਹੋ? main theek haan. tuseen kiven ho? You: ਰੱਬ ਰਾਖਾ। rabb raakhaa.

Unit 2

Dialogue 1 exercises

1 a False b False c True 2 Jeevan – Panjabi John – English
Ram – Gujarati

Dialogue 2 exercises

1 Ashok: ਹਾਂ ਜੀ, ਮੈਂ ਅਸ਼ੋਕ ਹਾਂ। haan jee, main ashok haan.
Mrs Sharma: ਮੇਰਾ ਹਾਲ ਠੀਕ ਹੈ। meraa haal theek hai. Kiran: ਨਹੀਂ,
ਮੇਰੇ ਮਾਤਾ ਜੀ ਇੱਥੇ ਨਹੀਂ ਹਨ। naheen, mere maataa jee iththe naheen
han. 2 a ਮੈਂ ਕਿਰਨ ਹਾਂ। main kiran haan. b ਕੀ ਤੁਸੀਂ ਅਸ਼ੋਕ ਹੋ? kee
tuseen ashok ho? c ਉਹ ਇੱਥੇ ਨਹੀਂ ਹਨ uh iththe naheen han. 3 1 Panjabi 2 English 3 Class 4 Mrs Sharma 5 Hindu

End exercises

1 are, hai, ਹੋ 2 a ਕੀ ਤੁਸੀਂ ਅਸ਼ੋਕ ਹੋ? kee tuseen ashok ho? b ਕੀ ਤੁਸੀਂ
ਕਿਰਨ ਹੋ? kee tuseen kiran ho? c ਮੈਂ ਕਿਰਨ ਹਾਂ main kiran haan d ਉਹ
ਅਸ਼ੋਕ ਹੈ uh ashok hai 3 a ਹੈਂ hain b ਹਾਂ haan c ਹਨ han 4 1st line
2nd letter 3rd line 1st letter 4th line 2nd letter

Unit 3

Dialogue 1 exercises

1 a False b False c True d False e True 2 ਕਰੇਲਾ karelaa
ਸ਼ਲਗਮ shalgam ਭਿੰਡੀ bhindee ਗੋਭੀ gobhee ਟਮਾਟਰ tamaatar
ਮਟਰ mater

Dialogue 2 exercises

1 miththaa, bitter, ਸੁਆਦ 2 a ਇਹ ਦੁਕਾਨ ਹੈ। ih dukaan hai. b ਇਹ
ਚੰਗੀ ਦੁਕਾਨ ਹੈ। ih changee dukaan hai. c ਇਹ ਮਿਠਿਆਈ ਦੀ ਦੁਕਾਨ ਹੈ।
ih mithiaaee dee dukaan hai. d ਇਹ ਚੰਗੀ ਮਿਠਿਆਈ ਦੀ ਦੁਕਾਨ ਹੈ। ih
changee mithiaaee dee dukaan hai.

End exercises

1 a ਛੋਟਾ chotaa b ਵੱਡਾ vaddaa c ਛੋਟੀ chotee d ਵੱਡੀ vaddee e ਛੋਟਾ
chotaa f ਵੱਡਾ vaddaa 2 Mr Singh: samosaa, pakaurhe, bhindee
Jane: samosaa, laddoo, pakaurhe Henry: rasmalaaee, bhindee,
gobhee 3 a ਗੁਲਾਬ ਜਾਮਣ gulaab jaamanh b ਬਰਫੀ barfee c ਸਮੋਸਾ
samosaa d ਪਕੌੜੇ pakaurhe 4 a ਉਹਨਾਂ ਦੇ uhnaan de b ਮੇਰੇ mere
c ਸਾੜੀਆਂ saadeeaan d ਤੁਹਾੜੀਆਂ tuhaadeeaan

Unit 4

Dialogue 1 exercises

1 b ਕੀ ਇਹ ਸੀਟ ਖ਼ਾਲੀ ਹੈ? kee ih seet khaalee hai? ਹਾਂ ਜੀ, ਖ਼ਾਲੀ ਹੈ।
haan jee, khaalee hai. c ਮੈਂ ਅਧਿਆਪਕਾ ਹਾਂ। main adhiaapkaa haan.
d ਤੁਸੀਂ ਕੀ ਕਰਦੇ ਹੋ? tuseen kee karde ho? 2 a ਮੈਂ ਵੀ ਬਰਮਿੰਘਮ ਰਹਿੰਦ

ਹਾਂ main vee barmingham rahindaa haan. **b** ਮੈਂ ਦਿੱਲੀ ਤੋਂ ਹਾਂ main dillee ton haan **c** ਤੁਸੀਂ ਕੀ ਕਰਦੇ ਹੋ? tuseen kee karde ho? **3 1** c **2** a **3** b **4** e **5** d

Dialogue 2 exercises

1 a True **b** True **c** False **2 a** ਮੇਰਾ ਨਾਮ (____) ਹੈ। meraa naam (____) hai. **b** ਮੈਂ (____) ਹਾਂ। main (____) haan. **c** ਮੈਂ (____) ਤੋਂ ਹਾਂ। main (____) ton haan. **d** ਮੈਂ (____) ਰਹਿੰਦਾ/ਰਹਿੰਦੀ ਹਾਂ। main (____) rahindaa/rahindee haan.

End exercises

1 a True **b** False **c** False **d** False **2 a** Mrs Sharma **b** Mrs Khan **c** Dr Singh **3 a** direct **b** oblique **c** direct **d** oblique **e** oblique **4 b** ਮੇਰੀਆਂ ਬੇਟੀਆਂ ਸਕੂਲ ਵਿਚ ਪੜ੍ਹਦੀਆਂ ਹਨ। mereeaan beteeaan sakool vich parhhdeeaan han. *My daughters study in school.* **c** ਤੁਹਾਡੇ ਲੜਕੇ ਕਿੱਥੇ ਰਹਿੰਦੇ ਹਨ? tuhaade larkhe kiththe rahinde han? *Where do your sons live?* **d** ਕੀ ਉਹ ਮੁੰਡੇ ਪੰਜਾਬੀ ਬੋਲਦੇ ਹਨ? kee uh munde panjaabee bolde han? *Do those boys speak Panjabi?*

Unit 5

Dialogue 1 exercises

1 a ਨਮਸਤੇ, ਤੂੰ ਕੀ ਕਰ ਰਹੀ ਹੈਂ? namaste, toon kee kar rahee hain? **b** ਮੈਂ ਜੇਬਾਂ ਲਗਾ ਰਹੀ ਹਾਂ। main jebaan lagaa rahee haan. **c** ਮੈਨੇਜਰ ਸਾਡੀ ਤਨਖ਼ਾਹ ਨਹੀਂ ਵਧਾ ਰਿਹਾ। mainejar saadee tankhaah naheen vadhaa rihaa. **2 1** machine **2** work **3** salary **4** pockets **5** time **6** needle

Dialogue 2 exercises

1 1st line 2nd letter 2nd line 1st letter 3rd line 3rd letter 4th line 2nd letter. **2 a** ਸੁਮੀਤ ਫ਼ਿਲਮ ਦੇਖ ਰਹੀ ਸੀ। sumeet filam dekh rahee see. **b** ਬੱਚੇ ਖੇਡ ਰਹੇ ਸਨ। bachche khed rahe san. **c** ਸੁਮੀਤ ਦਾ ਪਤੀ ਕਾਰ ਧੋ ਰਿਹਾ ਸੀ। sumeet daa patee kaar dho rihaa see.

End exercises

1 a ਤੁਸੀਂ ਸਮਾਂ ਜ਼ਾਇਆ ਕਰ ਰਹੇ ਹੋ। tuseen samaan zaaiaa kar rahe ho. **b** ਤੁਸੀਂ ਕੰਮ ਕਿਉਂ ਛੱਡ ਰਹੇ ਹੋ? tuseen kanm kiun chadd rahe ho? **c** ਤੁਸੀਂ ਠੀਕ ਕਹਿ ਰਹੇ ਹੋ। tuseen theek kahi rahe ho. **2** patee, house/home, ਕੱਲ੍ਹ **3 b** ਤੁਸੀਂ ਕੀ ਪੁੱਛ ਰਹੇ ਸੀ? tuseen kee puchch rahe see? *What were you asking?* **c** ਉਹ ਕੀ ਕਰ ਰਹੇ ਸਨ? uh kee kar rahe san? *What were they doing?* **d** ਉਹ ਕਾਰ ਧੋ ਰਿਹਾ ਸੀ। uh kaar dho rihaa see. *He was washing the car.* **4 a** ਗੀਤਾ ਟੈਨਸ ਖੇਡ ਰਹੀ ਹੈ। geetaa tainas khed rahee hai. *Geeta is playing tennis.* **b** ਅਵਤਾਰ

ਖਾਣਾ ਖਾ ਰਿਹਾ ਹੈ। avtaar khaanhaa khaa rihaa hai. *Avtar is eating food.* **c** ਸੀਤਾ ਤੇ ਗੀਤਾ ਪੰਜਾਬੀ ਬੋਲ ਰਹੀਆਂ ਹਨ। seetaa te geetaa panjaabee bol raheeaan han. *Sita and Geeta are speaking Panjabi.* **d** ਮੁੰਡਾ ਕਿਤਾਬ ਪੜ੍ਹ ਰਿਹਾ ਹੈ। mundaa kitaab parhh rihaa hai. *The boy is reading a book.*

Unit 6

Dialogue 1 exercises

1 a ਪਵਨ ਲੰਡਨ ਸੀ। pavan landan see. *Pavan was in London.* **b** ਪਵਨ ਦੀ ਭਤੀਜੀ ਦਾ ਵਿਆਹ ਸੀ। pavan dee bhateejee daa viaah see. *It was Pavan's niece's wedding.* **c** ਮਾਨਚੈਸਟਰ maanchaistar *Manchester* **d** ਤਕਰੀਬਨ ੧੦੦ ਬੰਦੇ takreeban 100 bande *about 100 people* **2 a** ਤੁਸੀਂ ਐਤਵਾਰ ਕਿੱਥੇ ਸੀ? tuseen aitvaar kiththe see? **b** ਤੁਸੀਂ ਕੱਲ੍ਹ ਕਿੱਥੇ ਸੀ? tuseen kallh kiththe see? **c** ਤੁਸੀਂ ਹਫ਼ਤੇ ਦੇ ਅਖ਼ੀਰ ਕਿੱਥੇ ਸੀ? tuseen hafte de akheer kiththe see?

Dialogue 2 exercises

1 ਇਸਤਰੀ, woman ਇਕੱਠ, gathering ਪ੍ਰਾਹੁਣੇ, praahunhe ਕਾਲਜ, college ਭਾਬੀ, bhaabee **2 a** informal **b** informal **c** formal

End exercises

1

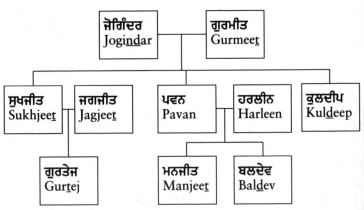

2 a ii **b** iii **c** i **3 a** True **b** False **c** True **4 b** ਉਹ ਹਫ਼ਤੇ ਦੇ ਅਖ਼ੀਰ ਲੰਡਨ ਨਹੀਂ ਗਏ ਸਨ। uh hafte de akheer landan naheen gae san. ਕੀ ਉਹ ਹਫ਼ਤੇ ਦੇ ਅਖ਼ੀਰ ਲੰਡਨ ਗਏ ਸਨ? kee uh hafte de akheer landan gae san? **c** ਅਸੀਂ ਇਕੱਠੇ ਟੈਨਸ ਨਹੀਂ ਖੇਡਦੇ ਸੀ। aseen ikaththe tainas naheen khedde see. ਕੀ ਅਸੀਂ ਇਕੱਠੇ ਟੈਨਸ ਖੇਡਦੇ ਸੀ? kee aseen ikaththe tainas khedde see? d ਉਹ ਪੰਜਾਬੀ ਨਹੀਂ ਬੋਲਦੀ ਹੁੰਦੀ ਸੀ। uh panjaabee naheen boldee hundee see ਕੀ ਉਹ ਪੰਜਾਬੀ ਬੋਲਦੀ ਹੁੰਦੀ ਸੀ? kee uh panjaabee boldee hundee see?

Unit 7

Dialogue 1 exercises

1 a ਜ਼ਰੂਰ zaroor b ਕੱਲ੍ਹ kallh c ਕਿੰਨੇ ਵਜੇ kinne vaje 2 4 2 3 1

Dialogue 2 exercises

1 a ਤੁਸੀਂ ਕੀ ਪੀਓ ਗੇ? tuseen kee peeo ge? b ਕੀ ਤੁਸੀਂ ਟੀ ਵੀ ਦੇਖੋ ਗੇ? kee tuseen tee vee dekho ge? c ਕੀ ਤੁਸੀਂ ਰਸ ਲਵੋ ਗੇ ਜਾਂ ਚਾਹ? kee tuseen ras lavo ge jaan chaah? 2 1st line 1st letter   3rd line 3rd letter 5th line 2nd letter

End exercises

1 a ਤੂੰ ਸੁਣ toon sunh b ਤੁਸੀਂ ਸੁਣੋ tuseen sunho c ਤੁਸੀਂ ਸੁਣੋ ਜੀ tuseen sunho jee d ਜ਼ਰਾ ਸੁਣਨਾ ਜੀ zaraa sunhnaa jee 2 1 ਦਸ ਵਜੇ ਹਨ das vaje han 2 ਢਾਈ ਵਜੇ ਹਨ dhaaee vaje han 3 ਪੌਣੇ ਛੇ ਵਜੇ ਹਨ paunhe che vaje han 4 ਸਵਾ ਅੱਠ ਵਜੇ ਹਨ savaa athth vaje han 5 ਬਾਰ੍ਹਾਂ ਵਜੇ ਹਨ baar-h-aan vaje han 6 ਸੱਤ ਵਜੇ ਹਨ satt vaje han 3 a ਮੈਂ ਚਾਹ ਪੀਵਾਂ ਗਾ main chaah peevaan gaa b ਮੈਂ ਚਾਹ ਪੀਵਾਂ ਗੀ main chaah peevaan gee c ਅਸੀਂ ਚਾਹ ਪੀਵਾਂ ਗੇ aseen chaah peevaan ge d ਅਸੀਂ ਚਾਹ ਪੀਵਾਂ ਗੀਆਂ aseen chaah peevaan geeaan 4 a ਹਾਂ ਜੀ, ਧੰਨਵਾਦ haan jee, dhannvaad b ਹਾਂ, ਕੱਲ੍ਹ ਮੈਂ ਆਵਾਂ ਗਾ haan, kallh main aavaan gaa c ਨਹੀਂ ਮੈਂ ਕਾਹਲ ਵਿਚ ਹਾਂ naheen main kaahal vich haan d ਚੰਗਾ ਫਿਰ, ਮੈਂ ਉਡੀਕਾਂ ਗਾ changaa phir, main udeekaan gaa

Unit 8

Dialogue 1 exercises

1 1 ਸਿਤਾਰ sitaar 2 ਡਾਲਰ daalar 3 ਖ਼ਰਚਾ kharchaa 4 ਫਿਰਨਾ phirnaa 2 a ii   b iii   c i

Dialogue 2 exercises

1 a ਸਾਨੂੰ ਥੋੜੀ ਬਹੁਤੀ ਪੰਜਾਬੀ ਆਉਂਦੀ ਹੈ। saanoon thorhee bahutee panjaabee aaun dee hai. b ਅਸੀਂ ਕਨਾਟ ਪਲੇਸ ਜਾਣਾ ਚਾਹੁੰਦੀਆਂ ਹਾਂ। aseen kanaat pales jaanhaa chaahundeeaan haan. c ਜੀ ਕੀ ਤੁਸੀਂ ਦੋ ਮਹੀਨੇ ਰਹਿਣ ਦੀ ਆਗਿਆ ਦੇਵੋ ਗੇ। jee kee tuseen do maheene rahinh dee aagiaa devo ge. 2 a ਤੁਸੀਂ ਦੋ ਸਵਾਰੀਆਂ ਹੋ ਤੇ ਸਮਾਨ ਵੀ ਬਹੁਤ ਹੈ। tuseen do savaareeaan ho te samaan vee bahut hai. b ਸਾਡੇ ਕੋਲ ਕੇਵਲ ਇੱਕ ਮਹੀਨੇ ਦਾ ਵੀਜ਼ਾ ਹੈ। saade kol keval ikk maheene daa veezaa hai. c ਅਨੰਦ ਮਾਣੋ! anand maanho!

End exercises

1 a ਚਾਹੀਦੀ chaaheedee b ਚਾਹੀਦਾ chaaheedaa c ਵਜਾਉਣ vajaaunh 2 a ਉਸ ਨੂੰ ਕੀ ਚਾਹੀਦਾ ਹੈ? us noon kee chaaheedaa hai? b ਧੀਓ, ਤੁਹਾਨੂੰ ਕੀ ਚਾਹੀਦਾ ਹੈ? dheeo, tuhaanoon kee chaaheedaa hai? c ਤੂੰ ਕਿਹਨਾਂ ਨੂੰ ਦੱਸਿਆ ਸੀ? toon kihnaan noon dassiaa see? d ਕੀ ਸਾਨੂੰ ਜਾਣਾ ਚਾਹੀਦਾ ਹੈ? kee saanoon jaanhaa chaaheedaa hai? 3 a ਘਰ ਵਾਲਾ ghar vaalaa b ਟੈਕਸੀ ਵਾਲਾ taiksee vaalaa c ਸਬਜ਼ੀ ਵਾਲਾ sabzee vaalaa 4 a four b Ashoka Hotel c Rs50 agreed d 10 miles e none f yes

Unit 9

Dialogue 1 exercises

1 a ਮੈਨੂੰ ਫਿੱਕੇ ਰੰਗ ਦਾ ਕਪੜਾ ਚਾਹੀਦਾ ਹੈ। mainoon phikke rang daa kaprhaa chaaheedaa hai. b ਮੈਨੂੰ ਮੋਟਾ ਅਤੇ ਹੰਢਣਸਾਰ ਕਪੜਾ ਚਾਹੀਦਾ ਹੈ। mainoon motaa ate handhanhsaar kaprhaa chaaheedaa hai. c ਅੱਜ ਕੱਲ੍ਹ ਦੇ ਰਵਾਜ ਦੀ ਛਪਾਈ ਚਾਹੀਦੀ ਹੈ। ajj kallh de ravaaj dee chapaaee chaaheedee hai. d ਕੀਮਤ ਬਹੁਤ ਜ਼ਿਆਦਾ ਨਹੀਂ ਹੋਣੀ ਚਾਹੀਦੀ। keemat bahut ziaadaa naheen honhee chaaheedee. 2 vadheeaa, good ਵਧੇਰੇ, vadhere ਕੀਮਤ price mukaablaa, comparison ਸਭ ਤੋਂ ਵਧੀਆ, best.

Dialogue 2 exercises

1 a ਕੀ ਤਕਲੀਫ਼ ਹੈ? kee takleef hai? b ਕੀ ਤੈਨੂੰ ਬੁਖ਼ਾਰ ਹੈ? kee tainoon bukhaar hai? c ਹੁਣ ਮੈਂ ਸਮਝਿਆ। hunh main samajhiaa. 2 You: ਤਬੀਅਤ tabeeat Doctor: ਤਕਲੀਫ਼ takleef You: ਪੇਟ pet, ਦਰਦ dard, ਬੁਖ਼ਾਰ bukhaar Doctor: ਬੁਖ਼ਾਰ bukhaar, ਠੰਡ thand Doctor: ਦਵਾਈ davaaee, ਅਰਾਮ araam

End exercises

1 Horizontal: 1st line 1st letter 2nd line 2nd letter 3rd line 1st letter 4th line 3rd letter 5th line 2nd letter Vertical: 1st column 3rd letter 2nd column 2nd letter 3rd column 2nd letter 4th column 1st letter 5th column 1st letter 2 a ਮੈਨੂੰ ਠੰਡ ਲੱਗਦੀ ਹੈ। mainoon thand laggdee hai. b ਮੇਰਾ ਸਿਰ ਦੁੱਖਦਾ ਹੈ। meraa sir dukhkhdaa hai. c ਮੇਰੇ ਪੇਟ ਵਿਚ ਦਰਦ ਹੈ। mere pet vich dard hai. d ਮੈਨੂੰ ਬੁਖ਼ਾਰ ਹੈ। mainoon bukhaar hai. 3 a ਮੈਂ ਕੱਲ੍ਹ ਨਹੀਂ ਆ ਸਕਦਾ/ਸਕਦੀ। main kallh naheen aa sakdaa/sakdee. b ਕੀ ਤੁਸੀਂ ਪੰਜਾਬੀ ਬੋਲ ਸਕਦੇ ਹੋ? kee tuseen panjaabee bol sakde ho? c ਅਸੀਂ ਪਹਿਲੇ ਉੱਥੇ ਜਾ ਚੁਕੇ ਹਾਂ। aseen pahile uththe jaa chuke haan. d ਉਹ ਪਹਿਲੇ ਖਾ ਚੁਕੇ ਹਨ। uh pahile khaa chuke han. 4 a ਜਿਹੜਾ jihrhaa b ਜਿਸ jis c ਜਿਹੜੇ jihrhe d ਜੋ jo

Unit 10

Dialogue 1 exercises

1 a True b False c False 2 i c ii b iii a iv d

Passage exercises

1 a ਨਾਨਾ ਜੀ ਤੇ ਨਾਨੀ ਜੀ ਕੋਲ naanaa jee te naanee jee kol b ਗੁੜ gurh c ਕਹਾਣੀਆਂ ਸੁਣੀਆਂ kahaanheeaan sunheeaan d ਦੁੱਧ dudhdh 2 pind, village ਖੂਹ, waterwell vihrhaa, court yard ਖੇਤ, khet ਗੰਨਾ, sugarcane

End exercises

1 a ਖਾਣਾ ਖਾ ਕੇ ਅਸੀਂ ਸੌਂ ਗਏ! khaanhaa khaa ke aseen saun ge! b ਦੁਕਾਨ ਤੇ ਜਾ ਕੇ ਦੁੱਧ ਲਿਆ! dukaan te jaa ke dudhdh liaa! c ਕੰਮ ਖਤਮ ਕਰ ਕੇ ਤੂੰ ਘਰ ਨੂੰ ਚਲੇ ਜਾ! kanm khatam kar ke toon ghar noon chale jaa! d ਜਲੰਧਰ ਹੋ ਕੇ ਅੰਮ੍ਰਿਤਸਰ ਜਾਓ! jalandhar ho ke anmritsar jaao! 2 a ਖਾਧੇ khaadhe b ਰੋਈ roee c ਸੁਣਾਈ sunhaaee d ਕਟਿਆ katiaa 3 You: ਬਹੁਤ ਸੁਹਣੀ ਰਹੀ। ਮੈਂ ਟਰਾਫ਼ਾਲਗਰ ਸਕੁਅਰ (ਗਈ/ਗਿਆ) ਅਤੇ ਨੈਲਸਨ ਕਾ ਕਾਲਮ ਦੇਖਿਆ। ਮੈਂ ਬਕਿੰਘਮ ਪੈਲਸ ਵੀ (ਗਈ/ਗਿਆ)। bahut suhnhee rahee. main taraafaalgar sakuar (gaee/giaa) ate nailsan daa kaalam dekhiaa. main bakingham pailas vee (gaee/giaa). You: ਮੈਂ ਔਕਸਫ਼ੋਰਡ ਸਰਕਸ (ਗਈ/ਗਿਆ) ਅਤੇ ਕੁਝ ਕਪੜੇ ਖਰੀਦੇ। main auksford sarkas (gaee/giaa) ate kujh kaprhe khareede. You: ਮੈਂ ਕੇਵਲ ਪੀਜ਼ਾ ਖਾਧਾ। main keval peezaa khaadhaa. 4 1 ਖੂਹ waterwell 2 ਮੱਝ majhjh 3 ਗੰਨਾ gannaa 4 ਘਰ ghar 5 ਖੇਤ khet

Unit 11

Dialogue 1 exercises

1 a ਟਿਕਟ ਬਾਬੂ b ਜਸਪ੍ਰੀਤ c ਟਿਕਟ ਬਾਬੂ d ਸਿਮਰਨ e ਜਸਪ੍ਰੀਤ 2 a ਅਸੀਂ ਅੱਜ ਜਾਣਾ ਚਾਹੁੰਦੀਆਂ ਹਾਂ। b ਨਵੀਆਂ ਥਾਂਵਾਂ ਦੇਖਣਾ ਚੰਗੀ ਗੱਲ ਹੈ। c ਇਹ ਹਨ ਤੁਹਾਡੀਆਂ ਦੋ ਟਿਕਟਾਂ।

Dialogue 2 exercises

1 i c ii a iii d iv b 2 1 gold 2 dome 3 visitors 4 world 5 city 6 guru Mystery word: Amritsar

End exercises

1 a ਸ਼ਾਨੇ ਪੰਜਾਬ b ਸੈਲਾਨੀ, ਜਾਂਦੇ c ਲਛੜੀ, ਅੰਮ੍ਰਿਤ ਦਾ ਸਰੋਵਰ d ਹੋ ਰਿਹਾ ਕੀਰਤਨ, ਸ਼ਾਂਤੀ, ਸਵਰਗਾ 2 a ਗੁਰੂ ਰਾਮ ਦਾਸ b ਅੰਮ੍ਰਿਤ ਦਾ ਸਰੋਵਰ c ਗੁੰਬਦਾਂ ਤੇ ਸੋਨਾ ਲੱਗਾ ਹੋਇਆ ਹੈ 3 You: ਮੈਂ ਅੱਜ ਦਿੱਲੀ ਜਾਣਾ (ਚਾਹੁੰਦਾ) ਹਾਂ। ਸਭ ਤੋਂ ਚੰਗੀ ਦਿੱਲੀ ਜਾਣ ਵਾਲੀ ਗੱਡੀ ਕਿਹੜੀ ਹੈ? You: ਕੀ ਮੈਥੋਂ ਸੈਕੰਡ ਕਲਾਸ ਵਿਚ ਸੀਟ ਮਿਲ ਜਾਏ ਗੀ। You: ਨਹੀਂ, ਮੈਨੂੰ ਵਾਪਸੀ ਟਿਕਟ ਚਾਹੀਦੀ ਹੈ। ਅੰਮ੍ਰਿਤਸਰ ਤੋਂ ਗੱਡੀ ਕਿੰਨੇ ਵਜੇ ਚਲਦੀ ਹੈ? You: ਅੱਛਾ, ਮੈਨੂੰ ਇੱਕ ਸੈਕੰਡ ਕਲਾਸ ਦੀ ਟਿਕਟ ਦੇਵੋ।

Unit 12

Dialogue exercises

1 a False b True c False d True 2 a ਜਰਮਨ, ਅੰਗਰੇਜ਼ੀ, ਪੰਜਾਬੀ b ਤਾਜ ਮੱਹਲ c ਸਹਿਮਤ, ਮੁਕਾਬਲਾ d ਅੰਮ੍ਰਿਤਸਰ

Letter exercises

1 lagaataar, continuously ਪਿਆਰੇ, dear <u>khush</u>, happy ਗਰਮੀ, garmee ਵਾਰੀ, instance. 2 a ਉਹਨਾਂ ਨੇ ਉਹ ਮਕਾਨ ਦੇਖਿਆ ਜਿੱਥੇ ਉਹਨਾਂ ਦੇ ਮਾਤਾ ਪਿਤਾ ਰਹਿੰਦੇ ਹੁੰਦੇ ਸੀ b ਬਾਰਸ਼ c ਅਬਾਦੀ ਤੇ ਟਰੈਫ਼ਿਕ ਬਹੁਤ ਹੈ d ਬਹੁਤ ਸੁਗਾਤਾਂ

End exercises

1 a ਮੈਂ ਖਾ ਚੁਕਾ ਹਾਂ। b ਮੈਂ ਖਾ ਚੁਕੀ ਹਾਂ। c ਉਹ ਬੋਲ ਚੁਕੇ ਸਨ। d ਉਹ ਦਸ ਮਿੰਟ ਤੋਂ ਬੋਲ ਰਿਹਾ ਸੀ। 2 ਜੂ. ਐਸ. ਡਾਲਰ ੪੦੦ ਡਾਲਰ ੩੫ ਰੁਪਏ ਵੱਧ ਅਮਰੀਕਨ 3 ਪਿਆਰੇ ਫੇਰੀ ਜਗ੍ਹਾ ਹਰਿਮੰਦਰ ਸਾਹਿਬ ਮੁਕਾਬਲਾ ਸ਼ਬਦਾਵਲੀ ਹੁੰਦੇ ਤਾਂ ਆਉਂਦਾ।

Unit 13

Exercises to matrimonial advertisement

1 a Yes b Yes c No 2 Not a suitable match! 3 a ਲੜਕੀ ਵਿਹਾਰੀ ਨੌਕਰੀ ਤੇ ਲੱਗੀ ਹੋਣੀ ਚਾਹੀਦੀ ਹੈ। b ਤਲਾਕ ਸ਼ੁਦਾ ਲੜਕੀਆਂ ਨੂੰ ਲਿਖਣ ਦੀ ਲੋੜ ਨਹੀਂ। c ਲੜਕੀ ਦੀ ਉਮਰ ੨੫ ਸਾਲ ਤੋਂ ਵੱਧ ਨਾ ਹੋਵੇ। d ਲੜਕਾ ਸੱਚੀ ਮੁੱਚੀ ਸੁਹਣਾ ਹੈ।

Dialogue exercises

1 a 2 b 1 c 4 d 3 2 a Edinburgh b Ilford c Manjit Singh d Kanwaljit Kaur e Gurbax Singh and Jasvir Kaur Kalsi f North London g May 23 h 9.30 a.m. i 10.00 a.m. j 12.00 noon

End exercises

1 Matrimonial advertisement ਲੰਡਨ ਵਿਚ ਰਹਿ ਰਹੇ ਸਿੱਖ ਮਾਪਿਆਂ ਦੀ ਲੜਕੀ ਲਈ ਰਿਸ਼ਤੇ ਦੀ ਲੋੜ ਹੈ। ਲੜਕੀ ਦੀ ਉਮਰ ੨੫ ਸਾਲ ਦੀ ਹੈ ਅਤੇ ਕੱਦ ਪੰਜ" ਹੈ। ਲੜਕੀ ਸੁਹਣੀ ਤੇ ਪੜ੍ਹੀ ਲਿਖੀ ਹੈ। ਬੈਂਕ ਵਿਚ ਕੰਮ ਕਰਦੀ ਹੈ। ਲੜਕਾ ਪਤਵੰਤੇ ਪਰਵਾਰ ਦਾ, ਬ੍ਰਿਟਿਸ਼ ਸ਼ਹਿਰੀਅਤ ਵਾਲਾ ਅਤੇ ਵਿਹਾਰੀ ਨੌਕਰੀ ਤੇ ਲੱਗਾ ਹੋਵੇ। 2 a ਜਿਹਾ b ਆਪਣੇ c ਆਪਣੀਆਂ d ਜਿਹੇ 3 a ਉਬਲੇ ਹੋਏ b ਡਰਿਆ ਹੋਇਆ c ਪੜ੍ਹਿਆ ਲਿਖਿਆ 4 a ਡੇਬਰਾ b ਜੀਤੀ ਦਾ c ਨਹੀਂ d ੨੮ ਜਨਵਰੀ e ਉਹ ਵਿਆਹ ਦੀਆਂ ਰਸਮਾਂ ਬਾਰੇ ਜਾਣਨਾ ਚਾਹੁੰਦੀ ਹੈ।

Unit 14

Dialogue 1 exercises

1 a ਪਾਪਾ ਜੀ! ਕੀ ਤੁਸੀਂ ਮੇਰੇ ਸ਼੍ਰੇਣੀ ਅਧਿਆਪਕ ਨੂੰ ਮਿਲੇ ਸੀ? b ਉਹ ਸਾਨੂੰ ਚੰਗੀ ਤਰ੍ਹਾਂ ਪੜ੍ਹਾਂਦਾ ਨਹੀਂ c ਤੈਨੂੰ ਪੜ੍ਹਾਈ ਵਿਚ ਮਿਹਨਤ ਕਰਨੀ ਚਾਹੀਦੀ ਹੈ। 2 1 teacher 2 Ramesh 3 homework 4 maths 5 careless

Dialogue 2 exercises

1 kaanoo<u>n</u>n ਬੀਬੀ, madam ਕਾਗ਼ਜ਼ਾਤ, kaa<u>gh</u>zaa<u>t</u> maaf, pardon ਉਲੰਘਣਾ, to disobey 2 mobile phone, officer, licence, minute, car

Dialogue 3 exercises

1 a ਮੈਂ ਸਮਾਜ ਸੇਵਕ ਹਾਂ। b ਕੀ ਗੱਲ ਹੈ? c ਅੰਦਰ ਆ ਜਾਓ d ਮੇਰੇ ਲਈ ਇਹ ਮੁਸ਼ਕਲ ਹੈ। 2 a ਆਇਆ b ਸਕਦੀ c ਚਲੇ ਜਾਂਦੇ d ਕਰਾਂ ਗੀ।

End exercises

1 a ਦੇ ਨੇੜੇ b ਦੇ ਅੰਦਰ c ਤੋਂ ਬਾਅਦ d ਦੀ ਜਗ੍ਹਾ 2 a ii b iii c iv d i 3 a ਦਫ਼ਤਰ b ੧੦ ਮਿੰਟ c ਨਹੀਂ d ਕਾਗ਼ਜ਼ਾਤ ਪੇਸ਼ ਕਰਨੇ ਹਨ 4 ਅਧਿਆਪਕ, ਇਲਾਵਾ, ਹਿਸਾਬ, ਕੰਮ, ਕਲਾਸ, ਡਾਕਟਰ, ਦੂਜੇ, ਪੜ੍ਹਉਣਾ, ਪਾਪਾ, ਬਾਰੇ, ਮਜ਼ਮੂਨਾਂ, ਮਿਹਨਤ, ਲਿਆਕਤ, ਵਰਤਣਾ, ਸ਼੍ਰੇਣੀ।

Unit 15

Dialogue 1 exercises

1 b ਵੈਸਾਖੀ ਮੇਲਾ c 1 ਫ਼ਸਲਾਂ ਕਟਣਾ 2 ਸਿੱਖ ਕੌਮ ਦਾ ਜਨਮ ਦਿਨ d ਜਲੇਬੀਆਂ ਅਤੇ ਪਕੌੜੇ e ਗਤਕਾ f 1 ਨੁਮਾਇਸ਼ 2 ਭੰਗੜਾ

2 village people harvest season Sikh religion the new year
3 True True False False

Folk song exercise

a Yes b No c No d No

End exercises

1 a ਜਿਹੜਾ, ਉਹ b ਜਿਵੇਂ, ਉਂਵੇਂ c ਜਿੱਥੇ, ਉੱਥੇ d ਜਦੋਂ, ਉਦੋਂ 2 b ਬਾਹਰ ਜਾਣ ਦੇਵੇ c ਪੀਣ ਦੇ d ਦੇਖਣ ਦੇਵੇ/ਦਿਉ 3 a ਕੰਮ ਤੇ ਜਾਣ ਲਈ ੧੫ ਮਿੰਟ ਲੱਗਦੇ ਹਨ। b ਇੱਕ ਫ਼ਰਸਟ ਕਲਾਸ ਟਿਕਟ ਲਈ ਕਿੰਨੇ ਪੈਸੇ ਲੱਗਦੇ ਹਨ? c ਮੈਨੂੰ ਗਰਮੀ ਲੱਗਦੀ ਹੈ। d ਬਾਰਸ਼ ਹੋਣ ਲੱਗੀ। e ਅਸੀਂ ਬਾਹਰ ਜਾਣ ਲੱਗੇ ਸੀਂ।

Unit 16

Dialogue 1 exercises

1 a True b False c False d True 2 a ਮੈਨੂੰ ਭੰਗੜਾ ਪਸੰਦ ਹੈ। b ਮੈਨੂੰ ਭੰਗੜਾ ਗਿੱਧੇ ਨਾਲੋਂ ਜ਼ਿਆਦਾ ਪਸੰਦ ਹੈ। c ਭਾਵੇਂ ਤੁਸੀਂ ਪੰਜਾਬ ਜਾ ਬਾਹਰ ਹੋ, ਭੰਗੜਾ ਦੇਖ ਸਕਦੇ ਹੋ। d ਆਓ ਆਪਾਂ, ਨੱਚੀਏ। 3 a drum b long wooden pole c spoon

Dialogue 2 exercises

1 Canada Uganda Malaysia England 2 a ਅਵਤਾਰ ਤੇ ਤਰਲੋਕ b ਮਲੇਸ਼ੀਆ c ਲਾਇਲਪੁਰ d ਯੂਗੰਡਾ e ਧੋਬੀ ਦਾ ਕੁੱਤਾ ਨਾ ਘਰ ਦਾ ਨਾ ਘਾਟ ਦਾ 3 a ਕਿਉਂ ਕਿ ਉਹ ਫ਼ੌਜ ਵਿਚ ਭਰਤੀ ਹੋ ਗਏ ਸਨ। b ਕਿਉਂ ਕਿ ਉਹ ਗ਼ਦਰ ਪਾਰਟੀ ਵਿਚ ਸ਼ਾਮਲ ਹੋ ਗਏ ਸਨ। c ਕਿਉਂ ਕਿ ਪੰਜਾਬ ਦਾ ਬਟਵਾਰਾ ਹੋ ਗਿਆ ਸੀ। d ਕਿਉਂ ਕਿ ਉਹ ਰੇਲਵੇ ਬਣਾਉਣ ਗਏ ਸਨ।

End exercises

1 b ਸਾਡੇ ਕੋਲ ਨਾ ਪੈਂਸਲਾਂ ਹਨ, ਨਾ ਕਾਪੀ ਹੈ। c ਸਾਡੇ ਕੋਲ ਨਾ ਘੜੀਆਂ ਹਨ, ਨਾ ਰੇਡੀਓ ਹੈ। d ਸਾਡੇ ਕੋਲ ਨਾ ਬੋਤਲਾਂ ਹਨ, ਨਾ ਪਾਣੀ ਹੈ। 2 b ਨਾ ਸਿਰਫ਼ ਇਹ ਕਿਤਾਬ ਲੰਬੀ ਹੈ, ਸਗੋਂ ਮੁਸ਼ਕਲ ਵੀ ਹੈ। c ਨਾ ਸਿਰਫ਼ ਅਸੀਂ ਭੰਗੜਾ ਪਸੰਦ ਕਰਦੇ ਹਾਂ, ਸਗੋਂ ਗਿੱਧਾ ਵੀ ਪਸੰਦ ਕਰਦੇ ਹਾਂ। d ਭਾਵੇਂ ਤੁਸੀਂ ਪੰਜਾਬ ਵਿਚ ਹੋ ਭਾਵੇਂ ਬਾਹਰ, ਤੁਸੀਂ ਭੰਗੜਾ ਦੇਖ ਸਕਦੇ ਹੋ। e ਮੰਨੋ ਜਾਂ ਨਾ ਮੰਨੋ, ਵੈਨਕੂਵਰ ਦਾ ਮਾਹੌਲ ਪੰਜਾਬ ਵਾਂਗੂੰ ਹੈ। 3 ਤਰਲੋਕ: ਇੰਗਲੈਂਡ, ਕੈਨੇਡਾ, ਯੂਗੰਡਾ ਅਵਤਾਰ: ਮਲੇਸ਼ੀਆ, ਕੈਨੇਡਾ, ਲਾਇਲਪੁਰ, ਜਲੰਧਰ

topic vocabulary

English	Transliteration	ਪੰਜਾਬੀ
Parts of the body	*sareer de ang*	ਸਰੀਰ ਦੇ ਅੰਗ
arm	baa<u>n</u>h	ਬਾਂਹ
back	piththh	ਪਿੱਠ
beard	<u>d</u>aarhhee	ਦਾੜ੍ਹੀ
body	sareer / jisam	ਸਰੀਰ / ਜਿਸਮ
chest	<u>ch</u>aa<u>t</u>ee	ਛਾਤੀ
ear	ka<u>n</u>n	ਕੰਨ
eye	akhkh	ਅੱਖ
face	moo<u>n</u>h / chihraa	ਮੂੰਹ / ਚਿਹਰਾ
finger	u<u>n</u>glee	ਉਂਗਲੀ
foot	pair	ਪੈਰ
hair	vaal	ਵਾਲ
hand	ha<u>t</u>hth	ਹੱਥ
head	sir	ਸਿਰ
knee	godaa	ਗੋਡਾ
leg	la<u>t</u>t	ਲੱਤ
moustache	mu<u>chch</u>aan	ਮੁੱਛਾਂ
mouth	moo<u>n</u>h	ਮੂੰਹ
neck	gar<u>d</u>an	ਗਰਦਨ
nose	nakk	ਨੱਕ
shoulder	modhaa	ਮੋਢਾ
stomach	dhidd / pet	ਢਿੱਡ / ਪੇਟ
throat	gal / galaa	ਗਲ / ਗਲਾ
tongue	jeebh / zabaan	ਜੀਭ / ਜ਼ਬਾਨ
tooth	<u>d</u>and	ਦੰਦ

Vegetables	*sabzeeaan*	ਸਬਜ਼ੀਆਂ
bitter gourd	karelaa	ਕਰੇਲਾ
brinjal / egg plant	vataaoon / bainganh	ਵਤਾਊਂ / ਬੈਂਗਣ
cabbage	band gobhee	ਬੰਦ ਗੋਭੀ
capsicum	shimlaa mirach	ਸ਼ਿਮਲਾ ਮਿਰਚ
carrot	gaajar	ਗਾਜਰ
cauliflower	gobhee	ਗੋਭੀ
courgette	raam toree	ਰਾਮ ਤੋਰੀ
mushrooms	khunbaan	ਖੁੰਬਾਂ
mustard leaves	sar-h-on de patte (saag)	ਸਰੋਂ ਦੇ ਪੱਤੇ (ਸਾਗ)
okra	bhindee	ਭਿੰਡੀ
peas	matar	ਮਟਰ
potato	aaloo	ਆਲੂ
spinach	paalak	ਪਾਲਕ
tomatoes	tamaatar	ਟਮਾਟਰ
turnip	shalgam / gongloo	ਸ਼ਲਗਮ / ਗੋਂਗਲੂ

Fruit	*phal*	ਫਲ
apple	seb	ਸੇਬ
apricot	khurmaanee	ਖੁਰਮਾਨੀ
banana	kelaa	ਕੇਲਾ
grapes	angoor	ਅੰਗੂਰ
lemon	ninboo	ਨਿੰਬੂ
mango	anb	ਅੰਬ
orange	santraa	ਸੰਤਰਾ
peach	aarhoo	ਆੜੂ
pear	naakh / naashpaatee	ਨਾਖ / ਨਾਸ਼ਪਾਟੀ
pineapple	anaanaas	ਅਨਾਨਾਸ
plums	alooche / aaloobukhaaraa	ਅਲੂਚੇ / ਆਲੂਬੁਖ਼ਾਰਾ
pomegranate	anaar	ਅਨਾਰ

Places	*thaanvaan*	ਥਾਂਵਾਂ
church	girjaa	ਗਿਰਜਾ
college	mahaan vidiaalaa	ਮਹਾਂ ਵਿਦਿਆਲਾ
community kitchen	langar	ਲੰਗਰ
enquiry office	puchch gichch daa daftar	ਪੁੱਛ ਗਿੱਛ ਦਾ ਦਫ਼ਤਰ

exhibition	numaaish / pardarshanee	ਨੁਮਾਇਸ਼ / ਪਰਦਰਸ਼ਨੀ
factory	kaarkhaanaa	ਕਾਰਖ਼ਾਨਾ
fort	kilhaa	ਕਿਲ੍ਹਾ
Hindu place of worship (temple)	mandar	ਮੰਦਰ
hospital	haspataal	ਹਸਪਤਾਲ
library	pustakaalaa	ਪੁਸਤਕਾਲਾ
market	mandee	ਮੰਡੀ
museum	ajaaib ghar	ਅਜਾਇਬ ਘਰ
Muslim place of worship (mosque)	masjid / maseet	ਮਸਜਿਦ / ਮਸੀਤ
office	daftar	ਦਫ਼ਤਰ
palace	mahhal	ਮੱਹਲ
park	baagh	ਬਾਗ਼
police station	thaanhaa / pulas chaunkee	ਥਾਣਾ / ਪੁਲਸ ਚੌਂਕੀ
post office	daakkhaanaa	ਡਾਕਖ਼ਾਨਾ
roadside restaurant	dhaabaa	ਢਾਬਾ
school	vidiaalaa / madrasaa	ਵਿਦਿਆਲਾ / ਮਦਰਸਾ
shop	dukaan / hattee	ਦੁਕਾਨ / ਹੱਟੀ
Sikh place of worship	gurdavaaraa / gurduaaraa	ਗੁਰਦਵਾਰਾ / ਗੁਰਦੁਆਰਾ
zoo	chirheeaa ghar	ਚਿੜੀਆ ਘਰ
Occupations	*peshe*	*ਪੇਸ਼ੇ*
carpenter	tarkhaanh	ਤਰਖਾਣ
cook / chef	laangree	ਲਾਂਗਰੀ
doctor	daaktar	ਡਾਕਟਰ
farmer	kisaan	ਕਿਸਾਨ
gardener	maalee	ਮਾਲੀ
judge	jajj	ਜੱਜ
lawyer	vakeel	ਵਕੀਲ
mechanic	mistaree	ਮਿਸਤਰੀ
milkman	dudhdh vaalaa	ਦੁੱਧ ਵਾਲਾ
policeman	pulas vaalaa	ਪੁਲਸ ਵਾਲਾ
postman	daakeeaa	ਡਾਕੀਆ
priest (Sikh)	garanthee	ਗਰੰਥੀ

singer	gaaik	ਗਾਇਕ
teacher	adhiaapak	ਅਧਿਆਪਕ
writer	lekhak	ਲੇਖਕ

Colours	*rang*	*ਰੰਗ*
black	kaalaa	ਕਾਲਾ
blue	neelaa	ਨੀਲਾ
brown	badaamee	ਬਦਾਮੀ
gold / golden	sunahiree	ਸੁਨਹਿਰੀ
green	haraa / sabaz	ਹਰਾ / ਸਬਜ਼
grey	saletee	ਸਲੇਟੀ
khaki	khaakee	ਖ਼ਾਕੀ
maroon	laakhaa	ਲਾਖਾ
orange	santaree	ਸੰਤਰੀ
pink	gulaabee	ਗੁਲਾਬੀ
purple	jaamnee	ਜਾਮਨੀ
red	laal	ਲਾਲ
saffron	kesaree	ਕੇਸਰੀ
white	chittaa / safed	ਚਿੱਟਾ / ਸਫ਼ੇਦ
yellow	peelaa	ਪੀਲਾ

Directions	*dishaavaan*	*ਦਿਸ਼ਾਵਾਂ*
behind	pichche	ਪਿੱਛੇ
down	thalle	ਥੱਲੇ
east	poorab	ਪੂਰਬ
far	door	ਦੂਰ
in front	agge	ਅੱਗੇ
left side	khabbe	ਖੱਬੇ
near	nerhe / nazdeek	ਨੇੜੇ / ਨਜ਼ਦੀਕ
north	uttar	ਉੱਤਰ
right side	sajje	ਸੱਜੇ
south	dakhkhanh	ਦੱਖਣ
straight	sidhdhaa, sidhdhe	ਸਿੱਧਾ / ਸਿੱਧੇ
that side	us paase	ਉਸ ਪਾਸੇ
this side	is paase	ਇਸ ਪਾਸੇ
up	uppar	ਉੱਪਰ
west	pachcham	ਪੱਛਮ

Animals	*jaanvar*	ਜਾਨਵਰ
bear	richch	ਰਿੱਛ
buffalo	majhjh	ਮੱਝ
camel	ooth	ਊਠ
cat	billee	ਬਿੱਲੀ
cow	gaan	ਗਾਂ
deer	hiran	ਹਿਰਨ
dog	kuttaa	ਕੁੱਤਾ
elephant	haathee	ਹਾਥੀ
fox	loonbarh	ਲੂੰਬੜ
horse	ghorhaa	ਘੋੜਾ
monkey	baandar	ਬਾਂਦਰ
mouse	choohaa	ਚੂਹਾ
pig	soor	ਸੂਰ
sheep	bhed	ਭੇਡ
tiger	sher	ਸ਼ੇਰ
Moods	*birteeaan*	ਬਿਰਤੀਆਂ
angry	gussaa	ਗੁੱਸਾ
anxious	pareshaan	ਪਰੇਸ਼ਾਨ
contented	santushat	ਸੰਤੁਸ਼ਟ
curious	utsuk	ਉਤਸੁਕ
depressed	udaas	ਉਦਾਸ
determined	nishchit	ਨਿਸ਼ਚਿਤ
disgusted	upraam	ਉਪਰਾਮ
frightened	dariaa hoiaa	ਡਰਿਆ ਹੋਇਆ
happy	khush	ਖ਼ੁਸ਼
irritated	khijhiaa hoiaa	ਖਿਝਿਆ ਹੋਇਆ
lazy	susat	ਸੁਸਤ
loving	piaaraa	ਪਿਆਰਾ
sad / unhappy	ghamgeen	ਗ਼ਮਗੀਨ
surprised	hairaan janak	ਹੈਰਾਨ ਜਨਕ
thoughtful	vichaarsheel	ਵਿਚਾਰਸ਼ੀਲ
Travel and transport	*safar te aavaajaaee*	ਸਫ਼ਰ ਤੇ ਆਵਾਜਾਈ
aeroplane	havaaee jahaaz	ਹਵਾਈ ਜਹਾਜ਼
airport	havaaee addaa	ਹਵਾਈ ਅੱਡਾ

bicycle	saaikal	ਸਾਇਕਲ
boat	berhee	ਬੇੜੀ
booking clerk	tikat baaboo	ਟਿਕਟ ਬਾਬੂ
bus	bas	ਬਸ
bus station	basaan daa addaa	ਬਸਾਂ ਦਾ ਅੱਡਾ
car	kaar / gaddee	ਕਾਰ / ਗੱਡੀ
fare	kiraaiaa	ਕਿਰਾਇਆ
foot (on)	paidal	ਪੈਦਲ
horse carriage	taangaa / yakkaa	ਟਾਂਗਾ / ਯੱਕਾ
journey	yaatraa / safar	ਜਾਤਰਾ / ਸਫਰ
passenger	savaaree	ਸਵਾਰੀ
road	sarhak	ਸੜਕ
rickshaw	rikshaa	ਰਿਕਸ਼ਾ
ship	samundaree jahaaz	ਸਮੁੰਦਰੀ ਜਹਾਜ਼
ticket	tikat	ਟਿਕਟ
train	rel gaddee	ਰੇਲ ਗੱਡੀ
(to) travel	safar karnaa	ਸਫਰ ਕਰਨਾ
traveller	yaatree	ਜਾਤਰੀ
vehicle	vaahanh	ਵਾਹਣ
waiting room	udeek ghar / musaafar khaanaa	ਉਡੀਕ ਘਰ / ਮੁਸਾਫ਼ਰ ਖ਼ਾਨਾ

Personal identification	*nijjee shanaakhat*	*ਨਿੱਜੀ ਸ਼ਨਾਖ਼ਤ*
age	umar	ਉਮਰ
birthday	janam din	ਜਨਮ ਦਿਨ
(to be) born	janmnhaa	ਜੰਮਣਾ
caste	zaat	ਜ਼ਾਤ
family name	got	ਗੋਤ
height	kadd	ਕੱਦ
maiden name	pekaa naan	ਪੇਕਾ ਨਾਂ
man	aadmee	ਆਦਮੀ
(to be) married	viaahiaa honhaa	ਵਿਆਹਿਆ ਹੋਣਾ
name	naam / naan	ਨਾਮ / ਨਾਂ
nation	kaum	ਕੌਮ
nationality	kaumeeat	ਕੌਮੀਅਤ
place of birth	janam asthaan	ਜਨਮ ਅਸਥਾਨ

religion	dharam / mazhab	ਧਰਮ / ਮਜ਼੍ਹਬ
(to be) unmarried	kanvaaraa honhaa	ਕੰਵਾਰਾ ਹੋਣਾ
young	javaan	ਜਵਾਨ

House and home	*makaan te ghar*	ਮਕਾਨ ਤੇ ਘਰ
bathroom	ghusal khaanaa / ishnaan ghar	ਗ਼ੁਸਲ ਖ਼ਾਨਾ / ਇਸ਼ਨਾਨ ਘਰ
bed	manjaa / palangh	ਮੰਜਾ / ਪਲੰਘ
bedroom	saunh vaalaa kamraa	ਸੌਣ ਵਾਲਾ ਕਮਰਾ
building	imaarat	ਇਮਾਰਤ
bungalow	banglaa	ਬੰਗਲਾ
carpet	daree	ਦਰੀ
ceiling	andarlee chatt	ਅੰਦਰਲੀ ਛੱਤ
cooker	chullhaa	ਚੁੱਲ੍ਹਾ
court yard	vihrhaa	ਵਿਹੜਾ
dining room	khaanh vaalaa kamraa	ਖਾਣ ਵਾਲਾ ਕਮਰਾ
door	darvaazaa	ਦਰਵਾਜ਼ਾ
floor	farash	ਫ਼ਰਸ਼
garden	bagheechaa	ਬਗੀਚਾ
key	taalee, chaabee	ਤਾਲੀ, ਚਾਬੀ
kitchen	rasoee	ਰਸੋਈ
light	roshnee	ਰੋਸ਼ਨੀ
lock	taalaa / jandraa	ਤਾਲਾ / ਜੰਦਰਾ
roof	baaharlee chatt	ਬਾਹਰਲੀ ਛੱਤ
room	kamraa	ਕਮਰਾ
sink	chubachchaa	ਚੁਬੱਚਾ
sitting room	baithak	ਬੈਠਕ
stairs	paurheeaan	ਪੌੜੀਆਂ
storey	manzal	ਮੰਜ਼ਲ
tap	nalkaa	ਨਲਕਾ
utensils	bartan / bhaande	ਬਰਤਨ / ਭਾਂਡੇ
wall	deevar / kandh	ਦੀਵਾਰ / ਕੰਧ
window	baaree / khirhkee	ਬਾਰੀ / ਖਿੜਕੀ

Nature	*kudrat*	ਕੁਦਰਤ
climate	paunh paanhee	ਪੌਣ ਪਾਣੀ
earth	dhartee	ਧਰਤੀ

flowers	phull	ਫੁੱਲ
forest	jangal	ਜੰਗਲ
grass	ghaah	ਘਾਹ
lake	jheel	ਝੀਲ
land	zameen	ਜ਼ਮੀਨ
lightning	bijlee dee chamak	ਬਿਜਲੀ ਦੀ ਚਮਕ
moon	chann	ਚੰਨ
mountains	parbat / pahaarh	ਪਰਬਤ / ਪਹਾੜ
river	dariaa	ਦਰਿਆ
sea	samundar	ਸਮੁੰਦਰ
seasons	ruttaan	ਰੁੱਤਾਂ
sky	asmaan	ਅਸਮਾਨ
star	taaraa	ਤਾਰਾ
sun	sooraj	ਸੂਰਜ
tree	darakhat	ਦਰਖ਼ਤ

Weather	*mausam*	*ਮੌਸਮ*
breeze	havaa	ਹਵਾ
cloud	baddal	ਬੱਦਲ
cold	thand	ਠੰਡ
drought	sokaa	ਸੋਕਾ
drizzle	boondaa baandee	ਬੂੰਦਾ ਬਾਂਦੀ
dry	khushak	ਖ਼ੁਸ਼ਕ
flood	harhh	ਹੜੁ
fog	dhund	ਧੁੰਦ
frost	koraa	ਕੋਰਾ
hailstones	garhe	ਗੜੇ
heatwave	loo	ਲੂ
hot	garmee	ਗਰਮੀ
rain	baarash / meenh	ਬਾਰਸ਼ / ਮੀਂਹ
shade	chaan	ਛਾਂ
snow	baraf	ਬਰਫ਼
sunshine	dhupp	ਧੁੱਪ
thunder	garaj	ਗਰਜ
wet	sillaa	ਸਿੱਲਾ

Numerals	ginhtee	ਗਿਣਤੀ	
0	sifar	ਸਿਫ਼ਰ	o
1	ikk	ਇੱਕ	੧
2	do	ਦੋ	੨
3	tinn	ਤਿੰਨ	੩
4	chaar	ਚਾਰ	੪
5	panj	ਪੰਜ	੫
6	che	ਛੇ	੬
7	satt	ਸੱਤ	੭
8	athth	ਅੱਠ	੮
9	naun	ਨੌਂ	੯
10	das	ਦਸ	੧੦
11	giaaraan	ਗਿਆਰਾਂ	੧੧
12	baar-h-aan	ਬਾਰ੍ਹਾਂ	੧੨
13	ter-h-aan	ਤੇਰ੍ਹਾਂ	੧੩
14	chaud-h-aan	ਚੌਦ੍ਹਾਂ	੧੪
15	pandraan	ਪੰਦਰਾਂ	੧੫
16	solhaan	ਸੋਲ੍ਹਾਂ	੧੬
17	sataar-h-aan	ਸਤਾਰ੍ਹਾਂ	੧੭
18	athaar-h-aan	ਅਠਾਰ੍ਹਾਂ	੧੮
19	unnee	ਉੱਨੀ	੧੯
20	veeh	ਵੀਹ	੨੦
21	ikkee	ਇੱਕੀ	੨੧
22	baaee	ਬਾਈ	੨੨
23	te-ee	ਤੇਈ	੨੩
24	chauvee	ਚੌਵੀ	੨੪
25	panjhee	ਪੰਝੀ	੨੫
26	chabbee	ਛੱਬੀ	੨੬
27	sataaee	ਸਤਾਈ	੨੭
28	athaaee	ਅਠਾਈ	੨੮
29	unattee	ਉਨੱਤੀ	੨੯
30	teeh	ਤੀਹ	੩੦
31	ikkatee	ਇੱਕਤੀ	੩੧
32	battee	ਬੱਤੀ	੩੨
33	tetee	ਤੇਤੀ	੩੩
34	chauntee	ਚੌਂਤੀ	੩੪

35	pai<u>nt</u>ee	ਪੈਂਤੀ	੩੫
36	<u>ch</u>attee	ਛੱਤੀ	੩੬
37	sai<u>nt</u>ee	ਸੈਂਤੀ	੩੭
38	a<u>th</u>a<u>tt</u>ee	ਅਠੱਤੀ	੩੮
39	u<u>nt</u>aalee	ਉਨਤਾਲੀ	੩੯
40	chaalee	ਚਾਲੀ	੪੦
41	ik<u>t</u>aalee	ਇਕਤਾਲੀ	੪੧
42	ba<u>t</u>aalee	ਬਤਾਲੀ	੪੨
43	<u>t</u>ir<u>t</u>aalee	ਤਿਰਤਾਲੀ	੪੩
44	chu<u>t</u>aalee	ਚੁਤਾਲੀ	੪੪
45	pa<u>nt</u>aalee	ਪੰਤਾਲੀ	੪੫
46	<u>ch</u>i<u>t</u>aalee	ਛਿਤਾਲੀ	੪੬
47	sa<u>nt</u>aalee	ਸੰਤਾਲੀ	੪੭
48	a<u>tht</u>aalee	ਅਠਤਾਲੀ	੪੮
49	unh<u>nj</u>aa	ਉਣੰਜਾ	੪੯
50	pa<u>nj</u>aah	ਪੰਜਾਹ	੫੦
51	ikva<u>nj</u>aa	ਇਕਵੰਜਾ	੫੧
52	bava<u>nj</u>aa	ਬਵੰਜਾ	੫੨
53	<u>t</u>arva<u>nj</u>aa	ਤਰਵੰਜਾ	੫੩
54	chura<u>nj</u>aa	ਚੁਰੰਜਾ	੫੪
55	pachva<u>nj</u>aa	ਪਚਵੰਜਾ	੫੫
56	<u>ch</u>iva<u>nj</u>aa	ਛਿਵੰਜਾ	੫੬
57	sa<u>t</u>va<u>nj</u>aa	ਸਤਵੰਜਾ	੫੭
58	a<u>th</u>va<u>nj</u>aa	ਅਠਵੰਜਾ	੫੮
59	unhaah<u>th</u>	ਉਣਾਹਠ	੫੯
60	sa<u>thth</u>	ਸੱਠ	੬੦
61	ikaah<u>th</u>	ਇਕਾਹਠ	੬੧
62	baah<u>th</u>	ਬਾਹਠ	੬੨
63	<u>t</u>reh<u>th</u>	ਤ੍ਰੇਹਠ	੬੩
64	chau<u>nh</u><u>th</u>	ਚੌਹਠ	੬੪
65	pai<u>nh</u><u>th</u>	ਪੈਂਹਠ	੬੫
66	<u>ch</u>iaah<u>th</u>	ਛਿਆਹਠ	੬੬
67	sa<u>t</u>aah<u>th</u>	ਸਤਾਹਠ	੬੭
68	a<u>th</u>aah<u>th</u>	ਅਠਾਹਠ	੬੮
69	unha<u>tt</u>ar	ਉਨਹੱਤਰ	੬੯

70	sattar	ਸੱਤਰ	੭੦
71	ikhattar	ਇਕਹੱਤਰ	੭੧
72	bahattar	ਬਹੱਤਰ	੭੨
73	tihattar	ਤਿਹੱਤਰ	੭੩
74	chauhattar	ਚੌਹੱਤਰ	੭੪
75	pachattar	ਪਚੱਤਰ	੭੫
76	chihattar	ਛਿਹੱਤਰ	੭੬
77	satattar	ਸਤੱਤਰ	੭੭
78	athattar	ਅਠੱਤਰ	੭੮
79	unaasee	ਉਨਾਸੀ	੭੯
80	assee	ਅੱਸੀ	੮੦
81	ikaasee	ਇਕਾਸੀ	੮੧
82	biaasee	ਬਿਆਸੀ	੮੨
83	triaasee	ਤ੍ਰਿਆਸੀ	੮੩
84	churaasee	ਚੁਰਾਸੀ	੮੪
85	pachaasee	ਪਚਾਸੀ	੮੫
86	chiaasee	ਛਿਆਸੀ	੮੬
87	sataasee	ਸਤਾਸੀ	੮੭
88	athaasee	ਅਠਾਸੀ	੮੮
89	unhaanven	ਉਠਾਨਵੇਂ	੮੯
90	navve	ਨੱਵੇ	੯੦
91	ikaanven	ਇਕਾਨਵੇਂ	੯੧
92	baanven	ਬਾਨਵੇਂ	੯੨
93	triaanven	ਤ੍ਰਿਆਨਵੇਂ	੯੩
94	churaanven	ਚੁਰਾਨਵੇਂ	੯੪
95	pachaanven	ਪਚਾਨਵੇਂ	੯੫
96	chiaanven	ਛਿਆਨਵੇਂ	੯੬
97	sataanven	ਸਤਾਨਵੇਂ	੯੭
98	athaanven	ਅਠਾਨਵੇਂ	੯੮
99	narhinven	ਨੜਿਨਵੇਂ	੯੯
100	sau	ਸੌ	੧੦੦
1,000	ikk hazaar	ਇੱਕ ਹਜ਼ਾਰ	੧,੦੦੦
10,000	lakhkh	ਲੱਖ	੧੦੦,੦੦੦
10,000,000	karorh	ਕਰੋੜ	੧੦,੦੦੦,੦੦੦

Panjabi–English glossary

ਉਸ	us	*that*
ਉਹ	uh	*he, she, that, they*
ਉਖੜਨਾ	ukharhnaa	*to be displaced, to be uprooted*
ਉਡੀਕਣਾ	udeeknhaa	*to wait*
ਉਤਸੁਕ	u<u>t</u>suk	*anxious, awaiting*
ਉੱਥੋਂ	u<u>thth</u>on	*from there*
ਉਮਰ	umar	*age* (f.)
ਉਮੀਦ	umee<u>d</u>	*hope* (f.)
ਉਰਦੂ	ur<u>d</u>oo	*Urdu* (m. / f.)
ਉਲੰਘਣਾ	ula<u>n</u>ghnhaa	*to disobey, to break*
ਊਠ	ooth	*male camel* (m.)
ਅੱਸਲਾਮ ਅਲੈਕਮ	asslaam alaikam	Muslim greeting
ਅਸੀਂ	asee<u>n</u>	*we*
ਅਸੀਂ ਸਾਰੇ	asee<u>n</u> saare	*all of us, we all*
ਅਸੀਂ ਦੋਨੋਂ	asee<u>n</u> <u>d</u>ono<u>n</u>	*both of us*
ਅਖਾਣ	akhaanh	*proverb, saying* (m.)
ਅਖ਼ੀਰ	a<u>kh</u>eer	*end*
ਅਗਲਾ	aglaa	*next* (v.)
ਅੰਗਰੇਜ਼	a<u>n</u>grez	*English* (m. / f.)
ਅੱਛਾ	a<u>chch</u>aa	*OK, alright*
ਅੱਜ	ajj	*today*
ਅੱਜ ਕੱਲੂ	ajj kallh	*these days*
ਅਜ਼ਾਦੀ	azaa<u>d</u>ee	*freedom, independence* (f.)

ਅੰਤਰ ਰਾਸ਼ਟਰੀ	antar raashtaree	*international*
ਅੰਦਰ	andar	*inside*
ਅਤੇ	ate	*and*
ਅਜ਼ਾਦੀ ਲਈ ਜਦੋ ਜਹਿਦ	azaadee laee jado jahid	*struggle for independence* (f.)
ਅਜੋਕਾ	ajokaa	*modern*
ਅਨੰਦ ਮਾਣੋ	anand maanho	*enjoy yourself*
ਅਨਾਰਕਲੀ	anaarkalee	*name of classic Urdu film* (f.)
ਅਪਰਾਧ	apraadh	*offence* (m.)
ਅਫ਼ਸਰ	afsar	*officer* (m. / f.)
ਅਫ਼ਸੋਸ	afsos	*regret, sorry*
ਅਬਾਦੀ	abaadee	*population* (f.)
ਅਮਰੀਕਾ	amreekaa	*America* (m.)
ਅੰਮ੍ਰਿਤ	anmrit	*nectar, holy water* (m.)
ਅਰਥ	arth	*meaning* (m.)
ਅਰਾਮ	araam	*rest* (m.)
ਆ ਜਾ	aa jaa	*come* (informal request)
ਆਉਣਾ	aaunhaa	*to come*
ਆਓ	aao	*come* (formal)
ਆਸ ਪਾਸ	aas paas	*around and about*
ਆਗਿਆ	aagiaa	*permission* (f.)
ਆਪਣਾ	aapnhaa	*one's own*
ਆਲੂ	aaloo	*potato(es)* (m.)
ਅਧਿਆਪਕ	adhiaapak	*teacher* (m. / f.)
ਅਧਿਆਪਕਾ	adhiaapkaa	*teacher* (f.)
ਐਨੇ ਸਾਰੇ	aine saare	*so much*
ਐਤਵਾਰ	aitvaar	*Sunday* (m.)
ਇਸ	is	*it, this*
ਇਸ ਕਰ ਕੇ	is kar ke	*that is why*
ਇਸਤਰੀ	istaree	*lady* (f.)
ਇਸ ਵਾਰੀ	is vaaree	*this time*
ਇਹ	ih	*he, she, it, this*
ਇੱਕ	ikk	*one, a*
ਇੱਕ ਪਾਸੇ	ikk paase	*one side*
ਇੱਕ ਸੌ ਵੀਹ	ikk sau veeh	*120*
ਇਕੱਠ	ikathth	*gathering* (m.)

ਇਕੱਠੇ	ikaththe	*together*
ਇੱਕੋ	ikko	*same*
ਇੰਤਜ਼ਾਮ	intzaam	*arrangements* (m.)
ਇੱਥੇ	iththe	*here*
ਇਨਸ਼ਾ ਅੱਲਾ	inshaa allaa	*hopefully* (lit: if God wishes)
ਈਸਟ ਅਫ਼ਰੀਕਾ	eest afreekaa	*East Africa* (m.)
ਏ	e	*is (informal)*
ਸਹਿਮਤ	sahimat	*agree*
ਸ਼ਹਿਰ	shahir	*city* (m.)
ਸ਼ਹਿਰੀਅਤ	shahireeat	*citizen* (f.)
ਸਹੁਰੇ	sahure	*in-laws* (m.)
ਸਹੇਲੀ	sahelee	*friend* (f.)
ਸਕਣਾ	saknhaa	*can, to be able to*
ਸਕੂਲ	sakool	*school* (m.)
ਸਗੋਂ	sagon	*but also*
ਸੱਚ	sachch	*true, truth* (v.)
ਸੱਚੀ ਮੁੱਚੀ	sachchee muchchee	*genuinely*
ਸਤਿ ਸ੍ਰੀ ਅਕਾਲ	sat sree akaal	Sikh greeting
ਸਥਿਤੀ	sathitee	*situation* (f.)
ਸੱਦਾ ਪੱਤਰ	saddaa pattar	*invitation* (m.)
ਸਨਿਚਰਵਾਰ	sanicharvaar	*Saturday* (m.)
ਸ਼ਨਾਖ਼ਤੀ ਕਾਰਡ	shanaakhtee kaard	*identity card* (m.)
ਸਪਤਾਹ	saptaah	*week* (m.)
ਸੰਪਰਕ	sanparak	*contact* (m.)
ਸਬਜ਼ੀ	sabzee	*vegetable* (f.)
ਸਫ਼ਰ ਕਰਨਾ	safar karnaa	*to travel*
ਸਭ	sabh	*all, every*
ਸਭ ਕੁਝ	sabh kujh	*everything*
ਸਭ ਪਾਸੇ	sabh paase	*everywhere*
ਸਭ ਤੋਂ ਵਧੀਆ	sabh ton vadheeaa	*the best*
ਸਮਝਣਾ	samjhnhaa	*to understand, to comprehend*
ਸਮਾਂ	samaan	*time* (m.)

ਸਮਾਂ ਪਾ ਕੇ	samaa<u>n</u> paa ke	*after a while, after some time*
ਸਮਾਜ ਸੇਵਕ	samaaj sevak	*social worker* (m. / f.)
ਸਮਾਨ	samaan	*luggage, things* (m.)
ਸਮੁੰਦਰ	samu<u>n</u>dar	*sea* (m.)
ਸਮੁੰਦਰੀ ਡਾਕ	samu<u>n</u>daree daak	*sea mail* (f.)
ਸਮੋਸਾ	samosaa	*triangular stuffed pastry* (m.)
ਸਰਦਾਰ ਸਾਹਿਬ	sar<u>d</u>aar saahib	*Mr* (m.)
ਸਰਦੀ	sar<u>d</u>ee	*winter* (f.)
ਸ਼੍ਰੇਣੀ	shrenhee	*class* (f.)
ਸਰੋਵਰ	sarovar	*pool* (m.)
ਸ਼ਲਗਮ	shalgam	*turnip* (m.)
ਸਵਰਗ	savarag	*heaven* (m.)
ਸਵਾਰੀ	savaaree	*installation* (f.)
ਸਵਾਰੀਆਂ	savaareeaa<u>n</u>	*passengers, travellers* (f.)
ਸਵੇਰੇ	savere	*in the morning*
ਸਾਹਿਬ	saahib	*sir* (m.)
ਸਾਡਾ	saadaa	*our*
ਸ਼ਾਂਤੀ	shaa<u>n</u>tee	*peace* (f.)
ਸਾਫ ਕਰਨਾ	saaf karnaa	*to clean*
ਸ਼ਾਬਾਸ਼	shaabaash	*well done*
ਸ਼ਾਮਲ	shaamal	*to be present, to join in, participate*
ਸਾਲ	saal	*year* (m.)
ਸਾਰਾ ਮਾਹੌਲ	saaraa maahaul	*whole atmosphere* (m.)
ਸਾਰੇ	saare	*everyone, all* (v.)
ਸਾੜ੍ਹੀ ਵਾਲੀ	saarhhee vaalee	*the one wearing the sari* (f.)
ਸਿਆਣਾ	siaanhaa	*wise, mature* (v.)
ਸਿਹਤ	siha<u>t</u>	*health* (f.)
ਸ਼ਿਕਾਇਤ	shikaai<u>t</u>	*complaint* (f.)
ਸਿੱਖਾਂ ਦੇ	sikhkhaa<u>n</u> <u>d</u>e	*of the Sikhs*
ਸਿਤਾਰ	si<u>t</u>aar	*sitar* (f.) (stringed classical musical instrument)
ਸੀਟ	seet	*seat* (f.)
ਸ਼ੀਸ਼ਾ	sheeshaa	*mirror* (m.)

ਸੀਨਾ	seenaa	*bosom, heart* (m.)
ਸੁਆਦ	suaad	*taste* (m.)
ਸੁਆਦੀ	suaadee	*tasty*
ਸੁਹਣਾ	suhnhaa	*nice, pretty* (v.)
ਸ਼ੁੱਕਰਵਾਰ	shukkarvaar	*Friday* (m.)
ਸ਼ੁਕਰੀਆ	shukreeaa	*thank you* (m.)
ਸੁਨਣਾ	sunhnaa	*to listen*
ਸੁਨਹਿਰੀ	sunahiree	*golden*
ਸ਼ੁਭ ਇਛਾਵਾਂ	shubh ichaavaan	*best wishes* (f.)
ਸੁਰੱਖਿਅਤ ਸਫ਼ਰ	surakhkhiat safar	*safe journey*
ਸ਼ੁਰੂ ਹੋਣਾ	shuroo honhaa	*to start, to begin*
ਸ਼ੁਰੂ ਕਰਨਾ	shuroo karnaa	*to begin, to commence*
ਸੂਈ	sooee	*needle* (f.)
ਸੇਵਾਦਾਰ	sevaadaar	*volunteer* (m. / f.)
ਸੈਲਾਨੀ	sailaanee	*tourist* (m. / f.)
ਸੋਚਣਾ	sochnhaa	*to think*
ਸੋਨਾ	sonaa	*gold* (m.)
ਸੋਮਵਾਰ	somvaar	*Monday* (m.)
ਸੌ (੧੦੦)	sau	*100*
ਸ਼ੌਕ	shauk	*fondness, enjoyment, like* (m.)
ਸੌਖਾ	saukhaa	*easy, simple* (v.)
ਹਜ਼ਮ	hazam	*digest*
ਹੰਢਣਸਾਰ	handhanhsaar	*durable, hardwearing*
ਹਫ਼ਤਾ	haftaa	*week* (m.)
ਹਫ਼ਤਾ	haftaa	*Saturday* (m.)
ਹਫ਼ਤੇ ਦੇ ਅਖ਼ੀਰ	hafte de akheer	*weekend* (**m.**)
ਹਰ ਪਾਸੇ	har paase	*everywhere*
ਹਰਿਮੰਦਰ ਸਾਹਿਬ	harmandar saahib	*Golden Temple* (m.)
ਹਵਾਈ	havaaee	*by air*
ਹਵਾਈ ਅੱਡਾ	havaaee addaa	*airport* (m.)
ਹਵਾਈ ਡਾਕ	havaaee daak	*air mail* (f.)
ਹਾਲ	haal	*condition* (m.)
ਹਾਂ ਜੀ	haan jee	*yes* (polite)

ਹਿਸਾਬ	hisaab	*maths* (m.)
ਹਿੰਦੂ	hindoo	*Hindu* (m. / f.)
ਹੁਣ	hunh	*now*
ਹੋਸਟਲ	hostal	*hostel* (m.)
ਹੋਣਾ	honhaa	*to be*
ਹੈ	hai	*is*
ਕਈ	kaee	*several*
ਕਈ ਤਰ੍ਹਾਂ	kaee tar-h-aan	*different types*
ਕਹਿਣਾ	kahinhaa	*to speak*
ਕਟਣਾ	katnhaa	*to cut*
ਕੱਦ	kadd	*height* (m.)
ਕਦਰਾਂ	kadraan	*values* (f.)
ਕਦੀ	kadee	*sometimes*
ਕਦੋਂ	kadon	*when*
ਕਪੜਾ	kaprhaa	*cloth* (m.)
ਕਮਰਾ	kamraa	*room* (m.)
ਕਮਜ਼ੋਰੀ	kamzoree	*weakness* (f.)
ਕੰਮ	kanm	*job, work task* (m.)
ਕੰਮ ਕਰਨਾ	kanm karnaa	*to work*
ਕਰਨਾ	karnaa	*to do*
ਕਰਾਰਾ	karaaraa	*spicy* (v.)
ਕਰੇਲਾ	karelaa	*bitter gourd* (m.)
ਕੱਲ੍ਹ	kallh	*yesterday, tomorrow*
ਕਲਾਸ	kalaas	*class* (f.)
ਕਾਹਲਾ	kaahlaa	*impatient, hasty* (v.)
ਕਾਹਲ ਵਿਚ	kaahal vich	*in a hurry*
ਕਾਗ਼ਜ਼ਾਤ	kaaghzaat	*papers, documents* (m.)
ਕਾਫ਼ੀ ਕੁਝ	kaafee kujh	*quite a lot, plenty*
ਕਾਨੂੰਨ	kaanoonn	*law* (m.)
ਕਾਰ	kaar	*car* (f.)
ਕਾਲਜ	kaalaj	*college* (m.)
ਕਿ	ki	*that*
ਕਿਉਂ	kiun	*why*
ਕਿਉਂ ਕਿ	kiun ki	*because*
ਕਿਹਾ ਜਾਂਦਾ ਹੈ	kihaa jaandaa hai	*is said, is called*

ਕਿਹੜਾ	kihrhaa	which
ਕਿੱਥੇ	kiththe	where
ਕਿੰਨਾ	kinnaa	how much?
ਕਿੰਨੇ	kinne	how many?
ਕਿੰਨਾ ਚਿਰ ਤੋਂ	kinnaa chir ton	since when, for how long?
ਕਿੰਨੀ ਦੂਰ	kinnee door	how far?
ਕਿੰਨੇ ਦਾ ਮੀਟਰ	kinne daa meetar	how much per metre?
ਕਿੰਨੇ ਵਜੇ	kinne vaje	what time
ਕਿਰਪਾ	kirpaa	blessings (f.)
ਕਿਰਾਇਆ	kiraaiaa	rate, fare, rent (m.)
ਕਿਵੇਂ	kiven	how
ਕਿਵੇਂ ਰਿਹਾ	kiven rihaa	how did it go?
ਕੀ	kee	what
ਕੀਮਤ	keemat	price (f.)
ਕੀਨੀਆ	keeneeaa	Kenya (m.)
ਕੀਰਤਨ	keertan	singing of hymns (m.)
ਕੁੱਤਾ	kuttaa	dog (m.)
ਕੋਈ	koee	any
ਕੋਈ ਨ ਕੋਈ	koee na koee	some one or another
ਕੋਸ਼ਿਸ਼ ਕਰਨਾ	koshish karnaa	to try
ਕੋਲ	kol	with, next to, in possession of
ਕੌਣ	kaunh	who
ਕੌਮ	kaum	nation, community (f.)
ਕੌੜਾ/ਕਸੈਲਾ	kaurhaa / kasailaa	bitter (v.)
ਕੇਵਲ	keval	only
ਕੈਮਰਾ	kaimraa	camera (m.)
ਖ਼ਤਮ ਕਰਨਾ	khatam karnaa	to finish, to complete
ਖ਼ਤਰਨਾਕ	khatarnaak	dangerous
ਖਤਰੀ	khatree	Khatri (m. / f.) (caste)
ਖ਼ਰਚਾ	kharchaa	expense, expenses (m.)
ਖਲੋਣਾ	khalonhaa	to be stood, to stand
ਖੜ੍ਹਨਾ	kharhhnaa	to stand, to park
ਖ਼ਾਸ	khaas	special
ਖਾਣਾ	khaanhaa	to eat
ਖ਼ਾਲੀ	khaalee	empty, vacant

ਖ਼ਿਲਾਫ਼	khilaaf	against
ਖ਼ੁਸ਼	khush	happy
ਖ਼ੁਸ਼ੀ	khushee	good (f.) (lit. happiness)
ਖ਼ੁਦਾ ਹਾਫ਼ਿਜ਼	khudaa haafiz	Muslim departing phrase
ਖੁੱਲ੍ਹਾ	khullhaa	open, plenty (v.)
ਖੇਡਨਾ	khednhaa	to play
ਖ਼ੈਰ	khair	anyway
ਗੱਡੀ	gaddee	car, vehicle (f.)
ਗੱਡੀ	gaddee	automobile, train (f.)
ਗਤਕਾ	gatkaa	a Sikh martial art, like fencing (m.)
ਗ਼ਦਰ	ghadar	mutiny (m.)
ਗ਼ਦਰ ਪਾਰਟੀ	ghadar paartee	Gadar Party (f.)
ਗ਼ਮੀ	ghamee	sadness (f.)
ਗਰਮੀ	garmee	summer, heat (f.)
ਗਰੇਡ	gared	grade (m.)
ਗੱਲ	gall	matter, news (f.) (lit. talk)
ਗ਼ਲਤ	ghalat	wrong
ਗੱਲਾਂ	gallaan	conversation (f.)
ਗਾਜਰ	gaajar	carrot (f.)
ਗਾਣਾ	gaanhaa	to sing
ਗਾਲੜੀ	gaalrhee	talkative
ਗਿੱਧਾ	gidhdhaa	women's folk dance (m.)
ਗੀਤ	geet	song (m.)
ਗ਼ੁਸਲ ਖ਼ਾਨਾ	ghusal khaanaa	bathroom (m.)
ਗੁਜਰਾਤੀ	gujraatee	a person from Gujarat or of Gujarati origin (m. / f.)
ਗੁੰਬਦ	gunbad	dome (m.)
ਗੋਭੀ	gobhee	cauliflower (f.)
ਗੋਰੀ	goree	fair, white (v.)
ਘਰ	ghar	house, home (m.)
ਘਰ ਦਾ ਕੰਮ	ghar daa kanm	homework (m.)
ਘਰਵਾਲਾ	gharvaalaa	husband (m.)

ਘੱਟ	ghatt	less, lower
ਘੱਟ ਕਰਨਾ	ghatt karnaa	to reduce, to lessen
ਘੱਟੋ ਘੱਟ	ghatto ghatt	at least
ਘਾਟ	ghaat	place where clothes are washed on the bay (m.)
ਘੁੰਮਣਾ	ghunmnhaa	to go around
ਘੁੰਮਣਾ ਫਿਰਨਾ	ghunmnhaa phirnaa	to travel around
ਘੋੜੀ	ghorhee	mare (f.)
ਚੰਗੀ	changee	good (v.)
ਚਮਕੀਲਾ	chamkeelaa	glittering, shining (v.)
ਚਮਚਾ	chamchaa	spoon (m.)
ਚਰਖਾ	charkhaa	spinning wheel (m.)
ਚਲਣਾ	chalnhaa	to go
ਚੜੁਦੀ ਕਲਾ	charhhdee kalaa	high spirits
ਚੜੁਨਾ	charhhnaa	to be upon, to ride
ਚਾਹੁਣਾ	chaahunhaa	to need, to want
ਚਾਚਾ ਜੀ	chaachaa jee	uncle (m) (father's brother)
ਚਿੱਠੀ	chiththee	letter (f.)
ਚਿਰ	chir	length of time
ਚੀਜ਼	cheez	thing (f.)
ਚੁਕਣਾ	chuknhaa	to be settled, finished
ਚੁੱਕਣਾ	chukknhaa	to lift, to pick
ਚੋਣ	chonh	choice, selection (f.)
ਚੋਥੇ ਗੁਰੂ	chauthe guroo	fourth Guru (m.)
ਚੋੜਾ	chaurhaa	wide (v.)
ਛਕਣਾ	chaknhaa	to take, to consume
ਛੱਡਣਾ	chaddnhaa	to leave, to quit
ਛਪਾਈਵਾਲਾ	chapaaeevaalaa	the printed one (m.)
ਛੱਲੀ	challee	corn on the cob (f.)
ਛਾਪਾ	chaapaa	print (m.)
ਛੁੱਟੀਆਂ	chutteeaan	holidays (f.)
ਛੋਟਾ	chotaa	small (v.)
ਜਗ੍ਹਾ	jag-h-aa	place, location (f.)
ਜਦੋ ਜਹਿਦ	jado jahid	struggle (f.)

ਜਨਮ	janam	*birth* (m.)
ਜਨਮ ਅਸਥਾਨ	janam asthaan	*birthplace* (m.)
ਜਨਮ ਦਿਨ	janam din	*birthday* (m.)
ਜੰਮਪਲ	janmpal	*raised, born and bred*
ਜੰਮਣਾ	janmnhaa	*to be born*
ਜ਼ਮਾਨਾ	zamaanaa	*times* (m.)
ਜਰਮਨ	jarman	*German* (m. / f.)
ਜ਼ਰੂਰ	zaroor	*definitely*
ਜਲੂਸ	jaloos	*procession, parade* (m.)
ਜਾਂ	jaan	*or*
ਜ਼ਾਇਆ ਕਰਨਾ	zaaiaa karnaa	*to waste time*
ਜਾ ਚੁਕਣਾ	jaa chuknhaa	*have (already) been*
ਜਾਂਞੀ	jaannjee	*members of the groom's wedding party* (m. / f.)
ਜਾਣਨਾ	jaanhnaa	*to know*
ਜ਼ਿਆਦਾ	ziaadaa	*too much*
ਜਿਸ	jis	*which* (oblique)
ਜਿਹਾ	jihaa	*sort of, rather*
ਜਿਹੜਾ	jihrhaa	*that, which*
ਜਿੱਥੇ	jiththe	*where*
ਜੀ	jee	honorific particle signifying respect
ਜੀ ਆਇਆਂ ਨੂੰ	jee aaiaan noon	*welcome*
ਜੀਵਨ	jeevan	*life* (m.)
ਜੁਮਾ	jumaa	*Friday* (m.)
ਜੁਮੇਰਾਤ	jumeraat	*Thursday* (f.)
ਜੇ	je	*if*
ਜੇਬਾਂ	jebaan	*pockets* (m. / f.)
ਝਾਕਣਾ	jhaaknhaa	*to stare, to look at*
ਝੂਟੇ	jhoote	*rides* (m.)
ਟਮਾਟਰ	tamaatar	*tomato(es)* (m.)
ਟਿਕਟ	tikat	*stamp* (f.)
ਟੀ. ਵੀ.	tee vee	*TV (television)* (m.)
ਟੇਕਣਾ	teknhaa	*to bow down*
ਟੈਲੀਫ਼ੋਨ	taileefon	*telephone* (m.)
ਟੈਲੀਫ਼ੋਨ ਕਰਨਾ	taileefon karnaa	*to call by telephone*

ਠੰਡ	thand	cold (f.)
ਠਹਿਰਨਾ	thahirnaa	to stay
ਠੀਕ	theek	fine / OK / alright / right
ਠੀਕ ਕਰਨਾ	theek karnaa	to fix, to correct
ਠੀਕ ਠਾਕ	theek thaak	OK, fine
ਡਾਕ	daak	mail, post (f.)
ਡਾਕਟਰ	daaktar	doctor (m. / f.)
ਡਾਂਗ	daang	long wooden pole (f.)
ਡਾਲਰ	daalar	dollar (m.)
ਡੋਲੀ	dolee	ceremony bidding farewell to the bride (f.)
ਢੋਲ	dhol	big drum (m.)
ਢੋਲਕੀ	dholkee	small drum (f.)
ਤਸ਼ਰੀਫ਼ ਰੱਖੋ ਜੀ	tashreef rakhkho jee	please have a seat
ਤਕਰੀਬਨ	takreeban	about, approximately
ਤਕਲੀਫ਼	takleef	trouble, irritation, bother (f.)
ਤਨਖ਼ਾਹ	tankhaah	pay, salary (f.)
ਤਬੀਅਤ	tabeeat	state of health, condition (f.)
ਤਰ੍ਹਾਂ	tar-h-aan	way, style
ਤਲਾਕ	talaak	divorce (m.)
ਤਾਂ	taan	then
ਤਾਂ ਕਿ	taan ki	so that
ਤਿਉਹਾਰ	tiuhaar	celebration, festival (m.)
ਤੁਸੀਂ	tuseen	you (formal)
ਤੁਹਾਡਾ	tuhaadaa	your (formal)
ਤੁਹਾਡਾ ਕੀ ਹਾਲ ਹੈ	tuhaadaa kee haal hai	how are you?
ਤੁਹਾਡੀ ਕਿਰਪਾ ਹੈ	tuhaadee kirpaa hai	by your blessings
ਤੁਹਾਡੇ ਬਾਰੇ	tuhaade baare	about you
ਤੁਰਨਾ	turnaa	to walk, to depart, to leave

ਤੂੰ	toon	*you* (informal)
ਤੇ	te	*and, on*
ਤੇਰਾ	teraa	*your* (informal)
ਤੋਂ	ton	*from*
ਤੋਂ ਇਲਾਵਾ	ton ilaavaa	*apart from, besides*
ਤੋਂ ਪਹਿਲੇ	ton pahile	*before*
ਤੋਂ ਬਾਅਦ	ton baa-a-d	*after*
ਤੋਂ ਬਿਨਾਂ / ਬ.ਗੈਰ	ton binaan / baghair	*without*

ਥਾਂ ਥਾਂ	thaan thaan	*each and every place* (m.)
ਥੋੜੀ ਬਹੁਤੀ	thorhee bahutee	*more or less, to some extent*

ਦਫ਼ਤਰ	daftar	*office* (m.)
ਦਰਸ਼ਕ	darshak	*participant, visitor* (m. / f.)
ਦਰਦ	dard	*pain, hurt* (f.)
ਦਵਾਈ	davaaee	*medicine* (f.)
ਦਾ	daa	*of*
ਦਿਸਣਾ	disnhaa	*to be visible, to be seen*
ਦਿਖਾਉਣਾ	dikhaaunhaa	*to show*
ਦਿਨ	din	*day* (m.)
ਦਿਲ	dil	*heart* (m.)
ਦਿਲਚਸਪ	dilchasp	*interesting*
ਦਿਲ ਲੱਗਣਾ	dil laggnhaa	*to feel at home, to be settled, to live happily*
ਦਿੱਲੀ	dillee	*Delhi* (f.)
ਦੀ ਜਗ੍ਹਾ	dee jag-h-aa	*in place of*
ਦੁਕਾਨ	dukaan	*shop* (f.)
ਦੁਕਾਨਦਾਰ	dukaandaar	*shopkeeper* (m.)
ਦੁਨੀਆਂ	duneeaan	*world* (f.)
ਦੂਜਾ ਦਿਨ	doojaa din	*second day*
ਦੂਜੇ	dooje	*others*
ਦੂਰ	door	*far, distant*
ਦੂਰ ਤੋਂ	door ton	*far from / away from*
ਦੇ ਉੱਪਰ	de uppar	*above, upon*

ਦੇ ਅੰਦਰ	de andar	*inside*
ਦੇਸ਼	desh	*country* (m.)
ਦੇਸੀ	desi	*Indian, Panjabi, home*
ਦੇ ਸਾਹਮਣੇ	de saahmanhe	*opposite, facing*
ਦੇਖਣਾ	dekhnhaa	*to see, to watch*
ਦੇਣਾ	denhaa	*to give*
ਦੇ ਥੱਲੇ	de thalle	*below*
ਦੇ ਨੇੜੇ	de nerhe	*near*
ਦੇ ਪਿੱਛੇ	de pichche	*behind*
ਦੇ ਬਾਹਰ	de baahar	*outside*
ਦੇ ਬਾਵਜੂਦ	de baavjood	*in spite of*
ਦੇ ਬਾਰੇ	de baare	*about, concerning*
ਦੇ ਲਈ	de laee	*for*
ਦੇ ਵਾਸਤੇ	de vaaste	*for*
ਦੋਸ਼	dosh	*charge* (m.)
ਦੋਨੋਂ	donon	*both*
ਧੰਨਵਾਦ	dhannvaad	*thanks* (m.)
ਧੀਆਂ	dheeaan	*daughters* (f.)
ਧੂਮ ਧਾਮ	dhoom dhaam	*bang, pomp and show*
ਧੋਣਾ	dhonhaa	*to wash*
ਧੋਬੀ	dhobee	*washerman* (m.)
ਨਹੀਂ	naheen	*no*
ਨਗਰ ਕੀਰਤਨ	nagar keertan	*religious procession* (m.)
ਨੱਚਣਾ	nachchnhaa	*to dance*
ਨਮਕੀਨ	namkeen	*salty*
ਨਮੂਨਾ	namoonaa	*pattern, design* (m.)
ਨਰਮ ਸੁਭਾ	naram subhaa	*kind natured*
ਨਾਂ	naan	*name* (m.) (informal)
ਨਾ ਕੇਵਲ	naa keval	*not only*
ਨਾਮ	naam	*name* (m.) (formal)
ਨੀਲਾ	neelaa	*blue* (v.)
ਨੁਮਾਇਸ਼	numaaish	*exhibition* (f.)
ਨੌਕਰ	naukar	*male servant* (m.)
ਨੌਕਰੀ	naukaree	*job, employment* (f.)
ਨੌਜੁਆਨ	naujuaan	*youth* (m.)

ਪਸੰਦ	pasa<u>nd</u>	*like, pleasing*
ਪਕੌੜਾ	pakaurhaa	a type of deep-fried pastry similar to fritters (m.)
ਪਹਿਲੀ ਵਾਰੀ	pahilee vaaree	*first time*
ਪਹਿਲੇ	pahile	*before*
ਪਹੁੰਚਾ ਦੇਣਾ	pahu<u>n</u>chaa <u>d</u>enhaa	*to deliver, to cause to arrive*
ਪੰਜਵਾਂ	pa<u>n</u>jvaa<u>n</u>	*fifth*
ਪੱਛਮ	pa<u>chch</u>am	*west* (m.)
ਪੰਜ ਵਜੇ	pa<u>n</u>j vaje	*five o'clock*
ਪੰਜਾਬ	pa<u>n</u>jaab	*Panjab* (m.)
ਪੰਜਾਬੀ	pa<u>n</u>jaabee	a person from Panjab or of Panjabi origin (m. / f.)
ਪੱਤਝੜ	pa<u>tt</u>jharh	*autumn* (f.)
ਪਤਨੀ	pa<u>t</u>nee	*wife* (f.)
ਪਤਲਾ	pa<u>t</u>laa	*thin, slim* (v.)
ਪਤਵੰਤੇ	pa<u>t</u>va<u>nt</u>e	*respectable* (v.)
ਪਤਾ	pa<u>t</u>aa	*to know*
ਪਤੀ	pa<u>t</u>ee	*husband* (m.)
ਪਰ	par	*but*
ਪਰਸੋਂ	parso<u>n</u>	*day before yesterday / day after tomorrow*
ਪਰਤਣਾ	par<u>t</u>nhaa	*to return*
ਪਰਵਾਰ	parvaar	*family* (m.)
ਪਰਵਾਰਕ	parvaarak	*family* (relating to family)
ਪ੍ਰਾਹੁਣੇ	praahunhe	*guests* (m.)
ਪਲੇਟ	palet	*plate* (f.)
ਪੜਦਾਦਾ	parh<u>d</u>aa<u>d</u>aa	*great grandfather* (m.)
ਪੜ੍ਹਨਾ	parhhnaa	*to read, to study*
ਪੜ੍ਹਾਉਣਾ	parhhaaunhaa	*to teach*
ਪੜ੍ਹਾਈ	parhhaaee	*studies* (f.)
ਪੜ੍ਹਿਆ ਲਿਖਿਆ	parhhiaa likhiaa	*educated* (v.)
ਪਾਸਪੋਰਟ	paasport	*passport* (m.)
ਪਾਸੇ	paase	*direction, way*
ਪਿਆਰ	piaar	*love, affection* (m.)
ਪਿਆਰ ਕਰਨਾ	piaar karnaa	*to love*

ਪਿਆਰੇ	piaare	dear, beloved (v.)
ਪਿੰਡਵਾਲਾ	pindvaalaa	villager (m.)
ਪੀਣਾ	peenhaa	to drink
ਪੀਰ	peer	holy man (m.)
ਪੀਰ	peer	Monday (m.)
ਪੁੱਛਣਾ	puchchnhaa	to ask
ਪੁੱਤਰ	puttar	son (m.)
ਪੁਰਸ਼	purash	gentleman (m.)
ਪੂਰਬ	poorab	east (m.)
ਪੂਰੀਆਂ	pooreeaan	fulfilling
ਪੇਸ਼	pesh	to present
ਪੇਸ਼ ਕਰਨਾ	pesh karnaa	to present, to produce
ਪੇਸ਼ਾਵਰ	peshaavar	professional (m. / f.)
ਪੇਕੇ	peke	bride's family, bride's parents (m.)
ਪੇਟ	pet	stomach, belly (m.)
ਪੇਂਡੂ	pendoo	of the village, village-like (m. / f.)
ਪੈਂਸਲ	painsal	pencil (f.)
ਪੈਸੇਵਾਲੇ	paisevaale	wealthy people (m.)
ਪੈਣਾ	painhaa	to act, to fall
ਪੌੜੀਆਂ	paurheeaan	stairs (f.)
ਫਸਲਾਂ	fasalaan	crops (f.)
ਫਿਕਰ	fikar	worry (m.)
ਫਿੱਕਾ	phikkaa	light, pale (v.)
ਫਿਰ	phir	again
ਫਿਰਨਾ	phirnaa	to travel
ਫ਼ਿਲਮ	filam	film (f.)
ਫੋਟੋ	foto	photograph (f.)
ਫ਼ੌਜ	fauj	military (f.)
ਬਸੰਤ	basant	spring (f.)
ਬਹੁਤ	bahut	very
ਬਹੁਤ ਅੱਛਾ	bahut achchaa	very good (v.)
ਬਹੁਤ ਸਾਰੇ	bahut saare	a lot, many
ਬਹੁਤ ਸੁਹਣਾ	bahut suhnhaa	very nice, excellent (v.)
ਬਹੁਤ ਜ਼ਿਆਦਾ	bahut ziaadaa	far too much

ਬਗੀਚਾ	bagheechaa	garden (m.)
ਬਚਪਨ	bachpan	childhood (m.)
ਬੱਚੇ	bachche	children (m.)
ਬਟਵਾਰਾ	batvaaraa	division, partition (m.)
ਬਣਨਾ	banhnaa	to become
ਬਣਵਾਉਣਾ	banhvaaunhaa	to get built
ਬਦਲਣਾ	badalnhaa	to change, to exchange
ਬੰਦ	band	closed, off
ਬੰਦ ਕਰਨਾ	band karnaa	to close
ਬੰਦੇ	bande	people (m.)
ਬਰਸਾਤ	barsaat	rainy season (f.)
ਬਰਮਿੰਘਮ	barmingham	Birmingham (m.)
ਬਰਾਤ	baraat	procession of the groom's relatives and friends (f.)
ਬਲਕਿ	balki	but also
ਬੜੀ	barhee	very (v.)
ਬਾਅਦ ਦੁਪਹਿਰ	baa-a-d dupahir	afternoon
ਬਾਹਰੋਂ	baahron	from outside / from abroad
ਬਾਰਸ਼	baarash	rain (f.)
ਬਾਲ	baal	male child (m.)
ਬਿਮਾਰ	bimaar	ill, sick
ਬਿਮਾਰ ਹੋਣ ਤੋਂ ਪਹਿਲੇ	bimaar honh ton pahile	before falling ill
ਬਿਲਕੁਲ	bilkul	absolutely, perfectly
ਬੀਬੀ	beebee	madam (f.)
ਬੁਖ਼ਾਰ	bukhaar	fever / temperature (m.)
ਬੁੱਧਵਾਰ	budhdhvaar	Wednesday (m.)
ਬੇਟਾ	betaa	son (m.)
ਬੇਟੀ	betee	daughter (f.)
ਬੇਨਤੀ	bentee	request (f.)
ਬੇਬੀ ਸਿਟਰ	bebee sitar	baby sitter (m. / f.)
ਬੈਠਕ	baithak	sitting room (f.)
ਬੈਠਣਾ	baithnhaa	to sit
ਬੈਠੋ ਜੀ	baitho jee	please sit down (formal)
ਬੋਰ ਹੋਣਾ	bor honhaa	to be bored, to feel bored
ਬੋਲਣਾ	bolnhaa	to speak

ਬੋਲੀ	bolee	*language* (f.)
ਬੋਲੀਆਂ	boleeaan	*folk verse couplets* (f.)
ਭੰਗੜਾ	bhangrhaa	*bhangra* (m.) (style of Panjabi dance)
ਭਤੀਜੀ	bhateejee	*niece* (f.)
ਭਰਤੀ	bhartee	*join*
ਭਰਾ	bharaa	*brother* (m.)
ਭਲਕ/ਭਲਕੇ	bhalak/bhalke	*tomorrow*
ਭਲੀ	bhalee	*look after, watch over*
ਭਾਈ ਸਾਹਿਬ	bhaaee saahib	*brother* (m.)
ਭਾਬੀ	bhaabee	*sister-in-law* (f.) (brother's wife)
ਭਾਰਤ	bhaarat	*India* (m.)
ਭਾਰਤੀ	bhaartee	*Indian* (m. / f.)
ਭਿੰਡੀ	bhindee	*okra* (type of vegetable) (f.)
ਭੁੱਖ	bhukhkh	*hunger* (f.)
ਭੇਜਣਾ	bhejnhaa	*to send, to post*
ਭੈਣ	bhainh	*sister* (f.)
ਮਹਿੰਗਾ	mahingaa	*expensive, costly* (v.)
ਮਸ਼ੀਨ	masheen	*machine* (f.)
ਮਹਿੰਦੀ	mahindee	*henna* (f.)
ਮਹੀਨਾ	maheenaa	*month* (m.)
ਮਕਾਨ	makaan	*house* (m.)
ਮੰਗਣਾ	mangnhaa	*to request, to ask for, to charge*
ਮੰਗਲਵਾਰ	mangalvaar	*Tuesday* (m.)
ਮੰਗਾਂ	mangaan	*demands* (f.)
ਮਜ਼ਮੂਨ	mazmoon	*subject* (m.)
ਮਟਰ	matar	*peas* (m.)
ਮਤਲਬ	matlab	*meaning, definition* (m.)
ਮੱਦਦ ਕਰਨਾ	maddad karnaa	*to help*
ਮਨ	man	*mind* (m.)
ਮਨਪਰਚਾਵੇ	manparchaave	*entertainment, enjoyment* (m.)

ਮਨਾਉਣਾ	manaaunhaa	to pray, to believe, to celebrate
ਮੰਨੋ ਜਾਂ ਨਾ ਮੰਨੋ	ma<u>n</u>no jaa<u>n</u> naa ma<u>n</u>no	believe it or not
ਮਾਤਾ ਜੀ	maa<u>t</u>aa jee	mother (f.)
ਮਾਫ਼	maaf	pardon, excuse
ਮਾਫ਼ ਕਰਨਾ	maaf karnaa	sorry, to pardon
ਮਾਨਚੈਸਟਰ	maanchaistar	Manchester (m.)
ਮਾਪੇ	maape	parents (m.)
ਮਾਰਨਾ	maarnaa	to hit
ਮਿਹਰਬਾਨੀ	miharbaanee	thanks, please (f.)
ਮਿਟਣਾ	mitnhaa	to finish, to vanish
ਮਿੰਟ	mi<u>n</u>t	minute (m.)
ਮਿੱਠਾ	miththaa	sweet (v.)
ਮਿਠਿਆਈ	mithiaaee	Panjabi sweet (f.)
ਮਿਲ ਜਾਣਾ	mil jaanhaa	to get, to receive
ਮਿਲਣਾ	milnhaa	to meet
ਮੁੱਖ	mukhkh	face (m.)
ਮੁਕਾਬਲਾ	mukaablaa	comparison, competition (m.)
ਮੁਫ਼ਤ	mufa<u>t</u>	free
ਮੁੜਨਾ	murhnaa	to turn around, to return
ਮੇਖ	mekh	nail (f.)
ਮੇਰਾ	meraa	my
ਮੇਰੇ ਕੋਲ ਨਹੀਂ	mere kol naahee<u>n</u>	not with me, not in my possession
ਮੇਰੇ ਨਾਲ	mere naal	with me
ਮੇਲ	mel	meeting, combination (m.)
ਮੇਲਾ	melaa	fair (m.)
ਮੈਂ	mai<u>n</u>	I
ਮੈਨੇਜਰ	mainejar	manager (m. / f.)
ਮੋਚੀ	mochee	cobbler (m.)
ਮੋਟਾ	motaa	fat, thick (v.)
ਮੌਕਾ	maukaa	opportunity, occasion (m.)
ਮੌਜਾਂ ਕਰਨਾ	maujaa<u>n</u> karnaa	to enjoy

ਯਾਦ	yaa<u>d</u>	*memory, remembrance* (f.)
ਯੁਵਕ	yuvak	*youth* (m.)
ਯੂਗੰਡਾ	yooga<u>n</u>daa	*Uganda* (m.)
ਯੋਗ	yog	*suitable*
ਰਸ	ras	*(fruit) juice* (m.)
ਰਸਮ	rasam	*custom, ritual* (f.)
ਰਸੋਈ	rasoee	*kitchen* (f.)
ਰਹਿਣਾ	rahinhaa	*to stay, to live*
ਰੱਖਣਾ	rakhkhnhaa	*to put*
ਰੰਗ	ra<u>n</u>g	*colour* (m.)
ਰੰਗਦਾਰ	ra<u>n</u>gdaar	*colourful*
ਰੰਗਲਾ	ra<u>n</u>glaa	*colourful* (v.)
ਰਚਨਾ	rachnaa	*composition* (f.)
ਰਲ ਮਿਲਣਾ	ral milnhaa	*to be mixed*
ਰਵਾਜ	ravaaj	*fashion* (m.)
ਰੜਕਣਾ	rarhkanhaa	*to prick, to rub against*
ਰਾਹਾਂ	raahaa<u>n</u>	*roads, routes* (f.)
ਰਾਹੀਂ	raahee<u>n</u>	*via, by*
ਰਾਜ	raaj	*rulership, kingdom* (m.)
ਰਾਜਾ	raajaa	*king* (m.)
ਰਿਸ਼ਤਾ	rish<u>t</u>aa	*(marriage) relation* (m.)
ਰਿਸ਼ਤੇਦਾਰ	rish<u>t</u>edaar	*relatives* (m. / f.)
ਰੁਪਇਆ	rupaiaa	*rupee* (m.)
ਲਈ	laee	*for, in order to*
ਲੱਗਣਾ	laggnhaa	*to be covered, laden, to feel*
ਲਗਵਾਉਣਾ	lagvaaunhaa	*to get covered*
ਲੰਗਰ	la<u>n</u>gar	*community kitchen* (m.)
ਲਗਾਉਣਾ	lagaaunhaa	*to stitch, to apply, to put on*
ਲਗਾਤਾਰ	lagaa<u>t</u>aar	*continuously, on going*
ਲੰਡਨ	la<u>n</u>dan	*London* (m.)
ਲੱਡੂ	laddoo	*a type of Panjabi sweet* (m.)
ਲਫਜ਼ੀ	lafzee	*literal*
ਲੰਬਾ	la<u>n</u>baa	*long, lengthy* (v.)

ਲੱਭਣਾ	labhbhnhaa	*to find*
ਲਾ ਪਰਵਾਹ	laa parvaah	*careless*
ਲਾਇਸੈਂਸ	laaisains	*licence* (m.)
ਲਾਹੋਰਵਾਲੀ ਔਰਤ	laahaurvaalee aurat	*the woman from Lahore* (f.)
ਲਾਲ	laal	*red*
ਲਾੜਾ	laarhaa	*groom* (m.)
ਲਿਖਣਾ	likhnhaa	*to write*
ਲਿਆਉਣਾ	liaaunhaa	*to bring*
ਲਿਆਕਤ	liaakat	*ability* (f.)
ਲੈਣਾ	lainhaa	*to take, to have*
ਲੋਕ	lok	*people* (m.)
ਲੋਕ ਨਾਚ	lok naach	*folk dance* (m.)
ਲੋੜ	lorh	*require, necessity, want* (f.)
ਵੱਸ	vass	*authority, jurisdiction* (m.)
ਵਸਾਉਣਾ	vasaaunhaa	*to establish, to habilitate*
ਵਕਤ	vakat	*time* (m.)
ਵੱਜਣਾ	vajjnhaa	*to be played, to be beaten*
ਵਜਾਉਣ ਦਾ ਸ਼ੌਕ	vajaaunh daa shauk	*fond of playing, enjoy playing*
ਵਜਾਉਣਾ	vajaaunhaa	*to play (music), to beat*
ਵਡੱਕਿਆਂ	vadkkiaan	*ancestors, forefathers* (m.)
ਵੱਡਾ	vaddaa	*big, large* (v.)
ਵੱਧ	vadhdh	*high, more*
ਵਧਾਉਣਾ	vadhaaunhaa	*to increase*
ਵਧਾਈ	vadhaaee	*congratulations* (f.)
ਵਧੀਆ	vadheeaa	*good quality*
ਵਧੇਰੇ	vadhere	*more*
ਵਰਗਾ	vargaa	*like* (v.)
ਵਰਤਣਾ	varatnhaa	*to use*
ਵਰਤਾਉਣਾ	vartaaunhaa	*to serve*
ਵੱਲ	vall	*towards*
ਵੱਲੋਂ	vallon	*on behalf of*
ਵਾਜਬੀ	vaajbee	*reasonable, fair, right*
ਵਾਜੇ ਵਾਲੇ	vaaje vaale	*band of musicians* (m.)

ਵਾਲੈਕਮ ਅੱਸਲਾਮ	vaalaikam asslaam	response to Muslim greeting
ਵਾਪਸ	vaapas	*return, back*
ਵਾਰੀ	vaaree	*turn, instance* (f.)
ਵਿਆਹ	viaah	*wedding* (m.)
ਵਿਹਾਰੀ ਨੌਕਰੀ	vihaaree naukaree	*professionally employed* (f.)
ਵਿਕਣਾ	viknhaa	*to be sold*
ਵਿਚ	vich	*in*
ਵਿੱਚੋਂ	vichchon	*from within*
ਵਿਦਿਆਰਥੀ	vi<u>d</u>iaar<u>th</u>ee	*student* (m. / f.)
ਵੀ	vee	*also*
ਵੀਹ (੨੦)	veeh	*20*
ਵੀਜ਼ਾ	veezaa	*visa* (m.)
ਵੀਰਵਾਰ	veervaar	*Thursday* (m.)
ਵੇ	ve	subjunctive particle
ਵੇਖਣਾ	vekhnhaa	*to see*
ਵੇਲੇ	vele	*period, time* (m.)
ਵੈਸਾਖ	vaisaakh	one of the Indian months (m.)
ਵੈਸਾਖੀ	vaisaakhee	a Sikh festival (f.)

English–Panjabi glossary

a	ਇੱਕ	ikk
a lot	ਬਹੁਤ ਸਾਰੇ	bahut saare
ability	ਲਿਆਕਤ	liaakat
able to: to be ~	ਸਕਣਾ	saknhaa
about (approximately)	ਤਕਰੀਬਨ	takreeban
about (concerning)	ਦੇ ਬਾਰੇ	de baare
about you	ਤੁਹਾਡੇ ਬਾਰੇ	tuhaade baare
above	ਦੇ ਉੱਪਰ	de uppar
absolutely	ਬਿਲਕੁਲ	bilkul
act: to ~	ਪੈਣਾ	painhaa
affection	ਪਿਆਰ	piaar
after	ਤੋਂ ਬਾਅਦ	ton baa-a-d
after a while	ਸਮਾਂ ਪਾ ਕੇ	samaan paa ke
afternoon	ਬਾਅਦ ਦੁਪਹਿਰ	baa-a-d dupahir
again	ਫਿਰ	phir
against	ਖ਼ਿਲਾਫ਼	khilaaf
age	ਉਮਰ	umar
agree	ਸਹਿਮਤ	sahimat
air mail	ਹਵਾਈ ਡਾਕ	havaaee daak
airport	ਹਵਾਈ ਅੱਡਾ	hvaaee addaa
all	ਸਭ, ਸਾਰੇ	sabh, saare
all of us	ਅਸੀਂ ਸਾਰੇ	aseen saare
also	ਵੀ	vee
America	ਅਮਰੀਕਾ	amreekaa
ancestors	ਵਡੱਕਿਆਂ	vadkkiaan

and, on	ਅਤੇ, ਤੇ	ate, te
anxious	ਉਤਸੁਕ	utsuk
any	ਕੋਈ	koee
anyway	ਖ਼ੈਰ	khair
apart from	ਤੋਂ ਇਲਾਵਾ	ton ilaavaa
apply: to ~	ਲਗਾਉਣਾ	lagaaunhaa
around and about	ਆਸ ਪਾਸ	aas paas
arrangements	ਇੰਤਜ਼ਾਮ	intzaam
ask: to ~	ਪੁੱਛਣਾ	puchchnhaa
at least	ਘੱਟੋ ਘੱਟ	ghatto ghatt
authority	ਵੱਸ	vass
automobile	ਗੱਡੀ	gaddee
autumn	ਪੱਤਝੜ	pattjharh
awaiting	ਉਤਸੁਕ	utsuk
away from	ਦੂਰ ਤੋਂ	door ton
baby sitter	ਬੇਬੀ ਸਿਟਰ	bebee sitar
back	ਵਾਪਸ	vaapas
band of musicians	ਵਾਜੇ ਵਾਲੇ	vaaje vaale
bang, pomp and show	ਧੂਮ ਧਾਮ	dhoom dhaam
bathroom	ਗ਼ੁਸਲ ਖ਼ਾਨਾ	ghusal khaanaa
be: to ~	ਹੋਣਾ	honhaa
beat: to ~	ਵਜਾਉਣਾ	vajaaunhaa
beaten: to be ~	ਵੱਜਣਾ	vajjnhaa
because	ਕਿਉਂ ਕਿ	kiun ki
become: to ~	ਬਣਨਾ	banhnaa
before	ਤੋਂ ਪਹਿਲੇ, ਪਹਿਲੇ	ton pahile, pahile
before falling ill	ਬਿਮਾਰ ਹੋਣ ਤੋਂ ਪਹਿਲੇ	bimaar honh ton pahile
begin: to ~	ਸ਼ੁਰੂ ਕਰਨਾ	shuroo karnaa
behind	ਦੇ ਪਿੱਛੇ	de pichche
believe: to ~	ਮਨਾਉਣਾ	manaaunhaa
believe it or not	ਮੰਨੋ ਜਾਂ ਨਾ ਮੰਨੋ	manno jaan naa manno
belly	ਪੇਟ	pet
beloved	ਪਿਆਰੇ	piaare
below	ਦੇ ਥੱਲੇ	de thalle

besides	ਤੋਂ ਇਲਾਵਾ	ton ilaavaa
best: the ~	ਸਭ ਤੋਂ ਵਧੀਆ	sabh ton vadheeaa
best wishes	ਸ਼ੁਭ ਇਛਾਵਾਂ	shubh ichaavaan
bhangra (style of Panjabi dance)	ਭੰਗੜਾ	bhangrhaa
big	ਵੱਡਾ	vaddaa
Birmingham	ਬਰਮਿੰਘਮ	barmingham
birth	ਜਨਮ	janam
birthday	ਜਨਮ ਦਿਨ	janam din
birthplace	ਜਨਮ ਅਸਥਾਨ	janam asthaan
bitter	ਕੌੜਾ / ਕਸੈਲਾ	kaurhaa/kasailaa
bitter gourd	ਕਰੇਲਾ	karelaa
blessings	ਕਿਰਪਾ	kirpaa
blue	ਨੀਲਾ	neelaa
bored: to be ~, to feel bored	ਬੋਰ ਹੋਣਾ	bor honhaa
born: to be ~	ਜੰਮਣਾ	janmnhaa
born and bred	ਜੰਮਪਲ	janmpal
bosom	ਸੀਨਾ	seenaa
both	ਦੋਨੋਂ	donon
both of us	ਅਸੀਂ ਦੋਨੋਂ	aseen donon
bother	ਤਕਲੀਫ਼	takleef
bow down: to ~	ਟੇਕਣਾ	teknhaa
bride's family, bride's parents	ਪੇਕੇ	peke
bring: to ~	ਲਿਆਉਣਾ	liaaunhaa
brother	ਭਰਾ, ਭਾਈ ਸਾਹਿਬ	bharaa, bhaaee saahib
built: to get ~	ਬਣਵਾਉਣਾ	banhvaaunhaa
but	ਪਰ	par
but also	ਸਗੋਂ, ਬਲਕਿ	sagon, balki
by	ਰਾਹੀਂ	raaheen
by air	ਹਵਾਈ	hvaaee
by your blessings	ਤੁਹਾਡੀ ਕਿਰਪਾ ਹੈ	tuhaadee kirpaa hai
camel	ਊਠ	ooth
camera	ਕੈਮਰਾ	kaimraa

can	ਸਕਣਾ	saknhaa
car	ਕਾਰ, ਗੱਡੀ	kaar, gaddee
careless	ਲਾ ਪਰਵਾਹ	laa parvaah
carrot	ਗਾਜਰ	gaajar
cauliflower	ਗੋਭੀ	gobhee
celebrate: to ~	ਮਨਾਉਣਾ	manaaunhaa
celebration	ਤਿਉਹਾਰ	ṯiuhaar
ceremony bidding farewell to the bride	ਡੋਲੀ	dolee
change: to ~	ਬਦਲਣਾ	ba<u>d</u>alnhaa
charge	ਦੋਸ਼	<u>d</u>osh
charge: to ~	ਮੰਗਣਾ	mangnhaa
childhood	ਬਚਪਨ	bachpan
children	ਬੱਚੇ	bachche
choice	ਚੋਣ	chonh
citizen	ਸ਼ਹਿਰੀਅਤ	shahireea<u>t</u>
city	ਸ਼ਹਿਰ	shahir
class	ਸ਼੍ਰੇਣੀ, ਕਲਾਸ	shrenhee, kalaas
clean: to ~	ਸਾਫ਼ ਕਰਨਾ	saaf karnaa
close: to ~	ਬੰਦ ਕਰਨਾ	ban<u>d</u> karnaa
closed off	ਬੰਦ	ban<u>d</u>
cloth	ਕਪੜਾ	kaprhaa
cobbler	ਮੋਚੀ	mochee
cold	ਠੰਡ	than<u>d</u>
college	ਕਾਲਜ	kaalaj
colour	ਰੰਗ	rang
colourful	ਰੰਗਦਾਰ, ਰੰਗਲਾ	rangdaar, ranglaa
combination	ਮੇਲ	mel
come (formal)	ਆਓ	aao
come (informal request)	ਆ ਜਾ	aa jaa
come: to ~	ਆਉਣਾ	aaunhaa
community	ਕੌਮ	kaum
community kitchen	ਲੰਗਰ	langar
comparison	ਮੁਕਾਬਲਾ	mukaablaa
competition	ਮੁਕਾਬਲਾ	mukaablaa
complaint	ਸ਼ਿਕਾਇਤ	shikaai<u>t</u>
complete: to ~	ਖ਼ਤਮ ਕਰਨਾ	<u>kh</u>a<u>t</u>am karnaa

composition	ਰਚਨਾ	rachnaa
condition	ਹਾਲ, ਤਬੀਅਤ	haal, ṯabeeaṯ
congratulations	ਵਧਾਈ	vadhaaee
consume: to ~	ਛਕਣਾ	chaknhaa
contact	ਸੰਪਰਕ	sanparak
continuously	ਲਗਾਤਾਰ	lagaaṯaar
conversation	ਗੱਲਾਂ	gallaan
corn on the cob	ਛੱਲੀ	challee
correct: to ~	ਠੀਕ ਕਰਨਾ	theek karnaa
costly	ਮਹਿੰਗਾ	mahingaa
country	ਦੇਸ਼	desh
covered: to be ~	ਲੱਗਣਾ	laggnhaa
covered: to get ~	ਲਗਵਾਉਣਾ	lagvaaunhaa
crops	ਫਸਲਾਂ	fasalaan
custom	ਰਸਮ	rasam
cut: to ~	ਕਟਣਾ	katnhaa
dance: to ~	ਨੱਚਣਾ	nachchnhaa
dangerous	ਖ਼ਤਰਨਾਕ	khaṯarnaak
daughter	ਬੇਟੀ	betee
daughters	ਧੀਆਂ	dheeaan
day	ਦਿਨ	din
day after tomorrow / day before yesterday	ਪਰਸੋਂ	parson
days: these ~	ਅੱਜ ਕੱਲ੍ਹ	ajj kallh
dear	ਪਿਆਰੇ	piaare
deep-fried pastry, similar to fritters	ਪਕੌੜਾ	pakaurhaa
definitely	ਜ਼ਰੂਰ	zaroor
definition	ਮਤਲਬ	maṯlab
Delhi	ਦਿੱਲੀ	dillee
deliver: to ~	ਪਹੁੰਚਾ ਦੇਣਾ	pahunchaa denhaa
demands	ਮੰਗਾਂ	mangaan
depart: to ~	ਤੁਰਨਾ	ṯurnaa
design	ਨਮੂਨਾ	namoonaa
different types	ਕਈ ਤਰ੍ਹਾਂ	kaee ṯar-h-aan
digest	ਹਜ਼ਮ	hazam

direction	ਪਾਸੇ	paase
disobey: to ~	ਉਲੰਘਣਾ	ulanghnhaa
displaced: to be ~	ਉਖੜਨਾ	ukhrhnaa
distant	ਦੂਰ	door
division	ਬਟਵਾਰਾ	batvaaraa
divorce	ਤਲਾਕ	talaak
do: to ~	ਕਰਨਾ	karnaa
doctor	ਡਾਕਟਰ	daaktar
documents	ਕਾਗ਼ਜ਼ਾਤ	kaaghzaat
dog	ਕੁੱਤਾ	kuttaa
dollar	ਡਾਲਰ	daalar
dome	ਗੁੰਬਦ	gunbad
drink: to ~	ਪੀਣਾ	peenhaa
drum: big ~	ਢੋਲ	dhol
durable	ਹੰਢਣਸਾਰ	handhanhsaar
each and every place	ਥਾਂ ਥਾਂ	thaan thaan
east	ਪੂਰਬ	poorab
East Africa	ਈਸਟ ਅਫ਼ਰੀਕਾ	eest afreekaa
easy	ਸੌਖਾ	saukhaa
eat: to ~	ਖਾਣਾ	khaanhaa
educated	ਪੜ੍ਹਿਆ ਲਿਖਿਆ	parhhiaa likhiaa
employment	ਨੌਕਰੀ	naukaree
empty	ਖ਼ਾਲੀ	khaalee
end	ਅਖ਼ੀਰ	akheer
English	ਅੰਗਰੇਜ਼	angrez
enjoy: to ~	ਮੌਜਾਂ ਕਰਨਾ	maujaan karnaa
enjoy playing	ਵਜਾਉਣ ਦਾ ਸ਼ੋਕ	vajaaunh daa shauk
enjoy yourself	ਅਨੰਦ ਮਾਣੋ	anand maanho
enjoyment	ਸ਼ੋਕ, ਮਨਪਰਚਾਵੇ	shauk, manparchaave
entertainment	ਮਨਪਰਚਾਵੇ	manparchaave
establish: to ~	ਵਸਾਉਣਾ	vasaaunhaa
every	ਸਭ	sabh
everyone	ਸਾਰੇ	saare
everything	ਸਭ ਕੁਝ	sabh kujh
everywhere	ਸਭ ਪਾਸੇ, ਹਰ ਪਾਸੇ	sabh paase, har paase

excellent	ਬਹੁਤ ਸੁਹਣਾ	bahut suhnhaa
exchange: to ~	ਬਦਲਣਾ	badalnhaa
excuse	ਮਾਫ਼	maaf
exhibition	ਨੁਮਾਇਸ਼	numaaish
expense(s)	ਖ਼ਰਚਾ	kharchaa
expensive	ਮਹਿੰਗਾ	mahingaa
extent: to some ~	ਥੋੜੀ ਬਹੁਤੀ	thorhee bahutee
face	ਮੁੱਖ	mukhkh
facing	ਦੇ ਸਾਹਮਣੇ	de saahmanhe
fair	ਮੇਲਾ, ਗੋਰੀ, ਵਾਜਬੀ	melaa, goree, vaajbee
family	ਪਰਵਾਰ	parvaar
family (relating to family)	ਪਰਵਾਰਕ	parvaarak
far	ਦੂਰ	door
far from	ਦੂਰ ਤੋਂ	door ton
far too much	ਬਹੁਤ ਜ਼ਿਆਦਾ	bahut ziaadaa
fare	ਕਿਰਾਇਆ	kiraaiaa
fashion	ਰਵਾਜ	ravaaj
fat	ਮੋਟਾ	motaa
feel: to ~	ਲੱਗਣਾ	laggnhaa
feel at home: to ~	ਦਿਲ ਲੱਗਣਾ	dil laggnhaa
festival	ਤਿਉਹਾਰ	tiuhaar
fever	ਬੁਖ਼ਾਰ	bukhaar
fifth	ਪੰਜਵਾਂ	panjvaan
film	ਫ਼ਿਲਮ	filam
find: to ~	ਲੱਭਣਾ	labhbhnhaa
fine	ਠੀਕ	theek
finish: to ~	ਖ਼ਤਮ ਕਰਨਾ, ਮਿਟਣਾ	khatam karnaa, mitnhaa
finished: to be ~	ਚੁਕਣਾ	chuknhaa
first time	ਪਹਿਲੀ ਵਾਰੀ	pahilee vaaree
five o'clock	ਪੰਜ ਵਜੇ	panj vaje
fix: to ~	ਠੀਕ ਕਰਨਾ	theek karnaa
folk dance	ਲੋਕ ਨਾਚ	lok naach
folk verse couplets	ਬੋਲੀਆਂ	boleeaan
fond of playing	ਵਜਾਉਣ ਦਾ ਸ਼ੋਕ	vajaaunh daa shauk

fondness	ਸ਼ੌਕ	shauk
for	ਦੇ ਲਈ, ਦੇ ਵਾਸਤੇ, ਲਈ	<u>d</u>e laee, <u>d</u>e vaas<u>t</u>e, laee
for how long	ਕਿੰਨਾ ਚਿਰ ਤੋਂ	ki<u>n</u>naa chir <u>t</u>on
forefathers	ਵਡੱਕਿਆਂ	vadkkiaa<u>n</u>
fourth Guru	ਚੌਥੇ ਗੁਰੂ	chau<u>th</u>e guroo
free	ਮੁਫ਼ਤ	mufa<u>t</u>
freedom	ਅਜ਼ਾਦੀ	azaa<u>d</u>ee
Friday	ਸ਼ੁੱਕਰਵਾਰ, ਜੁਮਾ	shukkarvaar, jumaa
friend	ਸਹੇਲੀ	sahelee
from	ਤੋਂ	<u>t</u>on
from abroad, from outside	ਬਾਹਰੋਂ	baahro<u>n</u>
from there	ਉੱਥੋਂ	uth<u>th</u>o<u>n</u>
from within	ਵਿੱਚੋਂ	vichcho<u>n</u>
fulfilling	ਪੂਰੀਆਂ	pooreeaa<u>n</u>
Gadar Party	.ਗਦਰ ਪਾਰਟੀ	<u>gh</u>adar paartee
garden	ਬ.ਗੀਚਾ	ba<u>gh</u>eechaa
gathering	ਇਕੱਠ	ikath<u>th</u>
gentleman	ਪੁਰਸ਼	purash
genuinely	ਸੱਚੀ ਮੁੱਚੀ	sachchee muchchee
German	ਜਰਮਨ	jarman
get: to ~	ਮਿਲ ਜਾਣਾ	mil jaanhaa
give: to ~	ਦੇਣਾ	<u>d</u>enhaa
glittering	ਚਮਕੀਲਾ	chamkeelaa
go: to ~	ਚਲਣਾ	chalnhaa
go around: to ~	ਘੁੰਮਣਾ	<u>gh</u>u<u>n</u>mnhaa
gold	ਸੋਨਾ	sonaa
golden	ਸੁਨਹਿਰੀ	sunahiree
Golden Temple	ਹਰਿਮੰਦਰ ਸਾਹਿਬ	harma<u>nd</u>ar saahib
good	ਚੰਗੀ	cha<u>n</u>gee
good (lit. happiness)	ਖ਼ੁਸ਼ੀ	<u>kh</u>ushee
good quality	ਵਧੀਆ	va<u>dh</u>eeaa
grade	ਗਰੇਡ	gared
great grandfather	ਪੜਦਾਦਾ	parh<u>d</u>aa<u>d</u>aa

groom	ਲਾੜਾ	laarhaa
guests	ਪ੍ਰਾਹੁਣੇ	praahunhe
happy	ਖ਼ੁਸ਼	<u>kh</u>ush
hardwearing	ਹੰਢਣਸਾਰ	ha<u>nd</u>hanhsaar
hasty	ਕਾਹਲਾ	kaahlaa
have: to ~	ਲੈਣਾ	lainhaa
have (already) been	ਜਾ ਚੁਕਣਾ	jaa chuknhaa
he	ਇਹ, ਉਹ	ih, uh
health	ਸਿਹਤ	siha<u>t</u>
heart	ਦਿਲ, ਸੀਨਾ	<u>d</u>il, seenaa
heat	ਗਰਮੀ	garmee
heaven	ਸਵਰਗ	savarag
height	ਕੱਦ	ka<u>dd</u>
help: to ~	ਮੱਦਦ ਕਰਨਾ	ma<u>dd</u>ad karnaa
henna	ਮਹਿੰਦੀ	mahi<u>nd</u>ee
here	ਇੱਥੇ	i<u>thth</u>e
high spirits	ਚੜ੍ਹਦੀ ਕਲਾ	charhh<u>d</u>ee kalaa
high	ਵੱਧ	va<u>dhdh</u>
Hindu	ਹਿੰਦੂ	hi<u>nd</u>oo
hit: to ~	ਮਾਰਨਾ	maarnaa
holidays	ਛੁੱਟੀਆਂ	<u>ch</u>uttee<u>aan</u>
holy man	ਪੀਰ	peer
holy water	ਅੰਮ੍ਰਿਤ	a<u>n</u>mrit
home	ਘਰ, ਦੇਸੀ	ghar, <u>d</u>esi
homework	ਘਰ ਦਾ ਕੰਮ	ghar <u>d</u>aa ka<u>n</u>m
honorific particle signifying respect	ਜੀ	jee
hope	ਉਮੀਦ	umee<u>d</u>
hopefully (lit. if God wishes)	ਇਨਸ਼ਾ ਅੱਲਾ	inshaa allaa
hostel	ਹੋਸਟਲ	hostal
house	ਮਕਾਨ	makaan
how	ਕਿਵੇਂ	kive<u>n</u>
how are you?	ਤੁਹਾਡਾ ਕੀ ਹਾਲ ਹੈ	<u>t</u>uhaadaa kee haal hai
how did it go?	ਕਿਵੇਂ ਰਿਹਾ	kive<u>n</u> rihaa

how far?	ਕਿੰਨੀ ਦੂਰ	kinnee door
how many?	ਕਿੰਨੇ	kinne
how much?	ਕਿੰਨਾ	kinnaa
how much per metre?	ਕਿੰਨੇ ਦਾ ਮੀਟਰ	kinne daa meetar
hunger	ਭੁੱਖ	bhukhkh
husband	ਘਰਵਾਲਾ, ਪਤੀ	gharvaalaa, patee
I	ਮੈਂ	main
identity card	ਸ਼ਨਾਖ਼ਤੀ ਕਾਰਡ	shanaakhtee kaard
if	ਜੇ	je
ill	ਬਿਮਾਰ	bimaar
impatient	ਕਾਹਲਾ	kaahlaa
in	ਵਿਚ	vich
in a hurry	ਕਾਹਲ ਵਿਚ	kaahal vich
in order to	ਲਈ	laee
in place of	ਦੀ ਜਗ੍ਹਾ	dee jag-h-aa
in spite of	ਦੇ ਬਾਵਜੂਦ	de baavjood
in the morning	ਸਵੇਰੇ	savere
increase: to ~	ਵਧਾਉਣਾ	vadhaaunhaa
independence	ਅਜ਼ਾਦੀ	azaadee
India	ਭਾਰਤ	bhaarat
Indian	ਭਾਰਤੀ, ਦੇਸੀ	bhaartee, desi
in-laws	ਸਹੁਰੇ	sahure
inside	ਅੰਦਰ, ਦੇ ਅੰਦਰ	andar, de andar
installation	ਸਵਾਰੀ	savaaree
instance	ਵਾਰੀ	vaaree
interesting	ਦਿਲਚਸਪ	dilchasp
international	ਅੰਤਰ ਰਾਸ਼ਟਰੀ	antar raashtaree
invitation	ਸੱਦਾ ਪੱਤਰ	saddaa pattar
irritation	ਤਕਲੀਫ਼	takleef
is	ਏ, ਹੈ	e, hai
is called, is said	ਕਿਹਾ ਜਾਂਦਾ ਹੈ	kihaa jaandaa hai
it	ਇਸ, ਇਹ	is, ih
job	ਨੌਕਰੀ, ਕੰਮ	naukaree, kanm
join	ਭਰਤੀ	bhartee
join in: to ~	ਸ਼ਾਮਲ	shaamal

juice (fruit)	ਰਸ	ras
jurisdiction	ਵੱਸ	vass
Kenya	ਕੀਨੀਆ	keeneeaa
Khatri (caste)	ਖਤਰੀ	kha<u>t</u>ree
kind natured	ਨਰਮ ਸੁਭਾ	naram subhaa
king	ਰਾਜਾ	raajaa
kingdom	ਰਾਜ	raaj
kitchen	ਰਸੋਈ	rasoee
know: to ~	ਜਾਣਨਾ, ਪਤਾ	jaanhnaa, pa<u>t</u>aa
laden: to be ~	ਲੱਗਣਾ	laggnhaa
lady	ਇਸਤਰੀ	istaree
lady teacher	ਅਧਿਆਪਕਾ	a<u>dh</u>iaapkaa
language	ਬੋਲੀ	bolee
large	ਵੱਡਾ	vaddaa
law	ਕਾਨੂੰਨ	kaanoo<u>n</u>n
leave: to ~	ਛੱਡਣਾ, ਤੁਰਨਾ	<u>ch</u>addnhaa, <u>t</u>urnaa
length of time	ਚਿਰ	chir
lengthy	ਲੰਬਾ	la<u>n</u>baa
less	ਘੱਟ	ghatt
lessen: to ~	ਘੱਟ ਕਰਨਾ	ghatt karnaa
letter	ਚਿੱਠੀ	chiththee
licence	ਲਾਇਸੈਂਸ	laaisai<u>n</u>s
life	ਜੀਵਨ	jeevan
lift: to ~	ਚੁੱਕਣਾ	chukknhaa
light	ਫਿੱਕਾ	phikkaa
like	ਵਰਗਾ	vargaa
like (pleasing)	ਪਸੰਦ, ਸ਼ੌਕ	pasan<u>d</u>, shauk
listen: to ~	ਸੁਣਨਾ	sunhnaa
literal	ਲਫ਼ਜ਼ੀ	lafzee
live: to ~	ਰਹਿਣਾ	rahinhaa
live happily: to ~	ਦਿਲ ਲੱਗਣਾ	<u>d</u>il laggnhaa
location	ਜਗ੍ਹਾ	jag-h-aa
London	ਲੰਡਨ	la<u>n</u>dan
long	ਲੰਬਾ	la<u>n</u>baa
long wooden pole	ਡਾਂਗ	daa<u>n</u>g

look after	ਭਲੀ	bhalee
look at: to ~	ਝਾਕਣਾ	jhaaknhaa
love	ਪਿਆਰ	piaar
love: to ~	ਪਿਆਰ ਕਰਨਾ	piaar karnaa
lower	ਘੱਟ	ghatt
luggage	ਸਮਾਨ	samaan
machine	ਮਸ਼ੀਨ	masheen
madam	ਬੀਬੀ	beebee
mail	ਡਾਕ	daak
male child	ਬਾਲ	baal
male servant	ਨੌਕਰ	naukar
manager	ਮੈਨੇਜਰ	mainejar
Manchester	ਮਾਨਚੈਸਟਰ	maanchaistar
many	ਬਹੁਤ ਸਾਰੇ	bahut saare
mare	ਘੋੜੀ	ghorhee
maths	ਹਿਸਾਬ	hisaab
matter	ਗੱਲ	gall
mature	ਸਿਆਣਾ	siaanhaa
meaning	ਅਰਥ	arth
meaning	ਮਤਲਬ	matlab
medicine	ਦਵਾਈ	davaaee
meet: to ~	ਮਿਲਣਾ	milnhaa
meeting	ਮੇਲ	mel
members of the groom's wedding party	ਜਾਂਞੀ	jaannjee
memory	ਯਾਦ	yaad
military	ਫੌਜ	fauj
mind	ਮਨ	man
minute	ਮਿੰਟ	mint
mirror	ਸ਼ੀਸ਼ਾ	sheeshaa
mixed: to be ~	ਰਲ ਮਿਲਣਾ	ral milnhaa
modern	ਅਜੋਕਾ	ajokaa
Monday	ਸੋਮਵਾਰ, ਪੀਰ	somvaar, peer
month	ਮਹੀਨਾ	maheenaa
more	ਵਧੇਰੇ	vadhere
more or less	ਥੋੜੀ ਬਹੁਤੀ	thorhee bahutee

mother	ਮਾਤਾ ਜੀ	maataa jee
Mr	ਸਰਦਾਰ ਸਾਹਿਬ	sardaar saahib
Muslim departing phrase	ਖ਼ੁਦਾ ਹਾਫ਼ਿਜ਼	khudaa haafiz
Muslim greeting	ਅੱਸਲਾਮ ਅਲੈਕਮ	asslaam alaikam
mutiny	ਗ਼ਦਰ	ghadar
my	ਮੇਰਾ	meraa
nail	ਮੇਖ	mekh
name (formal)	ਨਾਮ	naam
name (informal)	ਨਾਂ	naan
nation	ਕੌਮ	kaum
near	ਦੇ ਨੇੜੇ	de nerhe
necessity	ਲੋੜ	lorh
nectar	ਅੰਮ੍ਰਿਤ	anmrit
need: to ~	ਚਾਹੁਣਾ	chaahunhaa
needle	ਸੂਈ	sooee
news (lit. talk)	ਗੱਲ	gall
next	ਅਗਲਾ	aglaa
next to	ਕੋਲ	kol
nice	ਸੁਹਣਾ	suhnhaa
niece	ਭਤੀਜੀ	bhateejee
no	ਨਹੀਂ	naheen
not in my possession	ਮੇਰੇ ਕੋਲ ਨਹੀਂ	mere kol naheen
not only	ਨਾ ਕੇਵਲ	naa keval
not with me	ਮੇਰੇ ਕੋਲ ਨਹੀਂ	mere kol naheen
now	ਹੁਣ	hunh
occasion	ਮੌਕਾ	maukaa
of	ਦਾ	daa
of the Sikhs	ਸਿੱਖਾਂ ਦੇ	sikhkhaan de
of the village	ਪੇਂਡੂ	pendoo
offence	ਅਪਰਾਧ	apraadh
office	ਦਫ਼ਤਰ	daftar
officer	ਅਫ਼ਸਰ	afsar
OK (alright)	ਅੱਛਾ	achchaa
OK (fine)	ਠੀਕ ਠਾਕ	theek thaak
okra (type of vegetable)	ਭਿੰਡੀ	bhindee

on	ਤੇ	<u>t</u>e
on behalf of	ਵੱਲੋਂ	vallo<u>n</u>
one	ਇੱਕ	ikk
one hundred	ਸੌ (੧੦੦)	sau
one hundred and twenty	ਇੱਕ ਸੌ ਵੀਹ	ikk sau veeh
one side	ਇੱਕ ਪਾਸੇ	ikk paase
one's own	ਆਪਣਾ	aapnhaa
on-going	ਲਗਾਤਾਰ	lagaa<u>t</u>aar
only	ਕੇਵਲ	keval
open	ਖੁੱਲ੍ਹਾ	khullhaa
opportunity	ਮੌਕਾ	maukaa
opposite	ਦੇ ਸਾਹਮਣੇ	<u>d</u>e saahmanhe
or	ਜਾਂ	jaa<u>n</u>
others	ਦੂਜੇ	<u>d</u>ooje
our	ਸਾਡਾ	saadaa
outside	ਦੇ ਬਾਹਰ	<u>d</u>e baahar
pain, hurt	ਦਰਦ	<u>d</u>ar<u>d</u>
pale	ਫਿੱਕਾ	phikkaa
Panjab	ਪੰਜਾਬ	pa<u>n</u>jaab
Panjabi	ਦੇਸੀ	<u>d</u>esi
Panjabi sweet	ਮਿਠਿਆਈ	mithiaaee
papers	ਕਾਗ਼ਜ਼ਾਤ	kaa<u>gh</u>zaat
parade	ਜਲੂਸ	jaloos
pardon	ਮਾਫ਼	maaf
pardon: to ~	ਮਾਫ਼ ਕਰਨਾ	maaf karnaa
parents	ਮਾਪੇ	maape
park: to ~	ਖੜੂਨਾ	kharhhnaa
partition	ਬਟਵਾਰਾ	batvaaraa
participant	ਦਰਸ਼ਕ	<u>d</u>arshak
passengers	ਸਵਾਰੀਆਂ	savaareeaa<u>n</u>
passport	ਪਾਸਪੋਰਟ	paasport
pattern	ਨਮੂਨਾ	namoonaa
pay	ਤਨਖ਼ਾਹ	<u>t</u>an<u>kh</u>aah
peace	ਸ਼ਾਂਤੀ	shaa<u>n</u>tee
peas	ਮਟਰ	matar
pencil	ਪੈਂਸਲ	pai<u>n</u>sal

people	ਬੰਦੇ, ਲੋਕ	ban<u>de</u>, lok
perfectly	ਬਿਲਕੁਲ	bilkul
period, time	ਵੇਲੇ	vele
permission	ਆਗਿਆ	aagiaa
person from Gujarat or of Gujarati origin	ਗੁਜਰਾਤੀ	gujraa<u>t</u>ee
person from Panjab or of Panjabi origin	ਪੰਜਾਬੀ	pa<u>nj</u>aabee
photograph	ਫੋਟੋ	foto
pick: to ~	ਚੁੱਕਣਾ	chukk<u>n</u>haa
place	ਜਗ੍ਹਾ	jag-h-aa
place where clothes are washed on the bay	ਘਾਟ	ghaat
plate	ਪਲੇਟ	palet
play: to ~	ਖੇਡਣਾ	khed<u>n</u>haa
play (music): to ~	ਵਜਾਉਣਾ	vajaaunhaa
played: to be ~	ਵੱਜਣਾ	vajj<u>n</u>haa
please	ਮਿਹਰਬਾਨੀ	miharbaanee
please have a seat	ਤਸ਼ਰੀਫ਼ ਰੱਖੋ ਜੀ	<u>t</u>ashreef rakhkho jee
please sit down (formal)	ਬੈਠੋ ਜੀ	baitho jee
plenty	ਖੁੱਲ੍ਹਾ, ਕਾਫ਼ੀ ਕੁਝ	khullhaa, kaafee kujh
pockets	ਜੇਬਾਂ	jebaa<u>n</u>
pool	ਸਰੋਵਰ	sarovar
population	ਅਬਾਦੀ	abaa<u>d</u>ee
possession: in ~ of	ਕੋਲ	kol
post	ਡਾਕ	daak
post: to ~	ਭੇਜਣਾ	bhej<u>n</u>haa
potato(es)	ਆਲੂ	aaloo
pray: to ~	ਮਨਾਉਣਾ	manaaunhaa
present: to ~	ਪੇਸ਼, ਪੇਸ਼ ਕਰਨਾ	pesh, pesh karnaa
present: to be ~	ਸ਼ਾਮਲ	shaamal
pretty	ਸੁਹਣਾ	suh<u>n</u>haa
price	ਕੀਮਤ	keema<u>t</u>
prick: to ~	ਰੜਕਣਾ	rarhkanhaa
print	ਛਾਪਾ	<u>ch</u>aapaa
printed one: the ~	ਛਪਾਈਵਾਲਾ	<u>ch</u>apaaeevaalaa

procession	ਜਲੂਸ	jaloos
procession of the groom's relatives and friends	ਬਰਾਤ	baraat
professional	ਪੇਸ਼ਾਵਰ	peshaavar
produce: to ~	ਪੇਸ਼ ਕਰਨਾ	pesh karnaa
professionally employed	ਵਿਹਾਰੀ ਨੌਕਰੀ	vihaaree naukaree
proverb	ਅਖਾਣ	akhaanh
put: to ~	ਰੱਖਣਾ	rakhkhnhaa
put on: to ~	ਲਗਾਉਣਾ	lagaaunhaa
quite a lot	ਕਾਫ਼ੀ ਕੁਝ	kaafee kujh
rain	ਬਾਰਸ਼	baarash
rainy season	ਬਰਸਾਤ	barsaat
raised	ਜੰਮਪਲ	janmpal
rate	ਕਿਰਾਇਆ	kiraaiaa
rather	ਜਿਹਾ	jihaa
read: to ~	ਪੜ੍ਹਨਾ	parhhnaa
reasonable right	ਵਾਜਬੀ	vaajbee
receive: to ~	ਮਿਲ ਜਾਣਾ	mil jaanhaa
red	ਲਾਲ	laal
reduce: to ~	ਘੱਟ ਕਰਨਾ	ghatt karnaa
regret	ਅਫ਼ਸੋਸ	afsos
relation (marriage)	ਰਿਸ਼ਤਾ	rishtaa
relatives	ਰਿਸ਼ਤੇਦਾਰ	rishtedaar
religious procession	ਨਗਰ ਕੀਰਤਨ	nagar keertan
remembrance	ਯਾਦ	yaad
rent	ਕਿਰਾਇਆ	kiraaiaa
request	ਬੇਨਤੀ	bentee
request: to ~	ਮੰਗਣਾ	mangnhaa
require	ਲੋੜ	lorh
respectable	ਪਤਵੰਤੇ	patvante
response to Muslim greeting	ਵਾਲੈਕਮ ਅੱਸਲਾਮ	vaalaikam asslaam
rest	ਅਰਾਮ	araam
return	ਵਾਪਸ	vaapas
return: to ~	ਪਰਤਣਾ	partnhaa

English	Panjabi	Transliteration
ride: to ~	ਚੜੂਨਾ	charhhnaa
rides	ਝੂਟੇ	jhoote
right	ਵਾਜਬੀ	vaajbee
ritual	ਰਸਮ	rasam
roads	ਰਾਹਾਂ	raahaan
room	ਕਮਰਾ	kamraa
routes	ਰਾਹਾਂ	raahaan
rub against: to ~	ਰਝਕਨਾ	rarhkanhaa
rulership	ਰਾਜ	raaj
rupee	ਰੁਪਇਆ	rupaiaa
sadness	ਗ਼ਮੀ	ghamee
safe journey	ਸੁਰੱਖਿਅਤ ਸਫ਼ਰ	surakhkhiat safar
salary	ਤਨਖ਼ਾਹ	tankhaah
salty	ਨਮਕੀਨ	namkeen
same	ਇੱਕੋ	ikko
sari: the one wearing the ~	ਸਾੜ੍ਹੀਵਾਲੀ	saarhheevaalee
Saturday	ਸਨਿਚਰਵਾਰ, ਹਫ਼ਤਾ	sanicharvaar, haftaa
saying	ਅਖਾਣ	akhaanh
school	ਸਕੂਲ	sakool
sea	ਸਮੁੰਦਰ	samundar
sea mail	ਸਮੁੰਦਰੀ ਡਾਕ	samundaree daak
seat	ਸੀਟ	seet
second day	ਦੂਜਾ ਦਿਨ	doojaa din
send: to ~	ਭੇਜਣਾ	bhejnhaa
see: to ~	ਵੇਖਣਾ, ਦੇਖਣਾ	vekhnhaa, dekhnhaa
selection	ਚੋਣ	chonh
serve: to ~	ਵਰਤਾਉਣਾ	vartaaunhaa
settled: to be ~	ਚੁਕਣਾ	chuknhaa
several	ਕਈ	kaee
she	ਇਹ, ਉਹ	ih, uh
shining	ਚਮਕੀਲਾ	chamkeelaa
shop	ਦੁਕਾਨ	dukaan
shopkeeper	ਦੁਕਾਨਦਾਰ	dukaandaar
show: to ~	ਦਿਖਾਉਣਾ	dikhaaunhaa

sick	ਬਿਮਾਰ	bimaar
Sikh greeting	ਸਤਿ ਸ੍ਰੀ ਅਕਾਲ	saṭ sree akaal
Sikh festival	ਵੈਸਾਖੀ	vaisaakhee
Sikh martial art, like fencing	ਗਤਕਾ	gaṭkaa
simple	ਸੌਖਾ	saukhaa
since when	ਕਿੰਨਾ ਚਿਰ ਤੋਂ	kinnaa chir ṭon
sing: to ~	ਗਾਣਾ	gaanhaa
singing of hymns	ਕੀਰਤਨ	keerṭan
sir	ਸਾਹਿਬ	saahib
sister	ਭੈਣ	bhainh
sister-in-law (brother's wife)	ਭਾਬੀ	bhaabee
sit: to ~	ਬੈਠਣਾ	baithnhaa
sitting room	ਬੈਠਕ	baithak
situation	ਸਥਿਤੀ	saṭhiṭee
slim	ਪਤਲਾ	paṭlaa
small	ਛੋਟਾ	choṭaa
small drum	ਢੋਲਕੀ	dholkee
so much	ਐਨੇ ਸਾਰੇ	aine saare
so that	ਤਾਂ ਕਿ	ṭaan ki
social worker	ਸਮਾਜ ਸੇਵਕ	samaaj sevak
sold: to be ~	ਵਿਕਣਾ	viknhaa
someone or another	ਕੋਈ ਨ ਕੋਈ	koee na koee
sometimes	ਕਦੀ	kadee
son	ਪੁੱਤਰ, ਬੇਟਾ	puṭṭar, betaa
song	ਗੀਤ	geeṭ
sorry	ਮਾਫ਼ ਕਰਨਾ, ਅਫ਼ਸੋਸ	maaf karnaa, afsos
sort of	ਜਿਹਾ	jihaa
speak	ਬੋਲਣਾ	bolnhaa
speak: to ~	ਕਹਿਣਾ	kahinhaa
special	ਖ਼ਾਸ	khaas
spicy	ਕਰਾਰਾ	karaaraa
spinning wheel	ਚਰਖਾ	charkhaa
spoon	ਚਮਚਾ	chamchaa
spring	ਬਸੰਤ	basanṭ

stairs	ਪੌੜੀਆਂ	paurheeaa<u>n</u>
stamp	ਟਿਕਟ	tikat
stand: to ~	ਖਲੋਣਾ, ਖੜ੍ਹਨਾ	khalonhaa, kharhhnaa
stare: to ~	ਝਾਕਣਾ	jhaaknhaa
start: to ~	ਸ਼ੁਰੂ ਹੋਣਾ	shuroo honhaa
state of health	ਤਬੀਅਤ	tabeeat
stay: to ~	ਠਹਿਰਨਾ, ਰਹਿਣਾ	thahirnaa, rahinhaa
stitch: to ~	ਲਗਾਉਣਾ	lagaaunhaa
stomach	ਪੇਟ	pet
stood: to be ~	ਖਲੋਣਾ	khalonhaa
stringed classical musical instrument	ਸਿਤਾਰ	si<u>t</u>aar
struggle	ਜਦੋ ਜਹਿਦ	ja<u>d</u>o jahi<u>d</u>
struggle for independence	ਅਜ਼ਾਦੀ ਲਈ ਜਦੋ ਜਹਿਦ	azaadee laee ja<u>d</u>o jahi<u>d</u>
student	ਵਿਦਿਆਰਥੀ	vi<u>d</u>iaar<u>th</u>ee
studies	ਪੜ੍ਹਾਈ	parhhaaee
study: to ~	ਪੜ੍ਹਨਾ	parhhnaa
subject	ਮਜ਼ਮੂਨ	mazmoon
subjunctive particle	ਵੇ	ve
suitable	ਯੋਗ	yog
summer	ਗ਼ਰਮੀ	garmee
Sunday	ਐਤਵਾਰ	ai<u>t</u>vaar
sweet	ਮਿੱਠਾ	miththaa
take: to ~	ਛਕਣਾ, ਲੈਣਾ	<u>ch</u>aknhaa, lainhaa
talkative	ਗਾਲੜੀ	gaalrhee
task	ਕੰਮ	ka<u>n</u>m
taste	ਸੁਆਦ	suaa<u>d</u>
tasty	ਸੁਆਦੀ	suaa<u>d</u>ee
teach: to ~	ਪੜ੍ਹਾਉਣਾ	parhhaaunhaa
teacher	ਅਧਿਆਪਕ	a<u>dh</u>iaapak
telephone	ਟੈਲੀਫ਼ੋਨ	taileefon
telephone: to ~	ਟੈਲੀਫ਼ੋਨ ਕਰਨਾ	taileefon karnaa
temperature	ਬੁਖ਼ਾਰ	bu<u>kh</u>aar

thank you	ਸ਼ੁਕਰੀਆ	shukreeaa
thanks	ਧੰਨਵਾਦ,	<u>dh</u>annvaad,
	ਮਿਹਰਬਾਨੀ	miharbaanee
that	ਉਸ, ਕਿ, ਉਹ	us, ki, uh
that is why	ਇਸ ਕਰ ਕੇ	is kar ke
that, which	ਜਿਹੜਾ	jihrhaa
then	ਤਾਂ	<u>t</u>aa<u>n</u>
they	ਉਹ	uh
thick	ਮੋਟਾ	motaa
thin	ਪਤਲਾ	pa<u>t</u>laa
thing	ਚੀਜ਼	cheez
things	ਸਮਾਨ	samaan
think: to ~	ਸੋਚਣਾ	sochnhaa
this	ਇਹ, ਇਸ	ih, is
Thursday	ਜੁਮੇਰਾਤ, ਵੀਰਵਾਰ	jumeraa<u>t</u>, veervaar
time	ਸਮਾਂ, ਵਕਤ	samaa<u>n</u>, vaka<u>t</u>
time: this ~	ਇਸ ਵਾਰੀ	is vaaree
times	ਜ਼ਮਾਨਾ	zamaanaa
today	ਅੱਜ	ajj
together	ਇਕੱਠੇ	ikaththe
tomato(es)	ਟਮਾਟਰ	tamaatar
tomorrow	ਭਲਕ / ਭਲਕੇ, ਕੱਲੂ	bhalak / bhalke, kallh
too much	ਜ਼ਿਆਦਾ	ziaa<u>d</u>aa
tourist	ਸੈਲਾਨੀ	sailaanee
towards	ਵੱਲ	vall
train	ਗੱਡੀ	gaddee
travel: to ~	ਸਫ਼ਰ ਕਰਨਾ, ਫਿਰਨਾ	safar karnaa, phirnaa
travel around: to ~	ਘੁੰਮਣਾ ਫਿਰਨਾ	ghu<u>n</u>mnhaa phirnaa
travellers	ਸਵਾਰੀਆਂ	savaareeaa<u>n</u>
triangular stuffed pastry	ਸਮੋਸਾ	samosaa
trouble	ਤਕਲੀਫ਼	<u>t</u>akleef
true, truth	ਸੱਚ	sachch
try: to ~	ਕੋਸ਼ਿਸ਼ ਕਰਨਾ	koshish karnaa
Tuesday	ਮੰਗਲਵਾਰ	ma<u>n</u>galvaar
turn	ਵਾਰੀ	vaaree

turn around: to ~	ਮੁੜਨਾ	murhnaa
turnip	ਸ਼ਲਗਮ	shalgam
TV	ਟੀ ਵੀ	tee vee
twenty	ਵੀਹ (੨੦)	veeh
Uganda	ਯੂਗੰਡਾ	yoogandaa
uncle (father's brother)	ਚਾਚਾ ਜੀ	chaachaa jee
understand: to ~	ਸਮਝਨਾ	samjhnaa
upon	ਦੇ ਉੱਪਰ	de uppar
upon: to be ~	ਚੜ੍ਹਨਾ	charhhnaa
uprooted: to be ~	ਉਖੜਨਾ	ukhrhnaa
Urdu	ਉਰਦੂ	urdoo
use: to ~	ਵਰਤਣਾ	vartnhaa
vacant	ਖ਼ਾਲੀ	khaalee
values	ਕਦਰਾਂ	kadraan
vanish: to ~	ਮਿਟਣਾ	mitnhaa
vegetable	ਸਬਜ਼ੀ	sabzee
vehicle	ਗੱਡੀ	gaddee
very	ਬਹੁਤ, ਬੜੀ	bahut, barhee
very good	ਬਹੁਤ ਅੱਛਾ	bahut achchaa
very nice	ਬਹੁਤ ਸੁਹਣਾ	bahut suhnhaa
via	ਰਾਹੀਂ	raaheen
village-like	ਪੇਂਡੂ	pendoo
villager	ਪਿੰਡਵਾਲਾ	pindvaalaa
visa	ਵੀਜ਼ਾ	veezaa
visible: to be ~	ਦਿਸਣਾ	disnhaa
visitor	ਦਰਸ਼ਕ	darshak
volunteer	ਸੇਵਾਦਾਰ	sevaadaar
wait: to ~	ਉਡੀਕਣਾ	udeeknhaa
walk: to ~	ਤੁਰਨਾ	turnaa
want	ਲੋੜ	lorh
want: to ~	ਚਾਹੁਣਾ	chaahunhaa
wash: to ~	ਧੋਣਾ	dhonhaa
washerman	ਧੋਬੀ	dhobee
waste time: to ~	ਜ਼ਾਇਆ ਕਰਨਾ	zaaiaa karnaa

watch: to ~	ਦੇਖਣਾ	dekhnhaa
watch over	ਭਲੀ	bhalee
way (direction)	ਪਾਸੇ	paase
way (style)	ਤਰ੍ਹਾਂ	tar-h-aan
we	ਅਸੀਂ	aseen
we all	ਅਸੀਂ ਸਾਰੇ	aseen saare
weakness	ਕਮਜ਼ੋਰੀ	kamzoree
wealthy people	ਪੈਸੇਵਾਲੇ	paisevaale
wedding	ਵਿਆਹ	viaah
Wednesday	ਬੁੱਧਵਾਰ	budhdhvaar
week	ਸਪਤਾਹ, ਹਫ਼ਤਾ	saptaah, haftaa
weekend	ਹਫ਼ਤੇ ਦੇ ਅਖ਼ੀਰ	hafte de akheer
welcome	ਜੀ ਆਇਆਂ ਨੂੰ	jee aaiaan noon
well done	ਸ਼ਾਬਾਸ਼	shaabaash
west	ਪੱਛਮ	pachcham
what?	ਕੀ	kee
what time?	ਕਿੰਨੇ ਵਜੇ	kinne vaje
when?	ਕਦੋਂ	kadon
where?	ਕਿੱਥੇ, ਜਿੱਥੇ	kiththe, jiththe
which?	ਕਿਹੜਾ	kihrhaa
which (oblique)	ਜਿਸ	jis
white	ਗੋਰੀ	goree
who?	ਕੌਣ	kaunh
why?	ਕਿਉਂ	kiun
wide	ਚੌੜਾ	chaurhaa
wife	ਪਤਨੀ	patnee
winter	ਸਰਦੀ	sardee
wise	ਸਿਆਣਾ	siaanhaa
with	ਕੋਲ	kol
with me	ਮੇਰੇ ਨਾਲ	mere naal
without	ਤੋਂ ਬਿਨਾਂ / ਬ.ਗੈਰ	ton binaan / baghair
woman from Lahore	ਲਾਹੌਰਵਾਲੀ ਔਰਤ	laahaurvaalee aurat
women's folk dance	ਗਿੱਧਾ	gidhdhaa
work	ਕੰਮ	kanm
work: to ~	ਕੰਮ ਕਰਨਾ	kanm karnaa
world	ਦੁਨੀਆਂ	duneeaan

worry	ਫ਼ਿਕਰ	fikar
write: to ~	ਲਿਖਣਾ	likhnhaa
wrong	ਗ਼ਲਤ	ghalat
year	ਸਾਲ	saal
yes (polite)	ਹਾਂ ਜੀ	haan jee
yesterday	ਕੱਲ੍ਹ	kallh
you (formal)	ਤੁਸੀਂ	tuseen
you (informal)	ਤੂੰ	toon
your (formal)	ਤੁਹਾਡਾ	tuhaadaa
your (informal)	ਤੇਰਾ	teraa
youth	ਨੌਜੁਆਨ, ਜੁਵਕ	naujuaan, yuvak

taking it further

If you have enjoyed working your way through *Teach Yourself Panjabi* and are interested in enhancing your listening, speaking and reading skills, there are a number of different ways in which you can build upon your existing knowledge and skills. Here are a few suggestions which you might find helpful.

There are a range of different sources of information and places where you can look to for improving your understanding of Panjabi language and culture without having to venture too far away. Some satellite radio stations offer exclusively Panjabi programming, sometimes 24 hours a day, while others have specific slots given to Panjabi programmes:

- Desi Radio: **www.desiradio.org.uk**
- Panjab Radio: **www.panjabradio.co.uk**
- Akash Radio: **www.akashradio.com**
- BBC Asian network: **www.bbc.co.uk/ asiannetwork/**

These radio stations are available on the internet, so if you have access you can listen anywhere in the world. There are also a number of newspapers, both printed as well as on the internet. In the UK, *Des Pardes* and *The Punjab Times* are printed weeklies. The most popular newspaper in Panjab itself is *The Ajit* (**www.ajitjalandhar.com/**) which is available on the internet. A dual language paper from the UK, the *Sikh Times* is available for reading on the web also, at **www.sikhtimes.com**.

If you want to get a greater insight into Panjabi poetry and literary matters more generally then the website: **www.apnaorg.com** is the best resource available. There is also a feast of literature on the website, **www.likhari.com**. Many of these sites require you to download Panjabi fonts. There are many free fonts available on the internet as well as commercial packages. The most advanced software package in Panjabi includes a spellchecker and a converter for the many fonts, which is called 'Akhar' and details about it are available at: **www.akhar.net**.

Music and television are also a good source of exposure to Panjabi culture and language. There are a number of digital / satellite television channels, including Channel Punjab and Alpha ETC Punjabi which offer a rich view of Panjabi society, religion and culture. Broadcasts of music concerts, news and current affairs programmes are revealing of some of the current concerns of Panjab and Panjabis. Films, DVDs, music CDs are widely available in South Asian shopping areas too.

There are a growing number of Panjabi teaching and learning aides and books available from select sources. The Panjabi Language Development Board (PLDB) in Birmingham, UK, produces and distributes such materials, including dual language posters and workbooks for all levels (**www.panjabilang.org**). DTF (also in Birmingham, UK) offers an excellent mail order service (**www.dtfbooks.com**). Panjabi University, Patiala (India) hosts the best online learning materials in Panjabi at **www.advancedcentrepunjabi.org/intro1.asp**. There is also a very well made song of the Panjabi alphabet at **www.maa.com.au**.

In many places, Panjabi is no longer a 'foreign' language where Panjabi communities have settled in large numbers outside India, namely in the UK, Canada, the USA, East Africa, Australia and Singapore, to name a few places. This offers opportunities to brush up on your listening and spoken skills, even outside Panjab. Many people from India and Pakistan living in different parts of the world speak Panjabi. In fact, the largest population of native Panjabi speakers live in Pakistan. Our point is that when we look at the geographical spread of its speakers, inside and outside Panjab, Panjabi is very much a living language.

Visiting 'Indian' or 'Pakistani' restaurants and shopping areas such as the Broadway in Southall (UK), Soho Road in Birmingham (UK), Diwan Street in Chicago (USA) or Jackson Heights, New York (USA), to give a few examples, can provide a good opportunity to enjoy food and the experience of being in a Panjabi context, while also hearing and engaging in conversation with Panjabi speakers. Visiting a **gurdwara** (Sikh temple) is another place where you would come across native speakers. Congregations are generally very welcoming to new people and outsiders, Sikh and non-Sikh, who wish to visit the temple where **langar** (free community kitchen) is served to all, irrespective of religion, caste or creed. Of course, to completely immerse yourself in the language, a trip to Panjab (India or Pakistan) would be the best opportunity to improve your skills.

grammar and verb index